Buying In

Buying In

*Big-Time Women's College Basketball
and the Future of College Sports*

Aaron L. Miller

ROWMAN & LITTLEFIELD
Lanham • Boulder • New York • London

Published by Rowman & Littlefield
An imprint of The Rowman & Littlefield Publishing Group, Inc.
4501 Forbes Boulevard, Suite 200, Lanham, Maryland 20706
www.rowman.com

86-90 Paul Street, London EC2A 4NE

Copyright © 2022 by The Rowman & Littlefield Publishing Group, Inc.

All rights reserved. No part of this book may be reproduced in any form or by any electronic or mechanical means, including information storage and retrieval systems, without written permission from the publisher, except by a reviewer who may quote passages in a review.

British Library Cataloguing in Publication Information Available

Library of Congress Cataloging-in-Publication Data

Names: Miller, Aaron L. (Aaron Levi), 1980- author.
Title: Buying in : big-time women's college basketball and the future of college sports / Aaron L. Miller.
Description: Lanham : Rowman & Littlefield, [2022] | Includes bibliographical references and index.
Identifiers: LCCN 2021046385 (print) | LCCN 2021046386 (ebook) | ISBN 9781538166420 (cloth) | ISBN 9781538166437 (paperback) | ISBN 9781538166444 (ebook)
Subjects: LCSH: Basketball for women—United States—History. | College sports for women—United States—History. | College sports—Economic aspects—United States. | College sports—Social aspects—United States.
Classification: LCC GV886 .M46 2022 (print) | LCC GV886 (ebook) | DDC 796.323082—dc23/eng/20211215
LC record available at https://lccn.loc.gov/2021046385
LC ebook record available at https://lccn.loc.gov/2021046386

To Suzanne, for showing me how
to buy in to the banquet

Contents

	Acknowledgments	ix
	Prologue	xiii
Introduction	Big Time	1
Chapter 1	"We're Still Trying to Find Our Identity"	33
Chapter 2	The Engine of the Train	45
Chapter 3	Unselfish Play	71
Chapter 4	Enlightened Leadership	97
Chapter 5	A Coach of Coaches	127
Chapter 6	Everybody Is Capable, Everybody Is Fearless	143
Chapter 7	"Deep in the Woods"	173
Chapter 8	"I Am Stanford"	193
Chapter 9	"I Am Not a Celebrity at Stanford"	215
Chapter 10	"We Need People to Take Ownership"	249
Conclusion	Give Women's Sports a Chance	289
Epilogue	Big-Time College Sports amid Two Pandemics	295

Bibliography	307
Index	355
About the Author	373

Acknowledgments

This work is the product of many years and many fortunate relationships. Although my hands typed the words you read and I am responsible for any errors, none of these words would have been written without the people whose names follow. I have merely done my best to honor their good names.

First, I would like to thank my father, not just for laying concrete for a basketball hoop in our front yard on my sixth birthday, or for teaching me his patented left-handed hook shot, which as a righty I am still perfecting, but for showing me what it means to do good work in life, even when it's hard or when others might disagree.

Equally I thank my mother, whose powerful athleticism serves as a daily example of lifelong kinesthetic learning and self-care. For years I watched her rise early and join the day with an hour of movement that was entirely hers; now, as a parent myself, I am beginning to understand why such effort matters so much.

My mother is one of many great women in my family, in fact, and all these women were inspiration for this study in some peculiar way. It helped a lot that my inimitable sisters, cousins, aunts, and nieces all taught me to respect and revere women as a matter of course. To my sisters especially, it has been your constant example of love, intelligence, and empathy that has guided me every day of my life.

It was my Bobe Sarah who taught me, with her truly pioneering example, that anything is possible, in scholarship but also in life. Bobe's research on, and counsel of, child survivors of the Holocaust was powerful motivation during the many years I struggled to finish my first book, and during the many years I struggled to finish writing this one too. I love you, Bobe. (And Zaide, you're not so bad yourself!)

I am also deeply grateful to Jeremy Medovoy, my best friend and "big brother," who taught me how to play basketball, how to be an insatiable student of basketball, and how to be a true and loyal fan. In fact, Jeremy's boundless enthusiasm for, and in-depth knowledge of, sports has been a commonality among many of my friends, with whom I played basketball until the wee hours of the morning on warm summer nights. Their love of sports has become the bedrock of my theoretical perspective, in no small part because it is based on friendship, sportsmanship, love, and joy. Thank you each and thank you all.

Professionally, I would also like to acknowledge the great debts I owe to the many people who have either taken me under their wing and helped me grow as a scholar or taken more than a passing interest in my work. Academic life is busy, and there is always much to do, read, and write, but these people in particular carved out time for me, and for that I am very thankful.

In 2010 I moved to Kyoto University to become a member of the Hakubi Project, which provided the generous resources that I used to research the issues detailed in this book. Professors, mentors, and friends like Tanaka Koji, Fushiki Tohru, Hori Toshitaka, Inoue Yuki, Mizuno Hisayo, Nathan Badenoch, Simon Creak, and Jeremy Rappleye all helped me keep on the philosopher's path during that time, and to them I say, *Doumo arigatou gozaimashita!*

Beyond Kyoto, mentors, scholars, authors, and friends such as Roger Goodman, William Kelly, Kariya Takehiko, Sogawa Tsuneo, David Blake Willis, Ellis Krauss, George Selleck, Lee Thompson, Kuraishi Osamu, Victor Kobayashi, Sawai Kazuhiko, Tsukahara Fumio, Nakazawa Atsushi, Harumi Befu, Becky Beal, Rita Liberti, Missy Wright, Paul Carpenter, Robert Whiting, and Ikegami Tsuyoshi all offered gracious mentorship and kind friendship. Thank you!

I also leaned on many people at Stanford University, particularly in the athletic department and in the Center on Adolescence (COA). At the COA, William Damon and his outstanding team, especially Anne Colby, Heather Malin, Hyemin Han, Lisa Staton, and Elissa Hirsh, showed me the power we have to do research on exemplars in positive ways if we listen to the concerns of the world "out there" and join the public conversation.

At the athletic department, I would not have been able to start this project without the generosity of Paul "Bud" Anderson, who connected me with Coach Bobbie Kelsey, who was generous with her time and her connections, including her boss, Coach Tara VanDerveer. Eileen Roche was exceptionally hospitable and helpful, finding me tickets for games, directing me to appropriate places to find vital information, and showing genuine interest in my work. More than anything, Eileen always greeted me with a smile on her face, which meant more than she could even know!

To Stanford coaches Amy Tucker, Bobbie Kelsey, and Kate Paye, thank you for sharing your honest perspectives with me even though it must not have been at all clear how or why doing so might have been in your interest. To Heather Owen, thank you for your candid, instructional, and encouraging interview at a time that I needed it most, and to Joe Karlgaard, for your patience with my ignorance and for your generosity to free me of it.

To Coach Frank Brennan, Rosalyn Gold-Onwude, Jayne Appel, Kamba Tshionyi, Megan Boone, Danette Leighton, Kristin Acevedo, and dozens of other anonymous interviewees, thank you for helping me understand the increasingly complex landscape of college sports. To all the current or former Stanford athletes who spoke with me or answered one of my surveys, thank you. To Dr. Hans Steiner, thank you for your practical insights at Maples that day we met; it was a day that changed my thinking about life itself.

Last but obviously not least, I must express immeasurable gratitude to Coach Tara VanDerveer, who graciously opened practices to me, sat for many interviews, and even read drafts of this manuscript during its many iterations.

Other friends, colleagues, and family members generously took time out of their busy schedule to read earlier drafts too. Mike Singer helped me understand the meaning of "big time" and provided mentorship over the years that helped me navigate some treacherous academic waters. Tony Mirabelli kindly and thoughtfully helped with the book proposal. Becky Beal offered countless helpful suggestions, advice, and guidance. Rita Liberti read drafts and offered sensible advice, and Imoto Yuki enlightened me with some great conversations on a range of topics. Thank you to Burt Coombe, Todd Degnan, Jeff Vahid-Tari, and the late great Jil Plummer for reading draft chapters, too. Thank you to Peter Stern, Donna Lopiano, Mariah Burton Nelson, Jacqueline Grace, and Robert Whiting for helping me navigate the publishing world. To Henry and Rande Zaretsky, for the many timely articles you shared and for continued love and support, thank you.

To Kate Powers, Sarah Sichina, Jon Sisk, and Cindi Pietrzyk at Rowman & Littlefield, all of whom proficiently shepherded this project to completion, thank you for taking a chance on me. I also hired three excellent editors to help me along the way so special thanks must also go to Jason Nielsen, Alexandra Frankel, and Sangeeta Mishra, all of whom are consummate professionals. I enjoyed working with Jason and Alexandra on earlier drafts and with Sangeeta on the final revisions of this manuscript, which she read promptly and meticulously. All gave pointed advice and made wise suggestions for cuts. As a writer, I am often self-conscious about my work so I was particularly appreciative of Sangeeta's willingness to act a quasi-coach, helping me gain the confidence I needed to finish my book proposal and make a submission.

My final expression of gratitude has been reserved for the woman who has supported me through each draft and each revision and through each metaphorical win and loss: my lightning bolt, my bedrock, my cheerleader, and my catalyst for *all* things positive, Suzanne. Thank you for sharing your indomitable spirit, impressive patience, and enduring love. This book is above all dedicated to you and the three little gifts you have grown us. I love you.

Now, let the banquet begin!

Prologue

The Stories We Tell

This book is about the 2010–2011 Stanford University women's basketball team, big-time Division I NCAA women's college basketball, and the future of big-time Division I NCAA intercollegiate sports.

On a deeper level, though, it is also about the relationship between a researcher and his research, the tone and purpose of academic scholarship in the humanities and humanistic social sciences, and the potential for scholars to be a positive part of social change, in this case, the college sports reform movement.

The mainstream mass sports media dominates the way the American public thinks and feels about college sports, but the ways that scholars interpret the relationships between coaches and athletes and media and corporations, as well as how they judge the NCAA and athletic conferences, and universities who operate at the big-time level also matter, especially when it comes to progressive reform. We have voices, our arguments persuade, and what we write matters.

Sometimes the language we as scholars use and the theory we apply challenges our ability to make a public impact, and sometimes it may even prevent us from making any kind of practical contribution at all. Moreover, if we only look for problems to highlight, we may miss the forest for the trees or miss an opportunity to plant new ones.

The good news is that the way we choose to interpret and present the data that we collect can help mitigate these problems. The operators of big-time college sports undoubtedly can and sometimes do exploit and misuse young athletes. At the same time, big-time college sports can also serve to educate and uplift. It depends on the specific sport, institution, coach, boosters, and players involved. As scholars in the humanities and humanistic social sciences, isn't it our job to be open-minded about all possible ways of living, and specific about the how, who, when, what, where, and why of whatever we study so that our voices will be heard clearly, of course, but also so that others can understand what we are saying, and why?

Research Intentions and Research Reality

It was not my initial intention to write such a book or explore such issues. Instead, I was interested in the concept of education in sports on a global and cross-cultural level. I had written my doctoral dissertation on basketball coaches in Japan, and during my postdoc I set out to find a field site for further observational research in the hopes of doing comparative research with Japan and the United States.

But through the process of doing postdoctoral fieldwork, I came to see that there were bigger domestic issues at stake that demanded my attention first. I was fortunate that Coach Tara VanDerveer of Stanford University opened her team's practices to me, not for a day or two but for a whole season, and that she fielded my questions courteously even though it must not have been immediately clear what she might gain by welcoming an outsider into her world. Her generosity was not lost on me. Despite being an official member of the university—at the time, I was a visiting scholar in the Graduate School of Education—I was turned away from observing football practices and from men's basketball practices. One day, on my way home from a women's basketball practice, I stopped near the football practice field to peek through a hole in the fence. A man dressed in university attire came toward me and said, "We don't allow outside observers." On another occasion, when I showed up to a women's basketball practice too early one day, while the men were still practicing, and asked if I could work on my laptop while I waited, I was told, "I'm sorry. Practice is closed." A few days after that, I visited the university bookstore and I asked to see sales data regarding athletics-related merchandise. In short order I was turned away and told that such information was privileged. This secrecy hinted at the high stakes inherent in the big-time business that college sports have become. The entire university seemed to depend on these young athletes, and their trade secrets were protected as a large corporation might protect its own. In fact, so much of our consciousness of what big-time sports are is shaped by men's college football and basketball, especially the notion of big time, but that consciousness most often is filtered to us through the mass sports media.

Undeterred and still curious, I began watching the women's basketball team's daily trainings. I was in the stands at nearly every home game. I followed the team on long-distance road trips. I spoke with coaches and players about what women's basketball meant to them and the challenges they faced. I interviewed the team's former players, spoke with athletic department officials and athletic conference representatives, and listened to fans, boosters, alumni, and non-athlete students tell me what college sports in general, and women's basketball in particular, meant to them. I read everything about the school that I could get my hands on.

In allowing me to observe, Coach VanDerveer said she wanted to limit my access to the players and that this decision was made so they could focus on their studies. Reasonably, she wanted to protect her players and saw herself as their guardian. I understood; her legacy had been assured long before my arrival, but her players' legacies were still being written.

While I grew up an hour away from Stanford as an athlete and die-hard sports fan, there was much about women's sports I did not know. So I tried to spend as much time in the library as I did in the bleachers. As I read about the history of college sports in the United States, I noticed a need for a new comparative history of men's and women's college sports, especially the most significant of men's sports, football, which had been considered big-time for the longest, with women's basketball, which is today closest to being considered big-time. As I read and researched, I began to wonder why so few stories of big-time women's basketball include how college football became big-time. After all, that was how the big time came to be, and how a stage was set for women to buy in to it.

The same sexist thinking that sidelined women's college sports in the history of men's college sports also applied to contemporary college sports reform measures, which were and remain often structured around what to do with men's basketball and football, particularly, how to rein them in. Yet this focus on two male sports discolors our understandings of what college sports are and what they can be. Yes, they must be about money, but they are about so much more too.

That is why this book aims to be a celebration of college sports as part of higher education and a validation of the coaches who, when they serve as teachers first and foremost, contribute to it. Not all institutions and not all coaches will be able to prioritize education in the same way that the people in this study have, but my view nonetheless remains that balancing athletics and academics at the big-time level *is* possible, and that as scholars we can and ought to help the public recognize that possibility and fight to protect the notion that sports are and can remain educational tools.

On the Conscience of an Observational Fieldworker

For a long time I struggled to find the right theoretical framing for a biography of Tara VanDerveer—and the sport she coached. I was certainly influenced by various social theories that explained her marginality and the marginality of her peers, but sometimes I felt that these theories held me back from saying for myself what I thought about her and her experiences.

Women's college basketball teams like Stanford's assume a peculiar space in our culture—at once they are marginalized from the mainstream of big-time men's sports discourse but also often enjoy considerably more amenities and privileges than other women's sports (e.g., gymnastics, swimming) that do not generate the same levels of income or public attention. The athletes I observed were on full-ride athletic scholarships attending one of the finest academic universities in the world and would go on to become leaders in a wide-range of fields, and in some cases even become national celebrities. For these reasons, these big-time women's basketball players represented not only a marginalized group from the core of American sports culture but also an exemplary group that led, or would, by virtue of their Stanford degree, soon lead, comparatively privileged lives.

But in the media and cultural lexicon there is no medium time; you are either a big-time team or not, so I also struggled with the question of how to acknowledge both the accomplishments and the promise of these exemplary athletes and the failures of a commercialized and sexist college sports culture. How to simultaneously acknowledge sport's power to uplift some people and to hold others back? How to explore the tensions between the impressive educational growth that I observed taking place between coaches and players, the heart-felt emotions of American sports fans who craved a faithful escape, cheerleading journalists, and prolific scholars who focused primarily on college sport's (economic) exploitation?

I also struggled to frame the university that sponsored this team. The Stanford team—and the athletic department in which it is housed—is part of a prestigious academic university, and while the athletic department is not as integrated with the university as a counterpart would be at an NCAA Division III school, there remains great institutional faith that college sports are and should always remain an integral part of higher education. This is a faith that I will readily admit that I share myself. I believed in it before I arrived at Palo Alto, and it became stronger the longer I was there.

But sports are not simply educational pursuits at Stanford; they are big business too. Thanks to Coach VanDerveer and her staff, the basketball team has also been exceptionally successful on the court. This success led to the women's basketball program becoming a profitable part of the university's entertainment arm and allowed the university to market itself as a unique brand of higher education. The Stanford brand was an idea but also a commoditized logo that could be licensed in the same way that Stanford Athletics, which is a limited liability company called Cardinal Sports, could license multimedia rights for its sports broadcasts.[1] That was the case for Stanford men and women, and while the men by and large generated more revenue than the women, that did not mean that the women weren't, in their own way, big-time too. What did it mean to be part of a team that ticked both boxes: entertainment and education? Could a university truly strike a balance between the two?

Like her employer, Coach VanDerveer occupied an ambivalent place as head coach of a big-time women's college basketball team at an academically and athletically prestigious university. At once she was a pioneer of coaching who had cultivated numerous winning teams and helped hundreds of athletes graduate with enviable college degrees, but by simple virtue of being part of the system of big-time college sports, which had grown far beyond the system she had joined as a coach in the 1980s, she could not help but reproduce some of the less savory aspects of the system. She alone did not create this system, of course, nor did she alone sustain it, but she had a role to play nonetheless. One might say that Coach VanDerveer's role began when she bought in to the idea of the big time, as many women did after Title IX. The college basketball world that Coach VanDerveer entered was not the same one that I observed, though, nor would it be the same world she would leave when her coaching days were done. Like so many others who had come before her, and like so many who would come after her, she merely did the best she could within it a broken system to make the lives of people around her better. History and social change, it seemed to me, held the key to understanding her true place in the sports culture today, so I set out to situate her personal evolution with a historical narrative that examined what "the big time" meant, how it was made, and what it meant for women like her—and her players—to be participating in it.

I still had a difficult choice to make, especially in terms of selecting data from the reams of notes I took during my fieldwork. As an author with the power of the pen, I could choose to make Coach VanDerveer and her university the heroines of the story, or I could try to write a book that embraced nuance and examined tensions. Senior academic colleagues recommended the latter and suggested that it was the only way to fully acknowledge the power of this coach's approach as well as the flaws in the broader system. It would have been much more difficult, but I could have also tried to find fault in Coach VanDerveer's coaching ways or to be critical of Stanford's way of administering college sports.

Even if another scholar might judge VanDerveer and Stanford more harshly than I do, or consider them too unique to draw lessons from, I could not in good conscience do that myself. VanDerveer had opened her world to me. How could I overlook that gift she had given me? More importantly, though, there *was* also a lot to learn from studying her coaching style and her university's balance between education and athletics. To overlook her positive impact on countless athletes and coaches would amount to utter nonsense, if not revisionist history. It was simply not what I observed. So, I ultimately concluded, by only focusing on the flaws of the college system (and VanDerveer and Stanford's complicity within it) and in relative terms dismissing the transformative education taking place between these coaches and players would be akin to a rather blind application of neo-Marxist social theory rather than allowing my observations to guide my writing. I could not in good conscience do that. These young women were buying in to something that *they themselves* perceived to have great value. Who was I to interpret that choice in a negative light?

So I made a choice to show gratitude to Coach VanDerveer and to many others, and I made a choice to focus on the positive aspects of the sports culture I encountered. Indeed, the capacity to be grateful and positive is at the heart of this book's thesis, at the heart of my interpretation of women's basketball and big-time college sports, and even at the heart of my interpretation of the notion of buying in. No matter how marginalized we may be as scholars, women's basketball coaches or athletes, we all have choices. So above all, I have tried to highlight the laudable efforts my informants have made within a broken system that is in serious need of structural reform—in short, to focus on, and therefore try to learn from, the successes of those who have bought in.

Why Me and Why I Look at Sports This Way

I have studied sports coaches for fifteen years, in the United States and Japan, and there is no doubt that their positive, optimistic, and growth-minded worldview has shaped my own. Who better than coaches to offer scholars a better example of a positive growth-mindset applied to real life. Their inspirational locker room speeches can fire up even the most nihilistic academic, rouse his spirit, and refocus his pessimism on his ultimate purpose. Not that I am always so easily persuaded; undoubtedly some coaches, especially at the big-time level, can seem like drunken generals leading their charges into enemy territory to find the next distillery. But what I have learned from sports coaches like VanDerveer is that I most admire the ones whose vision, positivity, and determination invariably help their charges grow, no matter the cost.

Some scholars understand these qualities. One of my favorites is the literary theorist Hans Ulrich Gumbrecht, who in his book *In Praise of Athletic Beauty* notes the general criticality and negativity that intellectuals often have toward sports and their overwhelming inability to praise athletes for what they do.[2] Intellectuals, Gumbrecht argues, are unable to praise athletes because they "feel obliged to be *critical*—only and always critical."[3]

> When scholars, even scholars who love sports, apply the tools of their training to athletic events, they often wind up feeling obliged to interpret sports as a symptom of highly undesirable tendencies. Some academic critiques have gone so far as to denounce sports as [Foucauldian] biopolitical conspiracy that emerges from the delegation of state power to self-reflective micro-powers. Through practicing and watching sports, according to this view, we regulate and restrain our bodies against our individual self-interest.[4]

I had actually deployed such theory in my first book, but Gumbrecht helped me see that viewing sports in such a negative, beauty-less way diminishes their value and also our ability to revere and praise heroes and feel gratitude for them. Gumbrecht explains that he had a "determination to see and to value athletic beauty," which he calls *praise*. "And this capacity to praise," he adds, "is what we have lost—to the point where the very idea can seem embarrassing to us." He concludes, "I . . . feel gratitude for the pleasure of watching sports . . . and praising athletics . . . allows me to express this gratitude."[5]

Thus, in order to practice what I have come to call "positive anthropology"[6] and to highlight the beauty that these athletes and coaches bring us, I chose to make Coach VanDerveer, the Stanford women's basketball coaching staff, and the team's players the central characters in this story, and its heroines. Although I duly acknowledge and sufficiently explore the problematic aspects of the big-time college sports, I believe it is possible to showcase these women in a positive way, all without in any way sugarcoating the challenges they face.

"Taking It Like a Woman"

Ultimately there are both problems *and* promise in big-time college sports like women's basketball, and we must address them on both a micro-, interpersonal level, and a macro-, structural level. Nothing short of comprehensive reform will fulfill their promise and rid them of their many problems.

There *is* exploitation of big-time (male and female) college athletes but there is also great potential inherent in these pursuits to stimulate growth, education, and camaraderie. Sports may serve as a positive or negative force but it ultimately depends entirely upon how each person, coach, and university wields them as a tool (for personal gain, or for the liberation of another) and a symbol (of nationalism, or the valor in hard work, loyalty, and sacrifice). Since sports are both tools and symbols, and since we have the dexterity to wield them, then there is good reason to be hopeful and optimistic for their future, and for ours, since they are ultimately in our control.

In the case of women's big-time college basketball, the exciting but sometimes physically and mentally risky big-time level of competition is much more than a potential conduit for personal growth; it can also be a symbolic vehicle that encourages young women and girls to author their own lives, rather than accept the dictates of a patriarchal society.

In this regard, I am reminded of something inspirational that Coach VanDerveer said in 1996, after she led the U.S. Olympic team to a gold medal. As is customary, her players drenched her in a colorful sports drink, but Coach VanDerveer didn't flinch. "I took it like a woman," she said, in a no-nonsense, matter-of-fact way all her own. Perhaps VanDerveer knew that many young American girls would be listening when she upended a common cliché not only about gender but also about toughness. In my estimation, these six words constituted a remarkable philosophical summation of the on-court and off-court legacy of Coach VanDerveer, whose positive mindset has influenced thousands of athletes and millions of sports fans and has advanced our society one step closer not only to true gender equality but also to all of us leading richer lives of achievement, ambition, and growth.

In fact, it is the waves that ripple out from her work, touching her players, fans, and alumni, that begin to hint at why I argue in the pages that follow that big-time college sports reform should be focused on three pillars—pay, respect, and education—and should be focused on all big-time athletes, regardless of gender. After all, these realms of physical culture are first and foremost about our growth—as athletes, as students, and as people. It is only our collective fixation on profit that prevents us from seeing otherwise. In that regard, we must find a more balanced way to buy in without selling out that which matters most.

Notes

1. Zimbalist found a "dizzying" growth in money generated by licensing and merchandise, but his analysis also showed that much of this money was never seen by most universities and that anywhere from 15 to 20 percent was skimmed off the top by the licensing companies (*Unpaid Professionals*, 136–37).
2. Gumbrecht, *In Praise of*, 29.
3. Gumbrecht, *In Praise of*, 24.
4. Gumbrecht, *In Praise of*, 25.
5. Gumbrecht, *In Praise of*, 35.
6. A. Miller, "Corporal Punishment in Japan."

Introduction: Big Time

> Women's basketball is all about change. It's all about progression. It's all about opportunity.
>
> —Courtney Wicks[1]

When Two Streaks Collide, University of Connecticut, December 30, 2010

It was a late December evening, when I found myself standing in a long line that snaked outside the gates of Maples Pavilion, on the campus of Stanford University. A blanket of oak leaves covered much of the university's sprawling campus, and the gentle scent of eucalyptus drifted through a cloudless sky.

Thousands of basketball fans had lined up to see what was being billed as a battle of two powerhouses of NCAA (National Collegiate Athletic Association) women's college basketball: the Stanford University Cardinal versus the University of Connecticut (UCONN) Huskies. All 7,329 seats had been sold, and the ticketholders—students, professors, Silicon Valley techies—began taking their seats ninety minutes before tip-off. Condoleezza Rice—a Stanford professor, former U.S. secretary of state, and future leader in the movement for college basketball reform—was in attendance, along with several former star players from both schools.

UCONN entered the contest on a ninety-game winning streak and had firmly established itself as the nation's most successful college basketball team of the era. In its eighty-ninth win a few days earlier, UCONN had set a record for consecutive wins, surpassing the 1971–1974 University of California, Los Angeles (UCLA) men's basketball team, which had won eighty-eight consecutive games under legendary Coach John Wooden. UCONN was led by head coach Geno Auriemma and superstar forward Maya Moore, both of whom were considered living legends.

But Stanford, led by their own Hall of Fame coach Tara VanDerveer, presented an opponent more formidable than most. Like UCONN's, Stanford's players were accustomed to winning, even against elite opponents, and it was Stanford that had last defeated UCONN over two and a half years earlier.

Stanford was enjoying a winning streak of its own too—fifty-one straight home victories. Coming into the 2010–2011 season, the senior class had won *every* home game they played at Maples Pavilion. In fact, the Cardinal had not lost at Maples since March 2007, nearly four years prior. In 2009–2010, Stanford had attended the NCAA Final Four for the third straight year, solidifying their own top-tier status in women's college basketball.

At the end of the evening, and at the end of the year, one of these winning streaks would end. One team's new year would start with celebrations; the other's with wind sprints from the baseline.

For me, though, the evening ended with new questions about women's college basketball in particular, and big-time college sports in general, and set in motion a decade of research into what makes college sports great, and what would make college sports even better.

"A Rematch for Revenge"

The UCONN–Stanford game was set to be televised on ESPN's flagship channel, a rare occurrence for women's college basketball at that time. ESPN played up the drama and rivalry between two of the game's most accomplished coaches, UCONN's Auriemma and Stanford's VanDerveer, as if they were personally pitted in a boxing match, and highlighted the strengths of individual players, hoping to create a college sporting legend in real time. In particular, ESPN focused sharply on UCONN's standout forward, Maya Moore (who had been the leading scorer in the previous year's National Final, scoring twenty-three points and outshining junior Stanford forward Kayla Pedersen [fifteen points]), transforming her impressive biography into basketball mythology. Moore was certainly deserving of the praise, and when the starting lineups for the rematch were announced, Stanford fans cheered for her, showing respect and appreciation for what the twenty-two-year-old had accomplished during her college career.

Coming into the game, Moore was shooting over 50 percent from the floor, 40 percent from the three-point range, and 80 percent from the foul line, the kind of production that basketball coaches stay up all night dreaming about. In many ways, Moore was a complete basketball player—she could run, pass, rebound, score, defend, and dunk. Just halfway through her senior season, she was already the winningest individual player in college basketball history. By the end of her senior season, she would boast a team record of 150 wins with 4 losses, which amounted to an astonishing 97.4 four-year winning percentage. At the end of the 2010–2011 season, Moore would win her third Wade Trophy, the women's college basketball player of the year award, equivalent to the Naismith Award (men's college basketball) or Heisman Trophy (college football). It would be the first time any player would win this prestigious player of the year award three times (no one has done it again since). Almost as a matter of course, Moore would become the first overall pick in the Women's National Basketball Association (WNBA) draft, joining the Minnesota Lynx franchise and helping that team win four titles in the next eight seasons. She also became the first female athlete to sign with Michael Jordan's shoe and athletic apparel brand. Seemingly single-handedly, Moore was showing how far the women's game—and its marketability—had come. Moore was hardly the first woman to prove herself in or through the game of basketball, but she was something of a rarity among American female athletes, many of whom struggled in the face of the gendered disparity in media coverage to gain national attention on par with male athletes. When President Barack Obama invited Moore to the White House to play in an informal game on his birthday alongside various NBA stars, she was the only female player invited.

Moore was also the kind of player who showed up when it mattered most—what sports fans call a clutch player. Moore had burned Stanford in the 2010 NCAA Final, scoring eighteen of her twenty-three points in the second half, leading her team to another UCONN title. A few days before their December 2010 rematch at Maples, Moore had scored a career-high of forty-one points in a win over Florida State University, helping the Huskies secure their eighty-ninth consecutive win.

Moore's clutch play mattered beyond the court too since it helped ESPN hype up the game and attract a larger audience. Clutch players like Moore could be expected to deliver on the media's promise of an entertainment experience. They could be relied on to make good on the media's return on their financial investment in broadcasting and marketing a big game. Without such players, the hype would ring hollow. Was it any surprise that ESPN broadcasters referred to Moore as "Maya" during telecasts as if she were a friend of the network? In a certain sense, she was.

Like those of many Americans, my views of college sports in general, and women's basketball in particular, had long been shaped by the influence of mighty national sports media outlets like ESPN. While the media is hardly a homogenous entity, anyone who owns a television, reads a newspaper, or surfs the Internet knows that sports media outlets work hard to create a sensation, drive a drama, and draw in viewers. They also know that the rhetoric of battle is key, and that sports—for men or women—are portrayed as spiritual battles not unlike those found in war. At the same time, these media outlets aim to entertain first and foremost and believe that sports are primarily an escape for men and boys.

So it was that ESPN, the Connecticut-based, twenty-four-hour, all-sports, all-you-can-consume cable sports network that had long been American sports most dominant force, portrayed the UCONN–Stanford contest at Maples as a "rematch for revenge." It was true that the previous season, 2009–2010, Stanford had lost to UCONN in the championship match of the NCAA tournament. At the time, that game had pitted two seemingly equal teams against one another: UCONN was 38-0 and Stanford 36-1. UCONN managed to rally from a 20-12 halftime deficit to defeat the Cardinal and secure the title. That game had been a fierce defensive battle full of intense pressure: despite having some of the best shooters in basketball, Stanford made only 18 of their 68 shots, and UCONN was not much better at 18 out of 58.

But the language of revenge was far from accidental; rather, it reflected ESPN's specific attempt to capitalize on the fact that the game pitted two perennial title contenders of big-time women's college basketball, their choice to showcase the team's star players and coaches as protagonists in the show, and their perception that the best way to sell the show was to sell it as a battle.

"Tough and Together"

I watched Stanford practices the week before the UCONN game, where the mood was festive and fun. The players were focused but also committed to keeping practice loose. They were excited for their upcoming appearance on national television but also aware of the tall task at hand.

Keeping a balance between these goals was not easy. Being a college basketball player, male or female, requires managing one's body—eating right, getting enough sleep, training under the increasingly demanding counsel of sports science—and also managing the messages one sends into the mediated American sports landscape.

But with confident responses to the media, Stanford's senior captain, Jeanette Pohlen, deflected questions about exacting revenge against UCONN. Instead, she said, "We just want to protect our home court. We just want to get the 'W.' We want to show how we are improving each game . . . [that we] play well together. We want to show the country what we can do too.'" For her part, Pohlen's coach emphasized the seriousness of playing a nonconference matchup against powerhouse programs like UCONN, telling ESPN, "We play these [big] games to let us know where we are at." Coach VanDerveer was a longtime veteran of college basketball, and Pohlen was one of her senior players. As veterans, each instinctively knew that any basketball team can defeat the other on any given day, and that even if the media loved to market games that seemed like David versus Goliath, epic battles between strong and weak, all of the game's participants were exceptional athletes in their own right. No team was David, or more accurately, both teams were Goliath.

In the 2010–2011 campaign, Coach VanDerveer led an impressive group of intelligent, driven, and muscular athletes who hailed from all over the country. Only three players called California home.

All were playing basketball on scholarships, some of which were funded by generous alumni donations.

Six players on the Stanford team had at one time or another also worn the red, white, and blue of USA Basketball, the highest possible achievement

Table 0.1. Stanford University Basketball Team Roster, 2010–11

Name	Year	Position	Hometown	Height
Melanie Murphy	R-Sr.	G	Brooklyn, NY	5-9
Grace Mashore	Jr.	G	Washington, D.C.	5-10
Mikaela Ruef	So.	F	Beavercreek, OH	6-3
Chiney Ogwumike	Fr.	F	Cypress, TX	6-3
Kayla Pedersen	Sr.	F	Fountain Hills, AZ	6-4
Lindy La Rocque	Jr.	G	Las Vegas, NV	5-8
Hannah Donaghe	Sr.	G	Atascadero, CA	5-11
Sara James	Fr.	G	El Dorado Hills, CA	5-10
Jeannette Pohlen	Sr.	G	Brea, CA	6-0
Ashley Cimino	Sr.	F	Yarmouth, ME	6-3
Nnemkadi Ogwumike	Jr.	F	Cypress, TX	6-2
Toni Kokenis	Fr.	G	Oak Brook, IL	5-11
Sarah Boothe	R-So.	F/C	Gurnee, IL	6-5
Joslyn Tinkle	So.	F	Missoula, MT	6-3

Stanford alumni endow scholarships for athletes. Photo credit: *Aaron Miller*

for players of their age and at that stage of their basketball careers. Stanford players were versatile too. That season the Cardinal had several taller players who would normally play center or forward, but given their talents and abilities they were also able to play guard or forward, positions that were normally occupied by smaller players. Joslyn Tinkle was 6'3", but since Stanford's roster included several other players who were as tall or taller than her, VanDerveer could use Tinkle as either a forward or a guard. On most other teams, Tinkle would have likely played forward or center exclusively. Similarly, Pohlen was a 6'1" point guard, which was rare in women's college basketball.

A strong senior class led the Cardinal that year though Pohlen and Kayla Pedersen were the team's only senior starters. Pedersen could do it all—score, rebound, block shots, dribble, and defend—and she was on pace to become Stanford's all-time leading rebounder and was in the running to become the Stanford leader in total number of games played. Pohlen's stock was rising in her senior campaign as she shed her previous image as a three-point specialist. Pohlen had learned how to "post-up" smaller players in the "paint" and rebound over taller players, skills she had not apparently possessed earlier in her career. Longtime Stanford fans told me that in her four years at Stanford, Pohlen had improved more than any other player they had seen, diversifying her game to become one of the nation's premier guards. Junior standout

Nneka Ogwumike helped publicize the PAC-12 Conference and Stanford University. Source: PAC-12 Conference Women's Basketball Media Guide, 2011–2012 season

Nnemkadi (Nneka) Ogwumike rounded out what the university athletic department—and later, the national sports media—called Stanford's "Big Three."

In her junior year, Nneka would be named the Pac-10 Player of the Year and, after the season ended, would become the number one overall pick in the 2012 WNBA draft. Nneka was a lot like Moore: she was a superstar who could take over a game. But Coach VanDerveer also knew of the importance of recruiting an elite supporting cast of so-called role players, including redshirt sophomore Sarah Boothe, a 6'5" center, and a talented freshman class led by Nneka's younger sister Chiney and the speedster guard Toni Kokenis.

Stanford had a motto that year—"Tough and together"—which reflected their coach's philosophy about what made a good basketball team but perhaps also their university's desire to balance academics and athletics. There was no doubt the Cardinal was an entertaining team to watch. Their play was polished, the product of intense physical and mental preparation. In fact, these were not typical college athletes nor were their experiences representative of the experiences of other college athletes. What they delivered on the basketball court was nothing short of an elite entertainment product, and by all accounts they were also exceptional students in the classroom.

What fascinated me most about their experience—and what had brought me to do research at Stanford in the first place—was the fact that these young women were offered full-ride athletic scholarships (free tuition and room and board) to play basketball for an institution that was supposedly focused primarily on higher learning in the classroom. That arrangement was globally unique—most other big-time sports nations train their best athletes outside tertiary institutions of education—but in men's sports at least, it had been that way for over a century (see chapter 2).

But as they balanced their schoolwork with their courtwork, Stanford athletes contributed to a profitable business too, and for all intents and purposes they were employees of that business. At Stanford, intercollegiate sports like women's basketball were run by Stanford Athletics under the direction of the Department of Athletics and Physical Education and Recreation (DAPER), which operated a multimillion-dollar budget each year, part of which paid for these scholarships. Stanford Athletics generated revenue through ticket sales, TV revenue, and fundraising, which covered costs of intercollegiate sports programs (not intramurals or training gyms for regular students).

Moreover, the many universities that sponsor women's sports, like UCONN and Stanford, invest significant resources in women's basketball and have increasingly used the game to curry investment from outside sources. The Cardinal and Husky women's basketball teams were commercialized entities, with many games covered by at least local if not national media. Many Stanford games were either televised or broadcast on the local radio. The results from each game were written up in the university's student-run newspaper, the *Stanford Daily*, and many of their accomplishments and failures were compiled in the *San Jose Mercury News* and *San Francisco Chronicle*. The athletic department wrote press releases to inform the media of the latest goings-on too. Occasionally the Stanford women might even see their game highlights broadcast on ESPN, Fox Sports, CBS, NBC, or the Internet. Social media was making it easier than ever to publish reports and blogs about the team too. In short, women's college basketball may not have been as big time or as commercialized as men's sports, but it was still, in its own way, big time and commercialized.

In 2010 the median athletic budget for Division I-A schools was below $50 million (the median budget-to-endowment percentage was 9 percent). In 2010–2011 Stanford's athletic budget was $85.7 million, which represented 9 percent of the university's expenses for "administrative and auxiliary units."[2] That same year, Stanford Athletics had expenses and revenues of nearly $75 million. The men's football team took in $14.2 million and spent $13.5 million, the men's basketball team earned $6.1 million and spent $4.2

million, while the women's basketball team earned $1.3 million and spent nearly $2.7 million. Collectively, Stanford sports spent $44.3 million while only taking in $26.1 million, which means that only men's basketball and football were true money-makers. Between 2008 and 2010, Stanford Athletics lost approximately $5 million and did not have a balanced budget until fiscal year 2011.[3] The Stanford Athletics budget was listed as that of an auxiliary unit of the university, and yet the athletes of this university seemed to be anything but auxiliary to the building of Stanford's brand of higher education.

At the time of my research, DAPER included personnel from coaching staffs (thirty-five varsity teams plus club sports) as well as the departments of administration, compliance, development, human resources, facilities and operations, accounting, student services, recreation, community service, and media and marketing relations. Stanford's generous athletic endowment was an astonishing $500 million. The staff at DAPER consisted of 300 to 500 personnel (depending on whether part-time staff positions were tallied) entrusted to support 850 student-athletes in various ways.

Stanford employed an associate athletics director for business strategy whose role was to "manage strategic initiatives designed to enhance departmental revenue" and to "support the department's long-term business objectives." Each sport also had its own staff, which could be as small as two coaches (sailing) or as large as twenty-three coaches (football). Women's basketball had seven staff members. DAPER insisted that it operated a

Table 1.2. Stanford University, Department of Athletics and Physical Education and Recreation, Staff (2010–11 Figures)

Position Title	Number of people employed
Chief athletic director	1
Deputy athletic directors	2
Senior associate athletic directors	6
Accounting and finance	10
Development	15
Equipment	5
External relations	7
Facilities, operations and events	26
Human resources	3
Intercollegiate services	9
Marketing	6
Athletics communications and media relations	7
Physical education, recreation and wellness	15
Sports medicine/athletic training	25
Ticket sales	5

self-sufficient arm of the university, and Stanford Athletics was said to run independently of the main university, with two men's teams—basketball and football—effectively subsidizing the operations of all other teams.

Stanford's athletics scholarships were generous, valuable at the time and after graduation. In NCAA terminology, scholarships are divided into two categories—those given in "head count" sports, which means that all offers are full ride scholarships; and those given in "equivalency" sports, in which coaches give partial scholarships. Some coaches give the most money to the best players, others divide what they have to offer equally, and still others use it as a carrot to increase motivation for younger players or walk-ons (i.e., not recruited athletes). On the Stanford women's basketball team, all players were on full rides, which meant that these players were compensated as well as NCAA rules allowed them to be compensated and that in effect they were working for their coach and university. But their scholarships were not guaranteed, so if an athlete were injured or had a disagreement with her coach, her scholarship could be taken away (most were one-year agreements). Coaches at Stanford, as elsewhere, had the power to make decisions about who received a scholarship based primarily on whether that athlete could help their team win.

"She's Going to Challenge You and Push You"

Each Stanford practice leading up to the UCONN game was an exercise in efficiency not dissimilar to a factory floor, lending further credence to the idea that these players were working for the university. There was no down time, and no one ever stood idly on the sidelines. If an injured player was not able to practice a rebounding drill, she would be practicing free throws, riding a stationary bicycle, or engaging in dribbling practice. During full-court drills, which trained the team to be ready to run the floor in a fastbreak situation, Coach VanDerveer would yell, "If you are behind the ball you are SPRINNNNNTING!" or "Pick it *uuuuuuuup*!"

Coach VanDerveer slowly paced the court, and sharply focused on whatever task was at hand. She rarely smiled. Her longtime associate, Coach Amy Tucker, quietly strolled in a distinguished manner from one player to the next, finding ways to help. When she did speak, Coach Tucker enunciated words chosen carefully. Assistant Coach Kate Paye marched the court with purpose while remaining laser-focused on improving players' fundamental basketball techniques. Assistant Coach Bobbie Kelsey freewheeled, trying to lighten the mood and playfully coaxing players to "pick it up." Every member of the Stanford coaching staff had played basketball competitively and at a high level—Paye and Kelsey for Stanford, Tucker for Ohio State, and VanDerveer for Indiana. Coach Paye had even played professionally.[4]

Above all, the players seemed to trust Coach VanDerveer. One of VanDerveer's former players, Charli Turner Thorne, who would later become head basketball coach at Arizona State University, remembered that when Coach VanDerveer took over at Stanford, she set the bar high and set it high early: "You're going to be the best conditioned player you can be. She's going to get the best out of you. She's going to challenge you and push you. It helped me get the most out of my experience. I felt like I gave everything I had."[5]

"We're Not Losing Today"

The Maples crowd rose and roared for tipoff. The lights dimmed in the rafters, leaving a spotlight on the players on the court. The battle was underway.

Pohlen began brilliantly, slicing to the basket and shooting from long range. In the blink of an eye she scored ten points on two layups and two slingshot three-pointers, each shot from her right shoulder with the precision of an assassin. The Cardinal coaches directed several defenders at Moore, including the Ogwumike sisters, Tinkle, Boothe, and Pedersen. The strategy worked: Moore missed her first five shots, some badly.

In the first seven minutes of the game, Stanford raced out to a 17-4 lead. Nneka and Chiney took turns on offense, showing off their devastating combination of finely honed post moves and superior athleticism to put the Cardinal up 32-19. Just before halftime, Coach VanDerveer signaled for substitutes for the sisters, wanting them full of energy in the second half, especially if they were to continue chasing Moore around the court. But with the Ogwumike sisters on the bench, the Stanford offense froze, and UCONN cut Stanford's lead to 34-30.

Stanford remained resolute in the second half, led by Pohlen, who made play after play. When she drove to the basket, she put her head down like a ram. Every time UCONN made a run, it seemed that Pohlen had an answer. UCONN managed one final push, bringing the score to 61-55, but when Moore missed another shot and Chiney dropped in an easy fast-break layup, Stanford's lead stood strong again at eight, 63-55. Fouls and free throws punctuated the final minutes of the game, and when the clock ticked to zero, Stanford began to digest their victory, having felled a fellow Goliath, 71–59.

The victory had required a total team effort. Pedersen was formidable inside, grabbing eleven rebounds. Nneka chipped in twelve points and six rebounds, and Lindy LaRocque dished out six assists. The Cardinal held

UCONN to 32 percent shooting from the floor and they out-rebounded the Huskies by seven, 43-36. Stanford's defense had delivered a stalwart team performance in shutting down Moore. Their swarming, relentless resistance held the star to fourteen points, a little over half her average of 24.8. Moore made zero layups and shot one free throw.

But among an elite group of standout players, many of whom would ultimately go on to play professionally, Pohlen was outstanding, scoring a career-high thirty-one points, grabbing nine rebounds, and dishing out six assists. Even Pedersen, a steady senior who had carried the Cardinal for years, praised her teammate to the press: "She put this team on her back and told us, 'We're not losing today.'"

On a postgame television show, ESPN College Basketball Analyst Kara Lawson, herself a former star at the University of Tennessee and a gold-medal-winning Olympian, said, "UCONN was outplayed in every statistical category, but the key to Stanford's win was its defensive game plan. They stayed attached to Maya Moore at all times." The team's preparation routine in advance of the game had been calculated and methodical; Coach VanDerveer said she had watched every game that UCONN had played that year five times. All big-time college coaches scout opponents to learn their plays, but few were known to prepare like VanDerveer. All big-time college coaches were looking for an edge on their opponent, but few seemed as capable as her in finding it.

The players went about their business with similar professionalism. Even though the game took place at the end of the year and several players were battling winter colds, some coughing violently as they ran through warm-ups, the players never complained. Like their coach, they wanted to beat UCONN, and they were willing to put in the necessary time and make the necessary sacrifices. In practices, Cardinal players dove on the floor for loose balls. They discussed defensive tactics during water breaks. They pushed each other to get in game shape.

After the game, ESPN's highlight show, SportsCenter, went to some length to make it seem like the victory had been an improbable upset and that it couldn't have been done without individual stars like Jeannette Pohlen, Kayla Pedersen, and Nneka Ogwumike, but that said more about the sports media and its lust for underlining rivalry, hype, and drama than about Stanford's preparation.

At the time VanDerveer was in her thirty-second season as a head coach and twenty-fifth season at Stanford, and VanDerveer's teams had been collecting big-game victories and conference championships for years. Only once in VanDerveer's career had one of her teams lost more games in a

Coach Tara VanDerveer wins her 1,000th game. Photo credit: *Aaron Miller*

season than they won (1984–1985), and that was during her first year at Stanford, working with players she had not recruited herself. Excepting the 2000 season, Stanford had won every Pac-10 conference title in the new millennium, and during VanDerveer's tenure, Stanford had won over 80 percent of its games at Maples Pavilion. Two of VanDerveer's teams—1990 and 1992—had won national titles, elusive hardware for even the most accomplished college coaches. Beating UCONN was a variation on a theme that she, as a maestro of basketball greatness, had been conducting for over thirty years.

Big Time

Still, in the sports mediascape, a fantasyland where grown men and women leave reality to discuss the theater of American physical culture, the story of one team beating another in dramatic fashion was not enough. Media pundits made what they could of UCONN's now broken win streak, which they regularly noted surpassed even the streak of John Wooden's hallowed UCLA men's teams. For ESPN's Jeremy Schaap, UCONN's streak highlighted a battle that women's teams had been fighting against the public, particularly our "collective capacity to appreciate women's athletics." Every time UCONN played a game during its historic win streak, Schaap said "they were

Coach Tara VanDerveer surveys the court. Photo credit: *Aaron Miller*

fighting the battle of the sexes." Another ESPN writer, Michelle Voepel, took a different tack, stressing that in preparing to beat the Huskies, "Stanford wasn't really thinking all that much about the history, either its own against UCONN or that of women's basketball in general." Instead, Voepel continued, their focus was on strategy and execution, and the ultimate storyline ought to be that women athletes and women coaches were as serious, hard-working, and as talented as their male counterparts and approached their games as professionally.[6]

The ending of UCONN's streak—and the Stanford win—raised questions about the notion of big time. What exactly did "big time" signify, especially for female college athletes and the future of college sports?

The term denoted a strange space between the universities that invested in college sports and the media outlets who held the power to anoint a team or, alternatively, knock them off that imaginary pedestal.

First, there were structural issues. Institutions like Stanford and UCONN, which participate in the NCAA's highest level of competition, Division I (D-I), have larger stadiums and athletic department budgets, more elaborate practice facilities, and higher-paid coaches and athletic department staff than the other two NCAA tiers (D-II and D-III). The commercialization and professionalization of college football (see chapter 2) led to fractures among NCAA members, and the NCAA today oversees three divisions of college sports: D-I, which is the highest competition level of intercollegiate athletics, D-II, and D-III.[7]

While in principle "big time" refers to D-I, which offers (full) athletic scholarships, the lower divisions of intercollegiate competition also make attractive offers to prospective athletes. While D-II offers only partial athletic scholarships and D-III offers no athletic scholarships at all, exceptions to this general principle abound as NCAA rules do not penalize institutions that offer academic scholarships to promising athletes.[8] Still it is D-I's profitability that sets them apart. In the early 2010s, men's college sports, driven especially by college football, were nearly as formidable an economic juggernaut as the NFL, earning approximately $6 billion per year.[9] By 2018, profits from such arrangements (as well as ticket sales and donations) had grown; according to NCAA data, NCAA schools across all divisions and all sports generated over $10 billion dollars per year, most of which was generated by D-1 schools through their football programs.[10] Thus, if "big time" only indexed the amount of money being poured into college sports, football could truly stake a claim to be its king. Based on revenue alone, college football was the third most popular sport in the United States after professional football and professional basketball.

Table 0.3. Media Revenue for Major American Sports*

League	Year	Deal Partner	Media Revenue/Year (Approx.)
NFL	2012	CBS, Fox, NBC, ESPN, Verizon and Microsoft (for streaming games on mobile devices)	$5.23 billion
	2016	CBS, Fox, NBC, ESPN, Verizon and Microsoft (for streaming games on mobile devices)	Between $7 and $10 billion, plus another $2 billion for streaming rights fees
NBA	2012	Turner Sports, ESPN, ABC	$930 million
	2014	Turner Sports, ESPN, ABC	$2.667 billion
College football	2012	Various	$6 billion
	2018	Various	$10 billion (includes ticket sales and alumni donations)
MLB	2012	ESPN Fox and Turner Sports	$1.55 billion

* Sources: Travis, Clay. 2017. How Much Do the NFL and TV Partners Make a Year? March 1. https://www.outkickthecoverage.com/how-much-do-the-nfl-and-tv-partners-make-a-year-030117; Gaines, Cork. 2015. The amount networks are paying to broadcast NFL games is skyrocketing. November 23. http://www.businessinsider.com/nfl-tv-rights-revenue-2015-11; CNBC. 2018. Fox to pay more than $3 billion to broadcast 'Thursday Night Football' for five seasons, report says. https://www.cnbc.com/2018/01/31/fox-reaches-5-year-deal-with-the-nfl-to-broadcast-thursday-night-football.html; Rovell, Darren. 2017. Verizon, NFL agree to new 5-year deal worth nearly $2.5 billion. December 11. http://www.espn.com/nfl/story/_/id/21737823/verizon-nfl-agree-new-5-year-deal-worth-nearly-25-billion

Since the 1980s, each athletic conference has controlled the rights to college football revenue, crafted its own revenue and branding strategy, and has been concerned with maximizing profits (see chapter 2). The largest athletic conferences in the NCAA's D-I, sometimes referred to as the Power 5, sign contracts with television networks granting them the rights to broadcast college football in exchange for hundreds of millions of dollars per year and, therefore, operate much as the professional leagues do, which is to say as an entertainment (rather than an education) business.[11]

Meanwhile the NCAA controls the broadcast rights to men's and women's basketball and other sports, and like the conferences it seeks to maximize the profits it can derive from their entertainment value. In 2010 the NCAA signed a contract with Turner Sports and CBS for joint domestic production of the NCAA Men's Basketball tournament, which amounted to roughly $771 million annually over fourteen years. The NCAA signed with ESPN for approximately $46 million per year for the international broadcasting rights of the Women's Basketball Tournament and championship tournaments in ten other sports. Broadcast rights for the Women's Basketball Tournament championship game were therefore part of a larger television deal with ESPN that also included the College Baseball World Series and the national championships of twenty other minor sports. This deal was worth $55 million over three years (2010–2012), meaning that the total payout to be split each year was approximately $18.3 million (3.4 percent of the men's deal).[12] With a total of 126 game appearances, this amounted to $145,503 per team per game played, which paled in comparison to the $5.7 million per team per game played in the men's tournament.

This quantitative—rather than qualitative—notion of what constitutes the big time dominates mainstream understandings of American college sports. Take for example Charles Clotfelter, a professor of economics and law at Duke University and the author of *Big-Time College Sports in American Universities*, who notes that "big time" in college sports refers to the "the highly commercialized and widely followed competition . . . that is undertaken by several hundred American universities . . . featuring sizable revenues generated by ticket sales and television"[13] (he does not say specifically whether women's basketball teams like those of Stanford or UCONN would fit that bill). Clotfelter's primarily economic understanding of "big time" is unfortunate not only because many Americans overlook the formidable power college sports like basketball have in shaping the lives of young American women but also because a quantitative focus limits our ability to appreciate the social and cultural value that such endeavors hold not only for colleges, coaches, fans, and alumni but also in terms of the power that sports hold for the athletes themselves. Indeed, sports are both a big moneymaker *and* a forum for telling optimistic stories of effort leading to accomplishment for women and for men, stories that may be lost in a narrowly focused economic analysis of profits and losses.

Basketball is one of the most popular sports globally[14] and a growing number of those who play basketball are women and girls, particularly in the United States. In fact, basketball is the most-played sport among American high school girls,[15] and most U.S. colleges and universities field women's basketball teams.

But since the definition of "big time" in American sports is most often given in economic terms, some kind of qualitative—and historical—comparison between women's basketball and men's football also seems essential, especially one that more fully acknowledges the media's power to shape the narrative about who gets to be called big time, who does not, and what that status (or lack thereof) means.

"They've Made the Commitment"

ESPN was the pioneer in American cable sports media, and it remains the industry leader. Its in-your-face highlight presentations, which cleverly combine music, moving pictures, and witty banter bring sports-hungry audiences their fill of highlights any time of the day or night. In recent years the NFL, NBA, MLB, and NHL, not to mention network stalwarts NBC and CBS, have also developed dedicated sports networks, but the substance and presentation of these highlight shows generally mimic the ESPN model, and the cable sports network remains dominant.[16]

And yet ESPN's coverage of women's sports has long lagged behind the attention it gives to men's sports, which is why the UCONN–Stanford broadcast was something of an anomaly. In 2009, 1.4 percent of the airtime of ESPN's flagship program, SportsCenter, went to women's sports, and in 2010, 8 percent of ESPN's programming was on women's sports.[17] In 2013, sociologists Cooky, Messner, and Hextrum found that coverage of women's sports on local and national news was declining, having reached its lowest point since they began frequent longitudinal studies in 1989.[18] Even when the mainstream media covered women's sports, Cooky, Messner, and Hextrum's analysis showed that it was not covered in a "serious, respectful" way. Instead, coverage often focuses on athletes' femininity and sexuality, not their athleticism, often "presenting female athletes as sexual objects for consumption."[19] As a result, the authors argue that contrary to the popular claim that news media "give the viewers what they want," in fact, "news media build audiences for men's sport while silencing and marginalizing women's sport." (The marginalization of women in media coverage has been corroborated by several other studies in research regarding sports magazines,[20] newspapers,[21] and social media.[22])

The gender disparity in media coverage appeared to be changing in the fall of 2010 when ESPN introduced ESPNw, a dedicated network for women's sports that was launched after deep consideration.[23] ESPNw was unfurled cautiously, though, with executives testing it as a digital pilot project to see if such "niche programming" could ever become a full-fledged television channel. Some argued that the new network would serve as a "pink ghetto" and take pressure off male media executives to cover women fairly and regularly on ESPN's flagship channel. A group of female bloggers emerged against the idea of a sports network dedicated to women's sports because they saw ESPNw pitching them "something pink and putting sparkles on it."[24]

By 2013, ESPNw did not appear to have significantly changed the broader mass media, which generally derided women's sports as a sideshow to the real business of men's sports. According to research done that year by the University of Minnesota Tucker Center for Research on Girls and Women in Sport, while female participation in sports constituted 40 percent of all participation, the overall coverage of women's sports on local news broadcasts was 4 percent.[25]

"Because It's Boring"

In 2011, I spoke with an ESPN television producer, who agreed to speak on the condition of anonymity. She told me that ESPN's core business model had little place for women's sports and that ESPN producers operated under certain assumptions when they decided what the network would and would not air.

First, men's sports were always prioritized over women's sports because ESPN saw its main viewer base as male.

The second priority, the producer said, was anything that related to football, especially the NFL, because the league was far more lucrative than any other. In 2011, ESPN paid approximately $120 million for *each* NFL Monday Night Football game, which amounted to approximately $2 billion per season. But college football was no slouch. In late 2012, ESPN agreed to a deal that would allow it to broadcast the BCS Football Championship Playoffs for twelve years and agreed to pay $470 million each year for those rights, or $5.64 billion over a twelve-year period. After securing rights to broadcast the BCS Playoffs, ESPN president John Skipper said, "Because of college football's widespread popularity and the incredible passion of its fans, few events are more meaningful than these games. We are ecstatic at the opportunity to continue to crown a college football champion on ESPN's outlets for years to come, the perfect finale to our year-round commitment to the sport."[26] (Men's college basketball also garners huge bids from media outlets. For example, CBS paid $10.8 billion for the rights to the NCAA men's basketball tournament for the years 2011–2024.)[27]

The third priority was to broadcast anything about a star athlete, and the fourth was to broadcast anything that promoted a corporate brand. For the latter, the producer confided that one must not under any circumstance air segments that denigrated a corporate brand or one of the "cash-cow" leagues, especially the NFL.[28] Finally, ESPN producers were forbidden to broadcast anything suggesting that a particular sport was under-watched or considered minor because, in the words of the producer, "nobody cares."

As a leader in sports media, ESPN's production assumptions have long conditioned Americans to conclude that some sports matter and others do not. As I listened to the ESPN producer speak, I realized that I too had been conditioned each sport in a specific way, and that ESPN's assumptions reinforced the historical biases that have existed against women's sports for decades. Indeed, by prioritizing the NFL above all, these assumptions effectively shifted attention away from women's sports and toward the most graphic, violent, and profitable of men's sports such as football, men's basketball, and fight sports like the Ultimate Fighting Championship. The first two are among the sports I grew up playing and watching and are the sports I still watch with friends today. Rarely if ever do these friends watch women's basketball.

We are all conditioned in this way, but if I needed any more proof, it came when the ESPN producer also told me that *she* would never watch the WNBA. When I asked her why, she answered, "Because it's boring." Even as she recognized the many ways that ESPN's central broadcasting assumptions were biased against the production of women's sports, she herself had also come to believe that there was an inherent connection between gender and entertainment value and that women's sports could never provide the entertainment value that men's sports provide.

"That's a Kind of Chicken-Egg Thing"

If one only examines the question through a quantitative lens, it is hard to dispute the claim that women's basketball is smaller time than men's basketball, or men's football, since women's revenues are indeed lower than those of these sports. But our collective notion of what constitutes big time should not be solely dependent on how much money can be generated through marketing a particular sport but should also be dependent on more fundamentally qualitative issues such as culture; education; sex and gender; and aesthetics, ethics, and morality—as this book will show.

A critic might quibble that being dubbed big time hardly matters, but it does, and in fact, the stakes could not be higher. Surveys indicate that on average, young girls play youth sports, including basketball, to have fun, stay in shape, get exercise, improve skills, do something they're good at, be part of a team, and experience the excitement of competition. By contrast, it is interesting to note that these motivations for young women to play sports, which are listed in order of perceived importance, include several body-image related issues that boys in the same surveys do not list as being as important. For boys, motivations to play youth sport are to have fun, to improve skills, to experience the excitement of competition, to do something they're good at, to stay in shape, to meet the challenge of competition, to be part of a team, and to win.[29] If the media pours larger sums into men's sports than into women's, is it a surprise that young girls perceive sports participation in this way, not as a chance to improve skills or compete but instead to get the exercise they "need" to shape their bodies? As sociologist Cheryl Cooky has argued in the context of lackluster media coverage of women's sports, "young girls cannot be what they cannot see."[30]

Coach VanDerveer told me that being dubbed big time was not solely a problem experienced by female basketball players. The media are a big part of making a sport "big-time", she said, before adding:

> This season our women's volleyball team is #2 in the nation, and has beat the #1 and #3 teams, but there is no coverage. It's the same in soccer, where the media props up the men's teams. In postseason tournaments as well, such as men's basketball and football, teams are rewarded with big money. If women's teams got a similar amount of money, that would change things.[31]

Stanford assistant coach Kate Paye agreed, telling me that perceptions of women's basketball were constructed by the media, although she was also convinced that these perceptions could be changed: "Everything is market-driven. The media is going to presumably cover what people want to hear about but people kind of want to hear about what they know about so that's a kind of chicken-egg thing."[32]

In the post-game television coverage of Stanford's victory over UCONN, ESPN broadcasters were *still* asking whether the women's game had made it to the big time. It was a question that the cable pundits could keep asking each other ad nauseum and all the way to the bank while simultaneously keeping women's sports in its less than big-time place.

The more I thought about it, the more I realized that it was a misleading question anyway. After all, the UCONN–Stanford *was* a game between two elite teams watched by thousands of fans in person and hundreds of thousands if not millions more on television, with corporate sponsorship and print and radio media coverage to boot. The sold-out match was extremely exciting, profitable, and, arguably, a major cultural event. Wasn't *that* enough to be dubbed big time?

Still, the spotlights that lit up the stages for men's and women's sports had different strengths. Men's college sports generate bigger sums of money for their universities through media rights deals, but it is essential to note that that is not inherently because men are more talented or more entertaining. It is just that media outlets like ESPN are run largely by men who perceive sports to be spaces for men and boys, and that perception incentivizes those involved in the production of college sports to craft stories about men, not women. That tendency creates a vicious cycle, keeping the growth and popularity of women's sports relatively hamstrung. For example, despite consistent national success, Stanford's women's team still fails to draw the same media gaze as the often middling, and sometimes even mediocre, Stanford men's basketball team.

In short, there are powerful, if sometimes hidden, forces of sexism operating under the surface, unseen even in the bright spotlight that shines on college sports.

Even the issue of exploitation—and the supposed antidote for it, "pay for play"—suffers from these hidden forces. Since the late 2000s, NCAA D-I male college athletes in sports like basketball and football have been increasingly front and center in a national debate over whether athletes should be paid beyond the full-ride athletic scholarships they already received. In 2009, for example, around the time of the NCAA basketball tournaments, the *New York Times* posted a series of arguments on its "Room for Debate" blog that highlighted various proposals for how to reform college sports. Among the participants, it was professor of sport management Ellen J. Staurowsky who best summed up the hypocrisy of the NCAA, writing, "While college sports officials, coaches, and administrators would not make deals with corporate entities without adequate counsel to advise them and protect their interests at the negotiating table, the 'amateur' talent, in order to remain eligible, is barred according to NCAA regulations from having adequate legal counsel to represent them."

The chorus of those calling for more power for college athletes, and some of them proposing a more direct form of pay for play, seemed to reach a crescendo in the 2010s. In 2011, for example, in an essay in the *Atlantic* called "The Shame of College Sports," civil rights historian Taylor Branch blasted the NCAA's exploitation of big-time college athletes and compared the economic arrangement to the post–Civil War plantations of the South. Other similar essays followed.[33] Several former big-time college athletes also filed litigation against the NCAA and its corporate sponsors during this period, alleging that their names, images, and likenesses (NILs) were used without permission. These legal cases enticed more journalists than ever to squint a skeptical eye at big-time men's college sports. In response, in 2014 several big-time conferences agreed to cover the gap that had grown between what an NCAA grant-in-aid provided and the true cost of attendance (TCOA). The move seemed like one in the right direction, but as the journalist Christopher Smith wrote at the time, "No one is under the naive impression that this is the last train stop when it comes to compensating college athletes. It's more like a way-station."[34] For the next few years, pay-for-play calls seemed to go under the radar, but in 2017 a scandal rocked the nation back into the debate. That year, after an FBI investigation charged ten men, several of whom worked for the shoe and apparel manufacturer Adidas, with offering assistant coaches of D-I men's basketball teams bribes and kickbacks in exchange for sending promising players to their program. Soon there were calls for paying players *more than* the true cost of attendance. The discovery prompted the NCAA to appoint former Secretary of State and Stanford professor Condoleezza Rice to oversee the Commission on Collegiate Basketball and to officially consider whether or not to pay players beyond TCOA. Rice delivered her report in 2018, calling on leaders to "put the college back in college sports" and refocus reform measures not on pay-for-play but on raising rates of athletes receiving college degrees.

The next year, in late 2019, the state of California passed the first bill freeing college athletes to profit from their own NILs, prompting other states to draft similar bills and prompting U.S. senators Cory Booker and Richard Blumenthal to propose national legislation seeking large-scale college sports reform. Then in late December 2020, senators Booker and Blumenthal, along with two of their colleagues, introduced the College Athletes' Bill of Rights legislation, which included provisions to ensure that players in big-time sports were treated as employees and paid for their services to the university. Around the same time, the Supreme Court agreed to hear the so-called Kessler case, and ultimately ruled unanimously that universities could compensate athletes beyond their grant-in-aid if the money was for educational expenses.

The NCAA had all along insisted that paying players *in any way* would harm what it considered the integrity and "allure" of the college sports' product—amateurism—and "blur the lines between student-athletes and professionals", so the Kessler ruling was a major blow. What the NCAA feared was a full-blown free market for the services of college athletes. The system of capping their pay at the cost of an athletic scholarship (with or without TCOA) had been working fine for them and the universities that they represented.

Since they are rarely anointed with the crown of big time, women are largely left out of these debates, and while some women college athletes have begun to cash in on their NILs, their services to the university and compensation for it continue to be largely overlooked, even as many of the same universities that refuse to pay their big-time athletes advertise their institutions' educational offerings and institutional excellence with fancy billboards, pamphlets, and webpages of female athletes.

Thus there seems to remain a fundamental and commonplace sexism in American college sports, which is sometimes hidden but always made worse by a purely economic comparison of men's and women's sports, which keeps men on top and women looking up. This quantitative comparison prevents us from holistically assessing women's sports, let alone appreciating them aesthetically, and not in an objectified, sexualized way but in terms of appreciating athletes who shine, coaches who inspire, and games that move us emotionally, or ethically, games in which we not only see but also fully appreciate the value in all young people, regardless of gender, getting a chance to play, compete, and grow.

Agenda

As I began to organize this book, I had four goals in mind. First, I wanted to show how and why big-time women's basketball matters, and for me, this meant showing how tough the women of the big time are even if men have often (unjustifiably) kept that adjective to themselves throughout sports history.

Second, I wanted to emphasize that sports carry considerable educational potential, including this hidden curriculum for demonstrating toughness. As an athlete and former coach and as a current educator and researcher, I believe there is great potential to educate through sports despite the admittedly many problems that afflict college sports when played at the big-time level. The media may make much of scandals, but their existence does not necessarily mean we need to discard our belief in the power of sports to educate. We must not conflate the misguided acts of a few with the educational value of physical challenge and competition. Historically at many institutions, academics and athletics have been at odds, but in theory at least, they need not be. They can still be complementary endeavors, and students can exercise their bodies and minds to study and to play and to learn through these processes. Many have learned through sports because sports are among the most effective tools for teaching these values in that a greater number of children are interested in sports-based education who may not otherwise be interested in classroom-based education. Despite many critics who have said otherwise, sports remain real and important educational opportunities.

Third, I wanted to propose practical reforms of the big-time college sports system with education front of mind and to do so by studying a university, a team, and a coach that prioritized education over revenue generation (even if their way of doing things may not be perfect and may not work for everyone else). In philosophical terms, there is nothing inherently wrong with colleges participating in competitive, televised, mediated athletic contests that bring in extra revenue for the university nor with admitting athletes that will help them do so successfully, but if institutional safeguards are not implemented and adhered to, if educational priorities are not maintained, and if universities are not transparent about the entertainment businesses that they are in, the outcome may be a university culture that privileges the needs of athlete-students over non-athlete students. We have seen it happen time and again. At Stanford, by contrast, the question of athletics and academics is not an either-or equation but rather both-and. Sports do not overpower classroom education nor does classroom education overpower sports. Athletics are simply an important part of a broad-based education, and that balance suggests that the university expects great things from all its students, athletes or otherwise. There is much common sense in what we might call the Stanford standard (see chapter 8) since it is an ecosystem in which students can pursue academic and athletic greatness in tandem. Based on my observations, it seems that those who achieve such greatness do so when their coach and institution prioritize the values that are necessary to make that greatness possible to achieve, that is, where there are priorities set in a way that allow them to thrive. A classroom education can prepare the mind for one's whole life and help athletes move on with their lives after their physically demanding sporting careers are over, which is the most likely outcome for most athletes. For big-time athletes at universities where their brains are not sufficiently appreciated, much less their labor compensated, the story is different. But as scholars and as educators, shouldn't it be our job to help envision and then create an environment in which all athletes are realistically compensated, duly educated, and generally respected?

Big-time men's college sports, for many, are often seen as a ticket to a better life and a higher social class, a mechanism for upward social mobility. Parents, coaches, schools, media, and companies fuel these notions by (often implicitly) encouraging young people to invest themselves in sports. In recent years, some big-time college athletes have begun to realize that their chances of making the pros are much smaller than the sports culture has suggested and so have begun to resist these cultural forces and bring the widespread institutional exploitation of big-time college athletes to the front page. This all makes perfect sense: if you as a college athlete know that you are not going to go pro, then being paid for your athletic services to the university would logically become a more urgent matter to you.

But the experiences of big-time women athletes, for whom playing professionally is an opportunity but is not as lucrative, reminds us that upward mobility is more often—and often more effectively—achieved through educational attainment than through sports themselves. For too long, this fact has been ignored or overlooked in favor of simple pay-the-players conclusions, and far too often this only refers to discussions of big-time male athletes. For those who truly care about bringing an end to all exploitation and discrimination, the conversation about college sports must begin to include big-time women as much as it includes big-time men as well as proposals to better educate and respect and increase the compensation of these players.

This is especially the case for athletes who are not fortunate enough to receive a scholarship from a prestigious academic institution like Stanford. Does buying in to the big time—with its intense training and intense pressure—improve their lives, or does the market's commercial influence in college sports complicate their lives to a degree that reform is necessary?

I think the answer depends on the specifics of each case. The young women profiled in this book can be considered both privileged (having been given a free education and a chance to learn priceless lessons from a world-class coach) and exploited (for profit by their university and its partners extracting value from their labor and likeness) at the same time, but the story at other universities will be different.

The notion of exploitation is predicated too heavily on a quantitative, economic analysis of who earns what and who gets paid what, which largely ignores the social, educational, and psychological value of sport to the university and to the athlete. In effect, this focus on money limits our collective ability to see how some universities sometimes use, while others sometimes improve, the lives of young (female) athletes. Therefore, I believe we need to focus more attention on why college sports are and should remain an integral part of the higher education experience.

My fourth, and final agenda was to provide a more balanced theoretical approach to the study of college sports that blends the best of symbolic interactionist analysis and critical or cultural analysis in order to expose the problems of class conflict, racism, and sexism that undoubtedly exist but also to recognize the great role that real people see college sports playing in building their lives. It is my view that too many academics (and journalists) see only the economic exploitation of athletes—and this is a problem that I duly address herein—but since their views are disproportionately concerned with economic issues, and because their critical analyses focus on race, gender, or social class, they have often failed to recognize, or incorporate in their narrative, a full accounting of the social, cultural, educational, and psychological potential and benefits of college sports.

As a scholar, I know that I always have a choice to either focus on—and write about—the solutions we as human societies have already created or to focus on the solutions we have not yet come up with. That is, there are always many ways of looking at things, many ways of focusing our attention. One might see the big-time American college sports system as a microcosm of a free market and capitalistic economic system that encourages employers to exploit employees in order to gain for themselves. Alternatively, one might see that same economic system as an example of the rather miraculous human ability to create complex systems that can sustain the livelihoods of large numbers of people over time. Still others might see promise in the system as it stands but also wish to see it change in fundamental ways.

The college sports system in the United States is not a simple system, after all. It is not only an economic system, after all. It has both helped us create heroes to revere and hypnotize us out of our boredom, and it has also helped keep many people employed by creating new avenues for advertising dollars to move. It has encouraged people to try to keep their grades up so they can be eligible to go to college too. Although there are plenty of exceptions, our economic system generally rewards hard workers (in the case of basketball, the gym rats, in the case of school, the book worms, in the case of both, the scholar-athletes). Marginalized groups (such as African Americans and women) can and do use sports to become a little bit less marginalized too.

So money in education is not categorically a negative thing; rather, it depends on how it is used and whether it is allowed to distort other priorities, such as classroom education or the attainment of a quality college degree. Indeed, as chapters 2 and 3 show, financial sponsorship helped early American college athletes gain freedom from paternalistic faculty, and money was the legal rationale for the gender equity legislation known as Title IX. Green, can, under certain circumstances, be good.

Big-time sports are an important cultural institution, and yet scholars who study them rarely give the public the intellectual leadership they need to understand them in all their facets because they often begin their investigations of sport with a generally dismissive if not outright negative view of them. Some academic books on American college sports, such as those that primarily regard football and which foreground an economic analysis, have focused on how much money is wasted by corruption[35] and how these sports, as "circuses," largely serve to ruin undergraduate education by making college into one big party,[36] but these books often miss or take for granted the point of why these games matter socially, culturally, educationally, and symbolically, and, therefore, why many Americans are so willing to make sacrifices to watch, play, and consume them.

As a result, some of those who have studied sports academically, especially from a critical sociological perspective, have either chosen not to create a public space for scholarly voices on sports to be heard or have tried but have failed to provide a (balanced or positive) perspective on sport that speaks to sport's place—and power—in society. In recent years, the work of many social science scholars has borne the hallmarks of theories derived from Marx, the scholars of the Frankfurt School, Foucault, critical feminists, and postmodernism with varying degrees of emphasis on power, sexism, classism, and racism. In graduate school, the work of Marx and Foucault challenged my thinking about sports, which I realized had been quite conventional and shaped largely by the mass media. Yet upon deeper study, I realized that neither Marx nor Foucault squared with my worldview.

Then after a recommendation from my doctoral supervisor, I began to read Max Weber, who had studied why people work hard and try to join higher social classes. Whereas Marx posited that the lower classes, or proletariat, develop a collective consciousness and will one day revolt against the bourgeoisie class that oppresses them, for Weber, the situation was more fluid. Instead of clear lines between classes, "people in the same social class act in the same fashion in a given situation because others will hold them in esteem for making the right life-style decisions."[37] Thus, Weber concluded that the choice to pursue certain activities and not others amounted to an effort to join a certain class and to seek a certain kind of social status.

This argument suggested my own sense of the positive power of sport and the power inherent in the notion of buying in. If sports helped people join a chosen social class, then why did academics so often seem to condemn people for making that choice? I cannot deny that I am expressing my biases by applauding young people who buy in, which I do throughout this book, but without that dedication to themselves and their own education (in the classroom and on the court), I do not see how any society can function in an orderly way or how one generation can pass on its knowledge to the next.

So to provide a more balanced public intellectual guide, I set out to rethink not only big-time women's basketball but also how its story should be told. This story, it seemed to me, needed to include how women basketball players historically bought into a male-dominated and highly commercialized college sports system, replete with its professionalism and emphasis on victory, brand, and profit. But it also needed to include a discussion of what that act of buying in meant economically, educationally, and symbolically. After all, there is a great tension that lies between the rising commercialism[38] of big-time women's college sports and the considerable power that sports like basketball hold for the growth of the women who play them.

That being said, I neither propose that left-wing politics are "ruining college sports"[39] nor do I believe that we can or should take college sports as they are and conclude that "it is just what it is." There are myriad problems to address and significant reforms to be made, and we must solve them without throwing the baby out with the bathwater.

Chapter Summaries

In the chapters that follow, I trace women's basketball from its origins to the present day. I examine the history of women's basketball and women's sports with special reference to college football since it was football that first created our sense of what the big time in college sports is. Football players, coaches, and fans have excluded women from its domain and thereby created a gendered notion of what the big time is, actively shaping cultural ideals for manhood and womanhood, and masculinity and femininity, in and out of sport. Symbolically, football has also gendered some of the most important virtues of athletes who play sports such as hard work, toughness, and physical sacrifice, and that unfortunate fact has set up women who play for constant cultural comparison, much of which is unfair (see chapters 2 and 3). However, in response, women and girls have fought tirelessly to reclaim their sense of identity, dignity, and respect. *Buying In* thus spotlights the biography of Stanford University head women's basketball coach Tara VanDerveer and the experiences of one of her recent teams in order to put a face on this fight. Coach VanDerveer has long been active in the fight against the perception that sports are a "male preserve,"[40] combating a longstanding sexism that sadly still exists in sports. Women like Coach VanDerveer, who work tirelessly to help counteract the forces that keep sexism alive in sport, continue to challenge the idea that work in sports is work best suited to men (see chapters 3, 4, and 5). One of VanDerveer's recent teams experienced that sexism on a personal level so the following chapters attempt to describe both the power and problems that existed for them in rich detail. By following the team during its season and on its quest for a national championship, we will witness their ups and downs, setbacks and growth, and see what it means to be a big-time women's college basketball player today. For some, this means a chance to become a better athlete, to learn important life skills, or to find a place to belong. For others, it means branding oneself and one's university simultaneously, paving a path to celebrity and fame. For still others, it means finding a place where academics and athletics are not seen in antithetical terms and thriving in that place. Big-time female college athletes make courageous sacrifices with their bodies to play sports that are often extremely physical and sometimes violent. They do so because fierce competition means a great deal to them even if that competition might sometimes lead to physical pain and injury and mental stress (chapter 6). It is true that some colleges now use big-time college athletes to symbolically enhance their perceived brand value and create real revenue (chapter 7), but we must also acknowledge that the big time also affords young men and women a chance to learn and a chance to become part of something larger than themselves (chapter 8). At Stanford University, though, it is easier to buy in to this big-time arrangement because the university maintains policies that ensure that education matters for all students, including big-time athletes (chapter 9). Indeed, it is for that reason that the book's final chapter presents a summary of recommended reform measures to improve the lives of all big-time college athletes, organized around the mantra of "pay, respect, and better educate" (chapter 10). The book concludes by with a discussion of why fans should give women's sports a chance and an afterword on college sports amid the dual pandemics of COVID-19 and systemic racism.

Notes

1. Quoted in Mosbacher and Yacker. "Training Rules."
2. In 2012–2013, the Stanford Athletics budget was $97.4 million, in 2011–2012 $87.3 million, and in 2010–2011 $85.7 million. DAPER runs an investment fund to cover any shortfalls that may occur year to year.
3. Thomas and Drape, "Stanford Dominates"; see also Landicho, "Athletics Budget." Stanford Athletics eliminated twenty-five staff positions, froze salaries, and cut travel and facilities budgets, operating at a loss of $1.51 million for fiscal year 2009 and $156,000 for fiscal year 2010. But unlike some universities at the time, Stanford did not cut any sports programs.
4. Professional leagues for women did not exist at the time Coaches VanDerveer and Tucker graduated from college; accordingly, college basketball was the highest possible level they could play.
5. Antonucci, "Game On."
6. Voepel, "Stanford Snaps."
7. There are also National Association of Intercollegiate Athletics (NAIA) and "club sports," which are often self-organized. The NCAA established this three-division tiered system during the 1976–1977 academic year though some of the groundwork had been laid previously. In the early 1970s, the NCAA's major teams increased from 113 to 144. In 1978, the NCAA subdivided D-I into Division I-A, which a group of powerhouse football schools comprised, and Division I-AA. In 2006, Division I-A was renamed a football bowl subdivision, or FBS, and Division I-AA was renamed a football championship subdivision.
8. For example, a friend of mine who played soccer at Linfield College, in rural Oregon, which plays its games in D-III, did not receive an athletic scholarship but he was given a better financial aid grant than most of his non-athlete peers, with his financial aid amounting to 60 percent of his tuition fees. This deal was necessary to convince him to attend Linfield, which had a strong soccer program, and decide against being a walk-on for the soccer team at another bigger, bigger-time school. He had been an All-Oregon selection during his senior year of high school, scoring twenty-six goals in eighteen games, so being offered this financial aid served as important recognition of his accomplishments and an enticement to attend Linfield. D-III schools such as Lake Forest College, which is north of Chicago, also incentivize athletes to attend, and like Linfield they do so indirectly with financial aid that cannot be traced by the NCAA. Lake Forest gave a Canadian acquaintance of mine an academic scholarship to attend, but it was clear to him, as it had been for my Oregon friend, that the money he was receiving was because he was a promising hockey star and not because he was a stellar student. For these reasons, R. A. Smith in *Pay for Play* argues,

> The differences between Division I (big-time) and Division III (small-time) are ones of degree, not generally of kind . . . For the most part, with a few notable exceptions, the form of Division III athletics is similar to those of Division I. That is, there are profes-

sional coaches, professionalized recruiting, and professionalized advising; commercialized stadiums and arenas; lengthy schedules; prolonged training periods both daily and seasonally; play-offs and national championships; lowering of standards to bring less academically gifted athletes into the schools; "arms races" to build enticing athletic facilities; and a sports publicity office to carry the word to the alumni and general public (6–7).

See also Sage, Eitzen, and Beal, *Sociology*, 244.
 9. Nocera, "The Way to Run."
 10. NCAA. "14-Year Trends."
 11. According to 2011 research by Ortiz and Shih, college football revenue was increasing by "up to 20 percent annually . . . largely a result of increasingly valuable television and marketing rights, which accounted for 90% of all NCAA revenues" ("Media Contracts").
 12. The NCAA draws its own revenue from these media rights deals, too. Clotfelter found that in 1970 the NCAA earned approximately $1 for every ticket sold and $1 from media rights contracts, but by the late 2000s it was earning $1 from ticket sales but at least $6 dollars from media rights deals (*Big Time*, 56). Proceeds from such deals are distributed to NCAA member schools but not before the NCAA takes a 4 percent to 12 percent cut. In 2010–2011, March Madness was broadcast on four networks—CBS, TBS, TNT, and TruTV. In 2010–2011, a new contract was inked in 2010 between NCAA and CBS and Turner Broadcasting for a 14-year, $10.8 billion deal that would bring a sum of $740 million per year to divide between the NCAA and the schools with teams that made the men's tournament. The deal allowed all games to be televised, both digitally and online. It also expanded the field to sixty-eight teams from sixty-four teams. For brokering the deal, managing college sports, and ensuring a quality entertainment product that corporate sponsors could hang their hat on, the NCAA took in approximately $30 million per year, and the remaining $740 million would be sent to participating schools.
 13. Clotfelter, *Big Time*, xiii. Gerdy prefers the term "elite athletics" to describe those "competitive programs that cater not to the broad population of students who want to pursue athletics as an extracurricular activity, but rather to a select group of highly accomplished athletes, such as those sponsored at the NCAA Division I level, highly competitive high school programs, and youth league 'select' teams" (*Air Ball*, 9–10).
 14. Basketball has become one of the most popular sports in the world with, as of 2008, 213 nations registered with the *Fédération Internationale de Basketball Amateur* (FIBA) and more than 450 million participants globally (Nathan, "Review Essay," 738).
 15. National Federation of High School Sports, "2014–15 High School Athletics."
 16. ESPN is a huge moneymaker for its parent company, Disney. One ESPN producer, with whom I spoke in 2013, told me that ESPN is Disney's most lucrative arm—more profitable than, for example, ABC News.
 17. Messner and Cooky, "Gender in Televised Sports," 4.

18. Cooky, Messner, and Hextrum, "Women Play Sport," 203–30.
19. Hardin, Whiteside, and Ash. "Ambivalence on the Front Lines?" 46. See also Messner, Duncan, and Cooky. "Silence, Sports Bras"; and Carty, "Textual Portrayals."
20. Martin and McDonald, "Covering Women's Sport."
21. George, Hartley, and Paris, "The Representation."
22. Reichart-Smith, "The Less You Say."
23. ESPN planned the launch after consulting a variety of women's sports experts, including Billie Jean King, who told the *New York Times*, "I don't think there's ever been this much planning, research, and commitment before" (Thomas, "ESPN Slowly").
24. Quoted in Thomas, "ESPN Slowly."
25. PBS, *Media Coverage*.
26. Baysinger, "ESPN Reaches." See also Tracy and Rohan, "What Made College Football"; and CNN, "ESPN's $7.3 Billion."
27. Sage, Eitzen, and Beal, *Sociology*, 248.
28. In 2013, ESPN pulled out of a controversial joint documentary with PBS regarding the NFL's cover-up of its knowledge of the link between head injuries and long-term degenerative diseases such as CTE ostensibly because the documentary portrayed the league in an unfavorable light (PBS, *League of Denial*).
29. Sage, Eitzen, and Beal, *Sociology*, 197.
30. Cooky, "The Female Athlete."
31. Tara VanDerveer, letter to author, 2018.
32. Kate Paye, personal communication.
33. Berri, "Exploitation."
34. C. Smith. "Full Cost."
35. See Yost, *Var$ity Green*; Nixon, *The Athletic Trap*.
36. Sperber, *Beer and Circus*.
37. Besnier, Brownell, and Carter, *The Anthropology of Sport*, 99.
38. Note: Here I take "commercialism" to be the ideology that commerce should not only be allowed but also encouraged, and in the case of college sports, this has meant that colleges and universities encourage the signing of contracts with private and public businesses that increase the amount of revenue generated through the athletic activities of college athletes. By extension, I define the process of commercialization to be the making of a realm that was not previously a commercial realm—and thus not a profit-making vehicle—into one.
39. Travis, *Republicans Buy Sneakers*.
40. Dunning, "Sport as a Male Preserve"; Theberge, "Toward a Feminist Alternative."

CHAPTER 1

"We're Still Trying to Find Our Identity"

> It's the moment of truth. It's the moment where you realize that this race is going to be painful, and you have to make a decision as to whether or not you're going to embrace that and go for it, or whether you're going to back down. It's like the grind, [it's like] embracing the grind.
>
> —Joe Karlgaard

"Play February Defense in October"

In October, Stanford's season had begun with a number two ranking in the national polls. The Cardinal won two exhibition victories against Vanguard University (116-65) and UC San Diego (100-52) and earned hard-fought wins against Rutgers (63-50), Utah (62-53), and Gonzaga (84-78). Stanford then crushed South Carolina (70-32) in late November and Fresno State too (77-40), but the University of Texas managed to give the Cardinal a run for their money (93-78).

Throughout this early stage of the season, Stanford maintained a top five ranking and nearly every player contributed to the team's 6-0 record. Nneka Ogwumike was the team leader in points and rebounds. Kayla Pedersen racked up assists and rebounds. Jeannette Pohlen led the offense masterfully and shot three-pointers with precision. Chiney Ogwumike made a significant impact on the boards. Several freshman and sophomores, including Joslyn (aka Jos) Tinkle, Mikaela Ruef, Sarah Boothe, Toni Kokenis, and Sarah James, added solid contributions off the bench.

Coach VanDerveer had begun the season with high praise for her players, telling the team in late October that they were practicing better than any other team she had ever coached. "This is the most versatile team I have ever had. Your first seven practices are the best I have seen." She turned to seniors Jeanette and Kayla and junior Nneka. "You three have really set the pace."

It was high praise that seemed to propel everyone's hopes that another national championship trophy might be brought back to the Farm. Although Coach VanDerveer called the names of all her players during practices, when she said the name "Nneka," "Kayla," or "Jeannette," her voice seemed to rise higher, as if shining her brightest sunshine on the tallest redwoods she could find. By contrast, in various early season practices, Coach VanDerveer challenged the rest of the team's players to show why they deserved to be in the starting lineup. In one team huddle she said, "There's good news and bad news. We [the coaching staff] don't know who to play." She paused, as if to let the words sink in. "So you gotta help us figure it out!" She pushed, and they moved.

Versatility made Stanford a formidable opponent. The players' collective skill set defied traditional position designation where shorter players typically play guard and shoot from outside the paint while taller players stay inside the paint and bang bodies with opponents for rebounding position. Since nearly every player on the team could do a bit of everything, Stanford's coaches had the luxury of combining the players into the starting lineup in various ways depending on what the game's opponent required.

In early season practices, Toni Kokenis showed off her quickness and hustle, suggesting to her coaches that her insertion as a starter could create a fast, young, and energetic lineup. Chiney had long arms to steal the ball and block shots, and on offense she promised to bring the skills of a swingman and help with rebounding. Sarah Boothe could bolster the team's size advantage inside, filling up the scoreboard with short shots and making opponents' inside shots more difficult to convert. VanDerveer could also alternate between a young and energetic lineup or a steady and experienced lineup, or some combination of the two. Much of the team's top talent was relatively young, with two freshmen, Chiney and Toni, and two sophomores, Jos and Mikaela, in the running to play significant minutes. Junior Lindy (aka Lou) LaRocque had been an electric three-point shooter during her freshman year, but she had suffered a serious foot injury in her sophomore campaign, and even though she entered the season as the team's second starter at guard, she was seeing Toni slice into some of her playing time. Still, Lou courageously kept her head down and worked hard in practice as if she were the hungry junior player trying to supplant the senior player. She knew that if she showed VanDerveer great effort, the job could be hers again.

During one early season team meeting, Coach VanDerveer asked the players who they thought should start, and one by one each member voiced their opinions, lauding their teammates' accomplishments. It was a clever team-building activity as it encouraged each player to consider what was best for the team and praise each other at the same time.

One could start the season as a role player and end it as a starter, or one could start the season as a starter and end it as a role player. This meant, in effect, that one's spot in the lineup depended on talent as much as effort, and dedication and demonstration of hard work as much as heredity. The gate to the starting lineup was always open, and even if it was closed to a few players who warmed the bench, there was always another gate that led to more minutes of playing time. Jockeying for starting status continued well into December.

VanDerveer's approach to setting the starting lineup underscored the great expectations she had for all her players, whether as starter or role player. Some early season opponents had given the Cardinal all they could handle so VanDerveer implored her players "to play February defense in October," referring to the conventional wisdom that college teams often play better defense in the conference or postseason play when a season of practices has prepared them to play at their best, the games "count more," and there is more riding on the outcome. VanDerveer wanted postseason intensity all season long from superstar to last-woman-off-the-bench.

"We're Still Trying to Find Our Identity"

After an early season win against the University of South Carolina, which had been another blowout, Pohlen told the press that her team was focusing on long-term goals and spending little time relishing any one particular victory. "We're still trying to find our identity," she said. "We're trying to put it all together." At first her statement seemed like something any coach might have said, the kind of platitudinous "coach speak" that many college and professional sports coaches use when they speak to the media, eager to get off the podium and back to the locker room. To some degree, such coach speak is understandable since big-time coaches and athletes have to manage the sports media without creating a public stir or revealing too much of their game strategy to their future opponents.

But the longer I watched this team play, the more I realized how negative and cynical that initial interpretation was, how much it was shaped by the negativity of social science scholars, and how much it discounted, or at least denigrated, the great efforts and heroic determination of these young women and their coaches. Each member of this team saw the basketball season as an unfolding process, and as such, each wanted to improve her individual play and solidify a collective identity for their own long-term growth and for the long-term growth of the entire team. Pohlen's comment was not coach speak; it was honest and full of meaning.

"It's All about Mentality"

That honesty, often bordering on bluntness, was a hallmark of Coach VanDerveer, too, who routinely demonstrated in her actions and with her words how sports could help young women grow—physically, emotionally, and psychologically. She was a walking testament to this power of sports, having herself leveraged opportunities in basketball, however limited, for personal gain and at a time when it was not common for young women to do so. VanDerveer had come to see basketball as an educational conduit through which she could help cultivate winners, of course, but also instill in her players a deep belief in themselves, a belief that undeniably helped them *imagine* beating UCONN even as much of the sports mediascape seemed to think that outcome impossible. Without that faith in themselves, victory would have been impossible. After the 2010 NCAA final, which Stanford had lost to UCONN, Nneka Ogwumike told the *New York Times*, "It was kind of a realization, an epiphany. You know, [beating UCONN is] not impossible."[1] Nneka seems to have realized that basketball was more than a physical game; later in the interview, she added, "But it has to not be impossible for forty minutes. It's all about mentality."

Unshakable self-belief, precision game-planning, and consistent execution—it was a skillfully crafted blueprint Coach VanDerveer and her staff had drawn up to not only stop the streaking Huskies but also solidify the idea that hard work, perseverance, and mental and physical toughness could lead to a process of continual growth on and beyond the court.

Buying In to the Grind

As the season rolled on, I spoke with some of VanDerveer's former players. In one interview with a recent Stanford graduate, Rosalyn Gold-Onwude, aka "Ros," the former basketball player alerted me to the idea of buying in and its importance to her.[2] At the time I spoke with her, Ros was twenty-four years-old and a year from earning an MA in sociology.

Ros grew up in Queens and started playing basketball at age four.[3] She played basketball in junior high school, high school, and for a team in the

American Athletic Union, often with boys. Her mother, Patricia Gold, had been a roommate of Coach VanDerveer at SUNY, Albany in the 1970s, which gave both women the idea of Ros one day attending Stanford. Yet when Ros was being recruited, it was Ros's father who was most impressed by Coach VanDerveer's speech on education and athletics. The University of Maryland had been one of the first programs to recruit Ros out of Archbishop Molloy High School; Harvard, Rutgers, and Vanderbilt also made calls. However, after an injury plagued Ros's senior season and Stanford didn't renege on the scholarship it had previously offered her, Ros rewarded the Cardinal. Ros told me the choice was simple: Stanford was "Eden," offering better weather than she could find at colleges in the East, and it promised a great coach, great teammates, and a great education.

But Ros's experiences at Stanford did not begin well; in fact, she was considered something of a "problem child" in her freshman year.[4] She clashed with Coach VanDerveer daily, and Coach VanDerveer's admonishments occasionally appeared on Ros's Facebook page. "What play are you running? Mumbo jumbo? Be a point guard! Run the offense!" Once VanDerveer wrote, "Did you forget to plug in your brain today? That play is not for you to shoot, Ros. The play is called Money, remember? It's not called Funny!"[5] Ros felt like Coach VanDerveer was "on her all year"[6] and later recalled that her senior year was "The Tara and Ros Show."

But Ros made the most of her time at Stanford, a choice that she said boiled down to "buying in" to a "culture of accountability" that had been set by senior teammates and coaches before she arrived. "Oftentimes," she told me, "you find that your best player is slacking off," coasting on their talent and failing to lead others by example. "[But at Stanford] I had the luxury of being in a program where every year our best player was our hardest worker . . . You have a coach who instills this culture . . . where there is accountability. She identifies leaders and helps them come to a position where they can exert power . . . [Young players learned that] this is how you do things."

By the time Ros graduated, mutual respect had developed with Coach VanDerveer. Before the 2010 NCAA Championship Final against the UCONN Huskies, Ros delivered an inspirational pre-game speech, and in the game itself, VanDerveer entrusted her to guard UCONN's superstar guard Maya Moore. The 2009–2010 season was Ros's fifth year at Stanford, so her teammates nicknamed her "Grandma." Still, she played with a remarkable energy and tenacity and held her own against Moore.

After the season, the Pac-10 Conference, of which Stanford was a member, awarded her its Defensive Player of the Year award, and Coach

Rosalyn Gold-Onwude introduces Coach Tara VanDerveer to the Stanford crowd. Photo credit: *Aaron Miller*

VanDerveer lamented the loss of the team's "lockdown defender," adding, "I would hate to be playing in that rec gym and [Ros] shows up, because all of a sudden someone's going to be *guarding* you. It's not just gonna be running up and down having fun."[7] Looking back on her college career, Ros told me that playing basketball at Stanford was the "single greatest factor in my growth as a player and as a woman."

Ros's story intrigued me not only because of her success but also because of the language that she used to describe how it was achieved, most notably the expression "buying in." Although it was hard for her to see at first, buying in to "the way you do things" opened up a future path that she did not perceive beforehand. After Stanford, she trusted that her hard work and respect for authority would pay off and that her physical and emotional sacrifices for her teammates and coaches would be worth it. After graduation, she became a basketball analyst and sideline reporter for the Golden State Warriors television affiliate then later for the NBA and for ESPN, reaching tens of thousands of followers on social media under the motto "Queens stand up!" By 2017, Ros's Twitter followers numbered over 70,000; by 2018, it was up to 80,000; by 2019, it was 106,000; and by 2021, it was 114,000. By the time Coach VanDerveer won her 800th game, Ros was established enough as a sportscaster to be invited back to Stanford to interview VanDerveer in front of the Cardinal faithful, and on Christmas Day, 2021, she was the color commentator for the Warriors-Suns game on ESPN radio.

For Ros, buying in led to some serious cashing out.

Ros was not alone in these beliefs. In an interview with Stanford athletic department administrator Joe Karlgaard, who was Stanford's senior associate athletics director for development and chief fundraiser, I heard echoes of Ros's vocabulary, suggesting that the notion of buying in was part of a broader athletic culture at Stanford University. Like Ros, Karlgaard emphasized the willingness of Stanford athletes to buy in. Karlgaard, who had himself been a member of Stanford's cross-country team before becoming an athletics administrator, told me that various Stanford athletes used the term "buying in" to indicate how they "embraced the grind" of both big-time sports participation and high-level academics. He noted that Stanford's proximity to Silicon Valley and the venture capital hub of Sand Hill Road helped to crystallize the notion in their minds. After all, "buying in" has strong resonances with language used in American financial circles to indicate individual sacrifice (i.e., investment) for the sake of a firm (i.e., a business venture).

At the time we spoke, Stanford's football team was surging in the national rankings, and Karlgaard told me that he believed that while their success "was not something that many people would have predicted . . . the way that the staff was assembled, who was brought in . . . but [the fact that] they all bought in to this philosophy that the program has made what I previously thought was impossible, possible." He said he believed that the key to that transformation was because of the team's willingness to "grind": "There is an ethic on the football team that the game and the season is a 'grind,'" Karlgaard explained, "and they embrace it." On Twitter, Stanford's football players used the hashtag #grind to post stories of their training travails, and according to Karlgaard, they "believed that they were more capable of enduring the grind than kids at other schools." The football players "embraced the fact that they had to go to class every day, and that they had to study, and get in the weight room, and play through injuries." When Stanford recruited new football players, he added, coaches sought out players "who like to be challenged" and seemed like they would embrace this grind. "It's almost this very macho toughness," he continued, but was quick to add, "It applies to female athletes too." Stanford coaches would tell prospective Stanford athletes, "We want tough people who can persevere and grind," and then ask them, "Can you hang with us? Because if you can't hang, you need to go some other place." In his interpretation of the football team's success, Karlgaard suggested that these athletes played not primarily for the love of the game but for the "love of the grind," the thrill of the challenge to balance life on and off the court or field. He would have known, since he had been a member of the Stanford track and field team before pursuing a PhD and becoming an athletic administrator. As an athlete, he said he had personally experienced the grind.

> In a sport like track and field, you learn how to become really introspective. When you're running the 800 meters, there's this point that every half miler goes through a race and it usually happens somewhere between 500 and 700 meters into the race, where I call it the moment of honesty. It's the moment of truth. It's the moment where you realize that this race is going to be painful, and you have to make a decision as to whether or not you're going to embrace that and go for it or whether you're going to back down. It's like the grind, embracing the grind. I can think of the times where I truly embraced it. I can probably count them on one hand, and I ran dozens of races. It forces you into this moment where you have to look back and reflect on the race and say, You know what? When I was confronted with a real challenge and taking on the challenge would have been painful and uncomfortable for me, I backed down. What does that say about me? What does that mean about me? How can I improve as a human being by embracing that and by practicing and learning how to embrace that? That's what track did for me. All of the elements that went into preparing for the race . . . Did I bring everything to bear when I toed the line? Did I get enough sleep? Did I get the ice bath in? Did I get my morning run in? Did I stretch? Did I see the massage therapist? Did I do all the things that I could to prepare myself to be successful? That's the discipline aspect of it too. You learn that there is not a shortcut to it. It is a true meritocracy. You go out and the best person . . . the person who is willing to embrace that moment . . . is going to win.

Others on Stanford campus used the term "buying in" at the time too, and the language seemed to be part of the local zeitgeist.[8] One section of the *Stanford Daily* website was dubbed "The Grind," self-labeled as "Offbeat but on Point: A Snapshot of Campus Life, for Stanford Students, by Stanford Students," replete with articles such as "How (Not) to Apply for Internships," "What Does Being an Adult Mean?" and "When Stress-Induced Indulgences Are Okay." Stanford's administrators, athletes, and coaches, including VanDerveer and her staff, also used similar terms like "investment" and "ownership" (see chapter 9), justifying a given player's willingness or unwillingness to sacrifice for the team, coach, teammates, or university.

It seemed that when athletes adopted this language, they were echoing the language used by their coaches. If a Stanford coach told the media, "We are still looking for our identity" or "We have a very versatile team," days later I would read team captains echoing their coach's comments in the *Stanford Daily*. If the athletic director used a term like "buying in" one day, I would hear it again the next day from a player or a coach: "we bought in" or "we secured buy-in." Each time I heard or read it, it seemed to signify the seriousness, stress and significance of playing sports at Stanford and the importance of accepting the way of being a big-time college athlete, particularly at an academically elite institution.

In the months that followed, I would come to see the expression "buying in" also echoed throughout the greater San Francisco Bay Area,[9] particularly in Silicon Valley where blue skies, new digital technologies, and an innovation mindset created a zeitgeist in which investment in the future—and sacrifice in the present—set something of a new cultural standard.

But it was in observing Stanford's women basketball players demonstrate their buy in to the Stanford Athletics way of life in long, demanding, and physically intense practices, in high pressure, high stakes intercollegiate competition, and in general by investing body, mind, and spirit in the grind that assured me that Ros's recollections and Karlgaard's contentions were worthy of deeper inquiry. Like the grinders of the football team, VanDerveer's players gave their all in each practice, even dedicating considerable time to their own private training, both in the gym and in the weight and film rooms. They trusted that Coach VanDerveer's tough love approach to coaching would stimulate their growth as basketball players and that enduring it would be worth the considerable commitment required. They believed that putting time into their studies and into their training would one day pay off. They carried themselves seriously and proved their commitment with their daily actions, and, for some mysterious reason, using the coded performative language of buying in seemed to help.[10] It was as if the players were investment partners in a lucrative technology venture risking their fortunes on the equity of their sweat, betting that their wager would stand them in good stead long after their playing days were over.

Beyond Ros's personal experiences, and beyond what Joe Karlgaard had said about the Stanford football team, the expression "buying in" made sense to me on another level too: universities like Stanford accepting the market-driven, heavily commercialized state of college sports (i.e., college sports in a big-time form). After all, there would be no big-time college sports unless hundreds of universities agreed to sponsor these programs, and they wouldn't do that if they didn't perceive considerable value in doing so.

The notion of buying in also led me to try and understand the experiences of big-time athletes beyond Stanford, and while I did not undertake fieldwork at any other university—there was enough to digest at one university—I did read widely about such experiences.[11] While I thus cannot say whether Stanford's model of balance between academics and athletics would work elsewhere, I do believe that there is still great value in describing how this model operates and is perceived. Stanford occupied a unique position as both one of the nation's elite academic and athletic universities and one of the most ideal places to be a female athlete, but it was still a part of a broader national system that was the target of much public criticism and governed by the much-maligned NCAA.

Thus, I became fixated on the question: What was it like to buy in to the grind of balancing academics and athletics at Stanford? What I found was that Stanford University has refused to follow the herd in allowing football to commercialize the university to an excessive degree and thereby lower academic standards for athletes and compromise otherwise valuable educational objectives. In effect, that strict priority structure created a university culture that does not excuse the talented athlete who cares little about class.

Notes

1. Longman, "Education First."
2. Rosalyn Gold-Onwude, personal communication, 2011.
3. Longman, "Problem Child."
4. Longman, "Problem Child."
5. Longman, "Problem Child."
6. Longman, "Problem Child."
7. T. Taylor, "W. Basketball."
8. For example, the senior captain of Stanford's water polo team Maggie Steffens reflected on her team's national title in 2017: "There was 150 percent buy-in to what we were doing. Even when we were down, facing adversity, we could look into each other's eyes and be calm and know we could get it done. That's something that's really hard to create, really hard to find. That's ultimately what helped us win the finals—simply looking into each other's eyes and knowing we could do it" (Ramgopal, "Steffens"). Steven Fahy of the 2017 Stanford cross-country team, on his team's fourth place finish in the national title: "It's really a product of all the guys . . . and all the guys who have set the example. I think it's been our depth this year and having every single guy on the roster buy in and help us go on the podium even though it's not a perfect day" (Salinas, "Two Podiums"). This language and culture were echoed by coaches, such as Jerod Haase, who upon being hired to coach men's basketball in 2016 insisted that he was confident his players would buy in to his unselfish style. "I do believe there is going to be a great deal of buy-in from the team and a belief from the team that we can achieve great things. I would not be here if I didn't think we could compete at the highest level and do it fairly" (Ramachandran, "Jerod Haase"). Even sports performance coordinators like football's Shannon Turley

used the term. "If we're working to get some change from some of those young freshmen and get them to buy in to the way we want them to work, and they're immature and somewhat reluctant to do it and they see those great players that are now great NFL players here, training and doing it our way, seeking coaching and wanting to do it our way, well, it makes it a little easier for them to buy in. It makes my job easier. So, I'm happy to work with them and thrilled to have them around" (Shi, "Shannon Turley").

9. On October 31, 2012, Manager Bruce Bochy of the San Francisco Giants stood before tens of thousands of fans at Civic Center Plaza in San Francisco. His team had captured its second World Series in three years, a remarkable feat for an organization that before winning the first of these two had not won a championship since moving to San Francisco in 1958. When Bochy spoke of the team, which the local press had labeled a "team of misfits" that had put its fans through "torture," he insisted that they had won because "everyone put service ahead of self-interest" and because everyone on his team had "bought in."

10. Austin, "Performative Utterances"; Hall, K. "Performativity."

11. The language of buying in is not limited to Stanford sportspeople, of course, nor to people who live near Silicon Valley. As one North Carolina basketball coach and camp organizer wrote of high school coaches in 2016, "Coaches in every program have to work very hard to get their players to buy-in to their team's culture and them as a coach. The best teams have the most buy in from their players." The coach added that for other coaches to secure buy in they must admit that their players are not naturally inclined by human nature to buy in. He said players are skeptical, selfish, and sensitive, argued that coaches have to encourage players to ask the "why" questions and "trade skeptical for coachable," concluding that players who "understand WHY your coach believes the way he/she does" will find it "easier . . . to buy in" (Templeton, "Elevate Your Team").

CHAPTER 2

The Engine of the Train

Football is a game for mad men, and I'm the maddest of them all.

—Vince Lombardi

University of Texas, November 28, 2010

Long before there was big-time women's college basketball, big-time games like UCONN–Stanford, or even a distinction between big-time and small-time college sports, there was one game in town: college football.

That became clearer to me as Coach VanDerveer's Stanford team prepared to face their first ranked opponent, the University of Texas, for a nationally televised home game a few weeks before UCONN came to town in November. From the opening tip, when Stanford attacked the University of Texas man-to-man defense and took control of the game, the atmosphere in Maples Pavilion was electric. The crowd roared when a Stanford player made a basket and stomped their feet when the Longhorns played offense. The crowd's presence seemed to make a difference too, with the final score, 93-78, in favor of the home team.

But it wasn't the game itself but rather the Jumbotron hanging from the ceiling, which replayed game highlights, aired corporate advertisements, and delivered public address announcements, that caught my attention. During one of the game's scheduled TV timeouts,[1] I shifted my gaze from the court to the Jumbotron to take in a stream of ads. In one, Muscle Milk, a sports drink maker, showcased Chiney Ogwumike's training regimen. For the ad, the company had filmed the cheerful freshman performing weight-training exercises, her body attached to the wires of some sort of performance-measurement equipment, suggesting that Muscle Milk was associated with—or was somehow owed credit for—her impressive athleticism. In another video message, a local realtor announced an interactive Tees for Threes game. Whenever a Stanford player tossed in a three-point basket, tee-shirts embroidered with Stanford's logo and the logo of the realtor were tossed into the stands. The Jumbotron even enabled Stanford Athletics to thank its alumni donors for their help in funding scholarships.

One video message on the Jumbotron from the Stanford football team piqued my interest the most that day, speaking to the genesis of the big-time college sports culture in which such advertisements could dominate fan attention in the first place. In the video, dozens of stocky young men gathered to graciously thank Stanford's women's basketball fans, telling them that their support was a key ingredient to their football team's success. Support for Stanford's gridiron "Grinders," as the football team liked to call themselves, was at an all-time high too. The team had recently finished their regular season with a record of 11-1 and had received an invitation to participate in the Orange Bowl, one of the most prestigious—and lucrative—postseason bowl games on the holiday bowl calendar. For Stanford, the invitation was its first in many years, and the exceptional season came as a surprise to some since Cardinal fans had in recent years grown accustomed to middling squads.

Stanford football's record had been 10-23 under Buddy Teevens (2002–2004), 6-17 under Walt Harris (2005–2006), and 9-16 in Jim Harbaugh's first two seasons (2007–2009). It was not until quarterback Andrew Luck became the starter in 2009 that Stanford football re-emerged on the national stage. During Luck's Stanford career, the Cardinal tallied a 43-10 record and won two major bowl games. Luck put the athletic department's highest-profile team back in the national media conversation. In his senior season, Luck was a Heisman Trophy candidate, and following graduation with a degree in architecture, the Cardinal QB became the NFL's number-one overall draft pick.

The Stanford football players shown in the video at the Texas game that day were instantly recognizable to the women's basketball fans, and they received roaring cheers even though they were neither physically present nor sweating on the court that day.

As it is at other universities, football was a big deal "down on the farm" although it was not as central to the university culture as the sport was in some college towns. In the late summer, fall, and early winter, cable sports network broadcasts of football are default viewing on televisions in bars and restaurants across the country. The game dominates conversations around office water coolers, overtaking other topics such as politics, religion, and the weather. Games are played in palatial football arenas and stadiums. American football fans sometimes seem like religious zealots, wearing elaborate costumes, face paint, and roaring for their favorite teams and players with unbridled passion.[2] Some football fans are so passionate about their team that they will go to unbelievable lengths to support them. One college team's fans went so far as to chant, "A rope, a tree, hang the referee" when the calls did not go their way.[3] There can be little doubt that football is "the biggest game in the strongest and richest nation in the world"[4]—in some corners, it is known as "King Football." Every February when the two top professional teams meet in the Super Bowl for all the marbles, more Americans watch the game than vote in presidential elections.[5]

At Stanford, football was important but not more important than everything else. According to one study done by OSKR, a consulting firm, football teams generate as much 65 percent of the total revenue of major college athletic programs.[6] Stanford's administrators confirmed that to ensure the financial functioning of the entire athletic department, it was essential to invest in their football team. When I interviewed official representatives of the Stanford athletic department, several told me the football team was indispensable to the business operations of all Stanford athletics. One Stanford athletic director even explained that football is the "engine that drives the train" because "college sports are all about the money."[7]

And yet Stanford's players were recruited to play for the team and given scholarships, as elsewhere, but their admission was still predicated on academic achievements. Indeed, the same academic requirements were said to be expected of football players as were expected of incoming chemistry or computer science majors. Stanford fans too were passionate about their team, though not wild.

The atmosphere of the basketball game between Stanford and Texas hinted at the growing intensity and pressure surrounding women's college basketball, an electric energy that would nearly overload a month later when Stanford hosted UCONN.

Still, in many ways football remained the undisputed king, on the farm as elsewhere. Historically, football had a significant head start in the race to the big time, and women were still getting off the blocks. Stanford's women grinded just like Stanford football players, but the business of women's college basketball still paled in comparison to the business of college football, so the stakes of the grind were not quite the same.

Thus, a historical comparison between college football and women's college basketball seemed necessary to achieve both an understanding of the big time as well as an understanding of what it meant for college women to buy in not only to the grind of balancing academics and athletics but also to the commercialized form of college sports that created it.

Although college basketball is today highly profitable and undoubtedly an engine that drives college sports' big-time culture, college football was the first college sport to be that engine and remains by far the most profitable and influential of all college sports, thus making it integral to any study of how big time came to be and what it has meant for anyone to buy in to it. College football set the standard for all future big-time college sports, effectively raising the stakes of these games, bringing a heightened sense of seriousness and a more prevalent winning-at-any-cost mentality. It also brought a troubling sense that the game was inherently violent and potentially detrimental to the physical, and perhaps also mental, health of young men. The predominance of the college game predated pro football's cultural power by several decades, mimicking the festivals and carnivals of Europe[8] while also paving the way for the development of our perceptions of what professional, mediated sport and the big time signify. Football is thus a necessary mirror to understand how women athletes, women coaches, and women's athletics administrations learned of college sports in their big-time form and why some of them, when given the chance, choose to buy in to it. Such a history also affords us the chance to examine what that choice has meant to these people of course but also to the broader sports culture.

No sport has excluded women like football, nor is there any other sport that has so powerfully constructed our binary sense of masculinity and femininity. Football, more than any other sport, still genders notions of what American sports are, what an athlete can be, and what proper masculinity and femininity should look like. American football grew more popular than any other American sport not only because it engendered a sense of collective identity for universities, which it did, but also because it normalized notions of what ideal manhood was, which in turn invariably shaped what women could become.[9] Football is what Mariah Burton Nelson calls a "manly sport"—a sport that men use to construct their own masculinity, specifically the notion of toughness. What better way to do that than by fiercely seeking to exclude women from it and by, concurrently, insisting that by nature women are incapable of such toughness? In response, many women have come to use sports like basketball as a way of fighting back against the notion that football players are incomparably tough and that, ultimately, sports are the rightful domain of men and boys: a male "preserve" as some have called it.

Even if the grind of the big time at Stanford seemed in some ways to be less defined by gender than ever before, less a domain that only male athletes inhabited, it was not always that way. Indeed, as this chapter will show, college football first became king during the same era in which American men faced a masculinity crisis, so the game's big-time culture—commercialized, professionalized, exclusive—cannot be separated from the historical process by which character attributes such as toughness, hard work, and sacrifice were gendered masculine. In other words, college football itself became an assertion of male dominance in the form of a college extracurricular. It would take generations for women to recover let alone be considered grinders in their own right.

The Making of the Big Time

How exactly was the big time made and how did that process impact women in sports? The answer to that question can be found by investigating sport's early connections to religion, masculinity, character, commerce, and institutional rivalry: these were the props that would set the stage for the drama of the big time to develop.

Curiously, colonial Americans were initially skeptical of the value of recreational pursuits. In the seventeenth century, Puritans, particularly in the northeastern colonies, frowned upon what they saw as the hedonistic lifestyle known as "festive culture."[10] Sometimes they banned card and dice games and also football. The prevailing religious perspective at the time held that if and when sports were "all-absorbing" and therefore an "end in itself" that distracted "thought of one's higher duties ... one should stop engaging in it."[11]

After the American Revolution, political leaders echoed the Puritanical notion that the nation's men ought not to engage in "frivolous" activities, including what John Adams derided as "sports, diversions, and pleasures." "I was born for business," Adams said, "for both activity and study." Thomas Jefferson agreed, arguing that "games played with the ball and others of that nature are too violent for the body and stamp no character on the mind." Adams and Jefferson wanted Americans to live frugally, to work for the preservation of the republic, and they feared such diversions might lead Americans to a life of pleasure-seeking that could threaten the realization of that work.[12]

But Richard Baxter, a well-known English writer on Puritan ethics, argued that recreation could be a serious—and deeply religious—affair, and soon some Americans were following his lead. Baxter argued for what he called "lawful recreation," by which he meant that such activities could be disassociated from "traditional revelries" such as drinking alcohol as long as they were done "for the stimulation of the natural spirits" and "ultimately intended to fit the body and mind for their normal duty to God."[13] Americans were playing a range of games by the late nineteenth century, intent on using them to advance religious and educational agendas. During this time, American educators were often influenced by the work of upper-class English male educators who believed that games and sports could be beneficial for the development of young boys.[14] English writers such as Thomas Hughes and Charles Kingsley advanced the idea of muscular Christianity and "linked spirituality to physical vigor,"[15] positing that physical training could aid spiritual training and moral development and even solidify patriotism.[16] Hughes and Kingsley wanted to ensure the endurance of the established male patriarchy and aristocracy and, by extension, the British Empire.[17] Their ideas about sport entered the United States primarily through the writings of America's upper class. In particular, Thomas Wentworth Higginson—who was a minister, abolitionist, suffragist, temperance advocate, officer in the Civil War, poet, novelist, and historian, and who helped fund the raid by John Brown on Harpers Ferry in 1859—followed Hughes and Kingsley, adopting the view that physical activity was good for young American Christian boys. Urbanization and industrialization especially worried Higginson, who thought that boys needed a new way to become men now that they were no longer working in the fields and increasingly faced an array of urban temptations.[18]

It is also important to note here that there was a form of white male supremacy, coupled with race-based fears and imperial urges, that helped sport grow. The so-called great chain of being theory suggested to white Europeans (and their colonial descendants) that the white race had been blessed by Christ to reach a higher plateau of development than other races and therefore each English Christian gentlemen had a duty to "fulfill his God-given right to govern the inferior races in the far-flung corners of the British Empire."[19] Early English sports were expected to be the means to achieve these lofty goals.

In the process of molding good Christians, sports coaches and teachers—who were often the same person fulfilling two roles—also came to socialize their male and female students into a certain kind of work ethic that was highly gendered. The public schools of England were single-sex and rigidly hierarchical, and "authority was shared by the teachers and the older boys called 'prefects,'" "who were responsible for exerting authority over young boys in after-school hours."[20] Referred to as the "fagging system," this allowed a school's headmaster to "create a 'moral elite' among the prefects, who became his lieutenants in the aim of turning the boys into Christian gentlemen."[21] Therefore, at the same time that English sports educators were seeking the continuity of Christianity, they were also actively shaping dominant notions of what it meant to be a man (and by extension, what it meant to be a woman),[22] particularly in regard to work ethic and place of work.[23] After all, this fagging system did not exist for young female students nor were the ideologies of muscular Christianity and manliness[24] aimed at females. These were all gendered concepts that altogether excluded female students.

Class divisions also played a role. Some American sports enthusiasts wanted little to do with the Victorian moralism associated with upper-class England, and although many held tightly to white-black and male-female divisions in physical activity and leisure, some used sports to counter English amateur ideals.[25] The notion of amateurism was that true sportsmen played sports under a specific code of conduct guided by a desire to remain "noble, unpaid, and gentlemanly."[26] In America, some blue-collar workers often "turned to the pleasures and associations" that "frequently provided far more excitement, fulfillment, and sense of belonging than their work," eschewing Victorian culture and amateurism, while white-collar workers stood to gain from the increasing amounts of clerical work created by America's industrializing economy[27] and trusted Victorian values drew clear lines of expectation between males and females. Blue-collar workers often, though not always, felt less anxiety about women who played games and sports. As white-collar workers looked down on women as frail homemakers and questioned the femininity of women who played sports, some blue-collar workers encouraged women to play.[28]

These class tensions played out most strikingly in baseball, which began as an amateur affair but soon became a commercialized symbol of anti-Victorianism. Initially, a "baseball fraternity" formed as a group of sportsmen assured upper-class Americans that theirs was a game for upstanding, amateur men. They played sober, loved order, and preached discipline. They played for the love of the game not money or fame, and fair play was above all their most cherished value. Elite clubs for baseball promised only to admit amateur members of a certain social class, and to protect the purity of the game.[29] The baseball fraternity pitched its sport as the national game. This was a time of little national unity, with the Civil War threatening to divide the republic, and baseball was in some circles welcomed as a national savior.

Yet the amateurism of the game was called into question. Enterprising businessmen like William H. Cammeyer enclosed land they owned and began charging tickets to games played on it. This so-called enclosure movement spread, and other businessmen formalized what had been informal games to make a buck. Under-the-table payments to players became commonplace, and the most successful teams agreed to travel to challenge other teams in exchange for a share of the gate. Before long, baseball's culture, once seen as upstanding, was increasingly adopting a win-at-all-costs mentality (the more games a team won, the more money teams could charge at the gate). Intensified competition followed, hollowing out the substance of amateur rhetoric.[30]

There were also major divisions within baseball. The first professional league, the National League, was often dysfunctional since each individual club controlled itself and therefore put their own interests in front of league interests. In the 1870s, the National League expelled the Cincinnati Red Stockings for selling beer at its park, and five years later a group of six clubs, many with ties to breweries, formed the American Association in protest. The American Association, derisively called the Beer Ball League, did not try to appeal to Victorian morality, choosing instead to sell booze at games and allowing play on Sunday. Management in the National League did not want their players out late drinking or carousing, so they levied fines on errant players, and National League owners agreed to blacklist any player who had been dismissed from another team. They also instituted what was known as the reserve clause, which in effect gave the team that first signed a player a lifetime option on that player's services. Players revolted when Albert Spalding, the owner of the Chicago White Stockings and a founder of the National League, sold Mike "King" Kelly's contract to Boston for $10,000, and in 1890 they created what they called the Players' League. Players and management shared ownership duties and benefits, which enticed stars like Kelly to sign on, but ultimately the Players' League lasted one season because they played their games in the same cities and on the same days as the National League and because they chose to appeal to Victorian morality rather than sell beer and charge low prices for tickets like the American Association, which "reduced their appeal among those most likely to sympathize with them."[31]

Newspapers helped baseball move farther away from amateurism too, especially during circulation wars, when they found that expanding coverage of sport could help raise their sales figures. Joint stock companies were formed to raise funds to pay for the best baseball players, and some newspaper owners, including Joseph Medill of the *Chicago Tribune*, took ownership interest in clubs. In the process, teams came to represent not only the owners of the team but the cities and regions in which they played, prompting local businessmen and politicians to chase the publicity these "big games" could generate.³² Along the way, baseball found a friend in commerce, amateurism in baseball slowly waned, and leaders in other sports took note.

The Roots of the Amateur Ideal

Amateurism was an upper-class idea based on a Victorian sense of morality, a fact that becomes clearer if one considers the history of football, which followed a different path than baseball. The so-called football rush began in the 1820s as a rather spontaneous and often brutal initiation rite for freshmen in the elite colleges of the Northeast. It was a violent affair that included "melees" resulting in "black eyes, bloodied noses, sprained limbs, and shredded clothes."³³ By the 1860s and early 1870s, though, two kinds of football had emerged: one similar to association football of the United Kingdom, which Americans know today as soccer, and which prohibited the use of hands, and another that took hold around the Boston area that allowed the use of hands and therefore more closely resembled rugby. American football teams emerged in the last three decades of the nineteenth century at Ivy League schools such as Harvard, Yale, and Princeton, and the number of teams fielded grew exponentially between the 1880s and 1910s.³⁴

Not long after football's invention, an ideological battle ensued between those who wanted to use sport to maintain class divisions and those who wanted the players to be free to play as they wished. Freedom was perceived to take many forms. Some American colleges and universities, for example, were established in rural areas, which meant that students had to be put up in communal housing. There a religious professoriate guided young people in the classroom as well as outside it. These professors wanted to make "men of character" and believed this required moral and religious education. Echoing Adams and Jefferson, some professors at these colleges did not see the point in their students playing sports and diverting their attention from their studies.

Yet some early college students saw such parochial and religious education as paternalistic oppression, assailing a rigid educational curriculum and rote memorization. Their response was to establish their own extracurriculum, which by the 1850s included sports clubs. (Debate clubs and literary societies existed at Harvard and Yale before the American Revolution, and fraternities had begun to crop up in the 1830s and 1840s.) Thus, in his book *Sports and Freedom*, R. A. Smith argues that freedom was a key driver in why students wanted to play sports like football in nineteenth-century American colleges. Creative commercialization was also a factor. With baseball's example in mind, students made alliances with local businesses and alumni, who became boosters, or sponsors, which in turn allowed the students to play without permission from educators. Around the turn of the century, for example, Harvard students solicited alumni from the class of 1879 to help pay for a new, steel-reinforced football stadium.

National Loyalty

With its rough-and-tumble style, football fit its industrial era and also helped shape it, especially in terms of gender. The move from farm work to factory labor during the rapid industrialization of the 1890s sparked the so-called first crisis of American masculinity, which referred to the anxiety that American males might become soft as the nation's economy changed and the need to do daily physical labor declined.[35] At the time, America was growing into a world military and economic power, and some believed that to protect its new commercial, political, and military standing in the world it needed to ensure that what they saw as the prized Anglo-Saxon race, particularly its men, remained strong and fit. Naval men such as Alfred T. Mahan argued the United States risked losing its empire (as Rome had) if it "degenerated into . . . worship of comfort, wealth, and general softness."[36] The biggest threat to the maintenance of such tough masculinity was found in the "dyspeptic, shriveled up, and cowering scholar, only interested in gaining useless knowledge or cultivating an ineffectual spirituality."[37]

Among the economically elite, there was a similar paternalism: industrialists such as George Pullman, Henry Ford, and Andrew Carnegie sponsored sports programs for their workers, believing that they could control the vices of their factory workers. By 1918, "152 of the 400 largest manufacturers provided indoor recreational facilities and half of them sponsored outdoor recreation or annual picnics."[38] In fact, the first professional football teams, including teams that would later join the nascent National Football League (NFL), were organized in the early 1900s by industrialists in Western Pennsylvania and the Midwest to alleviate labor tension among, for example, millworkers and steelworkers.[39]

Opinions differed on what to do about male youth, including the sons of immigrants. There were nation builders who "saw youth sports as a tool for acculturating immigrant boys and creating a large pool of patriotic young men who would serve as soldiers as well as loyal workers"; social reformers who saw sports as a way of controlling young deviant boys; muscular Christians who saw in sports a chance to teach "God-based morality, self-discipline and overall development"; and playground movement advocates who saw sports as a chance for young boys to breathe fresh air and take "respite from suffocating urban neighborhoods."[40] Some industrialists believed that a public education system might induce independent farmers to submit to the new factory-based order and help grow their businesses in the process,[41] while some political leaders wanted mass public education to subdue the lower classes.[42]

For many, football seemed a particularly valuable weapon to combat the masculinity crisis for it was this game that had absorbed the values of muscular Christianity, industrialism, patriarchy, and whiteness and was therefore seen as a quintessentially American game. Football, many believed, could contribute to creating good environments, and a good coach was expected to dramatically impact the trajectory of one's behavior and one's life.[43] In this regard, football men were influenced by social Darwinism, believing that children would be molded into good workers if they were trained well and grew up in a good environment.[44] Team sports like football were said to create an environment that was conducive to building individual character but also to "building cohesion in an ethnically diverse population, and creating national loyalty."[45] Indeed, individual development toward maturity and national development toward social cohesion (or at least not outright ethnic conflict) were seen as complementary processes.

The Professional Spirit

Given this cultural context, it is little surprise that the moniker "Father of American football" would be given to Yale University's Walter Camp, who was himself married to the sister of Yale's most famous social Darwinist, William Graham Sumner. It was at Yale that Camp helped establish American football as America's most consequential sport and in the process helped professionalize the coaching industry and solidify the myth that college football was primarily about cultivating character, not commerce.

Camp was a multidimensional figure: a powerful businessman whose watch-making business was a major manufacturing concern, a shrewd university booster and fundraiser who used Yale Athletics to heighten the status of the university and its alumni, and a prolific author who promoted the gridiron game with both fiction and nonfiction writings. As chairman of the Yale Athletic Committee, Camp was instrumental in raising funds for Yale to construct the 80,000-capacity Yale Bowl in 1914, and as Yale's football coach for five years, Camp posted a record of 67-2, approaching the game with a dictatorial and authoritarian approach and earning the nickname for his regime, the "czar system."

Camp was also a polarizing figure who alienated opponents by setting rules for football that they said favored Yale's teams.[46] In this regard he symbolized the changing nature of the times, particularly the shift from amateurism to professionalism, winning at any cost, and triumphalism. Camp had been a star football halfback and baseball shortstop for Yale despite being a "spindle-shanked youth" and not "rugged enough for varsity athletics."[47] Yet Camp was also said to have played after his graduation from Yale and, therefore, beyond his eligibility, which raised questions about his integrity.

Camp penned many of football's rules and thereby effectively changed it from rugby into a quintessentially American pastime. For one, Camp changed the rugby style scrum by adding a line of scrimmage and introduced a "down and yardage" system (e.g., second down and five yards to go), which led to chalking the field and thus the nickname "gridiron game" since the field looked like a gridiron with burned white lines upon it. Camp has also been credited with transforming football from a fifteen-men-per-side game into an eleven-men-per-side game.

Yet his tactics in setting the rules of the game (as a member of college football's rules committee between 1878 and 1925) were not without controversy. As mentioned above, some grumbled that the rules he devised were intended to improve his own chances at victory. Further, Camp legalized tackling below the waist, which made the game more brutal than rugby. Around this time, the so-called V trick or flying V was invented, which was a "formation in which players formed a V with their arms encircling the players ahead of them . . . The new 'mass momentum' style of offense encouraged by [Camp's] legalization of the low tackle entailed massing players at a single point of attack."[48]

But Camp was more than a rule-maker; he was also an evangelist who wrote twenty books promoting the game and insisted that it had great value, particularly to male youth development. In 1893 a Harvard graduate began conducting a large-scale survey to assess the violence of the game. In a way, the survey was a referendum on the game's merits and demerits.[49] Camp was active in analyzing the survey's data, and being a former Yale football player, he selected the data that justified football's value. One of Camp's books, *Football Facts and Figures*, which was published the same year as the Harvard study, extolled the virtues of the game. Camp wanted to assure Victorians that his game was, while violent, primarily about cultivating disciplined young men, and he intentionally infused football with a moralism of character and sportsmanship, even exploiting the rationale of producing muscular Christians to do so.[50]

Other enthusiasts insisted that football was a positive form of control especially when aimed at young men who had the potential to do harm to themselves or to the community if their "virile passions" and "puerile judgment" went otherwise unchecked.[51] The president of the University of North Carolina F. P. Venable, for example, summed up the power of football to build character: "No half-way work will answer. A player must bring out every power, must develop to his utmost every faculty, must learn through self-control, must work for the team and not for himself, must make himself part of a perfectly working machine, must be full of nerve and pluck and strategy."[52] Francis A. Walker, who was a Civil War veteran and president of Yale, agreed, saying that the "competitive contests of our colleges" toughen the "cultivated classes" for roles as leaders.[53] Even President Theodore Roosevelt advocated a more "strenuous" life for young boys, believed football could provide it, and claimed that football could foster traits such as "integrity, reliability, and responsibility."[54] Roosevelt once said, "No amount of commercial prosperity can supply the lack of the heroic virtues," virtues which he deemed synonymous with an "American interpretation of muscular Christianity."[55]

And yet it did not take long before the prospect of winning intercollegiate contests had lured universities into hiring professional coaches whose concern with winning trumped concerns of character. As R. A. Smith notes, by the early 1900s, "the [college] coach's organization for victory was rather highly developed."[56] Nowhere was this more evident that in the rivalry between Harvard and Yale. Harvard hired William Reid, who played baseball and football at Harvard, as head football coach in 1901. Reid helped the Crimson beat Yale 22-0 in his first year, but Yale dominated the rivalry match in 1902 and 1903. Reid had left Harvard at the end of the 1901 season to become an assistant to his father at a Belmont, California, prep school, but after the next two year's losses, Harvard football players created the Harvard Graduate Football Association to lure Reid back east with a salary of $3,000 a season.

An internal debate at Harvard over the merits of professional coaches ensued, but those seeking victory prevailed, and by 1905 Reid was back with a salary of $3,500, and an additional $3,500 for "extraordinary expenses." At the time, $7,000 was double what the average Harvard professor earned, 30 percent more than the salary of the highest-paid Harvard professor, and nearly as much as then-Harvard president Charles Eliot, who had been Crimson chief for thirty-six years.

The salary seemed to influence Reid's coaching style. He was prone to worry, but he channeled that worry into detailed recruiting of all four thousand Harvard students, year-round football-focused training, and attention to players' cleanliness and hygiene. Reid told each player what his strengths and weaknesses were and what he needed to do during the offseason to get better. He bought state-of-the-art equipment. He was especially concerned that all his best athletes maintained their eligibility to play, and he even hired tutors and talked to parents to ensure they did. On one occasion, he secured employment for a star player to earn his board. Reid has thus been credited with bringing a rational approach to coaching that mirrored the scientific management principles of Frederick Taylor, who influenced the assembly-line production of the Ford Motor Company. Reid, though, only lasted two seasons at Harvard as "the pressure to produce victories began to mount on" him and his "constitution could not take it."[57] Still, in an article he wrote for *Harvard Graduate's Magazine* in 1906, he insisted that professional coaching was the way forward for Harvard, writing that a return to "charity coaching" would indicate a loss of "self-respect."[58] To some, like sportswriter Caspar Whitney, professional coaches were a "menace," and while he lamented Harvard's hiring of Reid, his words fell on deaf ears, and Harvard's athletic committee failed to pass a unilateral ban on professional coaching.[59] (The Rowing Association of American Colleges had tried to ban non-student coaches as early as 1873.) Even if Reid did not himself last long as a Harvard coach, he set a precedent at Harvard and for any other institution that wished to follow Harvard's lead.

After Walter Camp's death, contemporaries such as Dartmouth's Edward K. Hall, who was head of the NCAA committee, would remember him as a man who kept the game clean and its standards of sportsmanship high,[60] yet few men took larger steps toward creating what we know today as the big time. Camp also helped create the college sports arms race, which began with high salaries for coaches like Reid and now refers to the battle between rival schools to build the best arsenal of players, coaches, equipment, and facilities at their schools.[61] The professionalization of coaching also heightened the intensity and stakes of college football since the livelihoods of more individuals depended on victory.[62] Coaches wanted to win whatever the cost; indeed, that is what they were explicitly paid to do. Thus R. A. Smith concludes that "the saga of the professional coach does much to explode the myth that there was ever a lengthy period when the amateur spirit pervaded college athletics," adding that "intercollegiate athletics, almost from the first, had the professional spirit."[63]

Rock 'em, Sock 'em and the Shootout Spirit

Of course, students, alumni, and fans were similarly eager to see their favorite college win, which also helped football spread and become big-time.[64] In its early years, college football's game day was a social space that tied the academic community—and local community—together. Students, alumni, and other fans congregated each game day to feel a sense of shared unity, drink alcohol, and revel in a festival-like pageantry. Coaches and star quarterbacks became local legends in the process.

All this regional pride grew while the United States was becoming a much more urban nation; indeed, the two developments might be seen as parallel vectors. As the U.S. economy industrialized, salaries grew, and consumers spent their newfound disposable income watching young football men battle on the gridiron. Improved systems of communication and transportation advanced in the late-nineteenth and early-twentieth centuries, assisting the commercialization of sports, which became the object of adult entertainment as much as escape. The rules of sports were standardized on a national level to streamline the entertainment product being sold, newly designed watches helped keep more precise time in sporting matches, the spread of newspapers helped raise literacy rates, and all of the above helped in growing a market for writing about sports, especially football.[65]

Newspapers often carried stories about the big game days in advance not only to sell papers but also to sell tickets to the game. As John Thelin opines, this strategy "worked, to the delight of athletic directors, coaches, and college presidents."[66] Over time, football led America into what Benjamin Radar has called the "age of the spectator."[67]

Soon the universities sought to create "revenue-producing ... popular entertainment" products to sell to the public,[68] and teams across the country would come to promote their own local style of play, from rock 'em, sock 'em in the Midwest to the Wild West shootout spirit of the Southwest, all the while emphasizing their unique regional or ethnic identity.[69] In the South, some games played against Northern teams evoked memories of the Civil War, with some games even considered "reenactments."[70]

Before long, sponsors, alumni donors, and boosters were lined up to help colleges further commercialize the game. For sponsors, being affiliated with the game of football was a chance to associate their brand with the toughness, character, hard work, and grit of young football players and to sell their products to alumni who saw their alma mater as a defining characteristic of their identity.

And yet despite this commercialization and what one might call a failure to continue any sort of literal amateurism, Americans did not stop believing that college sports were amateur affairs that wholesomely brought the local community together. It was a wish as much as it was a dubious claim. Even as football was becoming a highly commercialized and professionalized ritual of inversion in which the escapist vices of drinking, violence, and gambling were either encouraged or not discouraged, making the big-time college football spectacle much less about love (for the game) and much more about hate (for one's rival) and the release of built-up masculine tension, Americans stood firm in their faith that the games were an important rite of passage for young men and therefore worthy of support.

Big Games, Tramp Athletes, and Professional Coaches

It wasn't long before the big time traveled west. The first Big Game, as the football contest between Stanford and the University of California would come to be called, was held on March 19, 1892, near the corner of Haight and Stanyan Streets. Stanford's coach in the game was none other than Walter Camp himself, who had agreed to travel west after Yale's season concluded (for a fee of course). At the time, football was by and large an Eastern game, and institutions like Stanford and Cal routinely looked east for educational ideas, athletic models, and football coaches.

The Big Game was the first major college football game in the western United States. A football team had formed down on the farm six months after the founding of Leland Stanford Junior University in 1891. In the team's third practice, Stanford team captain John Whittemore accepted a challenge from the University of California to tussle in a sandlot in San Francisco. Cal, which had been established in 1868, was considered the favorite in the game since Stanford had only been established the year before and did not have much experience. Cal students wondered whether California even needed two universities, and they derisively came to calling Stanford students "kidlets." The Haight Street Grounds had a capacity of fifteen thousand, but future U.S. president Herbert Hoover, who was Stanford's manager for the football and baseball teams at the time, underestimated the level of interest the game would generate so only ten thousand tickets were printed. As the kickoff approached, Hoover was shocked to see twenty thousand people turn up. Paper money did not yet exist, so gold and silver coins spilled over the registers.[71] It was Hoover's job to collect the gate, and he soon found his hands full with $30,000 in proceeds. Hoover was likely too busy counting it to see Stanford stun Cal 14-10 and win local bragging rights. In fact, it is remarkable that there was any gate at all. Hoover and his staff were so focused on organizing the game that they failed to realize that they had nothing to kick off, and the game was only saved when a businessman in the stands who happened to sell sporting goods offered to ride his horse to downtown San Francisco to retrieve a football. By the time the game started, the fans had been in their seats for an hour and a half.

Big Games and big controversy over professional coaches continued in the west. Although in 1895, Camp was hired to coach Stanford in the Big Game again, and Cal also hired former Yale and Princeton players to advise their teams in subsequent seasons, by 1900 Cal and Stanford had agreed to a system of graduate coaches to "avoid [coaching] professionalism".[72] At the end of 1904, however, this agreement expired, and although Stanford wanted to renew it, Cal wanted to once again hire coaches from the east. The *Stanford Alumnus* accordingly chided Cal in an editorial: "California has failed to develop in her large student body of alumni a coach with whom she is satisfied and has gone East for a coach with merely a professional interest in the results. Stanford has found an alumnus whom she believes to be for her the very best coach."[73]

Bringing Order to the Game

But it was not only professionalism that created football's controversy. Some claimed that the game was too violent, that training for it was too rigorous and to the detriment of education, and that "ringers" were being paid to play in big games. Some institutions, including Columbia University, dropped the sport altogether while others banned the sport temporarily. Educators, university officials, and others critical of the gridiron game fought to wrest managerial control of college football and reform it in such a way that its best traits could be preserved. In 1895 an intercollegiate conference of Midwestern university faculty was held and included seven colleges that were concerned by these trends. The faculty wanted to control football players' off-field behavior and stymie the off-field behavior of boisterous, drunken fans. At the same time, they did not want to give up the sport altogether since they still believed it successfully channeled players' energy and virility and they still considered many of them valued members of their respective colleges. Their desires led to the founding of the first college athletic conference—the Big Ten—in what was the nation's first attempt to manage and regulate college football.[74] But it was not enough. In 1905 and 1906, a series of muckraking journals published exposés detailing the vast influence of money, the brutality with which teams played the games,[75] and the blatant disregard for "gentlemanly behavior" of the players.[76] Then a player named Harold Moore died after sustaining injuries in a football game between Union College and New York University, precipitating a nationwide debate over the future of football.[77] In December 1905, the president of New York

University convened a group of colleges to form new rules for the game and establish the Intercollegiate Athletic Association (IAA), which five years later would become the National Collegiate Athletic Association (NCAA). Delegates at the conference gave the organization the power to create rules committees and formulate standards of conduct. The establishment of the IAA meant that colleges and their sporting activities were for the first time officially overseen by a national body. Yet that national body had little real power, thus "many colleges turned to regional associations or conferences [like the Big Ten Conference] to bring order to the game."[78] The assumption was that regional conferences, which were attended primarily by college faculty, would be better able to monitor each other and catch bad behavior. In reality, though, "faculty committees were often handpicked by the college presidents and were just as interested in the success of the football team as any other group."[79]

In 1906, Harvard president Charles W. Eliot tried to abolish football on the grounds that it had "become a brutal, cheating, demoralizing game." Eliot protested that football constituted terrible "preparation for the real struggles and contests of life" and prevented otherwise intellectual students from learning. But his outcry fell on deaf ears, the university's governing board outvoted him,[80] and the game's commercialization continued.[81] Thus early attempts by faculty, university presidents, and newly formed athletic conferences to control the management of college sport and limit the violence, gambling, and declining academic abilities of student-athletes by and large failed.

A "Rightful Place in the Cosmos"

Cal and Stanford took steps beyond banning professional coaches and tramp athletes and even abolished sponsoring intercollegiate football altogether, for a time replacing it with rugby. According to Roberta Park, rugby was in some circles seen as a "superior" game because "it was not professional or commercial . . . It was a 'game' rather than a 'spectacle'—a 'pastime' rather than a 'vocation'" that "could be played by small and light men as well as by larger and heavier men" and "did not lead to injuries like those which were incurred by the brutal American game."[82]

However, after many of the same excesses were found to be characteristic of rugby too,[83] football returned to Cal in 1915 and Stanford in 1919. In 1915, Cal students welcomed the game back with a large campus pep rally in part because being associated with American football made one "feel a bit proud to know that he is an American playing an American game the same as other great American universities."⁸⁴ And even though the *Daily Californian* began carrying reports of the same excesses and abuses (e.g., highly paid coaches, excessive training schedules, injuries, and academic problems) that had caused the school to drop football only a few years before, football was back to stay.

Meanwhile, Stanford president Ray Lyman Wilbur, who had been inaugurated in January 1916, went on record against football. To Wilbur, the game was still too professionalized, and he wanted sports coaches to "be concerned with the general student, not solely a small group of elite performers."⁸⁵ In 1917, though, Wilbur's hand was forced when Stanford was elected to host the Student Army Training Corps (SATC) for California, Nevada, and Utah, and army leaders said they believed that only football—and not rugby—could "develop the type of spirit needed by fighting men."⁸⁶ Wilbur reluctantly agreed to allow a football game to be played by SATC members from Stanford to raise money for the war effort. He insisted, however, that the football team did not represent Stanford University, and Cal dominated the SATC team, 67-0. A compromise was struck two years later when an agreement between Cal and Stanford was reached, with Cal president Wheeler concluding that action needed to be taken to dilute the intensity of the Big Game, and both universities agreed to plan matches in other sports and football games with other opponents as well as a second football game between the two schools each year. Feeling as if he had been met halfway, Wilbur agreed to a reformed version of the rivalry, and in 1919, eighteen thousand fans bought tickets to the first Stanford-Cal Big Game in fourteen years. Rugby would continue at both schools but on a relatively small scale, and American football was back in its "rightful place in the cosmos."⁸⁷

Give 'em the Axe

Football at Stanford and Cal came down to beating one's rival and by extension improving one's sense of communal self-worth. Alumni and boosters sought to build a winning team to enhance their affection for their university and their classmates, and students were similarly rabid about the big game, quibbling over specific rules.⁸⁸ Nationally, rivalries like the Big Game became incredibly serious affairs—in the words of one observer, "the most vitally folkloristic event in our culture"⁸⁹ and in the words of another, a spectacular event rich with "intense symbolism . . . [and] multiple layers of cultural performances . . . (e.g., rallies, dinners, alumni reunions, school colors, songs, etc.)."⁹⁰ This seriousness held true all across the country but especially so in regions where people saw football reflecting values of a bygone, pre-industrial era—toughness, hard work, and sacrifice—and where people wanted the game to help them solidify a sense of community.[91]

But to see how football symbolized these values and also carried with it the possibility of letting go and entering a wild fantasy land where the normal rules of society could be temporarily ignored or overlooked and otherwise alienated souls could find brotherhood, one need look no further than the Stanford Axe, the symbolic trophy that is awarded to the victorious team of the Big Game, to illustrate America's infatuation with the gridiron game. In 1899, a Stanford cheerleader named Billy Erb used an axe to behead a toy bear (Cal's mascot is a golden bear) and chop up blue-and-gold ribbons (Cal's official colors). As Erb did his decapitating, fellow Stanford students chanted,

Give 'em the axe, the axe, the axe!
Give 'em the axe, the axe, the axe!
Give 'em the axe, give 'em the axe,
Give 'em the axe, where?
Right in the neck, in the neck, in the neck!
Right in the neck, in the neck, in the neck!
Right in the neck, right in the neck,
Right in the neck! There!

Incensed, Cal men jumped the Stanford men in charge of guarding the axe, sawed off the axe's handle to make it easier to smuggle, and carried it east across San Francisco Bay on a ferry boat. In 1930, Stanford men posing as newspaper photographers asked to take a photograph of the axe after a Cal pep rally and then exploded smoke bombs and tear gas as the bulbs of their cameras began to flash. In the chaos that ensued, Stanford men wrestled the axe away from Cal guardsman, and returned it to Palo Alto.

In short, football rivalries manufactured an imagined community, belonging to which was as coveted as victories in the game itself. Big-time college football games were live, in-person revelries and sometimes almost religious events as a result. Some college games needed large "churches" to accommodate their growing congregations, which explains why, even after radio and television came on the scene, universities kept building bigger and bigger stadiums for live audiences.[92] After all, how else were football's faithful congregants to make meaning in their lives without a proper place of worship?

The gridiron game—in its big-time form—showed incredible staying power even in the face of considerable criticism. Among the game's critics were members of the Carnegie Foundation for the Advancement of Teaching, who in 1929 published a scathing report that concluded that physical educators had been used to "justify and create 'giant athletic agencies' in the nation's colleges and universities" and judged that only twenty-eight colleges operated "ethical" athletic programs.[93] The Carnegie Report, as the findings came to be known, also lamented the "secondary importance" of educational values and the prioritization of financial gain,[94] underscored recruiting improprieties and paying players under the table as its supporting evidence,[95] blamed sponsoring tobacco companies for "exploiting college athletics,"[96] and called on university presidents and faculties to confront their football teams. The sportswriter Paul Gallico, who wrote *Farewell to Sport* in 1938, similarly mourned the demise of the amateur spirit in college football, writing, "If there is anything good about college football it is the fact that it seems to bring entertainment, distraction, and pleasure to many millions of people. But the price, the sacrifice to decency, I maintain, is too high." In 1939, the president of the University of Chicago, Robert Maynard Hutchins, showed that he agreed, abolishing his university's football program and justifying his decision on the grounds that the game—and all sports—did more harm than good. The university's persistent mediocrity in football—it had not had a winning season in fifteen years—helped Hutchins convince regents that the sport should go. (Hutchins personally held a negative view toward sports and physical activity. He once said, "Whenever I feel a desire to exercise, I lie down until it goes away." He also wrote, "Education is primarily concerned with the training of the mind, and athletics and social life, though they may contribute to it, are not at the heart of it and cannot be permitted to interfere with it."[97])

Yet neither Roosevelt, Eliot, Gallico, Hutchins, nor the authors of the Carnegie Report could affect meaningful reform that would lead other institutions to abolish or significantly reform football. In fact, the general unpopularity of Hutchins's crusade at Chicago showed that even when a relatively powerful college president takes a stand, he cannot assure himself of victory against the forces of football. If they get too close, university presidents at that time—and many since—run the risk of burning themselves on the "engine of the train," and they more than anyone understand what one former head football coach at the University of Texas meant when he said, "In the final analysis, the public, not the colleges, runs college football."[98]

Conclusion

As football spread as a wildly popular form of entertainment, it held together tensions: at once it was a unifying force in an increasingly multi-ethnic society as well as a source of regional pride. American sports fans could not get enough of football's public drama, so it became the nation's new civil religion, replete with all the symbolic value formal religions carry: a moral code, a collective sense of belonging, and rituals to maintain one's sense of shared identity. At the same time, the game was a de facto tool of gender socialization that for many fit the times. While any young man who could withstand the physical pain that the game inflicted was assured an elevated status in society, women and girls were categorically excluded from stepping foot on the gridiron and thus from enjoying any accolades that would have otherwise accrued. In effect, promoters and sponsors of the game—including universities themselves—normalized these gender roles, none more than the notion that men should be physically tough in a way that proved them distinct from women, and in a way that proved their superior ability to make physical sacrifices. Women were left on the outside looking in, unable to step into the religion's inner circle where belonging felt strongest and important decisions were being made. Football's emphasis on physical toughness served to not only exclude women from that sport but as we will see in chapter 3, also raised questions about women's participation in other "manly" sports such as basketball. These manly sports were considered too tough and competitive for females, and playing them at all might suggest a mannish nature or, worse still, the development of one.

Notes

1. TV timeouts are carefully planned hiatuses from the action intended to carve out time for commercial enterprises to advertise their products and services to television viewers. They are not called by coaches to give their players a chance to catch their breath or hydrate.
2. Serazio, "Just How Much."
3. Ullian, "A Rope, a Tree."
4. Easterbrook, *The King of Sports*; Oriard, *King Football*.
5. Schlager, "More People."
6. Tracy and Rohan, "What Made College Football."
7. Tracy and Rohan, "What Made College Football."
8. Grundy and Rader, *American Sports*, 152.
9. Gems, *For Pride*.
10. Grundy and Rader, *American Sports*, 6–7.
11. Grundy and Rader, *American Sports*, 11.
12. Grundy and Rader, *American Sports*, 13–14.
13. Grundy and Rader, *American Sports*, 11. In an essay published in 1673, Baxter argued,

If you wish to avoid the sin and danger of unbiblical amusements masquerading as acceptable recreations—you must understand what acceptable or lawful recreation is, and its legitimate purpose. No wonder Christians sin, if they do not know what is right! Without doubt, some amusement and recreation is *lawful*, indeed, *necessary* to some people. Lawful recreation is the enjoyment of some natural thing, or participation in some activity which is not forbidden, for the stimulation of the natural spirits. It may be for the use of the mind, or the exercise of the body. It is some pleasurable activity or exercise, ultimately intended to fit the body and mind for their normal duty to God" ("Directions for Amusements").

14. In England, students in public schools, to which landed gentry and aristocracy sent their sons in part to reproduce their social class standing, initially led their own spontaneously created games. These students preferred often brutal games of poaching, shooting, and hare-and-hounds to the study of Latin and Greek, which they considered boring and irrelevant. But over time their games were coopted, with some English educators, and some public school headmasters, seeking to control them in order to implement their own educational agenda. Sports like rugby and cricket were developed and institutionalized with rules of conduct befitting the upper-class mores of English gentlemen, and an ideology of amateurism was deployed to ensure that upper-class values were reproduced. But in the process of adults taking control of what had once been youth-directed sports, an "educational revolution" took place since "the rough unorganized games that characterized the time became . . . organized and regulated." In time, "rules were agreed on and written down, and the headmasters and teachers began to support them." In time, some headmasters came to argue that sports were an effective way of raising good, upstanding muscular Christian boys who were tough, worked hard, and served God (Miracle and Rees, *Lessons*, 32).

15. Grundy and Rader, *American Sports*, 26.

16. As Miracle and Rees explain, "The essence of muscular Christianity was the belief that physical activity, especially team sports like cricket and rugby, made a significant contribution to the development of morality and patriotism, and the values learned sport at school would be transferred to other situations later in life" (*Lessons*, 32).

17. Mangan, *The Games Ethic*, 18.

18. Coakley, "Youth Sport," 88.

19. Miracle and Rees, *Lessons*, 35. See also American Anthropology Association, "Statement on Race." The AAA writes, "From its inception, this modern concept of 'race' was modeled after an ancient theorem of the Great Chain of Being, which posited natural categories on a hierarchy established by God or nature. Thus 'race' was a mode of classification linked specifically to peoples in the colonial situation. It subsumed a growing ideology of inequality devised to rationalize European attitudes and treatment of the conquered and enslaved peoples. Proponents of slavery in particular during the 19th century used 'race' to justify the retention of slavery." In a later form, the great chain of being held that white Christian men of European

stock sat atop the pinnacle of the human race and therefore should be the model for all humans and a blueprint for eugenic breeding (Lovejoy, *The Great Chain of Being*).

20. Miracle and Rees, *Lessons*, 33.
21. Miracle and Rees, *Lessons*, 34.
22. Various scholars have applied the Gramscian concept of cultural hegemony to sport, and it has been especially useful in understanding how manly sports shape a hegemonic masculinity. See, for example, Messner, *Power at Play*; Sabo and Panepinto, "Football Ritual"; and Light and Kirk, "High School Rugby."
23. While the idea that one could serve God spiritually and physically came to be known as muscular Christianity in religious circles, the sociologist Max Weber argued that it should be termed the "Protestant work ethic." Drawing on Baxter to prove his point, Weber noted that the theologian's "principal work [was] dominated by the continually repeated, often almost passionate preaching of hard, continuous bodily or mental labor" ("Protestant"). Weber concluded that the Protestant value accorded to physical and mental industriousness was a particularly powerful ideology that served the economies of the countries where it predominated.
24. According to Mangan, there was a "games ethic" in English public schools that

> held pride of place in the pedagogical priorities for the period public school. And by means of this ethic the public schoolboy supposedly learned *inter alia* the basic tools of imperial command: courage, endurance, assertion, control, and self-control. However, there was a further and important dimension of the later concept of "manliness": its relevance to both dominance and deference . . . initiative and self-reliance by also loyalty and obedience" (*The Games Ethic*, 18).

25. Grundy and Rader, *American Sports*, 23.
26. Allison, *Amateurism*, 39.
27. Grundy and Rader, *American Sports*, 24.
28. Grundy and Rader, *American Sports*, 24.
29. Riess, "Class and Sport."
30. Grundy and Rader, *American Sports*, 45.
31. Grundy and Rader, *American Sports*, 50–53.
32. Grundy and Rader, *American Sports*, 48–9.
33. Grundy and Rader, *American Sports*, 72–73.
34. Gems, "Football and Cultural Values," 1.
35. Messner, "Sports and Male Domination," 199–200.
36. Grundy and Rader, *American Sports*, 76.
37. Grundy and Rader, *American Sports*, 77.
38. Riess, *Sport in Industrial America*.
39. Riess, *Sport in Industrial America*.
40. Coakley, "Youth Sport," 88.
41. Goldstein, *The Teacher Wars*.

42. Ralph Waldo Emerson parodied these elite fears when he said, "This country is filling up with thousands of voters and you have to educate them to keep them from our throats" (Quoted in Chomsky, "Public Education," 28).

43. This was also the case for some in baseball. See Grundy and Rader, *American Sports*, 47.

44. Coakley, "Youth Sport," 87.

45. Coakley, *Sport in Society*, 72.

46. Sedgwick, "Walter Camp."

47. Sedgwick, "Walter Camp."

48. Grundy and Rader, *American Sports*, 74.

49. R. A. Smith, *Sports and Freedom*, 92.

50. Mechikoff, *A History and Philosophy*, 256–58.

51. Shulman and Bowen, *The Game of Life*, 7.

52. Quoted in Grundy and Rader, *American Sports*, 78.

53. Grundy and Rader, *American Sports*, 76.

54. Grundy and Rader, *American Sports*, 27.

55. Grundy and Rader, *American Sports*, 75; and Miracle and Rees, *Lessons*, 45.

56. R. A. Smith, *Sports and Freedom*, 6, 147. For a full history of professional sports coaches in rowing, which caught the Northeast's fancy in the mid-nineteenth century and which the elite colleges of the Northeast used to challenge each other's supremacy, see R. A. Smith, *Sports and Freedom*, 6, 40, and 147–54; see also, Sperber, "College Sports, Inc.," 17–31.

57. R. A. Smith, *Sports and Freedom*, 160.

58. R. A. Smith, *Sports and Freedom*, 161.

59. Quoted in R. A. Smith, *Sports and Freedom*, 164.

60. Barton, "Honoring Walter Camp."

61. In the late 1880s, for example, rival New England football teams, including Yale, began to play annual Thanksgiving Day games, and Camp was instrumental in this effort, helping to "transform football from a relatively insignificant fall pastime in colleges to a gigantic commercial attraction" (R. A. Smith, *Sports and Freedom*, 84).

62. Mrozek, *Sport and American Mentality*.

63. R. A. Smith, *Sports and Freedom*, 147–48.

64. R. A. Smith, *Sports and Freedom*, 148.

65. Grundy and Rader, *American Sports*, 20.

66. Thelin, "From Sports Page," 4.

67. Grundy and Rader, *American Sports*, 153.

68. Oriard, "Review of Smith."

69. Grundy and Rader, *American Sports*, 157.

70. Grundy and Rader, *American Sports*, 157.

71. Liebendorfer, *The Color*, 3.

72. Park, "From Football," 10–11.

73. Quoted in Park, "From Football," 12.

74. A. M. Frank, *Sports and Education*, 44.

75. In the year 1905, for example, eighteen students died playing football and another 160 were seriously injured (Nocera and Strauss, *Indentured*, 14).

76. Grundy and Rader, *American Sports*, 154.

77. Watterson, "The Gridiron Crisis."

78. Grundy and Rader, *American Sports*, 155.

79. Grundy and Rader, *American Sports*, 155.

80. Bok, *Universities*, 37.

81. Lambert and Bethell, "First and 100." Eliot was against other sports too, including basketball and hockey. Of the former he said, "Basketball is very objectionable. It is too rough, and there are too many chances for cheating" (quoted in *New York Times*, "Eliot against Basket Ball").

82. Park, "From Football," 24.

83. Park, "From Football," 20–24.

84. Quoted in Park, "From Football," 27–28.

85. Park, "From Football," 39.

86. Park, "From Football," 36.

87. Park, "From Football," 39.

88. Park, "From Football," 26.

89. Quoted in Guttmann, *Sports Spectators*, 93.

90. Park, "From Football," 8.

91. As Oriard argues, newly modern and urban ways in the early twentieth century were seen as a threat to those who grounded their identities in the local community. Whereas the church, community, and neighborhood were once the central institutions of local life, urban fashions and industrial factories were increasingly dictating the pace of rural and suburban life. As a result, local sports teams, and particularly college football teams, came to provide Americans with the emotional bond that they desired to keep their community tied together, and universities were more than happy to serve as the social hub (Oriard, *King Football*, 11–17).

92. The first college football radio broadcast was in 1921. Around the same time, three monumental stadiums were built for the sole purpose of hosting football games. Ohio State opened a 65,000-person stadium in 1922, and Soldier Field, holding 110,000, opened in Chicago the same year. The next year, 1923, the Los Angeles Coliseum, with a capacity of 105,000, followed suit.

93. Grundy and Rader, *American Sports*, 160.

94. Grundy and Rader, *American Sports*, 161.

95. Lumpkin, *Modern Sports Ethics*, 115.

96. Quoted in Sperber, "College Sports, Inc.," 18.

97. Quoted in Byers and Hammer, *Unsportsmanlike Conduct*, 40–41.

98. Quoted in Grundy and Rader, *American Sports*, 161.

CHAPTER 3

Unselfish Play

> Be strong in body, clean in mind, and lofty in ideals.
>
> —Dr. James Naismith

"It Was Really Unselfish Play": Fresno State University, December 12, 2010

In Stanford's 77-40 victory over Fresno State a few weeks after beating Texas and a few weeks before beating UCONN, Kayla Pedersen suffered a concussion when she slammed her head on the court. Kayla had been trying to hold her ground to take a charge. It was a tough and selfless play that symbolized the kind of player Kayla was and why her coaches and fellow players always sang her praises. In Kayla's absence, the Ogwumike sisters demonstrated their own team spirit, scoring eighteen points (Chiney) and seventeen points (Nneka). Afterward, Chiney told the press, "Fresno was a great test for us because they were aggressive from the start. We . . . worked hard to get open. It was really unselfish play."

"[We] Take No Chances with a Head Injury": Depaul University, December 16, 2010

Kayla sat and watched the game against DePaul a few days later as Coach VanDerveer said the coaches would "take no chances with a head injury."

At the time, the consequences of concussions in professional football were becoming national news, embroiling the NFL in scandal as investigative journalists Mark Fainaru-Wada and Steve Fainaru published a book called *League of Denial: The NFL, Concussions, and the Battle for Truth*, which alleged that the league had covered up knowledge of the links between football, concussions, and long-term brain health. Medical researchers were beginning to show a causal link between football and brain injury too, and in 2013, when the PBS *Frontline* program broadcast a documentary based on Fainaru-Wada and Fainaru's reporting (also titled *League of Denial*), the issue reached a fever pitch. *League of Denial* described instances in which the NFL seemed to have known that playing football could lead to long-term brain injury and to a newly diagnosed disease called chronic traumatic encephalopathy and yet had for years covered up the fact and hired sympathetic doctors to deny the connection. Some parents began to talk of removing their children from high school football teams.

For Pedersen, it was the first time in her career that such an injury had forced her to miss a game, and it could not have come at a worse time, during Stanford's first long-distance road trip. The injury presented a considerable challenge for the team's younger players, who had not yet seen big minutes in high-pressure games. Coach VanDerveer called upon Sarah James, Sarah Boothe, Lindy LaRocque, Mikaela Ruef, and Toni Kokenis to play more significant minutes in Pedersen's absence against the twenty-second-ranked DePaul Blue Demons on December 16, 2010, but it wasn't enough. Stanford launched a 15-5 attack to begin the first half, but that was the end of Cardinal control. Soon the Blue Demons took command, and without Pedersen, Stanford never stood a chance.

The loss prevented Coach VanDerveer, temporarily at least, from joining Pat Summitt, Jody Conradt, C. Vivian Stringer, and Sylvia Hatchell in the illustrious 800 Win Club. Ever selfless, VanDerveer dismissed the individual accomplishment to the press. "It's really totally irrelevant as far as I'm concerned," she said, before adding, "I honestly don't think about it at all. I'm really focused on the moment, this team, this game, looking at what combinations need to be out there."[1]

In the game's aftermath, VanDerveer made sure her comments to the press were precise reflecting on Kayla's concussion, "You know, we want the refs to allow some physicality. But we don't want anyone to get hurt."

"We're Not Going to Get Better Playing against Chumps": University of Tennessee, December 19, 2010

Kayla returned to the lineup against the University of Tennessee on December 19, 2010, when Stanford, ranked number two in the nation, traveled to Knoxville to play the number six Volunteers (Vols), but she did not seem fully recovered.

The game was held at cavernous Thompson-Boling Arena, which could hold 14,197 fans. It was the largest crowd that Stanford played for that year. Coach VanDerveer's counterpart, Pat Summitt, had coached the Vols to eight national titles, earned over one thousand wins, and had become such an icon of the sport that the University of Tennessee named the basketball court after her: the Summitt at Thompson-Boling Arena. The previous season, Stanford beat Tennessee at Maples, but Tennessee led the overall series, and Stanford had typically struggled when they played in Knoxville, having won only once, in 1996. Still, when it came to tough matchups against perennial powerhouses like the Vols, Coach VanDerveer took the long view. "That's why we play good teams: to get better. We're not going to get better in play against chumps."

The game was close, competitive, and entertaining, with the lead seesawing back and forth. With under a minute left to go in the game, Tennessee's standout freshman Meighan Simmons tied the game at 70-70. Stanford had possession of the ball. Near the bench, Cardinal players linked arms in anxious solidarity. To win, Stanford would have to run the length of the court and score. VanDerveer called on Kokenis to win the foot race and get a shot off before the buzzer. But her shot was offline, and the game went into overtime.

Thompson-Boling was rocking, and the crowd noise sowed chaos. Pohlen and Boothe fouled out, less than two minutes into the overtime period. The Vols took a 72-70 lead. Uncharacteristically, Pedersen made a sloppy pass and missed the front end of one-and-one, missing the chance to even the score. Tennessee stretched the lead to 75-70. With time on the clock ticking down, Stanford had little chance but to foul, and Tennessee iced the game at the free throw line, making the final score, 82-72, look more lopsided than the game had been. Stanford had mustered two points in the overtime period. Although Pohlen finished the game with twenty-four points, lasering six three-pointers through the net, her fouling out in overtime shot a hole in Stanford's chances. And it didn't help that Pedersen was not at full strength, still feeling the aftereffects of her concussion.[2]

For American women living in the early- to mid-twentieth century, competitive, physical, and intense sports, which is to say any activity that involved routine bodily collisions and risk of injuries like Kayla's, have been "contested terrain,"[3] in many ways an act seen as antithetical to properly meeting societal expectations. Participation in competitive, physical, and intense team sports was seen as a means to meet society's expectation of showing you were a tough man, and therefore it was forbidden to females, especially those who hailed from the upper and middle classes. No sport was more representative of these gendered expectations than college football, which women and girls were almost never allowed to play.

The consequences of this exclusion, both literal and ideological, were severe. First, it limited women's and girls' ability to lay claim to competitive sports participation as a normal activity. Second, it limited women and girls from using sports to build their confidence through competitive sports, which arguably impacted their ability to be confident in other realms of life. Third, it curtailed women's and girls' ability to leverage sporting success to create entertainment value, thereby stunting the commercial growth of sports like basketball, which itself further distorted people's notions about women's proper place in society and reinforced painful institutional systems of gender discrimination. Even how we talk about women in sport has been impacted. College women's sports are called just that: "college women's sports" (or sometimes "women's college sports"). We rarely use the term "men's college sports"; instead, we say simply "college sports" as if everyone should know that only women need the modifier.[4] It took years of hard work on and off the court for women to challenge these notions and begin to reverse these damaging trends, and much work remains.

Like male athletes, females who play competitive sports today must concern themselves not only with the potential for injury but also (unlike males) enduring societal norms that expect them to be tough on the court and maintain a conventionally feminine profile off it. Male athletes are expected to play sport in a way that shows they are men, and the physicality, injury risk, and toughness of their sports are rarely questioned.

At the same time, women's college sports, especially those played at the competitive big-time level, offer participants the chance to not only challenge themselves physically, mentally, and emotionally but also to challenge the received wisdom that highly physical realms like sports—where injury risk has always existed—are for men and boys alone. In that sense, competitive sports like basketball have become important arenas of resistance to historically gendered stereotypes as well as sites for challenging paternalistic notions of what femininity is and should be.

The Origins of Sports for Girls and Young Women

Much of the discrimination women face in contemporary sport can be traced to the social and cultural transitions that occurred during America's industrial modernization period, during which sports were invented and developed, and at a time in which upper-class Victorian values encouraged and incentivized women to be, act, and even think in a way that diminished their physical abilities and relative social standing vis-à-vis men.

We do not have a crystal-clear picture of the physical endeavors of women before modern sports were invented largely because women had little hand in writing their own histories, but we do know that in ancient times women were hailed for their *superior* physical strength. Women performed contests in honor of Zeus's wife, Hera, in the Olympic complex,[5] and ancient Cretan women performed amazing acrobatic feats at bullfights, right alongside men.[6] Moreover, for many centuries before the industrial period, women were depicted in art and folklore as symbols of physical strength and revered as superhuman creatures. In art in particular, the female form was used as an evocative symbol of beauty, re-creation, and strength.

Yet in Roman days a system of patriarchy and class stratification kept women out of physical activities and other important realms of social life. The record of exclusion from intense physical activity in modern times is clearer since modern sports were invented by men for boys, specifically to showcase male physical and mental strengths during a time in which men faced a masculinity crisis of their own and sought out refuges like football to emphasize their physical power. Many of the sports widely played or watched across the world today, such as soccer and rugby, were invented at seven English public schools (Rugby, Eton, Harrow, Charterhouse, Westminster, Winchester, Shrewsbury) and two universities (Oxford and Cambridge) that largely catered to boys and young men and therefore developed in the context of engendering manly virtues.

Even the Olympic Games in their modern incarnation did not include women at first. Their founder, the French Baron Pierre de Coubertin, who was also an avowed Anglophile and had studied at Oxford and therefore believed in the power of modern sports to socialize boys, banned women from participating when he established the modern Olympic Games in 1896. Although he would later reverse his view, allowing nineteen women to compete at the 1900 Olympic Games, de Coubertin's initial decision was a sign of the times.

Yet by the mid-nineteenth century, a small group of female educators, including Catherine Beecher (1800–1878), had come to believe that exercise and physical games might benefit women, and though they prescribed participation at a moderate level, often in the form of gentle calisthenics performed to music, it was the start of a period of change.[7] Beecher was a passionate advocate for girls' education although her advocacy of their physical education stopped short of encouraging competitive or physical play. Leading male physicians of the day similarly adhered to gendered protocol when they prescribed physical activity for women, thus limiting what girls could do.[8]

Access to sport was class based too. If women and girls were allowed to play sports just for fun, it was only among the upper class. In the late nineteenth century, for example, upper-class women were allowed to play golf and tennis, in some cases even allowed to practice against men[9] since these sports were considered proper pursuits of leisure for gilded groups. Only these supposedly amateur sports, which were neither inherently violent nor considered likely to make women manly, were considered tame enough to be considered appropriate for upper-class women and girls.

However, a battle for educational equality in the late nineteenth century began to make dents in the patriarchal hierarchy. In the 1870s, for example, as women sought suffrage, female political activism grew. Some women began to express themselves in political and social circles, fighting for their right to vote, the right to work, and the right to work for equal pay. Literary societies were a vital part of the co-education movement of the time, which sought to educate boys and girls together, and higher levels of women's educational attainment afforded them the knowledge of power inequalities that was prerequisite to challenging cultural norms.

From Safety Bicycle to Competitive Team Sports

By the 1890s, female college students had begun to seek more vigorous outdoor activities too, including athletics, and around the turn of the twentieth century, in a political and physical watershed, women began riding bicycles. The safety bicycle, which was designed to be safer than bicycles whose high center of gravity could send riders flying if they stopped short, gave women newfound freedom to roam outside the home. This was an important technological development because it removed the worry of some men that their wives and daughters would be in physical danger when riding on a bicycle.

The advent of the bicycle changed the way women lived but also how they thought about themselves and their rights. On February 2, 1896, Susan B. Anthony told *New York World*, "Bicycling . . . has done more to

Table 3.1. First Women's Sporting Events in American Colleges

Event (Participants/Host)	Year
First women's intercollegiate basketball game (Stanford University and the University of California[1])	1892
First women's intercollegiate track meet (aka "Field Day") (Vassar College[2])	1895
First Amateur Athletic Union national championships in swimming	1916
First women's international track meet[3]	1922
First Amateur Athletic Union national championships in track[4]	1924
First Amateur Athletic Union national championships in basketball[5]	1926

1. Liberti, R.M., 2002. Trailblazing in Marin: women's Dipsea hikes, 1918-1922. *California History*, 81(1), pp.54-65. P. 58.
2. See Liberti, R.M., 2002. Trailblazing in Marin: women's Dipsea hikes, 1918-1922. *California History*, 81(1), pp.54-65. P. 58.
3. Tuttle, Jane P. "Setting the Mark: Lucile Godbold and the First International Track Meet for Women." *South Carolina Historical Magazine* 102, no. 2 (April 2001): 135–52.
4. Cahn, S.K., 2015. *Coming on strong: Gender and sexuality in women's sport.* University of Illinois Press. pp. 44-5.
5. Cahn, S.K., 2015. *Coming on strong: Gender and sexuality in women's sport.* University of Illinois Press. pp. 44-5.

emancipate women than anything else in the world. It gives women a feeling of freedom and self-reliance. I stand and rejoice every time I see a woman ride by on a wheel . . . the picture of free, untrammeled womanhood."[10] In 1895, Frances Willard, the president of the Women's Christian Temperance Union, who learned how to ride at age fifty-three, also praised the bicycle and employed a cycling metaphor to call on suffragists to act: "I would not waste my life in friction when it could be turned into momentum."[11] By the year 1900, thirty thousand women owned and rode bicycles, and as Elizabeth Cady Stanton famously opined, "many a woman is riding to suffrage on a bicycle."[12] Although some critics claiming that riding a bicycle could risk "uterine displacement, spinal shock, pelvic damage and hardened abdominal muscles,"[13] overall it was a liberating technology and helped whet the appetite for females to participate in more competitive sports like basketball.

Women first played basketball in an intercollegiate contest on the west coast in 1892,[14] a year after Dr. James Naismith invented the game. By the 1910s and 1920s, women were beginning to participate in other sports such as running,[15] swimming, field hockey, and tennis, and the Summer Olympic Games expanded to include gymnastics and track and field events for women.

Play Days and Telegraphic Meets

Despite these gains, obstacles remained. While college football rivalries garnered more and more attention and the size of football stadiums continued to grow to accommodate ever-larger crowds, so-called sports days, play days, and telegraphic meets for middle- and upper-class white college women served to deemphasize any big-time competition for women.

At white colleges and universities, play days were special athletic events that emphasized sociality, not competition, thereby serving as a way of providing young women with healthy physical activity without their becoming too mannish. For play days, "athletes from several different colleges gathered for a day of competition and socializing,"[16] after which they drank tea and talked. Anyone could attend, and there were no rewards or trophies for victory. Educators also approved of telegraphic meets, which were supposed to provide an emotional outlet for those who aspired to greater competition.[17] Schools would hold their events independently and then telegraph the results to other schools so young women could measure themselves against one another and determine winners and losers.

Thus young women were allowed to compete but discouraged from doing so fiercely because of societal fears that such competitiveness would either further a win-at-any-cost attitude and thus breed dishonesty and corruption or lead to mannishness.[18] Institutions like the Women's Division of the National Amateur Athletic Federation even monitored the ways in which women participated in the sports they were allowed to play,[19] apparently in order to further so-called democratic values.[20] In other words, upper- and middle-class men—and some women—discouraged young women and girls from playing sports with intensity because they were expected to be pale-skinned and dainty and to focus their lives on attracting a male mate (derisively known as getting an MRS degree).[21]

Clothing Shows and Proper Posture

However, as Rita Liberti found in her historical research on 1930s basketball at Bennett College, an all-black college for women in North Carolina, being a lady in those days did not mean the same thing for every young American woman. Ruth Glover, a Bennett star player, explained the situation succinctly: "We were ladies, too, we just played basketball like boys."[22] While extramural play days for women reinforced dominant notions of white, middle-class femininity and echoed the ends sought by "clothing shows," "demonstrations of proper posture," and "courses to improve one's grammar,"[23] African American women like those at Bennett College had greater access to competitive sport in part because they faced different standards of etiquette.[24] Susan Cahn calls the phenomenon "female-controlled moderate sport," and at the time it was giving way as working-class women, African American women, and younger students began playing "highly competitive sport."[25]

But even when women were allowed to play, they were often still expected to conform to gendered standards of femininity that focused unfairly on their appearance and behavior rather than their athleticism. Until the 1920s, for example, white American women from the upper- and middle-classes were expected to conform to standards of Victorian femininity, but new styles in women's fashion emerged around the time that women were granted the right to vote (1920). In particular, the short-haired smoking and drinking flappers allowed some women to loosen the Victorian bodily restraints that had limited women's ability to participate in sports. And yet, as Liberti notes, "for conservative onlookers, these trends were scandalous as they symbolized all that was wrong with society."[26]

Out of this controversy over women's fashion, a "new type of athletic girl" emerged as the presumed frailty and submissiveness expected of women by Victorian mores to some degree gave way.[27] However even in a post–World War II baseball league for women, the All-Americans Girls Baseball League (AAGBL), women athletes were forced to follow a "femininity principle," and wear "league-mandated pastel-skirted uniforms, makeup, long hair," and adhere to "strict standards of off field dress and behavior."[28] In the 1940s, and especially during World War II, labor shortages had required that women enter the workforce in greater numbers, which renewed anxiety among men who worried that their women might become less feminine. So the AAGBL, which Cahn calls the "most viable professional organization in women's sports history," was marketed as a league that did not challenge conventional notions of femininity. AAGBL leaders such as Arthur Meyerhoff and William Wrigley saw no problem with promoting their star players as feminine women who had masculine athletic skill.[29] In promoting their league, AAGBL leadership made mandatory for all players a charm school where women went to learn about proper makeup, posture, fashion, and table manners, and the leadership also established a code of conduct for player behavior.[30] In other words, when American men finally did acknowledge the commercial appeal of women athletes, they focused not on women's interest in sports or on their ability to play them, but rather on how they looked and appeared to male spectators.

The Goddess and the Muscle Moll

While football players and coaches were capitalizing on the game's popular spectacles, female athletes were rarely anointed American sports heroes, and if and when they were, it was usually because of their looks not because of their abilities. A brief comparison between international tennis star and Frenchwoman Suzanne Lenglen and American Mildred "Babe" Didrikson proves the point. In the years after World War I, Lenglen gave her sport sex appeal, expanding the popularity of tennis. For instance, in 1920 at Wimbledon, Lenglen arrived at center court in an outfit that revealed her bare forearms and calves, shocking the staid upper-class fans, and when Helen Wills traveled to France to challenge her, Lenglen wore a "scandalously short skirt and a jeweled bandeau." Lenglen's off-the-court antics were as famous. According to one writer, she "wore ermine and partied on champagne, she traveled by chauffeured limo and private rail car, and she knew everyone who ever wrote a memoir about the Lost Generation."[31] The French press dubbed Lenglen *La Divine* (the Goddess), the French people called her *La Grande Suzanne*, and she was remembered as the first diva of tennis.

By contrast, the ascendance of Didrikson only stoked male fears that sports would produce mannish female athletes.[32] Didrikson excelled in every sport she picked up: basketball, track and field, golf, and she even qualified for the 1932 Los Angeles Olympics. She earned her nickname after she hit five home runs in a baseball game and people began comparing her to baseball legend Babe Ruth. But sportswriter Paul Gallico, who once personally lost a golf match to Didrikson, derisively labeled her the Muscle Moll, averring that she was "neither male nor female,"[33] and insensitively wrote in a 1932 issue of *Vanity Fair*, "She knows she is not pretty, that she cannot compete with the other girls in the very ancient and honored sport of man-trapping. She uses no cosmetics, creams, or powders. But she competes with girls, fiercely and hungrily, at everything else."[34] Another contemporary sportswriter suggested that Didrikson should better spend her time getting "prettied up and waiting for the phone to ring" rather than play sports.[35]

It was not until Babe Didrikson turned to golf that she began cultivating a more mainstream feminine appearance.[36] In 1947, Didrikson won seventeen out of the eighteen professional golf tournaments she entered, averaged seventy-seven strokes per round and hit the ball 280 yards off the tee, but the physical activity required in golf did not offend as many Americans as it did in basketball or track.

Thus, while the sexual appeal of Lenglen was enough to "lift women's tennis into the international sporting spotlight," female athletes like Didrikson struggled for popular acceptance.[37] In particular, women like Didrikson faced the unreasonable expectation of sexual appeal, an expectation that was not expected of male American athletes. To make matters worse, there were few female sportswriters in those days, which meant that the power of the pen only left a mark in one direction, further dividing rigidly delineated gender lines.

The Origins of Basketball for Girls and Young Women

Basketball exposed all these double standards too. Like football, it emerged out of anxieties surrounding masculinity, but since it was invented several decades after the Industrial Revolution, basketball was unique in its deliberate design to further Christian values and not to be as violent as football. In fact, for this reason, basketball was initially seen as a more feminine game than football.

Like football, basketball was invented by a man specifically for the educational and social benefit of young men, and therefore young women were not its intended audience. But young women and girls began playing it nonetheless, so much so in fact that basketball would eventually become the most popular sport for schoolgirls and young women.[38]

Basketball was invented by Dr. James Naismith in Springfield, Massachusetts, in 1891 and emerged during a time in which progressive social reformers, including physical educators such as Luther Gulick Jr as well as psychologists like G. Stanley Hall,[39] sought to improve society through education and activities that improved overall health.[40] In sports, this meant "adopt[ing] competitive team games as a means of molding the physical and social characteristics of young men and women."[41] A range of groups, including "private preparatory schools, churches, Public School Athletic Leagues (PSAL), city playground associations, and public high schools" became involved and created an era of "adult-directed sports" for youth.[42] The theory was that young boys were impressionable and required a positive environment in which they could grow.[43]

Basketball also had religious origins. Equipped with peach baskets fixed to a gymnasium wall and a football[44] in hand, Dr. Naismith drew up plans for basketball at the Springfield Young Men's Christian Association (YMCA), where he worked.

But it was Gulick Jr who also worked for the YMCA and developed its tripartite mission of physical, emotional, and intellectual education[45] and who urged Naismith to create a game that would toughen up young boys during the winter months between football and baseball seasons. Gulick Jr was the son of missionary and physician Luther Gulick Sr and brother and missionary

Sydney Gulick,[46] and his educational ideas were undoubtedly influenced by his religious upbringing and the ideology of muscular Christianity.[47] Like many of his contemporaries, Gulick feared that young boys would become too soft without physical training.

Gulick Jr developed an "evolutionary theory of play" that "gave physical activity a central role in child development" and argued that "organized, adult-monitored games constituted the most advanced form of play." To Gulick Jr, this form represented "man . . . the savage hunter" submitting to the leadership of a chief (i.e., the adult leader of a sport or physical activity). As a result of Gulick Jr. and Hall's religio-psychological work, American "adults increasingly looked to" organized and competitive sports, like those sponsored by the YMCA, as a way to teach male youth "teamwork, sportsmanship, and other components of what they called individual character."[48]

As a devout Christian, Naismith subscribed to Gulick's evolutionary theory of play but added that he could use it to "win men for the Master through the gym." At the time, Naismith was studying for a master's degree from Montreal's Presbyterian Theological College,[49] and he aimed to "put Christianity out there in front of people and try to influence them through positive character development" while "reserving his formal preaching for when he was a guest minister at area churches."[50] In other words, religious character development was a key existential pillar of Naismith's missionary project[51] and it followed in the tradition set not only by Hall and Gulick Jr but also by the YMCA itself.

Naismith envisioned basketball as an activity that would keep young male athletes active when hockey teams were not in town, but he also imagined it in response to his own growing uneasiness with football's violence, establishing a rule that there was to be no contact at all between players and no running with the ball. Above all, Naismith wanted players to exercise self-control since he believed that those who did represented the pinnacle of civilization.[52]

Football Suited to Feminine Capabilities

Basketball was an immediate hit, and before long many spectators, including some women like Senda Berenson, were visiting the Springfield YMCA to sneak a peek. Berenson, a Jewish woman whose family had immigrated from the Russian Empire (present day Lithuania) and who had been born Senda Valvrojenski, growing up speaking Yiddish on the streets of Boston, took a deep interest in the sport. Berenson had grown up in poor health and had enrolled at the Boston Normal School for Gymnastics in 1890 with the hope of strengthening her body. She wanted to eventually pursue a career in music, dance, or art. At the Boston Normal School for Gymnastics, she learned that there was a new form of art, that of physical education for women, and she began to see physical activity and exercise as a means of developing courage, endurance, and even mental acuity. Soon she began to pursue a career as a teacher of physical activity for women and was hired by all-women's Smith College in Northampton, Massachusetts. Ultimately, she rose to the rank of physical education director, and in 1892, after Berenson read about Naismith's game in the YMCA journal *Physical Education*, she decided to introduce it at Smith.[53]

Like many men of the time, Berenson believed that basketball had to be adapted to fit with prevailing views of female bodies and in a way that would not compromise the perceived femininity of its participants.[54] Berenson changed the rules to make the early forms of basketball palatable to anyone who believed women should avoid physically competitive sports.[55] These included dividing the court into three sections (mandating that players remain within the bounds of "their assigned areas"), limiting the ability of women to run fast or run into each other at high speed, allowing six players rather than five (a rule that testified to the belief that women could not and should not play with the same speed and intensity as men), and limited dribbling to one time (later, three times) while prohibiting players from making physical contact or attempting to hinder the shot of an opponent. She even enjoined women to be more cooperative than competitive and encouraged the "selfless" act of passing over "selfish" dribbling. Berenson's rules, which were codified in a rulebook published through the Spalding Sporting Goods Company, later became the rules adopted by the National Section on Women's Athletics (NSWA). These rules then spread across America, enabling women to play basketball without "compromising their femininity, and therefore, their acceptance in society."[56]

Berenson's rule changes were in keeping with what were mainstream gendered notions at the time. In the 1890s, girls were perceived to be biologically incapable of undertaking the hard labor required in competitive sports participation, and educators and medical professionals believed that "females had a limited amount of energy, which during puberty went to the development of reproductive organs."[57] Subjecting them to potentially physical sports like basketball might, some feared, compromise their ability to bear children. Even when allowed to participate, they were expected to wear floor length dresses (with hems they often tripped over), "heavy bloomers, "thick, black stockings," and a corset, which "restricted breathing, displaced ovaries and sometimes fractured ribs." (Male basketball players wore "short pants and long-sleeved shirts").[58] It seems that it was the gendered restrictions on women rather than the biological limits of the supposedly frail female frame that caused the most injury to athletic women in those days!

Berenson believed that team sports like basketball might help women achieve full social equality[59] and that the rules of basketball could be "reconfigured . . . to conform with the prevailing nineteenth-century medical, psychological, and social concepts of women's physical capabilities."[60] In 1903, Berenson argued that unlike other sports, basketball was "played with deep earnestness and utter unconsciousness of self," which she believed was necessary for women to be able to ignore many centuries of "false education" that had "made woman [too] self-conscious." Of basketball, Berenson wrote,

> It is impossible to pose . . . The game is too quick, too vigorous, the action too continuous to allow any element to enter which is foreign to it. It develops quick perception and judgment—in one moment a person must judge space and time in order to run and catch the ball at the right place, must decide to whom it may best be thrown, and at the same time must remember not to "foul." It develops physical and moral courage, self-reliance and self-control, the ability to meet success and defeat with dignity.[61]

While Naismith had wanted to use basketball to produce Christian men of good moral character, the Jewish Berenson insisted that the same game, if properly modified for women, could help them become less conscious of the ways they were pressured to conform to societal expectations. Faith in the power of basketball for women may have related to Berenson's struggles to find acceptance in the United States and particularly at a Christian institution, Smith College. According to Ralph Melnick, Berenson struggled to "fit into America," where she "would never completely lose her otherness, of marginalization as a Jew in a Christian world." Thus, he calls Berenson the "unlikely" founder of a women's game that was the result of "accident more than destiny."[62]

Like men's basketball, early forms of women's basketball did not involve much contact at all since there was no running with the ball allowed. In the men's game, with no rule forbidding players from grabbing the ball out of an opponent's hands, confrontations and physical play occurred, but Berenson banned grabbing.[63] In this sense, Berenson's variation of Naismith's game was, according to two historians who studied the game of basketball between 1892 and the 1930s, seen as "football modified to suit feminine capabilities."[64]

A Frenzy of Nervous Excitement

By the end of the nineteenth century, though, there were hysterical reports of bloody noses and other injuries in women's basketball games. In some accounts, uppercuts were apparently thrown to escape from a "wriggling heap," and in one southern California match "large chunks of anatomy were missing from various members of the teams."[65] Female physical educators took special aim at the issue of "emotional control," arguing that women and girls were losing their cool in basketball games; one even described a game in which "a frenzy of nervous excitement" included girls "pulling hair, hitting one another, tearing one another's clothing."[66] Men were quick to judge the competitive play too. For example, Al Treloar, physical director of the Los Angeles Athletic Club, "declared that competitive sports were not only dangerous for girls but suicidal to the race!"[67]

Basketball was therefore incorporated into female lives cautiously, in what Cahn calls a "campaign of suppression." Ironically, female physical educators led this campaign, effectively holding other women back from developing their sports commercially and their selves psychologically.[68] According to Cahn, there were five reasons why male and female educators were against the idea of "highly competitive sports" such as basketball for women. First, educators worried that females who participated in competitive sport might exceed "recommended restraints." Second, there were fears that an outsized emphasis on winning might alienate other non-athletic girls. At the time, a utilitarian perspective held sway, aiming to increase the total number of fit women (World War I had convinced many educators that the American populace was not fit enough). Third, allegedly scientific claims continued to abound regarding the risk to female athletes' reproductive capacities. Fourth, some educators worried that competitive sports might even change the nature of women altogether, making them more "physical, aggressive, competitive, and vocal," and in turn leave "the welfare of both men, women, and society" in a "disastrous" state. Female physical educators wanted women and girls to enjoy basketball, but they worried that in basketball in a "masculine" form, by which they meant led by male coaches or promoted by male promoters with games played in front of mixed-sex crowds, might be damaging to girls' perceived femininity.[69]

Basketball thus became perceived as a masculine game that was characterized by "ruggedness, explosive power, and technical precision."[70] To counteract "masculinization," the NSWA encouraged schools to hire female coaches and referees, fearing, for example, that a male coach might "masculinize" his female players,[71] and the NSWA codified rule changes and restrictions on space, movement, and touch as well as uniforms and stadium design.[72] Ultimately, female athletes who did not conform to these standards were ostracized or marginalized, and females who enjoyed playing sports were considered suspect and subject to homophobic slurs.[73]

Finally, some educators believed that competitive sport might leave female athletes "vulnerable to sexual and economic abuses." Competitive sport, the rationale held, would be more popular among spectators, and with more viewers there would less privacy. As the games became more popular, there would be an influx of male coaches, media, and promoters who would invariably lead women into "overexertion" and potentially sexualize their bodies.[74]

But this campaign of suppression against women's basketball ultimately failed.[75] As Cahn notes, most female basketball players in those days disagreed with physical educators who worried that extensive travel, fame, and success could take a toll on women; disagreed that commercial basketball would exploit women sexually and economically; and disagreed that beauty contests objectified women.[76] There was no stopping these women from playing.[77]

Female Athletes at Stanford University before Title IX

At Stanford University, women who played sports in the early-to-mid-twentieth century were also marginalized from the serious business of competitive athletics although their marginalization was uneven over the years. While few records remain of women's sports in the late nineteenth century, in April 1896 the Stanford women's basketball team challenged Berkeley to a game in the San Francisco Armory, with spectators being charged $0.50 per person at the gate.[78] Only women were allowed to watch the game, though. This was one of Berkeley's stipulations. Defending the decision, one fan, in a letter to *The Berkeleyan*, wrote that "playing in the open . . . in front of a lot of college men . . . seems to us to be lowering a certain standard of womanhood," adding that it was "the place of the co-ed, with her high education, to advance womanhood toward its ideal."[79] What exactly that ideal was, the author did not say.

In the immediate years after Stanford University was established, its female students took part in track, archery, boating, basketball, bicycling, and tennis. The physical health of Stanford students—both male and female—was of great importance to university founders Jane and Leland Stanford, who insisted in their Founding Grant that the nondenominational, coed university would be "for both sexes" and "qualify its students for personal success, and direct usefulness in life," eschewing the notion of an "ivory tower" academy.[80] Stanford has since insisted upon being "avowedly practical,"[81] "producing 'cultured and useful citizens.'" According to Altenberg, Stanford advanced such pragmatism by "carrying out the Declaration of Independence to women as well as men." As such, Stanford required its trustees "to afford equal facilities and give equal advantages in the University to both sexes."[82] In fact, Leland Stanford Sr was an early supporter of "women's rights, suffrage, participation politics and equal pay for equal work."[83]

However, in May 1899, Jane Stanford changed the university's course, amending the Founding Grant to limit the number of women enrolled at Stanford each year to five hundred at any given time. Leland Stanford Sr had died in the summer of 1893, but in making her decision, Jane cited her late son, Leland Stanford Jr's memory (he had died at age fifteen in 1884) and demonstrated what she perceived to be a societal need to admit and educate more young men.[84] For the next thirty-four years (1899–1933), women would not be admitted into Stanford as freely as they had been before.

Following Jane's lead, Stanford's Faculty Committee on Athletics (FCA) "took a dim view" of women's athletics in the early twentieth century, deciding to "curtail" women's intercollegiate competitions at the same time that it "systematized" men's intercollegiate competition.[85] Some Stanford officials believed that "their campuses were being feminized, literally and figuratively" and worried "that the arrival of more female students, who were typically older . . . than their male classmates," might "jeopardize their ascent as a premier institution devoted to the manly goals of useful knowledge and productive graduates."[86] Meanwhile, Stanford's football team was increasingly a "top institutional priority" as "senior officials were convinced that varsity sports" like football "would bolster the school's male ethos."[87] During the 1900s and 1910s, male athletes enjoyed better facilities and formal intercollegiate competition while women were generally confined to intramurals and occasional intercollegiate matches against local universities. The FCA "abolished intercollegiate basketball [for women] in 1915 because of repeated unpleasant experiences"[88] (especially when the opponent was Berkeley since games with this Bay Area rival led to rough play that officials deemed unseemly for women). Female students objected to the FCA's decision, but the institutional position remained firm, and in 1919 Stanford established a separate Faculty Committee on Women's Athletics (FCWA), which immediately and emphatically opposed all varsity intercollegiate athletics for women. Within the FCWA, which was headed by Dr. Clelia Duel Mosher (who was also its medical adviser) and Helen Bunting (who supervised physical education), there was personal and professional disagreement over the proper types of physical activity for Stanford's women. While

Dr. Mosher believed that it was "social expectations, not the physical body, [that] restricted female interests and aptitude" and argued that once they were liberated from such cultural myths, women could enjoy health and self-confidence by understanding their bodies, following the laws of hygiene, and engaging in vigorous activity, including intercollegiate sports, Bunting, by contrast, "advocated mass recreation and intramural games" and was generally more conservative about women's health. Bunting also feared that hard training and the publicity of it might be damaging to young athletic women, so while Stanford's female students managed to effect some changes, they still could not compete extramurally as varsity representatives of Stanford University. Bunting's views were shared by many male administrators at Stanford and also by officials at Berkeley and Mills College, which feared "the unpleasantness" of "intercollegiate competition," "Stanford's aggressive mindset," and "intensive practice and publicity."[89] Thus Bunting's ideas prevailed over Dr. Mosher's, and Stanford began prioritizing play days over intercollegiate competition.

In 1933, Jane Stanford's limitation on the number of women admitted into Stanford was lifted, and Stanford's female students again sought to persuade administrators to provide them with more opportunities that they deemed suitable to their interests and abilities. But that effort failed too, leaving Stanford women still sidelined from intercollegiate sport and participation in tough and competitive sports that were routinely offered to Stanford men. Accordingly, Stanford women had little choice but to build a "separate campus culture."[90]

Even decades later, female athletic accomplishments were still only acknowledged with a paternalistic, objectifying, and sexualizing air, as if their participation in sport was merely a conduit through which women could display their bodies to men. Consider for example a popular history of Stanford athletics written by Stanford sports information director Don Liebendorfer and published in 1972 under the title *The Color of Life Is Red: A History of Athletics at Stanford University*. While the book boasts itself a "complete history of athletics at Stanford University in all sports," it nearly overlooks women's participation in sports. Seven pages of the 331-page book are devoted to the "Distaff Side" of Stanford women's sports. Liebendorfer admits that when he began research for the book he knew nothing of Stanford women's sports history and had to enlist the support of women like Luell Weed Guthrie of the Women's Physical Education Department to educate him,[91] and in what little he does write about women, he focuses attention on women's outfits, appearance, or the man to whom a particular female athlete became married. For example, in one passage, Liebendorfer diminishes the athletic efforts of one Stanford swimmer by writing, "My personal candidate for the most beautiful of Stanford's greatest coed swimmers is the gorgeous Brendra Mersereau Helser . . . This striking brunette with the flashing brown eyes looked more like a beauty queen than a swimmer."[92] In another he writes, "Stanford coeds (bless 'em) started building the body beautiful almost as soon as their hairy-chested counterparts."[93] And in yet another, he boasts, "The [Stanford] Indian squaws, brazen hussies that they were, remained on the floor and continued to shoot at the basket . . . in spite of the stares of the repairmen, who were getting their first view of the daring bloomers."[94]

It seems that no matter what sport they chose or and no matter how they played it, female athletes who took part in Stanford athletics in the early and mid-twentieth century were appreciated more for how they looked than for how they performed. These young athletic women were considered beautiful figures in a masculine university that was practically determined to prioritize the education of young men who could improve the prestige and productivity of the university, and that meant, effectively, that women's sports were nothing more than a sideshow to the real business of men's sports, particularly football.

Conclusion

In her history of American physical education, *Active Bodies*, Martha Verbrugge writes, "The logic seemed simple: bodies differ, people differ, therefore activities must differ,"[95] noting that despite varied experiences in gym class, girls of all ages, social classes, and races were separated in physical education classes because of the perception that their bodies were biologically different from those of young boys. As a result, Verbrugge argues, physical educators reproduced gender discrimination through the body at the same time that they privileged so-called scientific understandings of gender, which were often themselves sexist.[96] These experiences in physical education—and the perceptions of gender and power that they helped solidify—later shaped women's experiences in competitive sports and in turn shaped the way many women and girls viewed their own bodies and also their sense of self and self-worth.

From the late nineteenth century to the 1970s, the idea of females playing competitive sports like basketball, let alone being entertainers through sport, was considered an abomination to white, upper- and middle-class patriarchal notions of what an ideal education for girls and young women should be. This customary way of thinking about sex, gender, and sport not only limited girls' and young women's opportunities to play but also reinforced the patriarchal notion that boys and men were physically superior, somehow more capable of making physical sacrifices or being tough, and accordingly, that sports should be protected preserves for boys and men alone.[97] As men's college sports became more popular and profitable forms of mass entertainment, the best a sporting woman could hope for was a spot on the sidelines holding pom-poms. Even though in the 1950s, American women were finally allowed to compete in international basketball competitions such as the FIBA Women's World Cup, they would still not be allowed to participate in basketball in the Olympics until 1976, fully four decades after 1936 when men played the same sport there. In college basketball, it wasn't until 1971 that women began to play basketball full court with the ability of all players to run, dribble, shoot, and block as the men did. In school basketball, girls' rules often depended on the community in which it was being played since there was little standardization by state governmental bodies, and thus girls' rules "never had the consistency of the boys game."[98] The result of these uneven laws and discriminatory customs was that even on the rare occasion that women and girls were allowed to play competitive sports, they could only do so under severe restriction or significant stress, hoping to perform well but not to sweat in a way that might offend the delicate sensibilities of traditional men. In 1953, for example, Pulitzer Prize-winning journalist Arthur Daley wrote in the *New York Times*, "There's nothing enchanting about a woman with beads of perspiration on her alabaster brow."[99] That view has sadly proved rather durable among many American men.

In sum, during the first seven decades of the twentieth century and even into part of the eighth, women athletes continued to "negotiate difficult terrain." Their athletic abilities were at once the source of both "intrigue and threat," their bodies generally seen as fit for relatively tame, less physically demanding individual sports like tennis and golf and unfit for intensely physical team sports like basketball, in which it was routinely expected that a masculine toughness was required, and a sweaty brow would develop.[100]

Exclusion from participation at the big-time level of competitive sports was not only a limitation to play, competition, or entertainment, though; it was also a limitation on one's ability to be seen as someone who could play, someone who was tough, some who could work hard, someone who made physical sacrifices, or someone who could entertain and make a livelihood from it.

But all of that would eventually begin to change, ushered in by the women's liberation movement of the 1960s and 1970s and the women who helped lead it, like Stanford's own Coach Tara VanDerveer.

Notes

1. Associated Press, "Kayla Pedersen."
2. Associated Press, "No. 6 Tennessee."
3. Messner, "Sports and Male Domination."
4. The term "female" denotes sex, a biologically determined category based on chromosomes delivered at birth, measures of testosterone and estrogen, and whether an individual human has a womb, ovaries, or can produce milk. The term "woman" is much more dependent upon time, place, and individual, and it connotes a status that is conferred only after an individual female does whatever society expects that individual to do.
5. Kyle, *Sport and Spectacle*, 21.
6. Russell, *A History*, 7.
7. Miracle and Rees, *Lessons*, 37.
8. For example, Boston physician Dr. Edward Clarke (1820–1877), who wrote *Sex in Education; Or, a Fair Chance for the Girls*, diagnosed young college women with "nervous disorders" that could only be cured with physical education. He argued that intellectual education taxed the female nervous system and took away vital energy needed for reproduction, so he advised physical activity to clear female minds. Still he only prescribed physical activity for health care and, arguably, the ultimate needs of men, and not for women's own joy, growth or playful escape (see Mechikoff, *A History*, 205). In the early 1870s, Dr. Clarke said, "Girls can do the same things as men and to the same extent, but not in the same way." Zschoche further explains, "Clarke called for a separate female system of higher education, one that took into account woman's 'peculiar' physical organization, arguing that female education that mimicked masculine methods of learning had already produced a frightful deterioration of health among women" ("Dr. Clarke Revisited," 545–46).
9. Grundy and Rader, *American Sports*, 132–33.
10. Quoted in Zirin, *A People's History*, 13.
11. Willard and O'Hare, *How I Learned*.
12. Liberti, "Trailblazing in Marin," 58.
13. Cahn, *Coming on Strong*, 16.
14. On November 18, 1892, UC Berkeley played the first of three basketball games against Miss Head's School, a private prep school, at Cal's Harmon Gymnasium (Emery and Toohey-Costa, "Hoops and Skirts," 138).
15. C. Williams, "Bay to Breakers," 62.
16. Cahn, *Coming on Strong*, 66.
17. Cahn, *Coming on Strong*, 66.
18. Eikleberry, "More Than Milk."
19. While the NAAF promoted sports for all girls, in 1923 it also set clear guidelines on the way that girls were to play and how sports were to be managed, stating that women's athletics should "be protected from exploitation for the enjoyment of

the spectator, the athletic reputation, or the commercial advantage of any school or organization" (Grundy and Rader, *American Sports*, 172).

20. As Brad Austin explains, during the Great Depression "most white women's athletic programs were a conscious reaction to the problems many women saw in the operation and orientation of men's college athletics and in women's industrial league athletics. Rejecting these two models of sport for a variety of ideological, pedagogical, and personal reasons, female physical educators argued that only by denying gifted athletes special opportunities not available to the others, deemphasizing competitions and the importance of victory, and allocating precisely the same amount of time and resources to all college women could women learn their role in the US democratic system" (*Democratic Sports*, xx). According to Austin, during the Great Depression,

> women athletic leaders warned repeatedly and vehemently about the corruption that could be caused by overemphasizing competition in women's athletics . . . In their eyes, competition was a masculine drive that was necessary for the continuation of American life as they knew it but that should be moderated very carefully in women. Women, the university educators held, should concentrate on "democratic" cooperation and companionship, not on the competitive fight for glory and personal achievement, and they argued that only properly trained women (themselves) could coordinate such a program. (*Democratic Sports*, xx–xxi)

21. Suggs, *A Place on the Team*.
22. Liberti, "We Were Ladies," 575.
23. Eikleberry, "More Than milk," 476.
24. Liberti, "We Were Ladies"; Hult and Trekell, *A Century*, 30.
25. Cahn, *Coming on Strong*, 55–56.
26. Liberti, "Trailblazing," 60–61.
27. Liberti, "Trailblazing," 64. See also Cahn, *Coming on Strong*, 7–30.
28. Cahn, *Coming on Strong*, 140–41.
29. Cahn, *Coming on Strong*, 148.
30. Cahn, *Coming on Strong*, 150–52.
31. Lidz, "Tennis, Everyone?"
32. Mrozek, "The 'Amazon.'"
33. Schwartz, "Didrikson Was a Woman"; Schwartz. "More Info."
34. Quoted in Grundy and Rader, *American Sports*, 104.
35. Quoted in Schwartz, "Didrikson Was a Woman."
36. Cahn, *Coming on Strong*, 216.
37. Quoted in Grundy and Rader, *American Sports*, 104.
38. Cahn, *Coming on Strong*, 83.
39. Hall, who was himself a devout Christian, was the first to conceptualize the life stage of adolescence. He also published a psychological profile of Jesus Christ (*Jesus, the Christ*).
40. Liberti, "Gendering the Gym," 155.

41. Horger, "Play by the Rules," ii. See also Johnson, "Walter Camp and James Naismith."

42. Grundy and Rader, *American Sports*, 99.

43. See Cavallo, *Muscles and Morals*; Macleod, *Building Character*; and Riess, *City Games*.

44. The first ball used to play the game was a football that was then replaced by a soccer ball. Only later was the ball we now know as a basketball introduced (Blanchard, *The Anthropology of Sport*, 208).

45. Miracle and Rees, *Lessons*, 46. Gulick Jr also founded the first Public School Athletic League, the Camp Fire Girls, and the Boy Scouts of America.

46. S. Taylor, *Advocate of Understanding*.

47. Watson, Weir, and Friend. "The Development," 9n26.

48. Grundy and Rader, *American Sports*, 99.

49. Kosloski, "How a Christian."

50. Zogry quoted in Kosloski, "How a Christian."

51. Kosloski, "How a Christian."

52. Johnson, "Walter Camp and James Naismith."

53. Melnick, *Senda Berenson*.

54. R. A. Smith, "The Rise of Basketball," 20. See also Cahn, *Coming on Strong*, especially chapter 4.

55. Johnson, "Walter Camp and James Naismith."

56. R. A. Smith, "The Rise of Basketball," 295.

57. Miracle and Rees, *Lessons*, 37.

58. Grundy and Shackelford, *Shattering*, 21.

59. Melnick, *Senda Berenson*.

60. Mechikoff, *A History*, 286.

61. Quoted in O'Reilly and Cahn, *Women and Sports*, 53. See also Berenson, *Basketball for Women*.

62. Melnick, *Senda Berenson*, 6.

63. R. A. Smith, "The Rise of Basketball."

64. Emery and Toohey-Costa, "Hoops and Skirts," 137.

65. Quoted in Emery and Toohey-Costa, "Hoops and Skirts," 140–42.

66. Cahn, *Coming on Strong*, 96.

67. Quoted in Emery and Toohey-Costa, "Hoops and Skirts," 149.

68. Cahn, *Coming on Strong*, 83ff.

69. Cahn, *Coming on Strong*, 55, 87.

70. Cahn, *Coming on Strong*, 99.

71. Cahn, *Coming on Strong*, 88.

72. Women standardized and unified basketball rules sixteen years before men did (1899 compared with 1915), and they began to govern their own basketball competitions in 1924 (Cahn, *Coming on Strong*, 100).

73. Grundy and Rader, *American Sports*, 173.

74. Cahn, *Coming on Strong*, 62–65.

75. The campaign to suppress women's basketball was more successful in the North than it was in the South where interschool competition continued (Cahn, *Coming on Strong*, 95).

76. Cahn, *Coming on Strong*, 104–5.

77. This fact ought to be underscored. Unfortunately, Cahn largely ignores the voices of these players in the final conclusions to her book *Coming on Strong* and instead foregrounds the reform efforts of women's physical educators to tame the game in a way that would limit the objectification of women athletes and prevent them from being sexualized, therefore concluding that the women educators who had this agenda were not "off base" in their critique (*Coming on Strong*, 107). While Cahn's study is rigorously researched and richly detailed, her overarching thesis—that sports have largely been a realm where the sexism of broader society has been recapitulated—prevents her from seeing, or at least giving more than limited attention to, the positivity in sport's liberating influence for women. Seemingly locked in a paradigm in which sports are seen as tools of marginalization, Cahn largely glosses over the positive aspects of female sports participation. (For basketball, Cahn waits until page 106, and even then, she largely ignores the power of sports for early-twentieth-century American women basketball players. Instead of using a more balanced amount of ink to highlight how much women loved basketball and how powerful that love for the game was in shaping their lives, Cahn writes that the central "significance of the basketball controversy lies in what it reveals about the ongoing effort to make masculine sport and womanhood compatible" (108). My reading of the history of women's basketball does not altogether support this thesis. There is no doubt that there were many men and women who wanted to gender basketball by either making women and girls sex symbols (commercial promoters) or by limiting physical activity to a level of moderation (male and female physical educators), but in the process of supporting her thesis Cahn fails to see the reasons why the sport grew popular in the first place: the excitement, the joy, and the positive opportunities for growth (83–109).

78. Guttmann, *Sports Spectators*, 95.

79. Emery and Toohey-Costa, "Hoops and Skirts," 138–39.

80. Stanford Digital Repository, "Grant Founding."

81. Stanford University, "Facts."

82. Stanford University, "Our History---Our Mission"; Altenberg, "Beyond Capitalism," 12–15.

83. In his first meeting with the new university's trustees, Leland Stanford said, "We deem it of the first importance that education of both sexes shall be equally full and complete, varied only as nature dictates. The rights of one sex, political and otherwise, are the same as those of the other sex, and this equality of rights ought to be fully recognized." Stanford also believed that women would be limited in the workplace because of maternity leave, but if there appeared to be other limitations to their production it was because of external forces, not inherent inabilities. In a bill he

proposed advocating worker cooperatives, which he believed would make American workplaces more humane and democratic, Stanford told the U.S. Senate in 1887,

> One of the difficulties in the employment of women arises from their domestic duties; but cooperation would provide for a general utilization of their capacities and permit the prosecution of their business, without harm, because of the temporary incapacity of the individual to prosecute her calling. And if this cooperation shall relieve them of the temporary incapacity arising from the duties incident to motherhood, then their capacity for production may be utilized to the greatest extent. Very many of the industries would be open to and managed as well by women in their co-operative capacity as by men. There is no reason why the women of the country should not greatly advance themselves by this act. Take the matter of clothing alone; there are sixty million people in America, and if each expends $10 a year for clothes, that makes $600 million; it might just as well go to cooperative associations of women as to these large partnerships which pay hardly living wages. At the same time the grade of women's labor would be advanced; they would become cutters, style-makers.

Stanford wanted cooperatives to help women and saw them as the answer to management's concern regarding maternity leave. He said, "Under cooperation they would draw wages when they could not labor, or the character of the labor could be changed for them."

84. On May 31, 1899, Jane Stanford wrote, "There is another subject upon which I feel deeply, and I speak of it at present, because this may be my last opportunity of meeting you face to face. Whereas the University was founded in memory of our dear son Leland, and bears his name, I direct, under the power given me in the original Grant, that the number of women attending the University as students shall at no time ever exceed five hundred." A Stanford board resolution dated May 11, 1933, authorized an increase in the number of women students beyond five hundred, and a court decree on March 9, 1973, deleted the restrictive provision on the enrollment of women.

85. Verbrugge, *Active Bodies*, 118.
86. Verbrugge, *Active Bodies*, 118.
87. Verbrugge, *Active Bodies*, 118.
88. Verbrugge, *Active Bodies*, 118.
89. Verbrugge, *Active Bodies*, 122. See also Cahn, *Coming on Strong*, 248.
90. Verbrugge, *Active Bodies*, 123.
91. Liebendorfer, *The Color*, 293.
92. Liebendorfer, *The Color*, 295–96.
93. Liebendorfer, *The Color*, 293.
94. Liebendorfer, *The Color*, 293.
95. Verbrugge, *Active Bodies*, 8.
96. Verbrugge, *Active Bodies*, 103–5.
97. Miracle and Rees. *Lessons*, 49–50.
98. Grundy and Shackelford, *Shattering*, 50.

99. Quoted in Earp, *Not Just a Game*. See also Festle, *Playing Nice*.
100. Grundy and Rader, *American Sports*, 166.

CHAPTER 4

Enlightened Leadership

Laws are sand, custom is rock.

—Mark Twain

Although fears of women athletes upending the status quo remained common even in the 1970s as intense and physical competition in sport continued to be frowned upon in white middle- and upper-class circles, young women like Tara Ann VanDerveer and the authors of Title IX—Patsy Mink and Edith Green—stood ready to emerge as pioneers in a movement for change.

On June 26, 1953, VanDerveer was born in Boston, Massachusetts, less than a hundred miles from where basketball was invented. She grew up during a time of considerable social upheaval in the United States, and in fact, VanDerveer's biography offers a lens through which we can observe some major historic transitions in American sports culture. No transition was more significant than the 1972 federal legislation of Title IX, which eventually established a new foundation upon which women athletes could challenge long-standing notions of gendered toughness and find a new sense of self-worth through competitive sports like basketball. Indeed, it was authors of Title IX—and the administrators of women's sports who embraced its spirit—who afforded future generations of women and girls the choice to buy in to the big time and thus also the choice to play and grow through fierce physical competition and commercialized popular entertainment.

The fight for females to have equal treatment within American life seems to have come to a head or at least to have reached an inflection point, in the late 1960s and early 1970s. During this period, America was in the throes of a contentious period of racial, generational, and sexual strife, which culminated in a series of laws aimed at equalizing opportunity, particularly for historically disenfranchised groups such as African Americans and women. This period is broadly remembered as the civil rights era, within which blacks and women, as well as their allies, fought for liberation and a public dignity not yet accorded to them by powerful American men. Prior to the late 1960s, there were few laws or regulations mandating that there was anything illegal, wrong, or unethical with institutionalized sexism. For all of America's history up until that point, white men had written American law, and they had largely excluded the interests and needs of anyone that did not look like them. It was also the case that few American colleges, which were also largely run by white men, offered competitive sporting opportunities for women, spending significantly larger amounts of money on men's sports like football than on women's sports.

"It Is Time to Change Our Operating Assumptions"

On an institutional level, this began to change with Title IX—which President Richard Nixon signed into law on June 23, 1972—that went into effect on July 1, 1972,[1] and read, "No person in the United States shall, on the basis of sex, be excluded from participation in, be denied the benefits of, or be subjected to discrimination under any education program or activity receiving Federal financial assistance."[2] However, because Title IX lacked substantial implementation guidelines, female athletes like VanDerveer, who had just turned nineteen and was a college basketball player at the time, would not realize its promise during their own playing days.

Congresswomen Edith Starrett Green and Patsy Matsu Takemoto Mink co-authored the first draft of the bill. Before Green was elected to the House in 1955, she had been a schoolteacher, legislative director for Oregon's Congress of Parents and Teachers, and a lobbyist for the Oregon Education Association. She made a name for herself in 1965 when she broke ranks with President Lyndon Johnson and voted against the president's request for funding to escalate war in Vietnam. Mink (born Matsu Takemoto), who was elected to the House in 1964, had faced her share of sexist and racist discrimination on her way to becoming the first woman of color and the first Asian American woman ever elected to the U.S. Congress. As a child in Hawaii, Mink loved basketball but was only allowed to play the game half-court; her teachers worried that girls might injure themselves if they ran the whole court. When she applied to medical school in her early twenties, her applications were all rejected, despite high grades and standardized test scores. Even when she was admitted to the University of Chicago Law School, she was forced to enroll as a foreign student. There she met John Mink, whom she would marry. Upon graduation, though, she was told that she could not take the Hawaii Bar Exam because John was from Pennsylvania, making her a resident-by-marriage of that state, rather than her birth state of Hawaii. Mink filed a rebuttal to the ruling, arguing that she and John Mink had never resided in Pennsylvania and therefore had never forfeited her Hawaii residency. The rebuttal worked, but still she found herself without job prospects. So Mink took matters into her own hands and started her own law firm. By 1956, Mink had entered politics and won a seat in Hawaii's Territorial House of Representatives (Hawaii became a U.S. state in August 1959). Eight years later in 1964, Mink was elected to the first of six consecutive terms in the U.S. House of Representatives, where she developed a reputation as an anti–Vietnam War legislator who prioritized education and the needs of women and children. Opponents sophomorically labeled her "Patsy Pink," tying her to communism, but Mink kept on fighting for her ambitious goals. As she wrote on the back of an envelope in preparation for a speech in support of civil rights in 1960, "How can America stand

Edith Green. Source: *Library of Congress: LC-USZ62-112920 DLC*

Patsy Takemoto Mink. Source: *Photographic print, b/w (gelatin silver), ca. 1965, Collection of the U.S. House of Representatives.*

as the golden land of opportunity if indeed there is only that opportunity for some but not all?"[3]

In the late 1960s, Green and Mink worked together to fight for equal opportunities for women and girls in formal classroom education and co-authored and co-sponsored a bill to amend the Higher Education Amendments. Ultimately this bill would become the 1972 Title IX amendments. Pragmatically, they focused their efforts on financial support. When the 1965 Higher Education Act expired in mid-1971, Green led an effort in the House to consolidate aid-to-education legislation, and Mink offered support in the Senate.

Mink and Green received support for these efforts from Birch Bayh, a Democrat from Indiana and the amendment's chief sponsor in the U.S. Senate. Bayh understood Mink's perspective well. While he had been admitted into every law school to which he applied, his wife had not been admitted to any despite the fact that Bayh was convinced that she was the smarter half of their couple. His personal experience led him to say on the Senate floor in 1972, in an effort to explain to his (mostly male) colleagues why Title IX mattered,

> We are all familiar with the stereotype of women as pretty things who go to college to find a husband, go on to graduate school because they want a more interesting husband, and finally marry, have children, and never work again. The desire of many schools not to waste a "man's place" on a woman stems from such stereotyped notions. But the facts absolutely contradict these myths about the "weaker sex" and it is time to change our operating assumptions.

While he noted that the impact of the amendments would be far-reaching, Bayh acknowledged that the law "is not a panacea. It is, however, an important first step in the effort to provide for the women of America something that is rightfully theirs—an equal chance to attend the schools of their choice, to develop the skills they want, and to apply those skills with the knowledge that they will have a fair chance to secure the jobs of their choice with equal pay for equal work."

"A Passion We Nurtured Ourselves"

VanDerveer grew up in Massachusetts and New York without the opportunity to play organized basketball. Neither her junior high nor high school fielded girls' basketball teams, and she had few chances to play basketball informally, otherwise known as pick-up. When she could, VanDerveer played basketball in her driveway with the neighborhood boys. She would bring the best basketball she could find to their impromptu matches so that even when they did not want her there, in her words, "they had to let me play." VanDerveer was so enthusiastic about the game that she tried out for her high school cheerleading team just to be closer her high school's basketball games. When she didn't make the cut for that, she became the basketball team's mascot. (After she was caught watching too much of the game and not doing enough mascotting, she was let go.)

There was only one place where VanDerveer was allowed to play freely: a summer vacation retreat called the Chautauqua Institution. Although she was largely discouraged from playing basketball during the school year, VanDerveer could play in the Boys' and Girls' Club Building that sat on the Chautauqua grounds. Chautauqua gave VanDerveer a chance to try her hand at other games and sports too, from sailing to tennis and swimming. She would recall that the male director of the Boys and Girls Club, Mel Lewellen, "promoted health and activity, as Chautauqua did," and he allowed VanDerveer to play with the boys.[4] She remembered it as a "very stimulating place" where she was surrounded by "many accomplished, upbeat people."[5]

By the time VanDerveer entered high school in 1967, girls in some parts of the United States were beginning to find their way into gymnasiums and onto sports fields (without being a cheerleader or mascot). However in the late 1960s and early 1970s, most female basketball players did not have the opportunity to play organized basketball until college, and even when they did, they had little or no financial support. In her memoir, VanDerveer remembers that female athletes had to wear "sneakers we paid for ourselves, uniforms we washed ourselves," and cultivate "a passion we nurtured ourselves." VanDerveer managed to play at Buffalo Seminary and later briefly at Albany State. But the teams were not exceptional, and VanDerveer wanted to "be in the big time," so in March 1972 she convinced a group of four friends to travel to Normal, Illinois, to watch the first ever Association for Intercollegiate Athletics for Women (AIAW) National Championships. VanDerveer's enthusiasm for basketball was not her only reason for attending the AIAW National Championship, though; she went with the express intent of finding a better college team that she could play on. Indiana University impressed her most since she "liked the camaraderie and work ethic" that she "saw on the floor."

VanDerveer became a Hoosier a few months after Title IX passed. She started as a guard for three seasons, but her experiences there continued to be shaped by sexism. There were no college scholarships for female athletes, and the regular season for women's college basketball was limited to seven games. When she sprained her ankle, VanDerveer missed five of her team's games—almost the entire season. Her team had to practice late in the evening too, after the men's team was done, and eat dinner at 10 p.m. or later, then wake up the next morning at 6 a.m. for class. Compared to Albany State, in some ways Indiana felt like the big time, but compared to the Indiana men, who presided in Bloomington like "big men on campus," it was hardly worth writing home about. Still, VanDerveer did not let the difficulties get her down; she made the dean's list every year and graduated with an honors degree in sociology. And while no one kept statistics on women's sports in those days, no one questioned that VanDerveer was a feisty team leader.

"Basketball Will Never Take You Anywhere"

VanDerveer remembers that during her childhood, her father would often say, "Tara, come on in and do your algebra. Basketball will never take you anywhere." But as VanDerveer's experiences in basketball expanded, she began to realize that it wasn't only about the chance to play the game. It was also about what playing the game could do for a young person like her. Sadly, this was a principle that was lost on many men—even her father—throughout the twentieth century.

Girls were not allowed to try—and fail—like the boys. For VanDerveer, this meant that while "school provided a structure and discipline that brought out her best work," sports remained an untapped forum for learning how to set goals and be self-disciplined, not to mention playfully create. As importantly, she did not have the confidence to "lay her talent and skill on the line and see if it measured up." Ultimately, VanDerveer would come to see this exclusion from sport as a missed opportunity. While boys "learned to figure out why they failed, then put it behind them and move on," girls were left behind. It was a lesson VanDerveer would never forget.

"How Basketball Should Look"

After graduating from college, in 1975, VanDerveer took a year off, lived at home, and mostly slept or played chess, until her father demanded she do something. At the time, VanDerveer was toying with the idea of going to law school, but when her father asked her to help coach her younger sister Marie's high school basketball team, things began to change. "I said, 'Dad, they just lost 99-11 last night.' He said, 'That's why [you're] going down there; they need some help.'" VanDerveer found her first coaching experience frustrating. The girls of Marie's team did not take the endeavor seriously, but VanDerveer realized that coaching was something she enjoyed and could do well, so she canceled her law school plans and began asking college teams to hire her as an unpaid graduate assistant. VanDerveer returned to Bloomington and enrolled in a coaching clinic led by Indiana's successful if incendiary Coach Bob Knight, who was growing a national reputation as something of a drill sergeant. (Knight's nickname was "the General," and the controversies surrounding him would later be immortalized by John Feinstein in the 1986 book *A Season on the Brink*, one of the best-selling sports books of all time.) There were 150 participants in Knight's clinic out of which 149 were men. VanDerveer sat in the front row, watching intently. Knight said he was surprised by her presence and asked her why she was there. Another attendee asked if she was lost. However overwhelmed she may have been by the men's boorish behavior, VanDerveer did not let it show. In time, VanDerveer would come to say that she appreciated Knight's coaching, later explaining, "Despite his barking and criticisms, he was the kind of coach I liked: someone who understood how basketball should look and did whatever it took to make sure his players understood too. I've turned out to be that kind of coach myself."

A Rising Star
At least attending Knight's coaching clinic appeared to have helped VanDerveer land her first job. In 1976 Ohio State University (OSU) hired her as an assistant coach to the varsity and head coach of the junior varsity teams. The OSU athletic director said he remembered VanDerveer's tenacity from her playing days at Indiana. In her first year on the job, the OSU junior varsity's record was 8-0.

Coach VanDerveer's curiosity for coaching grew. She watched OSU men's practices, and she asked visiting men's teams for permission to watch their practices, too. Her drive to learn was so considerable that friends concluded, "All she thought about was basketball." She began working every summer basketball camp she could, approaching other coaches with question after question. What's your favorite drill? What are you favorite out-of-bounds plays? Why do you play that defense? For Coach VanDerveer, it was a matter of "knowing everything and trying everything."

For VanDerveer, basketball and education were equally important. During this period, VanDerveer was offered an opportunity to take the head-coaching job at Old Dominion University, which would have come with a $15,000 per year salary, but she turned it down to complete her master's degree in sports administration even though doing so meant a considerably lower salary. (Ohio State waived tuition fees in exchange for her coaching and paid VanDerveer just $3,500.) The decision forced VanDerveer to live

Coach Tara VanDerveer (back row, third from the right) led the Ohio State basketball team. Source: Ohio State University Media Guide, 1984–1985 season.

off food stamps and other part-time income. At one time, VanDerveer had to live rent-free with a friend in a trailer.

After finishing her studies at age twenty-five, Coach VanDerveer accepted the head-coaching position of the women's basketball team at the University of Idaho, then a D-II program, in 1978. When Idaho's men's team coach, Don Monson, said he was going to run the summer girls' basketball camp, VanDerveer challenged him. "No, you're not running the camp," she said. "You don't care about girls' basketball. You just want the money. I am going to run the camp."[6]

Idaho's team was a perennial loser, but after two seasons there, VanDerveer had revived it, helping it ascend to the AIAW Tournament. It was such a dramatic improvement that VanDerveer was seen as "rising star in the coaching circles," and in 1980 after she had posted a two-season record of 42-14 at Idaho, OSU hired VanDerveer back, this time as its varsity head coach. On that team, Coach VanDerveer found Amy Tucker, a rangy player with a soft-spoken congeniality who complemented VanDerveer's passion and intensity. Tucker enjoyed playing for VanDerveer and decided to stay on as a graduate assistant and then join Coach VanDerveer on a move west. The pair would sit next to each other on the bench for the next thirty-two years.

The Ultimate Challenge
It was athletic director Andy Geiger who offered Coach VanDerveer the top gig at Stanford, but at first she turned him down. At the time the Pac-10 was dominated by USC, who were led by Coach Linda Sharp and star player Cheryl Miller, making success out west seem improbable.[7] VanDerveer's OSU team was rolling too, having made the Elite Eight the previous year, and the crowds for their home games had reached five figures. They could recruit any Ohio player they wanted. But after giving it further thought, VanDerveer changed her mind just in time to take the helm in Palo Alto before the 1985–1986 season. She would later say that she wanted an academically stimulating environment akin to Chautauqua, an institution that appreciated women and fostered their growth physically and cognitively. VanDerveer considered balancing academics and athletics at Stanford to be a "challenge" worth taking, and though it was not easy, she and Tucker envisioned turning the academically elite Stanford into an elite basketball program in part by selling the combination of "good school, good sports" to recruits. VanDerveer later recalled that she knew Stanford could sell itself to recruits: "Both my parents were teachers, and I liked the idea of being a teacher . . . It was all about education [at Stanford], and I felt like I could walk into a living room and sit down with parents and no one could offer something better [than Stanford]." As Coach Tucker would later put it, the combination of a "world-class education" and "Division I basketball" was a powerful "pitch that we could . . . make to recruits nationally." Before long, VanDerveer and Tucker were compiling a roster of nationally elite players, establishing the Cardinal as a Pac-10 power, and building a road to the big time.

Graveyard or Goldmine?
Coach VanDerveer was supremely confident that she could—and would—accomplish her goals at Stanford, and her belief in herself ensured her success. In 2011, Coach Tucker remembered the moment when Coach VanDerveer interviewed for the Stanford job as if it had happened the week before: "Tara met with the dean of admissions—obviously admissions dictates a lot of your success at Stanford—and told them that she thought she could win a national championship in five years . . . and she did. Five years exactly."

By taking her talents west, by building a program that refused to settle for anything less than national excellence in both academics and athletics, and by refusing to sacrifice one for the other, Coach VanDerveer and Coach Tucker helped make women's basketball the most popular women's team sport in America, helped make it the most profitable of all women's college sports, and helped inspire millions of American girls to dream bigger than even their own fathers had dreamed for them.

And in the process of bringing women's college basketball into the big time, Coach VanDerveer also assured her father, herself and the sportsworld that Stanford was anything but a graveyard for a basketball coach. In fact, in a way it was a coach's Garden of Eden, not the end of life but its beginning. For her part, VanDerveer recalled the decision to leave Ohio State with a wit all her own: "I was at OSU. We had a very good program there . . . [and] Stanford was 5-23. [There were] no fans [in Palo Alto] . . . Still, I felt Stanford was a goldmine job. My father said it was a graveyard." Then she paused, and added, "You know, though, we were both digging."

Implementing Title IX (at Stanford University and Elsewhere)

However, it wasn't only Coach VanDerveer and Coach Tucker who paved that path to the big time; Stanford's athletic department administrators also chose to buy in to the idea of investing in women's sports after Title IX, and since they did, they played a significant role in helping coaches like VanDerveer build their programs, strengthen their rosters, and set a foundation for other women to build big-time basketball programs. When Stanford hired VanDerveer and Tucker in the early 1980s, they made a financial and political commitment to the women's basketball program. That commitment, VanDerveer recalled in an interview in 2011, "was the difference between the great teams and the also-rans."

It's important to note that at that time, while Title IX was federal law and therefore compliance to it was theoretically mandatory, there was debate within Congress and the courts regarding its implementation and legality so there were other programs that merely paid it lip service and looked for ways to work around it, often pointing to a lack of clear governmental guidance as their justification. Some universities, such as the University of Iowa and Harvard University, took the opposite approach and initiated so-called women's sports enhancement programs, going above and beyond what Title IX expected.

Striving to honor the spirit of Title IX, Stanford set internal deadlines for the university to achieve gender equity either by creating new women's teams, elevating other women's teams to a higher status, or distributing extra funding to women's sports teams. The university's institutional commitment was therefore made not only to VanDerveer personally but to women's sports as a whole, and administrators and alumni alike matched it. All of this became clearer to me in October 2012 when the Stanford Historical Society

(SHS) held an event in a small auditorium near Maples Pavilion titled "40 Years of Women's Sports at Stanford."

It still took some time before Stanford's female athletes were truly treated equally due to the local university culture lagging behind the national law, but several financial and administrative moves amounted to steps in the right direction. Before Title IX, Stanford female athletes in sports such as the women's tennis and track teams had been confined to practice in Roble Gym, which was geographically miles away from Encina Gym, where the men's intercollegiate sports teams practiced, as well as "light years away" in terms of philosophy and funding. In contrast to Encina Hall, at Roble Gym, one Stanford female athlete would remember, "[women's] sports were exercise, period."[8] Before Title IX, and even for a few years after its passage, there was a particularly low standard in Stanford women's sports coaching, especially in basketball.[9] In the early 1970s, Stanford's women's basketball team was coached by a woman—Shirley Schoof—who had no background in basketball and did not approach games with a competitive spirit or much of a desire to win. Schoof, who taught PE classes and coached the bowling team, was asked to also coach basketball in 1972, and though she declined the offer several times, she reluctantly accepted when then-women's PE director Pamela Strathairn threatened to drop the program altogether. For three years, Schoof struggled to match the team's desire to win. She later recalled, "I went in with the attitude of playing every single person on my team and letting them do the best they could do. Winning was not the whole thing. We lost most of our games . . . We were horrible, just horrible." Schoof began suffering migraines, developed an ulcer, and upon the recommendation of her doctor, quit coaching altogether.

Among the panelists at the 2012 SHS event was Gary Cavalli, a former Stanford sports information director (SID) who had become author of *Stanford Sports* and a cofounder and CEO of one of the first professional basketball leagues for women, the American Basketball League (ABL), who began the event by declaring, "Stanford totally embraced Title IX." Cavalli recalled that Joe Ruetz, Stanford's athletic director between 1972 and 1979, "didn't try to get around" Title IX. (Ruetz had played college and pro football and had been an assistant coach on Stanford's football team before becoming athletic director in 1972.) In his hiring interview, Ruetz told Cavalli that "'the camaraderie' and 'relationships you build' in athletics 'mean an awful lot and [shouldn't] be sex-restricted.'"

In 1975, Ruetz consolidated the men's and women's athletic departments into one, merging the two programs into the new Department of Athletics, Physical Education, and Recreation (DAPER),[10] which was an uncommon move at the time. Other schools, such as UCLA and the University of Texas, kept men's and women's athletic departments separate, appointing athletic directors for each and siloing their management. Ruetz also required Cavalli to manage the sports information of all teams, and Cavalli began issuing press releases for women's sports even though few SIDs did so at the time. Ruetz also constructed one training room to accommodate all athletes, which was unusual at the time. He recognized that merging them would give female athletes access to the men's facilities on the east side of campus, space in the Encina locker room, and access to the weight room. In Cavalli's estimation, Ruetz showed "enlightened leadership."

Similarly, Stanford's administrators changed the way the sports teams generated funding, and the alumni stepped up to fund scholarships for female athletes. Before Title IX, men's teams had money generated from gate receipts in football and basketball. By contrast, women's teams required funding from the university's general fund, which meant that women did not have proper equipment that allowed them to pursue their sport with any level of seriousness.[11] For example, the uniforms Stanford's female athletes wore were often discarded by men's athletes, and the tennis balls the women used were worn out hand-me-downs.[12] In 2012, Donna Lopiano, the women's athletic director at the University of Texas, Austin, between 1975 and 1992, remembered that the NCAA in those days thought of women's sports "as extra-curricular activities, like taking a phys-ed class."[13]

But after Title IX, Stanford's alumni community stepped up to help fund athletic scholarships for female athletes. The Tiny Buck of the Month Club had been formed in 1934 in order "to raise funds from Stanford alumni and friends to pay the tuition costs for capable, worthy, and needy [male] student-athletes." Five years after Title IX was passed, during the 1977–1978 season, the Cardinal Club was established in order "to raise scholarship funds for women." The two clubs merged in 1987, calling themselves the "Buck and Cardinal Club," and ever since they have raised money for scholarships for both male and female athletes.[14] Even into the 1980s and 1990s, some female athletes at Stanford still did not receive athletic scholarships with the same regularity as men.[15] Yet for the ones who did, the change was monumental. Anne Connelly Gould, who was hired as the women's tennis coach in 1975, recalled, "All of a sudden, it was the big time. We were practicing at stadium courts, we had uniforms, we had balls, we had scholarships."[16]

Perhaps most significant was the fact that Stanford officials like Andy Geiger, who replaced Ruetz and was Stanford athletic director between 1979 and 1990, moved to actively implement Title IX. Had Geiger not been of a mind to do so, he may never have had the inkling to hire VanDerveer.

After all, at the time there were some on Stanford's campus who did not see the point of supporting women's sports, so Geiger's position was not without controversy. The hiring of VanDerveer began to normalize the presence of competitive intercollegiate women's sports on the farm, but it would not have been possible without a broader commitment from the athletic department and the university as a whole.

From Educational Model to Men's Commercial Model

Meanwhile, other universities did not make the same commitment to women's sports that Stanford did. Between 1972 and 1979, Title IX was a statement of what ought to be done but without a strong enforcement mechanism behind it or a precise guide for implementation, there was little to ensure that anything would happen, and so some universities chose to do little if anything. Specifically, it remained unclear whether colleges were legally required to provide equal opportunities or "to provide participation opportunities and equitable funding and support for those who participate."[17]

On a national level, Title IX threw the administration of university athletic programs into disarray as well as sowed confusion for the NCAA and the AIAW, which at the time was the primary institution that staged women's college sports championships, and which held firm to the idea of an "educational model."[18] As we saw earlier, female physical educators had long attempted to protect female athletes from commercial exploitation and the male gaze, which they believed posed threats if women were allowed to participate in competitive intercollegiate sports. Following the passage of Title IX, some female physical educators again feared that if women's sports were commercialized in the same way that men's sports like football had been, sport's value might dissipate, and women's bodies might be exploited as sexualized objects. Many of these educators supported the AIAW. Others began adopting what became known as the men's commercial model in order to change the perception that women had no business receiving equal funding for their sports.[19] According to Wushanley, while for "three quarters of a century" women's college sports were "sheltered within the sex-separate sphere of college campuses,"[20] with Title IX "sex-separation gave way to integration" in exchange for women giving up their long-held "educational model."[21] Since the NCAA wanted little to do with women's sports, in 1972 the AIAW began holding women's national championships for badminton, basketball, gymnastics, swimming, and volleyball with the philosophy that anyone who wanted to participate, could. As a result, Title IX also brought women who wanted women's sports to be big time in conflict with those who wanted women's sports to remain small-time pursuits where competition was de-emphasized.

Fierce battles over Title IX regarding how to interpret its implementation persisted, no more significantly than in the philosophical and territorial debate between the NCAA and the AIAW.[22] The law itself had not mentioned college sports so there was much room for debate regarding how it would be or should be implemented in this realm. There was even a "well-organized and financed campaign to reverse Title IX,"[23] and the NCAA drafted what was known as the Tower Amendment, "legislation that specifically exempted athletic departments from Title IX requirements."[24] NCAA director Walter Byers feared that Title IX would spell the "doom" of intercollegiate sports, suggesting that men's programs would be damaged irreparably if Title IX forced them to cut budgets and reduce scholarships.[25] The implication of the Tower Amendment was clear: the NCAA did not believe that the football team should have to pay for women's sports if the English department received federal funding. Although the Tower Amendment failed, the pressure Byers and the NCAA put on Congress further slowed the progress of women's sports and made Title IX appear toothless.

Table 4.1. US Department of Education Three-Part Test for Title IX Compliance

Participation	Athletic Financial Assistance	Treatment
Proportionality: If the ratio of male and female participants in the program are equal, then the institution is most likely in compliance with Title IX	Scholarships must be allocated in proportion to the number of female and male students participating in intercollegiate athletics. Funding for women's and men's programs does not have to be equal, but a significant disparity in funds does suggest that institutions could be found non-compliant in other program areas.	Title IX does not "require that each men's and women's team receive exactly the same services and supplies, but it looks at the entirety of the treatment the men's and women's programs receive as a whole."[1] The areas which are considered include: locker rooms, practice, and competitive facilities, equipment and supplies, scheduling of games and practice times, publicity, coaching, travel and daily allowance, academic tutoring, provision of medical training facilities, provision of housing and dining, recruitment of student athletes, and support services.

Source: Women's Sports Foundation.[2]

1. Hart, A. and Brooks, F.E., 2016. *The Student Athlete's Guide to College Success*. ABC-CLIO. P. 76.
2. Standard Language of Title IX; https://www.womenssportsfoundation.org/advocate/title-ix-issues/what-is-title-ix/standard-language-of-title-ix/ Retrieved October 9, 2017.

Seven years after Title IX, not one college or university had been fined for violating the 1972 law.[26]

But in 1979, the U.S. Department of Education created a section of the law that became known as the three-part test, making Title IX enforceable for the first time. The three-part test made it clear that universities had to pass one of three tests to ensure they were honoring Title IX and effectively providing male and female students with equal—or equitable—athletic opportunities. The question was not necessarily one of equal opportunity since that equation required some understanding of how much each student desired to play intercollegiate sport, but rather one of equity.

In 1980, after the three-part test had been established, the NCAA realized that their attempts to lobby for a reversal of Title IX were not likely to succeed[27] so they began holding intercollegiate championships for women in a range of sports "even though the AIAW already coordinated 750 state, regional, and national championships for its 970 member institutions." The NCAA justified their move as Title IX compliance; if they hosted men's championships, then they had to do the same for women. Given their earlier grumblings about the value of women's college sports, it seemed a strange thing for the NCAA to say, but the NCAA had something to offer that the AIAW did not: reimbursement for travel expenses and greater television exposure for teams that cut ties with the AIAW.[28] The AIAW had only a $2 million budget while the NCAA promised it would fold women's sports into its multi-million-dollar TV package.[29]

The NCAA and AIAW could not have been more different. The AIAW's policy of all-comers in championship participation—that is, any team that wanted to compete, could compete—held it back from cashing in on television contracts since the AIAW policy did not encourage the drama of Darwinian survival of the fittest that television executives believed attracted the most eyeballs and advertising dollars. The AIAW was also more progressive and athlete-centered than the NCAA. They wanted to eliminate any unfair advantage that bigger schools with more money might have in recruiting, so they asked prospective athletes to pay their own way to recruiting trips. Athletes had voting rights equal to those of coaches and administrators on the AIAW executive board too.

While the NCAA seemed much more interested in protecting the commercial interests of universities and their income-producing men's sports teams, arguing that the sports that had made money via building their income stream over many decades ought to be exempt from the calculations, the AIAW interpreted Title IX to mean that 50 percent of all resources a college chose to devote to athletics must be given to women's sports.

Women who played or managed college sports at the time had a difficult decision to make: choose the NCAA commercial model, which was managed primarily by men but promised a greater chance to be televised and showcase one's talents, or stay with the AIAW and retain female governance but likely have less television exposure (the NCAA ultimately promised women 16 percent governance on the NCAA Council and 18–24 percent on other committees).[30] Some female athletes, and some female administrators of women's sports teams, having felt the sting of being excluded from big-time sports for so long, wanted to give higher level competition a shot so they joined the NCAA. In their mind, to turn championships into equal-opportunity endeavors seemed antithetical to their goal of equal rights, and the AIAW's policy of all-comers did not suffice. Moreover, some felt that only by hosting competitive championships that selected participant teams—not all-comers—would real national exposure come to women's sports, grow the popularity of women's sports, and help it become income-producing. Thus, a group of AIAW members defected to the NCAA, and the NCAA began to actively recruit AIAW members to choose the NCAA to manage their end-of-season championships.

Now put yourself in the shoes of competitive sportswomen like Coach VanDerveer for a moment. You have seen big-time men's athletes enjoying the glory of college sports your entire life. You have witnessed the big men on campus firsthand and wondered why women were arbitrarily excluded from such fame. You have been fighting all your life to enjoy the same opportunities as boys and men. You have seen various other social groups fighting for their civil rights, and you want your own rights too, including the right to compete fiercely in an environment in which winners are crowned for their domination. You want to win and feel the rush of dominating an opposing team. You want national television exposure. You want to be able to play the sport you love. That which you have coveted for so long is now finally in your reach, and all you have to do is join an organization—the NCAA—that has demeaned you as a second-class human since its establishment. You are reassured by their assurance that this organization has changed its ways. To you, joining the NCAA may seem like a deal with the devil that cannot be refused, while to others it may appear the only option left on the table. In either case, the prospect of joining the big time may be too great to pass up.

For "stealing" their members, the AIAW sued the NCAA, arguing that the NCAA had "unlawfully used its monopoly power in men's college sports to facilitate its entry into women's college sports and to force AIAW out of existence."[31] The AIAW claimed that the NCAA guaranteed women travel expenses to hold their championships with them, that they unfairly used their longstanding connections to television networks to promote women's sports, and that they effectively blocked the AIAW from signing their own television contract. The AIAW added that the NCAA lured AIAW members to its postseason tournaments by using its powerful infrastructure and money.

The NCAA won the lawsuit. A district court judge ruled that the NCAA was an eleemosynary, or charitable, organization "that exist[s] primarily to enhance the contribution made by amateur athletic competition to ... higher education." The verdict was upheld by the court of appeals.[32]

The AIAW held its last championships in 1982 and folded in 1983. School after school declared their allegiance to an institution that had long questioned the value of female athletes and women's college sports were folded into a system that was dominated by men, commercial interests, and a competitive model that had long shaped men's college sports like football and basketball into big-time business.

The NCAA's legal victory over the AIAW did not mean that the battle over Title IX was over, though. One institution, Grove City College, sued the federal government, arguing that Title IX violated its rights. The small, private, liberal arts college believed it had the right to keep the federal government out of its business because it "accepted no federal grants and contracts" except for students' receipt of Basic Educational Opportunity Grants (BEOG). According to Graham, it also "rejected attempts by Washington officials during the Carter presidency to regulate its internal affairs."[33] As a result, Grove City College became "ensnared" in a Supreme Court battle over the extent to which civil rights legislation of the 1960s and 1970s entitled the federal government to put higher education policies under greater scrutiny.[34] In 1984, the Supreme Court ruled in the case of *Grove City College v. Bell* (1984) that Title IX ought not to apply to athletics if federal funds were accepted by a different department of the institution. Effectively, the verdict in *Grove City College v. Bell* weakened Title IX. If for example federal funds were only accepted by the English department, then there would be no requirement for the athletic department to fund men's and women's sports equally. But in 1987, after several years of divisive debate, Congress restored Title IX and passed the Civil Rights Restoration Act, which overturned the *Grove* decision and legislated that any institution that received federal funds of any kind, in any form (even scholarship funding or BEOGs), must comply with civil rights laws in all areas and not only in the particular program or activity that received the federal funding.[35]

The three-part test continues to be in place, allowing universities to find ways to prioritize men's sports over women's sports but arguably still failing to create genuine equity. In an NCAA 2015–2016 study it was found that females make up 57 percent of the college student population but only 43 percent of NCAA participant athletes are women. Moreover, male college athletes receive 55 percent of all college athletic scholarship dollars while women athletes get 45 percent.[36] Unsurprisingly, complaints and lawsuits against universities over Title IX violations now abound.[37]

The Power of Title IX

In his memoir *Unsportsmanlike Conduct*, Walter Byers, NCAA director from 1951 to 1988, suggested that it was culture, not law, that had historically kept women behind men. Accordingly, he blamed the "culture of the times" for the limited opportunities women athletes had pre–Title IX and for why the NCAA initially opposed welcoming women to the big time.[38] Byers, though, more than anyone could have changed that culture by drafting NCAA directives for the implementation of Title IX or for advancing the interests of sporting women in other ways; yet instead he more often doubled down on the NCAA's interests to protect the business of college football.

Byers's comments are doubly instructive because they speak to an enduring desire of many sportsmen to dismiss women's lack of access to the big time as a matter of choice, custom, or culture. The signs are everywhere. Even after there was a protocol for deciding whether a university was in compliance with the law—the three-part test—female athletes were still not receiving an equal share of athletic scholarships. During the 1998–1999 season, for example, women constituted 42 percent of all D-I athletes. While they received the same percentage of scholarship money, women only received 31 percent of recruiting budgets, 34 percent of coaching salary budgets, and 33 percent of total operating budgets.[39] And today athletic directors are still more often than not men as are most head coaches in both men's and women's sports. All of which suggests that the old-boy networks of big-time college sports remain in place long after Title IX and even implementation of the three-part test.

While Title IX did force all Americans—male and female—to at least consider the notion that men and women should be treated equally under the law and therefore given equal access to opportunities like sports, large swaths of the nation, including many men who ran universities and influenced the NCAA, were still not ready to hear that message.[40] While the law may have been changed, attitudes have taken longer to turn. Perhaps the legal emphasis on federal funding rather than the human right to be educated or the ethics of equality is ultimately to blame, or perhaps it reflects Mark Twain's astute observation that "laws are sand, custom is rock." Whatever the case, the law's focus on funding rather than justice or fairness has limited its impact and added to the enduring tension between male and female sportspeople.

A Battle for Scarce Resources?

In the 1990s and early 2000s some politicians tried to use Title IX as a campaign issue by suggesting that it required quotas[41] while others dubbed Title IX "affirmative action."[42] Some legal scholars argued that Title IX wrongly extended a legally justifiable end (ending discrimination) into a legally unjustifiable end (mandating that boys and girls receive equal participation, regardless of differing levels of interest)[43] and suggested that Title IX required colleges to offer women athletes equal opportunity, which necessarily meant taking money away from men's sports. As Jurewitz explained, the perception was that Title IX created "a battle for scarce resources between male and female athletes, and between revenue and nonrevenue-producing sports."[44]

However, this need not have been the case since Title IX did not explicitly compel universities to take opportunities away from male athletes.[45] Moreover, the resources in college sports were never scarce and have become even farther from scarce in the years since Title IX, especially as cable television and the Internet have increased the sums of sponsorship dollars that flow into college sports.

The legality and the spirit of the law have similarly been an enduring point of confusion. Historically, the determination of a Title IX violation has hinged upon whether an institution that received federal funding discriminated on the basis of sex or gender. Title IX, therefore, did not focus on increasing the access young female athletes had to sports per se nor did it underscore the inherent morality or ethics of giving both young men and women an equal chance to play. The law did not codify the liberation of women in any direct sense even if its authors were sympathetic to the feminist movement and even if advocacy groups such as the National Organization of Women (NOW) would later fight to protect Title IX.

Title IX effectively divided college sports along funding lines, which led to a conceptual dichotomy within college sports: one group of sports was called "income-producing" or "revenue-generating," and another was called "non-income-producing" or "non-revenue-generating." These terms have in some instances been seen as euphemistic code language for men's and women's sports although there are non-revenue-generating men's college sports and revenue-generating women's sports, so they are not perfect synonyms. Still the distinction has led to considerable tension between men's and women's sports, with the sports that generate revenue occasionally assuming a superiority and the sports that do not assuming something of an inferiority complex. As a result, Title IX underlined an unwritten conceptual hierarchy that prioritizes men's over women's sports, emphasizing that men's sports attracted the greatest number of fans and television viewers and generated the most dollars for one's university.

And yet the claim of some critics that Title IX led to a quota system and was therefore a zero-sum win for women and a zero-sum loss for men is unsubstantiated; in fact, Title IX led to record amounts of money for men's college sports and more media exposure too, which helped men's college sports grow into what they are today. Some critics have alleged that since Title IX mandated that universities provide more resources than they once had to women, this necessarily implied that it was an entitlement program that required that men get less,[46] and others have argued that Title IX compliance thereby led colleges to end some men's sports programs,[47] but Title IX in actuality accelerated the commercialization of college sports for both men and women. At some schools, the big-time men's teams of football and basketball were forced to—or chose to—find new ways to generate revenue so that non-revenue-generating sports would have enough money to make ends meet. At others, Title IX accelerated commercialization because women knew they had to find creative ways to pay their own way and fit into what was already a commercial model of college sports. In either case, though, after Title IX there was greater impetus than ever for members of college athletic departments to find outside money to fund college sports.

The claim that men's teams were cut to make room for women's teams is similarly dubious. Between 1982 and 1995, the number of women's sports teams participating in NCAA D-I grew from 2,011 to 2,576. At the same time, the number of men's teams held relative steady, growing from 2,829 to 2,853.[48] Moreover, according to 2001 data from the U.S. General Accountability Office (GAO), 72 percent of the colleges and universities that added women's teams after Title IX's implementation did so without cutting men's teams while a few cut or cut back men's football.[49] In 2007, the GAO also found that women's and men's college sports both increased in number between 1992 and 2007.[50]

In fact, all college sports have seen an increase in revenue, and that has less to do with Title IX than one might think. Instead, a 1984 Supreme Court verdict in *NCAA v. Board of Regents of the University of Oklahoma* coupled with the rise of cable television and the deregulation of the college sports broadcasting market opened the floodgates for money to pour into college sports like football and basketball.

Thus, blaming sportswomen for cuts to men's teams is a canard. Universities with sports-related financial trouble could have easily cut the number of men's football scholarships or hired cheaper football coaches but few chose to because they were reluctant to challenge the "king" sport whose revenues had historically been relied upon.

In fact, if there has been intra-university theft at all, it has not been by women's sports teams but rather by football, in that it has routinely required all enrolled students to pay fees to balance the books. For example, Indiana University, a public university, used a student fee of $24 per semester to help build its football stadium. The University of Texas, also a public university, enlarged its football stadium by building a fifteen-story physical education building behind it, funded by university endowment funds and student user fees.[51]

If anything Title IX brought more media attention, more corporate sponsorship, and more revenue to colleges and all of their sports teams, male and female, and in the process increased the commercialization of college sports as a whole. Athletic department officials have become more creative and have found more equitable ways to fund both men's and women's sports, and that has led to, in aggregate, more advertising dollars and alumni donations coming into the university from outside than ever before. The proof is in the pudding: big-time universities now routinely hire large marketing teams to engage local businesses in advertising and development officers to solicit outside funds.

A Watershed Time

Perhaps it is an inability to understand the notion that a rising tide raises all ships that partly explains why many men have seen Title IX as a threat to their chosen sport or have used the law as a scapegoat to save the status quo. But in fact, Title IX has opened new opportunities for both males and females by creating new markets for the commercialized product of college sports as entertainment.

Of course women athletes benefited most, but that is largely because they were starting from a such an impoverished position. After Title IX, women's sports teams sprouted up on college campuses across the nation, offering new athletic opportunities for millions of young American women.[52] Title IX's waves rippled widely too, increasing female sports participation at lower levels of school sport. For example, in 1971 one of twenty-seven girls participated in sports, but by the early 2010s, one out of three girls participated. In the late 2000s, the National Federation of State High School Associations estimated that 40 percent of all high school athletes were girls, and in states such as Colorado, Hawaii, and North Dakota, more girls played sports than boys.[53]

Title IX also deserves credit for increasing the total number of outstanding American female athletes, including those who have gone on to win Olympic medals and other world championships. At the 1996 Atlanta Olympics, 35 percent of all Olympic athletes were female, and at the 2012 London Olympics, there were more U.S. women participating than men. In 1996, the U.S. women's teams won Olympic gold in softball, soccer, and basketball. Anne Cribbs, a gold medal–winning swimmer for the United States at the Rome Olympics, called 1996 a "watershed time" because it was first group of "Title IX athletes." The U.S. Olympians that year were part of a generation that came of age during the decades in which the amendments were implemented widely, and these Olympians were the first female Americans to cut their teeth during college training.[54]

After Title IX, there was also great growth in the number of spectators consuming women's sports. Before the 1970s, women's sports at all levels drew much smaller crowds, garnered less revenue from advertising, merchandising, and ticket sales, and enjoyed less frequent media exposure than men's sports.[55] But after the passage of Title IX, the spectatorship and the big business of women's basketball began to grow. For example, basketball drew 12,000 fans in the first AIAW game at Madison Square Garden and grossed $4,500 at the first women's AIAW championship game in 1975.[56] NBC and ESPN soon signed television deals valued between $300,000 and $650,000, and corporate sponsorships followed.[57] Attendance at women's college basketball games has only grown since, from 6.4 million (or an average of 1,491 tickets sold per contest) in the 1999–2000 season to nearly 8.3 million (or an average of 1,586 tickets sold per contest) in the 2016–2017 season at the D-I level.[58] According to the NCAA, cumulative attendance at women's college basketball games exceeded 11 million fans during the 2010–2011 season.[59] By the 2015–2016 season, some teams like the University of Tennessee were averaging over 10,000 fans per home game.[60] Spectatorship can also be measured by television ratings for the women's NCAA championship game, which zigzagged between 1.9 (2.92 million) and 3.5 (5.58 million). In the year 2013, the women's championship game had a rating of 2.00 and a viewership of 3.20 million. Of course, these figures are rarely mentioned without reference to the men's game; in 2013, the men's title game rating was 14.0 and reached a viewership of 23.4 million. But given men's head start

Table 4.2. Television ratings for NCAA Men's and Women's Basketball Tournaments, 2013.

	Avg. Men's Rating	Avg. Women's Rating	Avg. Men's Viewership (millions)	Avg. Women's Viewership (millions)
Round 1	1.37	0.31	2.04	0.45
Round 2	3.35	0.37	5.17	0.51
Sweet 16	3.74	0.60	5.89	0.93
Elite 8	6.48	0.83	10.88	1.20
Final 4	9.45	1.60	15.80	2.65
Championship Game	14.00	2.00	23.40	3.20

Sources: SportsMediaWatch.com, "Women's Title Game Holds Up Better in Final Tally" http://www.sportsmediawatch.com/2018/04/womens-national-championship-ratings-espn/); "NCAA Men's Final Four Ratings Hub" http://www.sportsmediawatch.com/ncaa-final-four-ratings-history-most-watched-games-cbs-tbs-nbc/.

in the race to commercialize college sports, is such comparison even fair to begin with?

"This Is About Gold"

American female Olympians not only brought home more hardware after Title IX; they also helped usher in the first era of sustained professional sports leagues for women. Thanks to pioneers like VanDerveer, whose leaderhip of the 1996 Atlanta Olympic team helped establish the Women's National Basketball Association (WNBA), elite college women's players can now earn a living playing basketball too, something which was unheard of before Title IX. After she was hired, it did not take long before VanDerveer had transformed Stanford into a national contender, and as a testament to her college success, she was handed the reins to the USA women's national basketball team in 1996. The president of USA Basketball at the time, C. M. Newton, told her, "This isn't about bronze. This isn't about silver. This is about gold." VanDerveer asked Coach Tucker to take charge of the Stanford team for a year as she led the national team on an exhausting tour of exhibition games, all in the hope of making the women's game more popular and laying a solid marketing foundation for the establishment of the WNBA. NBA commissioner David Stern laid more pressure upon VanDerveer when he told her that "if [the National Team] didn't win the gold, all of the effort, money, and planning" for the WNBA, "would be wasted."[61] Coach VanDerveer coached the Olympic team in the only way she knew how—with a focus on physical and mental conditioning without letting the pressure distract her from her goals—an uncompromising approach that gave all her teams the necessary discipline to succeed. Sara Corbett, who wrote about the national team in *Venus to the Hoop*, remembered that VanDerveer "worked her players . . . harder than they wanted to be worked and [that] sometimes some of the players felt they weren't getting the playing time that they deserved."[62] But the team won all of its exhibition games and rolled to a gold medal. Over a calendar year the team went 60-0, and most of their victories were blowouts. The national team's success, which came two dozen years after Title IX, reinforced the symbolic value of the law by showcasing more female athletes as the heroines that their mothers had never had.

"A Total Fantasy" Becomes Reality
In this way, Title IX has been important in several ways that cannot be measured by economic analysis alone. It gave millions of American girls and women the opportunity to learn from and through their participation in sports, earn a degree (often with the benefit of an athletic scholarship), earn their own livelihood by playing a sport professionally, use the professional skills they learned in that sport in their chosen career, and be themselves in a group that fully accepted them. In other words, Title IX has had a ripple effect that started with economics and bled into education and psychological growth, on the court, in society, and within athletes themselves.

Coach VanDerveer's own story is instructive here again. In the stands in Atlanta's Georgia Dome where the 1996 Olympics were held and where VanDerveer's team won the gold medal, fans held up signs that read, "The REAL Dream Team," highlighting how far women had come to play, and how the moniker "Dream Team" actually meant something more to them than it did to the men's national team. Furthermore, without Title IX, and without pro leagues and Olympic golds, many current youth basketball players may never have started playing at all. Thus, Title IX's most lasting impact may not be on actual opportunities, for athletic women or otherwise, but on the psychology of female athletes. After all, Title IX opened the door for American girls and women to realize unprecedented educational access and employment options, and the knowledge that such access has given them has helped many build their own self-confidence. The law meant that it was now more socially acceptable than ever for girls to play outside, get dirty, and sweat but also to challenge fields of inquiry like medicine, business, and law, once deemed only suitable to boys and men. For many women, Title IX was a symbolic assurance that they could do what they wanted with their bodies and with their lives.[63]

Conclusion

Some myopic political commentators cannot seem to appreciate how monumental—and progressive—Title IX has become. Columnists such as George Will, for example, have focused unjustifiably on how women's college sports are a good example of "liberalism run amok." Will has written that women's sports in colleges amount to an ill-advised use of precious university resources and are the cause of the decline of men's sports teams. For him, market logic would be a better mechanism for apportioning funds for athletics, and by his estimation, if women's sports are not as popular as men's sports, so be it.[64] Similarly, Robert L. Shibley and Jessica Gavora have argued that Title IX has become a political weapon that is a "government-enforced quota regime" and a "monster that both the federal government and many college administrators treat as though it supersedes both the U.S. Constitution and hundreds of years of common law."[65]

But Will, Shibley, and Gavora all unjustifiably dismiss the fact that there is great value in college sports participation, which has been made possible by Title IX, and that such value is not always quantitatively measurable. Thus, even if Title IX is a quota regime, and even if it is not economically efficient, it still holds great value. Will, Shibley, and Gavora do not properly acknowledge the role of a largely patriarchal history in shaping the present, the power of a sexist media in shaping our perceptions thereof, or the educational, cultural, psychological, and social value of women's college sports participation. Will may point to the comparative popularity of men's sports over women's sports as reason enough for women's marginalization in sport, but this popularity is not something that arose out of a vacuum.[66]

In the end, the legacy of Title IX cannot be assessed only in simplistic economic terms. Title IX is about the values that money furthers, including the spirit of equal access to sport's pleasure and educational promise, which universities such as Stanford continue to further today.[67] Unfortunately, Title IX was not a panacea, and problems remain.[68] One of them—the inability of women to secure jobs as coaches of women's teams—is the subject of the next chapter.

Notes

1. Earlier civil rights legislation, particularly Title VI, which was part of the Civil Rights Act of 1964 and was an attempt to help federal contractors who were discriminated against on the basis of "race, color, or national origin," laid the foundation for Title IX. The spirit and language of Title VI was extended on October 13, 1967, to include sex when President Johnson signed Executive Order 11375 prohibiting federal contractors from employment practices that discriminated on the basis of sex. (Title VI originally read, "Prohibition against exclusion from participation in, denial of benefits of, and discrimination under federally assisted programs on ground of race, color, or national origin.") Officially, Title IX was an amendment to the 1972 reauthorization of the Higher Education Act, which was part of President Johnson's Great Society Program, and was passed in 1965 in order to strengthen the nation's programs of higher education by providing more federal funding and financial assistance to students, including low-interest loans. In the five years between Johnson's Executive Order 11375 in 1967 and the passage Title IX in 1972, organizations such as NOW lobbied Congress to change federal guidelines prohibiting organizations receiving federal funding from discriminating on the basis of sex in hiring and employment practices. The American political zeitgeist of the time was shifting toward a more progressive agenda particularly in terms of greater equality for women and racial minorities and less tolerance for discrimination of these groups. But it was also a time in which contract compliance was increasingly deemed important, especially in contracts between the government and its contractors or any organization receiving funding from the federal government, and these two social and legal trends effectively opened space for Title IX to be passed.
2. Title IX of the Education Amendments, 1972, 20 U.S.C. Â§1681 et seq.
3. Patsy T. Mink, undated handwritten notes for a speech given in support of a civil rights plank at the Democratic National Convention, Los Angeles, California, July 12, 1960, container 5, folder 2. Patsy T. Mink Papers, Manuscript Division, Library of Congress, https://www.loc.gov/rr/mss/images/mink_env_front_smst.jpg.
4. Kindberg, "VanDerveer Loves."
5. Follansbee, "Excellence, Community"; Kindberg, "VanDerveer Loves."
6. Purdy, "Tara VanDerveer's Victory."
7. Sharp was in the middle of a twelve-year stint at USC in which she won 271 of 370 games and two NCAA titles. The year before Coach VanDerveer began coaching at Stanford (1983–1984), USC won the first of these titles. Between 1984 and 1986, Miller won three straight Naismith National Player of the Year awards. Miller was the first of many star recruits for the Trojans, including Lisa Leslie, Tina Thompson, and Cynthia Cooper. Cooper is the WNBA's all-time leading scorer by points per game (21.0), and Leslie is second in total points (6,263), trailing only Thompson (6,413). In 1986, *Sports Illustrated* called USC's Cheryl Miller the best college basketball in America, male or female.
8. Anderson, "The Fight for Play."

9. Quoted in Anderson, "The Fight for Play."
10. Chapin, "Joe Ruetz."
11. Ally Hudson Richter, who graduated from Stanford in 1972 and took a class in track and field (there was no women's team at the time), remembers that the equipment was subpar: "When the boys got these nice, sleek aluminum hurdles, we got their old wooden hurdles. Half of us spent time at Cowell [the student health center] getting splinters pulled out of our butts" (quoted in Anderson, "The Fight for Play").
12. Rhode and Walker, "Gender Equity," 4.
13. Quoted in Dohrmann, "Chance."
14. Stanford University, "Our History."
15. Stanford didn't have a scholarship to offer star tennis players in the 1980s. The same was true in soccer. Stanford did not offer female soccer players athletic scholarships until the 1993–1994 season (personal communication, Frank Brennan).
16. Quoted in Anderson, "The Fight for Play."
17. Rintala, "Review," 340.
18. The AIAW, which was initially called the Commission on Intercollegiate Athletics for Women, was created in 1971 by a splinter group of the American Alliance for Health, Physical Education, Recreation, and Dance (AAHPERD). AAHPERD itself was founded in 1885 and was one of the first scholarly organizations in the United States to consider the health benefits of sports for the wider population (i.e., not only schoolchildren or professional athletes).
19. Wushanley, *Playing Nice*, 5.
20. Wushanley, *Playing Nice*, 5.
21. Wushanley, *Playing Nice*, 155.
22. Fields, "Review of Ying Wushanley, 189.
23. Cahn, *Coming on Strong*, 254.
24. Cahn, *Coming on Strong*, 255.
25. Cahn, *Coming on Strong*, 254–55.
26. Cahn, *Coming on Strong*, 255.
27. Dohrmann, "Chance to Be."
28. Cahn, *Coming on Strong*, 255–56.
29. Cahn, *Coming on Strong*, 257.
30. Cahn, *Coming on Strong*, 257.
31. *Association for Intercollegiate Athletics for Women v. NCAA*, 558.
32. *Association for Intercollegiate Athletics for Women v. NCAA*, 558; *Association for Intercollegiate Athletics for Women v. NCAA*, 735.
33. Graham, "The Storm over Grove," 407–9.
34. Graham, "The Storm over Grove," 407–9.
35. President Reagan vetoed the CRRA in 1988 on the grounds that it would allow Congress to "vastly and unjustifiably expand the power of the federal government over the decisions and affairs of private organizations, such as churches and synagogues, farms, businesses and state and local governments" but Congress overruled President Reagan's veto, marking a significant victory for advocates of Title IX

and women's participation in competitive intercollegiate sports (quoted in Marcus, "Reagan Vetoes").

36. Irick, NCAA Sports.
37. Jenkins, "Hundreds of Colleges".
38. Byers and Hammer, *Unsportsmanlike*, 247.
39. Zimbalist, *Unpaid Professionals*, 249.
40. S. Smith, "Basketball," 299.
41. Suggs, "Foes of Title IX."
42. Brake, "The Struggle for Sex," 8n33; Weistart, "Equal Opportunity."
43. Dudley and Rutherglen, "Ironies."
44. Jurewitz argues that Title IX "created severe unintended consequences" since athletic directors are pressed to reduce budgets while also increase the proportion of athletic opportunities for female athletes to comply with the regulations implementing Title IX. Athletic directors have chosen to try and have their cake and eat it too by eliminating men's athletic programs, particularly in nonrevenue-producing sports, and by providing equal athletic opportunities for women athletes. Thus "Title IX has . . . created a battle for scarce resources, [which] has led to distrust and closed communications between partisan groups seeking to further the interests of their members" ("Playing at Even," 283).
45. Jackson explains this point in her historical study of college sports at the University of North Carolina ("Title IX," x).
46. A 2012 report by the National Organization for Women and Girls in Education disputes this claim ("Title IX at 40).
47. Thomas, "Colleges Cut."
48. National Collegiate Athletic Association, "Participation Statistics," 90–117; Zimbalist, *Unpaid Professionals*, 65.
49. U.S. General Accounting Office, "Intercollegiate Athletics: Four-Year Colleges," 14.
50. U.S. General Accounting Office, "Intercollegiate Athletics: Recent Trends"; Cheslock, "Who's Playing?" 2.
51. Hobson and Rich, "Colleges Spend."
52. Zimbalist, *Unpaid Professionals*, 65.
53. Hyman, *Until It Hurts*, 45.
54. Longman, "Before Games."
55. Zimbalist, *Unpaid Professionals*, 72.
56. Lannin, *A History of Basketball*, 83.
57. Hult and Trekell, *A Century*, 316.
58. National Collegiate Athletic Association, "1999–2000 Attendance Figures"; National Collegiate Athletic Association, "2016–2017 Attendance Figures."
59. During the 2011–2012 season, Stanford averaged approximately five thousand fans per game while Tennessee and Louisville averaged over ten thousand. In the same year, ten programs topped an average of seven thousand fans per home game, with the University of Tennessee leading the way with twelve thousand fans per

game. Louisville and UCONN also routinely topped nine thousand per game (Stanford was not in the top ten in terms of attendance; National Collegiate Athletic Association, "Women's Hoops").

60. National Collegiate Athletic Association, "1999–2000 Attendance Figures."

61. S. Smith, "Basketball," 308.

62. Quoted in S. Smith, "Basketball," 308.

63. Castelnuovo and Guthrie, *Feminism and the Female Body*.

64. Will, "A Train Wreck."

65. Gavora, *Tilting the Playing Field*; Shibley, *Twisting Title IX*.

66. Cooky, Messner, and Hextrum, "Women Play Sport."

67. Auletta argues that Stanford—and the broader San Francisco Bay Area—incubates tolerant multicultural values that are relatively gender-neutral and progressive, technologically innovative, and religiously tolerant ("Annals").

68. Grundy and Shackelford, *Shattering*, 5–6.

CHAPTER 5

A Coach of Coaches

As the game evolved, what changed? Television coverage.

—Kim Mulkey[1]

"The Influx of Money Has Changed the Sport"

Before Title IX, many women's college basketball coaches, such as C. Vivian Stringer, struggled to make ends meet. In *Standing Tall*, Stringer explained, "I coached for eleven years without receiving a single paycheck for it. There's no question in my mind that the influx of money has changed the sport. Most of the people coaching basketball when I started . . . were women, and they did it for nothing except the chance to build the sport."[2]

After Title IX, there was an increase in the number of male coaches coaching women's college teams. Male coaches began to pay closer attention to women's sports, applied for jobs to coach them, and were hired in larger numbers than ever by (often male)[3] athletic directors who saw them as better qualified.[4] There was simply more money to be made in women's college sports after Title IX so male coaches jumped at the chance to coach women's teams.

As more men took up these positions, there was a decline of female coaches coaching women's teams as a result. At the time Title IX was passed, in 1972, 90 percent of all coaches of women's college sports teams at Stanford were women. Thirty-two years later in 2006, that percentage had fallen to 42 percent.[5] In 1977, as the implementation of Title IX was taking shape, women coached 79.4 percent of all U.S. women's college teams. By 2012, that percentage had fallen to 59.5 percent.[6] As recently as 2015, women made up just 38 percent of all women's sports team's coaches.[7]

The difficulty female coaches had finding coaching jobs after Title IX has been even worse for women of color, and particularly African American coaches like Stringer, because on top of sexist hiring practices, there has long been widespread racial prejudice against people of color in American sports. Between 2009 and 2011, for example, the Black Coaches and Administrators group found that five non-white coaches were hired among a total of eighteen hires (28 percent). Just a few years earlier, from 2007 to 2008, non-whites filled nine of sixteen coaching vacancies (56 percent). Although Stringer never blamed her misfortunes on prejudice within the coaching ranks, she did write in her memoir that the initiation of pay for women's college basketball coaches after Title IX helped create a world in which athletic directors, many of whom were male, hired other males to coach the women's teams.

> [If] I'm smoking a cigar and you're smoking a cigar, neither of us is going to mind the smoke. For there to be real equity, we have to look not just at the high-visibility positions, but at who's doing the hiring and firing . . . The more women like me there are working as head coaches, athletic directors, and university presidents, the more chances other women like me will have.[8]

What exacerbates these inequities is the fact that women rarely coach male athletes. In 2001, the NCAA reported that women coached 3 percent of all men's collegiate sports teams and that there were no women coaching men's college basketball.[9] In 2008, the Women's Sports Foundation found that these figures had dropped even further, with women coaching 2 percent of men's college sports teams.[10] By 2015, the trend had reversed only slightly, with women making up under 4 percent of all the head coaches coaching men's college sports teams.[11]

"It's Sexism"

In 2018, Coach VanDerveer lamented that "women are not getting the opportunities in men's basketball and . . . are getting pushed out of women's basketball," concluding that "sexism" prevents men from allowing women to coach men.[12] To Coach VanDerveer, coaching men's and women's basketball were "more the same than they are different," noting that patterns of practice, recruiting, game-planning, film study, were comparable.

Of course, she added, "the men . . . are bigger and stronger . . . you know . . . testosterone . . . but their competition is bigger and stronger, too." She noted that "professors and people in business" were "shocked that women don't coach men," especially considering that "female professors have men in their classes."

"It's sexism, I don't know that I can answer it any other way. I think that . . . athletics are the last bastion of all maleness . . . We still live in a world where there's sexual harassment and discrimination, and we have a way to go in our culture, and this is reflected in athletics."[13]

"The Most Influential Person in My Life"

VanDerveer's Stanford program was the epitome of stability. When I first met her in 2010, she had been coaching at Stanford for thirty-five years while the next-longest-tenured coach in the entire Pac-10 conference had twenty-two years of coaching experience and five of the ten Pac-10 teams were led by coaches with less than five years' experience. Coaching at the big-time level is a volatile profession, and given this clear sexism, many of Coach VanDerveer's female colleagues struggle to find work.

So VanDerveer challenged herself to help other women find opportunities to coach. VanDerveer has primarily hired female assistants and makes sure she is available to any female coach who wants her advice on team strategies—for example, the intricacies of the triangle offense. They are given the chance to learn from a coaching veteran up close, and they can ask her any coaching question they want. At the time that I followed Stanford's season

Table 5.1. Coach VanDerveer's coaching protégés (NCAA head coaches only, as of January 2020)

Name	Institution	Years Active
June Daugherty	Boise State University, University of Washington, Washington State University	1989–96, 1996–97, 2007–18
Trisha Stevens	Boise State University	1996–2002
Charli Turner Thorne	Arizona State University	1996–present
Katy Steding	Werner Pacific College, Boston University	2001–08, 2014–18
Molly Goodenbour	University of San Francisco, Chico State University, UC Irvine	1989–93, 2006–08, 2008–present
Lindsey Yamasaki	San Francisco Academy of Art	2008–present
Jennifer Azzi	University of San Francisco	2010–present
Bobbie Kelsey	University of Wisconsin	2011–16

unfold, eleven of VanDerveer's former players or assistant coaches were coaching at some collegiate or professional level, and countless more were coaching or had coached at high school or other levels.

No one better exemplified this mentorship than Coach Kate Paye, who was an assistant to VanDerveer that season. VanDerveer hired Coach Bobbie Kelsey and Coach Paye as assistant coaches in 2007. Both women had played for Stanford when it won its second national title under VanDerveer in 1992.

Coach Paye's serious, humorous, and humble approach mirrored VanDerveer's own. She was positive, upbeat, intelligent, strong, and laser-focused on helping each player grow during each practice, too. Like VanDerveer, Coach Paye balanced a witty sense of humor with seriousness, playful banter with a business-like approach. Like VanDerveer, Coach Paye paid careful attention to the fundamentals of the game, devouring Stanford's extensive game film library and pacing the court during practices looking for any player whom she thought was not practicing her drills perfectly.

In one early season dribbling drill, Coach Paye sprinted to the side of Jeanette Pohlen, who was guarding one of the team's volunteer practice players, a male undergraduate named Elon. "[If you dribble like that] you're not going to play like you did against Texas," she told her. "He [Elon] is being nice to you. C'mon! Get in triple threat [position]!" Coach Paye was fit and full of energy and expected the same intensity from the players.

Before becoming a coach, Coach Paye enjoyed a successful professional career outside basketball, but her heart remained in the game. After growing up in a family of stellar athletes—her father was a Stanford running back, and her brother John played for both the Stanford football and basketball teams in the early 1980s—Coach Paye was not recruited to play basketball by Stanford. But since she had grown up near Stanford and was loyal to the university, she passed on offers from Princeton, Harvard, and Dartmouth and enrolled at Stanford. Even though she was not offered a scholarship, she walked on and made the team, earning a scholarship in her second year. She worked her way into a starting role too and ultimately played professionally, in the American Basketball League (ABL) for the Seattle Reign. When the ABL folded in 1998, Coach Paye played for two seasons for the WNBA's Minnesota Lynx. Professional salaries for women were not significant so Coach Paye enrolled in law school hoping to become an attorney after her playing days were done. But after graduating with a JD and an MBA and working a desk job that she didn't care for, Coach Paye realized that practicing law was not a good fit. "As an attorney, I would wake up and say to myself, 'Just get through the day.' I was miserable."

Paye decided to try coaching. As a player at Stanford, Paye's teammates had told her that she would one day become a great coach but for years she defied their predictions. She was interested in game strategy, and she loved working summer camps with children, but, she said, it was "always one of those things . . . when people tell you that you are going to do something, you are determined not to."

One day Paye began to talk to herself into trying coaching. "[I said to myself], 'if you are ever going to try coaching, you better do it now.'" She recalled the transition from lawyer to coach as being "awesome," adding that "[in law] I was just unhappy. Now I get up and I am excited to do whatever it is I get to do."

Coach VanDerveer helped Paye make her way into basketball coaching as an assistant at Pepperdine University and then at San Diego State University. By 2007, she had returned to the farm to be VanDerveer's assistant. Looking back, Paye told me that Coach VanDerveer had taught her that basketball was a technical game that would be won by the most precise team, the team that executed best. But more importantly, she said, Coach VanDerveer was "the most influential person in my life (other than my parents)," and she credited Coach VanDerveer with teaching her how to be not only a good coach but also a good person.

> Tara has very high expectations and she is very demanding . . . Tara is a phenomenal teacher . . . She has a way of teaching without putting it in your face. She trusts that you are going to learn just by watching her and learning your own way . . . [She] puts it out there, and if you want to take advantage of it, [then] go for it . . . Tara always treats players with respect. She can yell at them, she will occasionally drop profanity, but very rarely, and she treats them with respect . . . That is something that I always aspire to . . . I have been around a lot of coaches who don't always treat the players and their staff with respect . . . Tara very rarely if ever uses sarcasm as a teaching tool. I have been around coaches that have. I slip into it sometimes, and I don't think that's necessarily a positive way to teach. But everyone has to do it their own way. You watch Geno [Auriemma of UCONN] and he is sarcastic every other comment. That is his primary teaching tool. Tara's very organized. She has a very clear purpose. Everything we do is for a purpose.

"The Jumps This Way Are Crazy"

Although Coach VanDerveer had helped cultivate the talents of dozens of women who have played professionally, I asked her if she considered herself a "coach of coaches," to which she answered,

Former Stanford Women's Basketball Players in the WNBA Photo credit: *Aaron Miller*

> Yes . . . for a long time . . . ever since I have been at Stanford. I like to have coaches come in and work with them and try to get them jobs, particularly female coaches, because I think men have enough help. They don't need me. Sometimes [a male coach] will ask, and I'll just say, "You don't need me. You've got a whole mechanism already working for you. I've got to help women who don't have that support."

Since VanDerveer has led the Cardinal, Stanford has had an all-female coaching staff. When I observed the team, all the coaching interns, trainer, and team managers were female too. Only the strength and conditioning coaches, who were hired by Stanford Athletics and worked for other Stanford sports too, were male.

Would Coach VanDerveer ever consider coaching a men's team?

> Yeah, I would. If they are going to pay you three times as much, you have to look at it. The thing about it—about anything—is you don't just go in at the top of anything . . . If you have women's basketball and you have men's basketball and you have pro basketball . . . it's not always this leap from one to the other. Now, people in men's basketball go into the women's game this

way. In fact . . . a director of men's basketball . . . can take the head job for the women—the jumps this way are crazy . . . Women are not necessarily given the opportunities . . . Here are resumes for my assistant job [at the time of the interview, the position had recently been vacated by Coach Kelsey, who was hired into a head coaching position elsewhere]. I would bet you . . . I can't even tell you how many would be men versus women . . . So part of what I see my job as is to mentor young women.

Others around VanDerveer agreed that there was good reason to hire female coaches. According to one female Stanford athletic director, male coaches often do not understand their female players.

Women players simply respond differently to women coaches. Certain players—I wasn't one of them—would break under a male coach . . . One player was a great shooter, but after [the male coach] broke her down, she never shot the ball anymore. Coach VanDerveer shows each player exactly what to do and when they do in the game, and when they win the game, that kind of coaching is validated. The players trust her.

College athletes spend more time with their coach than any other adult in college, thus women who are not coached by women are arguably denied an important same-sex mentor. When women are not hired into these positions, the aspirations of the next generation of young women may become more limited too.[14]

There are also glaring disparities in coaching salaries between male and female coaches. With the spread of professionalism and commercialism, and the arms race fanning the flames, colleges began paying college sports coaches larger, arguably exorbitant, salaries. Partly colleges could do this because they did not have to pay the players, and the media rights fees rose exponentially.

But there have been other justifications given for why these high salaries are necessary. First, college coaches across the country are essentially offering young athletes the same thing—a free education and a chance to play a sport—so their individual charisma and abilities in recruiting, leadership, and strategy purportedly carry greater importance. College sports are played primarily by young men and women 18–22. These athletes generally have a similar amount of prior athletic experience. The rules of the game are the same for everyone. Enter into that system the much more variable factor of coaching expertise, and you might begin to see why the most competitive college teams are willing to pay large salaries for the best college coaches. College coaches come from various walks of life and experience. Some coaches have more experience, and some have better coaching experiences than others. Some are better recruiters. Some are more charismatic or better trained in the art of persuasion.

There is also the matter of supply and demand, which dovetails with the notion that some coaches are much better than others. Big-time college sports programs want the best coaches, and their boosters, who may be asked to foot part of the bill for these salaries, or donate larger sums to the university, are often willing to pay for them too. Wealthy boosters want to donate money to "get their name out there," and what better way to do that than to donate to the campus event that generates more local buzz than any other and to a specific cause that everyone knows will have a great impact on your team's performance?

Salaries for college coaches began to go up in the late 1980s. Clotfelter found that between 1985–1986 and 2009–2010, football coaches' salaries ballooned 750 percent while full professors' salaries rose 32 percent and college presidents' salaries rose 90 percent.[15] In 2013 the *Chronicle of Higher Education* reported that thirty-three coaches and athletics directors at private universities across the country earned more than $1 million per year.[16] Fourteen of these thirty-three earned more than $2 million in total compensation. Some football and men's basketball coaches at public universities receive the highest salary of any state employee, including the governor and the university president at a time when these universities only hired 30 percent of their academic faculty full-time.

Some of the highest salaries for college sports coaches are astonishing, despite research that suggests that paying such high salaries does not lead to better-performing teams.[17] In 2011, Ohio State University agreed to pay football coach Urban Meyer $24 million over six years. In 2013, Nick Saban of the University of Alabama earned $5.5 million per year,[18] and by 2020 that salary had risen above $9 million.[19] Even at academically elite universities the numbers can be eye-popping. At Duke University, for example, head basketball coach Mike Krzyzewski made $5 million per year in the late 1990s[20] and by 2011 he was earning nearly $10 million.[21] At Stanford, head football coach David Shaw now earns approximately $4 million per season.[22] It's not just top-performing coaches who are rewarded handsomely either; many football and men's basketball coaches who do not succeed receive millions of dollars per year in total compensation from their universities, and some even receive severance payments and other perks after they are fired. You might think that Americans would be outraged or offended by this excess, yet few reforms are proposed let alone implemented, and college coaching salaries in the big-time sports continue to rise.[23]

It is not just coaching salaries, though; it is administrative salaries too. With fatter wallets and greater pull within the college as a whole, big-time coaches built out their staffs, which has meant higher overall athletic department spending. In fact, there was a 30 percent increase in the number of athletic department staff in the 1980s and 1990s,[24] including assistant coaches and strength and conditioning or performance coaches, all of whom were each earning several hundred thousand dollars a year.[25] Conference commissioners in the Pac-12, Big 10, and SEC are also hauling in large salaries, some even in the millions of dollars.[26] Everyone is getting rich except the players, especially the female ones.

Stanford apparently spends less on female athletes than on men. According to 2017 figures from the U.S. Department of Education, Stanford University spent more on athletics-related student aid (total) for male athletes than for female athletes, while the average amount spent per athlete was comparable. Recruiting and operating expenses were also greater for men's teams, as were revenues. However, in comparison to Duke University, a comparable private university that has a similar number of students, Stanford appears to spend less per athlete (except for football). Moreover, a comparison with close athletic and academic rival UC Berkeley reveals that Stanford spends much more per athlete except in football and basketball.

Since Title IX, coaches in women's sports have earned comparatively low salaries despite doing what is generally the same job as their male counterparts.[27] This trend has remained consistent over time, with female coaches typically earning 50 cents for every dollar male coaches earn.[28] The salaries of a few female coaches, such as Tennessee's Pat Summitt, Connecticut's Geno Auriemma, and Gail Goestenkors of Texas rose into the millions of dollars per year by the late 2000s. And yet in 2010–2011, while over thirty men's coaches in basketball alone surpassed $1 million in total compensation, just five coaches of college women's sports teams received the same or more.[29] It was not just the top-earning coaches who profited handsomely, though; even the median salary of men's college basketball coaches was twice that of women's college basketball coaches in 2010.

The University of Connecticut, whose men's and women's basketball teams are both considered elite, serves as a prime example of the gender wage gap in college coaching. In 2004, Geno Auriemma re-signed to coach the women's basketball team for an annual salary of $825,000. At the same time, Jim Calhoun, the men's basketball coach, received an annual salary that was almost double Auriemma's: $1.4 million per year. At that point in their coaching tenures, both coaches had won multiple NCAA titles and led teams that were widely considered elite. But Auriemma had collected

Table 5.2. A comparison of university athletics revenues and expenses, totals and averages. (2017 Figures)

University	Stanford	UC Berkeley	Duke
Enrollments	7,056	29,351	6,536
Men's teams' total participants	504	544	442
Athletically related student aid (total for men's teams)	$13.2 million	$6.7 million	$12.33 million
Athletically related student aid (average for male athlete)	$26,190	$12,316	$27,896

University	Stanford	UC Berkeley	Duke
Women's teams' total participants	479	473	334
Athletically related student aid (total for women's teams)	$12.4 million	$6.15 million	$10.3 million
Athletically related student aid (average for female athletes)	$26,887	$13,002	$30,838

University	Stanford	UC Berkeley	Duke
Athletically related student aid (average for male basketball player)	$58,142	$77,047	$234,828
Athletically related student aid (average for female basketball players)	$44,221	$35,886	$70,942
Athletically related student aid (average for football players)	$50,140	$58,377	$23,032

University	Stanford	UC Berkeley	Duke
Operating expenses (total for men's basketball)	$872,125	$1.39 million	$3.52 million
Operating expenses (women's basketball)	$619,096	$1.005 million	$1.064 million
Operating expenses (men's football)	$5.164 million	$6.95 million	$2.65 million

University	Stanford	UC Berkeley	Duke
Recruiting expenses (total for men's teams)	$1.05 million	$1.01 million	$1.11 million
Recruiting expenses (total for women's teams)	$452,792	$342,045	$474,777

University	Stanford	UC Berkeley	Duke
Revenues (Total for men's basketball)	$7.25 million	$8.01 million	$36.41 million
Revenues (Total women's basketball)	$2.03 million	$491,698	$3.81 million
Revenues (Total for football)	$46.85 million	$32.65 million	$37.84 million

Source: US Department of Education. N.d. "Equity in Athletics Data analysis." https://ope.ed.gov/athletics/#/

five national championships to Calhoun's two and could boast a 67 percent graduation rate, 40 percent higher than Calhoun's.[30] Both men had brought attention to their university and revenue too (although it would be impossible to measure exactly how much exposure was due to each man individually). Clearly Auriemma received a lower salary not because he was an inferior coach but because university administrators saw his sport—and therefore his coaching—as less important and valuable to the university than his counterpart's and therefore decided that he was less deserving of a salary comparable to Calhoun's. The question that remained was this: if UCONN women's basketball was perennially the best program of its kind in the nation, was this argument defensible? Moreover, what would the UCONN women's coach's salary have been if Auriemma were female?

How do universities get away with it and why aren't these salaries a violation of Title IX? Although the Equal Pay Act of 1963 prohibits discrimination in employment based on pay, universities use perks, bonuses, and third parties to provide men's coaches with more lucrative, and therefore more enticing, deals.[31]

Stanford apparently led the way by becoming one of the first colleges to pay the same base salary to its men's and women's team coaches,[32] although we don't know for certain what the university pays each of its coaches today since Stanford, as a private university, is not legally required to disclose this information to the public nor is it subject to a state or federal open records request. However, according to U.S. Department of Education figures, as recently as 2017 the average salary for coaches of women's teams still fell well short of salaries for men's teams not only at Stanford University but also at UC Berkeley and Duke University.

Although Internet speculators suggest that VanDerveer is among the nation's highest paid women's basketball coaches, it remains unclear whether Coach VanDerveer is underpaid in comparison with Stanford's men's basketball head coach. Johnny Dawkins, who coached Stanford's men's basketball team between 2008 and 2016, reportedly earned $900,000 in 2013 although this is an estimated figure.[33] In that eight-year period, Dawkins's record was 156-115, and 66-78 within the Pac-10. Only one of his teams, in 2013–2014, earned a berth to the NCAA Tournament. By contrast, VanDerveer's record during this time was 256-37, with just twelve losses coming in conference

Table 5.3. A comparison of average college head coaching salaries. (2017 Figures)

University	Stanford	UC Berkeley	Duke
Average Head coaching salary (men's sports)	$585,414	$348,291	$888,921
Average Head coaching salary (women's sports)	$222,922	$178,380	$217,429

Source: US Department of Education. N.d. "Equity in Athletics Data analysis." https://ope.ed.gov/athletics/#/

Coach Tara VanDerveer celebrates her 1,000th victory with her team. Photo credit: Aaron Miller

play. While the men's team at Stanford may sell more Stanford merchandise and tickets than the women's team (it is hard to know for certain because the bookstore will not respond to interview requests), garner better "prime time" slots for TV appearances, and perhaps generate greater numbers of alumni donations, if VanDerveer did earn less than Dawkins during this period, it would be curious. How could VanDerveer, who had won two national titles and in 2020 became the winningest head basketball coach in college basketball history earn less money than a coach who was fired after eight seasons (Dawkins)?

The outsized revenues that Stanford earns through men's basketball is not necessarily because of the team's coach but rather reflects the public's appetite for men's basketball over women's basketball; thus, coaching salaries are not completely reflective of a coach's abilities or accomplishments. Still pay disparities do seem unfair since the job of women's basketball head coach and men's basketball head coach are not substantially different in any meaningful sense. VanDerveer has to deal with the same number of players as Coach Dawkins did, has to make the same recruiting trips, and has to deal with the same members of the media.

Women's coaches have also struggled to stand out to potential corporate sponsors, and since there are no regulations limiting how much a private company can pay coaches to outfit their players in that company's apparel, this also adds to the gender pay gap for coaches. Male coaches cashed in when shoe companies began giving them free shoes and apparel alongside large sums of cash, but coaches of women's teams have never been offered the same kinds of deals.[34]

Some suggest there is a labor market rationale for paying higher salaries to male coaches; that is, male coaches should earn more because of supply and demand. Proponents accordingly argue that men's sports coaches generate more revenue than their female counterparts and therefore deserve higher salaries. This may seem logical since only one-quarter of coaching salaries is paid by universities, and according to Yost, the rest comes from sponsors, especially broadcasters who seem to have an unlimited budget when it comes to paying for sports broadcasting rights."[35] Another justification universities make for paying men's coaches high salaries is that the best among them will also be prime candidates for coaching positions in prosperous professional leagues such as the NBA and NFL (of which there are no analogs in women's professional sports), so universities feel they must pay professional salaries to compete in the labor market for the best coaching talent.

While it is true that coaches in big-time men's sports generate more money for their university and the demand for men's sports is larger than the demand for women's sports, women's sports coaches have a near impossible game to win. The disparity between the viewership of women's sports and men's sports is largely shaped by the perceptions of (mostly male) media executives regarding how desirable a particular sport may be to prospective viewers and by those prospective viewers who rather blindly watch "what is on." This is a problem far beyond the control of any individual coach; after all, women's basketball coaches cannot generate more revenue for their universities if media executives do not decide that there is potential value in broadcasting women's games as often as men's or in "prime time", nor will alumni follow the women's game with as much passion if the media coverage is not there, nor will companies have as much interest in promoting their products through women's sports if the media and alumni are not as involved as they are in men's sports. It is a vicious cycle, so the deck remains stacked against women coaches hoping for more-equitable salaries.[36]

Still it must be asked whether it is fair to determine coaches' salaries by revenue-generation alone since coaches (should be) performing various other roles that are similarly integral to the university mission, none more important than promoting the value of a quality college degree. This is a question that we will return to in the final two chapters of this book.

"A House for Half Price"

For women like VanDerveer, the choice to make a career of college coaching is effectively the choice to enter an industry in which just one-half of all possible jobs are accessible. There are eight coaching jobs for basketball on any given college campus—four for the men and four for the women, and yet women can only apply with confidence for half of them since few women have had any success breaking into the old-boy network of men's sports coaching. Male coaches, meanwhile, can and do apply for all these jobs and in most cases will be considered seriously for all of them. This is referred to as the glass wall problem; women can see the jobs through the wall but they cannot confidently apply for them. In the end, the problem comes down to sexism, to the labor market rationale used to justify it, and to an ignorance of these problems by men close enough to the game to know better.

In 2013, American women accounted for more than half of all college students, earned 57 percent of all undergraduate degrees and 60 percent of all master's degrees,[37] and had joined men in the ranks of nearly every industry, and yet vast inequalities remained in a labor market where some of the highest earners were the highest earners in the state, leading VanDerveer to protest,

> Let's just say I am on a plane or something. They say, "What do you do?" Sometimes I will say, "Yeah, I coach basketball at Stanford," and they will say, "Oh, which team do you coach?" I'm like, "I coach the women's team" because women only coach women, whereas a man could coach men or women . . . [By the time we] have a female president, we'll have one woman coaching women's college basketball.[38]

But VanDerveer probably summed it up best in her memoir when she wrote, "People think it is somehow okay to pay a woman less because she is a woman, as if we don't need money as much as a man does. Do they think that when we go to buy a house, people say, 'Okay, you're a woman, you get the house for half-price?'"[39]

Notes

1. Quoted in Ellwood, "Women of Troy."
2. Stringer and Tucker, *Standing Tall*, 69–70.
3. After Title IX, women also "lost departmental control of women's collegiate sports programs" as universities decided to merge women's and men's athletic departments (Stanford University, "Thinking about Sports"). The percentage of female

administrators of women's athletic programs, which had been as high as 90 percent in 1972, dropped to 17.9 percent by 2002 (Estler and Nelson, "Who Calls the Shots?"; Acosta and Carpenter, "Women in Intercollegiate Sport," 28; Ackerman, "Is Gender a Factor?").

4. In 2008, the Women's Sports Foundation found that "the insidious impact of historical discrimination against women in employment as coaches" persisted because various myths and stereotypes helped keep women from getting more coaching positions. These myths and stereotypes included the idea that female coaches "do not win as many championships" (perhaps true but if so, it is only because women are not given the same number of chances to win them); that "women are less intense and less demanding of their players" (a stereotype akin to asserting that "all football players are dumb" or "white men can't jump"); that "women turn other women off and that it is easier for women to be coached by a man" (this assumes various stereotypes about men and women, for example, that women are quiet while men are outgoing, weak where men are strong, passive where men are aggressive); and that "you do not have to be worried that the coach might be a lesbian if you hire a male coach" (this assumes that all female coaches are lesbians and that even if they were there would be something to worry about, such as sexual predation; Women's Sports Foundation, "Coaching").

5. Stanford University, "Thinking about Sports."
6. ESPN, "OTL."
7. Lapchick and Baker, "The 2015 Racial and Gender."
8. Stringer and Tucker, *Standing Tall*, 70.
9. ESPN Outside the Lines, "Women Coaching Men."
10. Women's Sports Foundation, "Coaching."
11. Acosta and Carpenter, "Women in Intercollegiate Sport," 28.
12. Stanford University (Lagunita), "Interview."
13. Stanford University (Lagunita), "Interview."
14. Rhode and Walker, "Gender Equity," 42.
15. Clotfelter, *Big Time*, 106.
16. Wolverton, "At Private Colleges."
17. Tsitsos and Nixon, "The Star Wars," 69, 80. See also Orszag and Orszag, "The Empirical," 11.
18. Coaches Hot Seat, "Salaries and Contracts."
19. Stripling and Fuller, "On Campuses."
20. Shulman and Bowen, *The Game of Life*, 236.
21. Berkowitz, "Duke's Krzyzewski."
22. Shaw's predecessor, Jim Harbaugh, reportedly earned approximately $1 million in 2010, and Shaw apparently earned approximately $4 million in total compensation in 2016 (*San Jose Mercury News*, "Stanford Football Coach"; it is unclear how the *Mercury News* acquired data on these salaries).
23. Easterbrook, *The King*, 101.
24. Byers and Hammer, *Unsportsmanlike Conduct*, 367.

25. Shi, "Shannon Turley"; Zimbalist, *Unpaid Professionals*, 131.
26. Shi, "Shannon Turley." See also Zimbalist, "Taxation of College Sports," 131.
27. *USA Today*, "An Analysis of Salaries."
28. Humphreys, "Equal Pay on the Hardwood"; Staurowsky, "March Money Madness"; Gentry and Alexander, "Pay for Women's Basketball."
29. *USA Today*, Men's Basketball Coaches."
30. Araton, *Crashing the Borders*, 106.
31. Gentry and Alexander, "Pay for Women's Basketball."
32. Zimbalist, *Unpaid Professionals*, 88.
33. Wilner, "Pac-12 Salaries."
34. For a study of the evolution of these deals, see Wetzel and Yaeger, *Sole Influence*; Sperber, "College Sports, Inc.: How Big-Time," 23–25; and Nocera and Strauss, *Indentured*, 37–50.
35. Yost, *Var$ity Green*, 10.
36. Messner, Cooky, and Hextrum, "Gender in Televised Sports."
37. National Science Foundation, "Women, Minorities."
38. VanDerveer and Ryan, *Shooting from the Outside*, 127.
39. VanDerveer and Ryan, *Shooting from the Outside*, 125–26.

CHAPTER 6

Everybody Is Capable, Everybody Is Fearless

> The sporting legend is above all else a story of the pain barrier, of going to the limits of endurance, of being drunk with "animal" fatigue and of getting a kick out of bruises, knocks, and injuries.
>
> —Jean Marie Brohm[1]

> In order to live a full human life, we require not only control of our bodies (though control is a prerequisite), we must touch the unity and resonance of our physicality, our bond with the natural order, the corporeal ground of our intelligence.
>
> —Adrienne Rich[2]

"We Are Now a Marked Team": University of California, January 2, 2011

A few nights after Stanford beat UCONN, I was nursing a cold at home and watching Comcast SportsNet Bay Area (CSNBA) bring a broadcast of the Stanford-Cal game into my bedroom. It was a unique luxury of doing fieldwork with a nationally ranked college basketball team: even when I could not make it to my fieldsite, the fieldsite sometimes came to me.

That evening Cal hosted Stanford at Haas Pavilion amidst the redwoods and oaks of Berkeley. The teams had competed against each other for over a hundred years, and Bay Area bragging rights were once again on the line. CSNBA played up the drama, giving the game a heightened importance that belied it being both teams' first Pac-10 game and a game that would not necessarily make or break the season.

Coach VanDerveer certainly did not play down the drama, saying in a press conference after the UCONN game, "We are now a marked team." She knew that all the team's future opponents would bring their best effort. But the matter-of-fact tone she took to utter these words suggested that she did not fear but rather relished being the target on every opponent's schedule. Stanford was on top of the mountain, and that meant that the team had to summon great strength to keep their breath in the thin air.

Cal's team appeared strong, coming into the game with an 8-3 record, but as soon as the ball left the referee's hands, the Cardinal proved to be a cut above. Stanford took control of the game, posting an early 15-4 lead, weathered a Cal run that cut the lead to 17-10, and overcame poor shooting to take a 33-18 advantage into halftime.

Like many contests in the Pac-10 (now called Pac-12) Conference, Stanford's match against Cal was physical. In watching the game on television, I was served with a close-up view of the action, which CSNBA's producers eagerly replayed again and again.

Early in the second half, the banging bodies began to take their toll. Nneka injured her shoulder and left the game. Chiney was smacked in the face and played through the pain. Kayla took a shot to the mouth. Mary Murphy, the color commentator for CSNBA, did not find the play problematic. In fact, of Cal's Talia Campbell, who had been involved in the plays that caused both Ogwumike injuries, she said, "Campbell loves to hit people and loves to tell you she loves to hit people." Stanford hit hardest on the scoreboard and won the game, 78-45. Yet the physical intensity of the game, and its impact on her players' health, was not lost on Coach VanDerveer. Nneka soon developed headaches from her injury, which were concerning enough that VanDerveer canceled practice the next day.

"Playing Out of Their Mind": University of Arizona, January 6, 2011

When practices resumed, Nneka didn't participate in contact drills. It was hard to know whether her headaches were related to the shoulder injury suffered against Cal, but by the time the Cardinal played the University of Arizona four days later, she was back in the starting lineup.

Ushers in red coats checked tickets and directed guests to their seats. The cheer squad warmed up for their halftime routine, and the band whipped the crowd into a frenzy. I took a seat in a section reserved for guests of the coaches and athletic directors. A generous Stanford athletic department official had given me a ticket to sit there, affording me a unique opportunity to rub elbows with the team's most loyal fans.

Near the bench, I spotted Mel Murphy, a redshirt senior on the Stanford team, wiping up sweat from the floor. Sidelined by a knee injury, Mel had yet to participate in a game that season, but she was determined to do her part even if she could not help the team on the court.

Both teams struggled to score early. "We came out sluggish," VanDerveer later said, and in the locker room, she said she "let her team have it," singling out captains Jeanette Pohlen and Kayla Pedersen, imploring them to take the initiative.[3] As seniors, Pohlen and Pedersen were used to Coach VanDerveer's red-faced halftime speeches. "We can kind of tell at halftime when she's happy with us and when she's not," Jeannette told the press. "She knows our potential. We've shown the whole country what we can do. When we don't . . . show that same style of play, she can be hard on us. [But] if she wasn't getting on us, there would be a problem."

Something in VanDerveer's halftime speech worked, and in the second half Stanford made over 70 percent of the shots they took and won the game handily, 87-54.[4] In a postgame interview, Coach VanDerveer praised Pohlen and Pedersen for the way they heeded her counsel: "I think it just shows what kind of leaders they are. I can get on them and they [can] respond in a positive way." Nneka scored twenty-four points and showed no visible effects from the injuries sustained at Cal.

After the game, Arizona's Coach Niya Butts acknowledged the role Stanford's size, strength, and ability played in the win in a begrudging tone. "When they're knocking down shots like that, there's not a lot you can do. The way they've been playing [lately] . . . they've been playing out of their mind."

"Eventually It Gets Demoralizing": Arizona State University, January 8, 2011

Arizona State University (ASU) came to town the following Saturday hoping to mimic Cal's approach to beat the Cardinal with physical play. The crowd roared loudest when Becca Tobin, a 6'4" forward for ASU, drew a foul for swinging her elbows, an act perceived to be so egregious that it stirred some of the generally reserved Maples fans out of their seats. One fan leaped to his feet and yelled, "That's unnecessary roughness, ref!"

Many conference opponents brought an intense, physical brand of play to Maples and even when the final scores were not close, the games were hard-fought contests to the bitter end. But when an opponent knew from the outset that they were overmatched, it seemed that they played even more physically. It was almost as if they felt that they had no other answer, no way to match the level of Stanford's talent, so they chose physicality as their primary strategy. Tobin's elbows weren't even half of it; the bodies of players for both teams rammed frequently, leading to countless hard falls on the Maples hardwood.

Nothing could stop Stanford, though, and the Cardinal won its twelfth game, 82-35. After the game, ASU coach Charli Turner Thorne, who had played for Coach VanDerveer at Stanford in the 1980s, lamented, "Stanford has it rolling . . . Eventually it gets demoralizing."

"It's More Mental Than Physical"

During the team's final practice before playing UCLA, Stanford's most formidable challenger in the Pac-10, Coach VanDerveer stopped practice and spoke.

> Put yourself in their shoes. We beat them how many times last year? Three. And the year before? Three more. What about a year before that? We lost once to them down there? They are *tiiiiired* of Stanford. These are all the same players. They are ranked in the top ten, but they haven't beaten us. They are gonna come in here and want to *kiiiiiick yooooour ass*! They are going to want it bad, just like DePaul wanted it bad, just like Stanford wanted it bad against Connecticut. You have to be ready. It's more mental than it is physical. You have to be *ready!*

The players sprang to their feet and bellowed, "Let's go CARD!" sending an echo high into the empty rafters. Then Coach VanDerveer reminded her starters, whose brows were dripping in sweat, "Look up there." She pointed to the banners on the Maples wall that catalogued Stanford's many conference championships. "*They* want what you have. Don't let that happen!"

University of California, Los Angeles, January 20, 2011

Altogether 4,300 fans filed into Maples to take in the Bruin-Cardinal clash. Mel was set to return to her first game action of the season. She had struggled through various injuries throughout her career—basketball had forced her into enduring four surgeries, including once to fix a torn anterior cruciate ligament (ACL) and another to fix a microfracture—and it had been a long road back from her latest knee injury, so when she made a huge steal at the end of the first half, I was among the first to stand for the ovation.

Despite the fact that both teams were ranked in the top ten, and despite the fact that UCLA's 2009–2010 record suggested that they had the firepower to challenge Stanford for conference supremacy, there was no television broadcast of the game, not even by the regional cable network, CSNBA. If the same game had pitted two men's teams in the top ten, it would have undoubtedly been on national TV.

Like so many games that year, Stanford dominated inside and outside the paint, showing an impressive balance of talent and skill from "bigs" and "smalls" alike. The final score was 64-38. Kayla had her best game since suffering her concussion, finishing the game with eighteen points and ten rebounds. Once again, the contest never really felt very close.

"Pushing Through Injuries"

Mel was a fan favorite but nearly every Stanford player had dealt with a knee, ankle, or some other kind of injury. A few, like Kayla, had suffered concussions too. Tears to the ACL are particularly problematic for women's basketball players, with research suggesting that playing basketball is riskier for the knees of female basketball players than it is for males.[5] For some, injuries developed into chronic conditions too. Jeannette, for example, sat out practices during "dead week" to rest her back, which often ailed her. One former Stanford star, Jayne Appel, who had graduated and gone on to play professionally, told me that she had "been pushing through injuries" since the end of her junior year at Stanford and that she had undergone two surgeries and immersed herself daily in ice baths to curtail inflammation. But Appel said cheerfully, it was "mind over matter" that helped her stay motivated to do the necessary rehabilitation.

The risk of injury was ever present and so always on the minds of the coaches, too. When I first began observing the Stanford team, I naively assumed that the coaches took the starters out of the game when they had a sizeable lead because they wanted to make sure that every player had a chance to play. I imagined, in a rather sexist way I must admit, that the coaches viewed broad participation and having a good time as just as important as victory and performance. At that point, I did not see the team as a big-time team, having been socialized in my own youth to see women's sports as less than that. But I later realized that I was failing to adequately recognize their big-time status and the high stakes associated with it. As the season progressed and I began to witness the physical cost of Stanford's dominance, I realized that the Stanford coaches often took the starters out of the game for a very different reason: they wanted to make sure their star players didn't get hurt and that they'd be as healthy as possible to compete in postseason play.

The injury risk to star players was enough of a coaching concern that they adopted a special training protocol for star players in practices. During the middle of conference play, the team's best players were not subjected to the same drills in practices as the second-string players because the coaches were wary of overworking them, which could increase their injury risk. Instead, they wanted to save them for the games and so allowed them to do the less laborious work of shooting around during Friday practices instead of going through a full practice regimen. Coach Kelsey told me, "We simply can't afford to have Nneka or Kayla get hurt."

"We Don't Want Our Players Peeing Down Their Legs": University of Washington, February 12, 2011

It was more business as usual when the Washington Huskies flew to the farm, on February 12. Before the game, Coach Kelsey addressed Stanford fans during a pre-game Chalk Talk inside Kissick Auditorium. Stanford's most curious and loyal fans gathered to see videos of Stanford's upcoming opposition, including game highlights and details regarding players' personal information and pertinent statistics. Kissick Chalk Talks were rather intimate gatherings, limited to roughly fifty fans, offering Stanford's fans a chance to explore the coaches' tactics and strategy and take an inside look at how the team was run. I felt lucky to get a seat myself.

One fan asked Coach Kelsey what fans could expect from the matchups against Washington. "We don't try to change much for each opponent," she answered. "We just try to tweak things." But Coach Kelsey paused and changed her tone to add that there had been many illegal screens in Stanford's first meeting against Washington and that she didn't think the referees called the "very physical" game fairly. (An illegal screen is when a player fails to stand her ground properly when attempting to block an opponent's path.) "[But] you can't worry about the refs," she said, pivoting back to an earlier point. "No matter what you do, they are going to be terrible!" The fans laughed and clapped in appreciation of the coach's humor. An older fan raised her hand to ask how the staff prepared the players for the physicality. "We don't want our players peeing down their legs," Coach Kelsey responded, her piercing brown eyes darting to the door as if she resented the question. She said the coaches wanted to make sure the players were prepared for all opponents, regardless of their size or aggression. In the case of Washington, she said, that meant preparing for Regina Rogers, the Huskies' biggest big. "She's twice as big as [6'5"] Sarah Boothe." Coach Kelsey smiled and declared playfully that Rogers was a "hefty girl."

Coach Kelsey stood over six feet so perceptions about who was big or hefty seemed relative in this sports subculture where even women who were 5'9" or 5'10" could be considered small or little. Curiously, women's college basketball players' weights were considered taboo, as I learned when I studied the teams' media guides. In Stanford's guide, the weights and heights of male college basketball were listed for the media whereas only women's heights were listed. Upon further examination, I could find women's weights listed neither on the Stanford Athletics Website nor on several popular websites devoted to covering women's basketball. Discussions of weight were apparently off limits.

In the early stages of the game, Washington kept the score close as Stanford's shooters started cold. Lindy was a lone bright spot. She played defense aggressively and dove to the floor for several loose balls, energizing the team and helping to build a six-point halftime lead, 24-18.

Once again, the contest was physical, but the referees were "letting 'em play," choosing not to call too many fouls. That is until the second half when they began to crack down, finally giving Coach Kelsey what she wanted.

However when Nneka collected her fourth foul, the Stanford faithful gasped. "Terrible game, ref!" one yelled bluntly. Jeannette made her first three-pointer of the game, but a referee blew his whistle and cancelled the shot. When she was smacked on a driving layup and a referee called a foul against her defender, Jeannette's father, who attended many Stanford games, yelled from the stands, "Finally!" with no small hint of sarcasm.

Stanford managed to hold on to record a 62-52 win. As usual, the Ogwumike sisters led the team with their scoring inside, combining for forty-three points and nineteen rebounds. Washington's coach, Tia Jackson, who had at one time been an assistant to Coach VanDerveer, was pleased with her team's effort, even in defeat, saying she "couldn't be prouder" of "the way they battled and competed." Her comments reflected the kind of moral victory that many Stanford opponents seemed happy to live with even if it required playing a bruising style of play to get it. After the game, Coach Tucker told me that the "very physical . . . battle . . . was what we expected" and "we have to be physical back."

"Your Big Dogs Have to Show Up": University of California, Los Angeles, February 20, 2011

In late February, Stanford played road matches against UCLA and USC but not before ESPN sent a camera crew to the farm to film a Cardinal practice. The crew of four men moved their cameras around the court with speed and precision, carefully framing jump shots by Jeannette, layups by Nneka or Chiney, and passes by Toni. I got to talking with the crew and asked them why they had been sent. "To get shots we can use in the Final Four," one member replied. "What happens if Stanford doesn't make it?" I asked, adding that there was no guarantee Stanford, or any other team for that matter, would make it that far. "Then we don't use the footage," another replied. "But," he continued, "we are confident *Stanford* will make it." I asked, "Did ESPN also send crews for men's teams and if so, which teams were they similarly confident would make the men's final four?" "No," a crew member answered. "There's no way of knowing who the men's teams will be, and it would cost too much to produce such footage for so many contenders. Anyway," he said, "a far greater percentage of the men's games are televised so we already have plenty of in-game footage to work with."

I made the trip to Los Angeles to see Stanford beat the USC Trojans, 78-64. Nneka sprained her ankle in that game, so Jos entered the starting lineup against UCLA as her replacement.

Once again, the Cardinal versus Bruin matchup was framed as a battle between conference title and NCAA title contenders. Stanford carried a perfect conference record into the UCLA game and the Bruins had only lost in conference play once themselves. Stanford entered the game with the number three ranking in the national polls, and UCLA clung to number nine. The match was held on a Sunday, which allowed a larger Los Angeles crowd to file in, and with the Pac-10 conference title hanging in the balance, this gave the game an added level of intensity. If the Bruins won, the title might be shared with the Cardinal. If Stanford won, they would win the conference outright for the seventh year in a row. UCLA head coach Nikki Caldwell felt the weight of the moment, telling her players before the game, "If you want to play with the big dogs, your big dogs have to show up. Stanford has done it over the years."

Over half the Pauley Pavilion seats were filled: 6,700 people in an arena that could hold 13,000. The game began with back-and-forth play. UCLA's Darxia Morris led the Bruins and Stanford enjoying balanced scoring in Nneka's absence. Toni ran the offense and showed just what ESPN

HoopGurlz meant when it called her crossover "deadly." Chiney filled her sister's void in the paint. In the game's first thirteen minutes, the two freshmen each tallied eleven points. Still, UCLA was making Stanford look much less dominant than they been all season, keeping the score close. At half, the score was tied, 28-28.

Toward the end of the first half, Mel advanced the ball up the court casually as the clock wound down. When Stanford failed to get off a good shot, Coach VanDerveer roared, gestured Mel to her side, and unloaded an earful. Although I could not make out what VanDerveer said, her gesticulations suggested that she was livid. VanDerveer often told players that while she could tolerate "physical mistakes"—e.g., falling down, missing a shot—she would not accept "mental" mistakes, especially from veteran players who "should know better" like Mel. Mel had thick skin, but I couldn't help but feel personally for her. If Mel had mistaken how much time was left on the clock, it seemed unfortunate that one mistake would end up costing her playing time in the second half but that is exactly what happened. There was a slim margin for error with Coach VanDerveer.

After halftime, Stanford gradually stretched its lead, continuing to ride the strong inside play of Chiney and the confident ball-handling of Toni. UCLA was not at all intimidated, but for everything the Bruins threw out, the Cardinal had an answer. When UCLA used its full court press to create turnovers, Stanford "broke the press" and converted transition baskets. The Cardinal pulled away and outscored the Bruins 39-25 in the second half, collecting another conference victory, 67-53, and securing at least a share of the Pac-10 crown.

"How Are You Hurtin' 'em?"
University of California, March 3, 2011

Stanford returned home to host Cal, seeking to close out an undefeated conference campaign against their longtime rival. Six thousand fans were in attendance, representing the biggest Maples crowd since the UCONN game. Stanford was now 27-2 on the season, and Cal, who was 15-12 overall and just 7-10 in conference play, was a heavy underdog looking to salvage a rather forgettable season. You could feel the tension in the air, and the presence of both the Cal and Stanford bands only served to thicken it.

Nneka was back in the lineup, having recovered from the ankle injury she suffered against USC. Cal started the game strong, playing with a level of inspiration that masked their season's struggles. The Bears even took an early lead, 13-9, and were controlling the pace of play. Cal's Rachelle Frederico hit two three pointers to push the lead to 19-16, and though Stanford regained the lead, 38-33 by halftime, Cal Coach Joanne Boyle later said she was "proud" of her team "for the way we came out."

Coach VanDerveer invited me into the locker room to hear her halftime speech. It was an opportunity that I had hoped she might offer at some point during the season, but I had never pressed the issue, especially at this later stage in the season, when I was particularly conscious not to get in the team's way. I did not want to do anything that might compromise their efforts to accomplish their goals.

After one practice, though, Coach Tucker told me that seeing Coach VanDerveer in the locker room would expose me to one of her "huge strengths . . . that people do not see,"[6] so I was intrigued to see VanDerveer "in her element," when she got her chance to perform. I fumbled with my voice recorder as I followed the team into the locker room. Somehow I managed to find the Record button, and I looked up to see Coach VanDerveer taking a deep breath to draw strength.

> **Coach VanDerveer:** Alright guys . . . the number one thing is being aggressive. We are not close enough to them . . . We are just being *punished* right now by their perimeter people. Kayla, how many fouls do you have? You're not close enough to people. They are shooting in your face. To play the three, Kayla, you have to get up on them! . . . Toni, I thought you did a good job. But again, how many fouls do you have?
>
> **Coach Paye:** One.
>
> **Coach VanDerveer:** Jeannette, you got that one . . . I am glad you didn't get another one. You guys you have to come out and *gooooo*! You're just sleepwalking defensively. The *nuuuumber* one thing is being aggressive. Their perimeter people are doing the damage. On the high on-ball screen, we are trapping. So that means you're going to have trap and rotate.
>
> [Coach VanDerveer begins drawing Xs and Os on an erasable whiteboard.]
>
> **Coach VanDerveer:** So when they're setting screens here, you have to get out, you have to be aggressive in this trap . . . Caldwell [Cal center Talia] can't step out and hit anything . . . so be aggressive and get [the ball] out of their guards' hands.
>
> **Coach Tucker:** The three perimeter players [Rachelle Federico, Lindsay Sherbert and Layshia Clarendon] have twenty-nine of their thirty-three points.
>
> **Coach Kelsey:** C'mon now!

[A pause, and the coaches take a brief moment to quietly discuss matters among themselves.]

Coach VanDerveer: So, you guys . . . we can only play people on the perimeter who we have confidence that they are going to play defense. Alright? Jeannette will play defense, Toni, you're working on your defense. Lindy, you gotta work harder. Mel, if you come in you got to work hard defensively. Get your hands active. Mikaela Ruef, I've got to know that you're gonna get in your stance and play defense. Chiney, play defense, alright? You could go out on a perimeter player. You could switch with Kayla, alright? So you'd be chasing people and you know you can guard people out there. That might be something we do at the beginning of the second half. Jos, I like your defense on the post. Nneka do you have any fouls?

Nneka: No.

Coach VanDerveer: Again, it's not about fouling, it's just [that you are too] passive. The ball is going where they want it to. They're making shots. [If] you're here, then you got to be up into 'em. The whole key for me is for people defensively being aggressive. Toni, get in the passing lane and get a steal. Jeannette, get a steal. You've got to get deflections and get a lot more active defensively. Maybe we'll switch it. Maybe we'll put you . . . put Chiney on Sherbert [Cal player Lindsay]. Put Kayla on one of their post players. Right now, we are *nooooot* getting the job done. It's *alllllll* about defense.

[All of a sudden, Coach VanDerveer's stops, and she seems to realize that her tone is overly critical, and that her players might need some positive motivation.]

Coach VanDerveer: We've had good chances. Toni had a nice layup. Lindy, nice layup. Goin' inside.

[Coach VanDerveer's tone changes back again.]

Coach VanDerveer: Eliminate silly [mental] mistakes. We cannot have moving screens. We cannot have three seconds,* things like that. You must box out. And then *goooo* [on the fastbreak]. Rama [N'Diaye] cannot run. The game is [too] slow. We're going to do 3 [a defensive play] and we've got to be aggressive in that. And you've got to move in that if we go 3. If we go with 2, you've got to really move and know who you're taking. And then we have to rebound. So, look to mix up our defenses a little bit. We might be going 3, we might be going 2. We'll start the people who started the beginning of the game, but you *cannnnot* start that way [in the second half]. You have to be much more active.

---

* A "three in the key" violation is called when a player does not leave the painted area near the basket within three seconds after entering it.

Kayla, you've got to help a lot more. Be much more active. Be much more aggressive. They know our stuff inside and out. It's not gonna be about *what* we're running. It's about *how* we run stuff. We could run Easy [an offensive play], [but] how were they playing [it]?"

[Coach VanDerveer turns to the assistant coaches.]

Other coaches: Soft. Way off.

[Coach VanDerveer raises her voice to a higher decibel.]

Coach VanDerveer: Be a screener and be a rebounder! Make 'em pay for leaving you. Be a screener so then someone else gets a shot. Like Jeannette. And *naaaail* somebody on a screen, legally.

[Coach VanDerveer turns to face Nneka.]

Coach VanDerveer: How are they playing you?

Nneka: They started playing me tight.

Coach VanDerveer: Then go to the basket. Rebound the hell out of it. And run on them. Kayla, how are they playing you?

Kayla: Tight.

Coach VanDerveer: Then let's get screens [for you] and get you on the block a little.

[Coach VanDerveer points at the dry erase board again.]

Coach VanDerveer: The problem is they're playing off of our fours and fives [power forward and center positions] so get people moving so you can curl. Or you could post and someone else is coming off the screens. We're running either Basic or . . . when the ball comes here, reverse the ball. Kayla . . . you've got to pass it back. You got to double screen for whoever is down there. Screen and move. Be much more active. Be ready to run 2. I can't see them being in a zone when . . . Who has number 9 instead of number 10 . . . look at this! Step up and guard people! Jeannette can only guard one of 'em! Lou, you got to be aggressive. Toni, you've got to be aggressive. I'm gonna put Chiney on one of 'em. You've got Sherbert. Number 32. Freshman. Three-point shooter. Guard her. Guard her! Kayla, if you're on her, you've got to guard her. She's been wide open. You guys are absolutely *sleepwalking* defensively!

Coach VanDerveer: Now offensively, they are gambling off of people. They're on Jeannette, but she's still hurtin' 'em. What's Jeannette got?

Coach Paye: Eleven points. Four for four.

Coach VanDerveer: So, Jeannette's hurtin' 'em. Kayla, are you hurtin' 'em? *How* are you hurtin' 'em? How many O-boards we got? How many O-boards we got, period?

Coach Paye: Seven.

Coach VanDerveer: How many times did we finish on those? Break it down for me. Who's scoring?

Coach Paye: For us?

Coach VanDerveer: Yes.

Coach Paye: Jeannette's got eleven. Nneka's got ten. Kayla's got six. Toni and Sarah Boothe have four. And Chiney has two.

Coach VanDerveer: Alright, so Chiney you gotta help us more on the O-boards. Screen and get people open. How many free throws have we got?

Coach Paye: Five for eight.

Coach VanDerveer: It's all about guarding people. And this is what's coming [in the NCAA Tournament]. I'm glad to see this. You gotta get out on people and guard people. If you can't do that and you're not committed to that, we're not going anywhere. Forget about beating Cal. So [what if] they're hot for one half? So, you decide. Jeannette, who do you want to guard? Who do you want to shut down? Who is the most important person for us again?

[Coach VanDerveer turns to Coach Tucker.]

Coach VanDerveer: You want Jeannette on number 23 [Cal's Layshia Clarendon]?

Coach Tucker: Yep.

Coach VanDerveer: Alright you guard her. She's *done*. So this means that Lindy, you have number 3. Chiney, you're on number 32 [Lindsay Sherbert]. So, you don't let her get the ball. Jeannette was working hard at that. Forget about helping in the post. Show your numbers. Be aggressive. Get deflections. Get the ball. We're going *doooown* the court! . . . Be ready to switch things up. This is about your pride. They are shooting in your *faaaace*. This is what I talked about in practice. *You cannnnnnnot come into a fight and wait to get a bloody nose* . . . Well, it's gushing right now. You have to come out and be aggressive! Let's *gooooooooooooo!*

Everyone gathered around VanDerveer and lifted a hand into the air. Suddenly, in unison they shouted, "Together!" unleashing a boisterous echo of camaraderie and determination that reverberated off the locker room walls. The players darted into the cold concrete tunnel and back to the bright lights of Maples Pavilion. I walked behind them, slowly, reflecting on the intense but sharply focused words of one of the winningest coaches in college basketball history. Watching Coach VanDerveer hold court in the locker room was like watching an army general command the attention of her soldiers. The players seemed mesmerized too, locked on to her every word.

Heeding VanDerveer's call and rising to meet the challenge, Kayla scored the second half's first bucket and then made a steal and converted a transition layup. Her passionate play lit a fire under her teammates, and before long Stanford had the lead, 46-33, and some breathing room. At the first television timeout of the second half, the Cal band began to play their fight song, "Fight for California," and their cheerleaders riled up the Bear fans in attendance. The Stanford band retorted with their perennial favorite, "All Right Now," by Free, the English rock band. With precise offensive passing and a flustering defensive swarm, Stanford extended the lead. Toni made a steal and raced the court for another fast-break layup, putting Stanford up by fifteen points, 61-46, with just under six minutes left. She later knocked in four more beautiful shots, adding to the Cardinal lead. Coach VanDerveer's mental challenges, and the gravity of her halftime speech, were working.

It was senior night, the final regular season game and a chance for the Stanford fans to pay tribute to the players whose NCAA eligibility had run its course. Kayla had done just as her coach had asked in the second half so even after she picked up her fourth foul, Coach VanDerveer left her in the game, honoring her with a privilege she would not have enjoyed in a regular game. The Cal players enjoyed no such privileges; when one of them fouled out of the game and was forced to take a seat next to her teammates, the rowdy Stanford student section counted each footstep to the bench. "Left! Right! Left! Right! Left! Right!" Then, as the player neared her seat, the crowd joined together to yell ferociously, "Siiiiiiiiiit down!"

Stanford's reserves saw their first playing time in the last minute and a half of the game. Kayla exited with just over one minute left in the game, awash in cheers from the now-standing Stanford faithful. Fellow senior Ashley Cimino entered the game to replace her and delivered some solid defense on the wing. Hannah Donaghe, who had been sidelined by a torn ACL all season, took to the court too. Donaghe's knee had not yet fully healed, though, so she stayed close enough to the bench to make sure she didn't further injure it. In effect, this meant that Stanford played out the last twenty-five seconds of the game with just four players, but it also meant that Donaghe could be honored for her service to the team.

The final score was 75-51, another lopsided victory in a game that had begun under very different terms. Stanford had assured themselves of a perfect

Pac-10 conference record as well as yet another conference championship to hang on the Maples wall. It also almost guaranteed a top seed in the upcoming Pac-10 tournament. After the game, Cal's Federico approached the Cardinal team huddle and said, "Go win a national championship."

"We Need a Break. We're Taking It."

With their regular season complete, the Cardinal found themselves worn thin. "We're taking three days off," Coach VanDerveer told the press. "Our team earned it; we need it. We barely had Christmas. I don't even remember it. We've been going, going, going. We need a break. We're taking it." It would be the team's longest hiatus from practice since November.

"Everyone Is a Capable Player. Everybody's Fearless": University of California, Los Angeles, March 12, 2011 (Pac-10 Tournament)

Like all Pac-10 contests, Stanford's matchups in the Pac-10 Tournament were highly physical. But the Pac-10's conference championship games were held in Staples Center in Los Angeles, where the NBA's LA Lakers and LA Clippers and the WNBA LA Sparks play their home games, adding to the pageantry and pressure that the players must have felt on a visceral level. Stanford beat the University of Arizona 100-71 in the semifinal of the tournament, largely the result of tremendous performances by the Ogwumike sisters (32 points and 10 rebounds for Nneka, and 21 points and 13 rebounds for Chiney) and another well-rounded stat-line delivered by Kayla: 16 points, 7 assists, and 6 rebounds. On the other side of the tournament bracket, Cal upset ASU in the quarterfinal to advance to the semifinal against UCLA, but lost there, 63-50, setting up a third meeting of the season between Stanford and UCLA in the tournament final. By then, Stanford was 28-2 and UCLA was 27-3, with two of UCLA's three losses on the year coming at the hands of the Cardinal. To further dramatize the meeting, play-by-play man Jim Watson of Comcast SportsNet said he saw the game as a chance for UCLA to finally "step out of the shadow of the Stanford tree."

At first it seemed that the Bruins had, frustrating the Cardinal and keeping the game close. At one point, UCLA even took a one-point lead, 19-18. But then UCLA's Darxia Morris hit a jumper and Coach VanDerveer called a time out. The Cardinal had gone cold, recording just one field goal in a six-minute span. Stanford's frustration seemed to climax when Kayla elbowed

UCLA's Jasmine Dixon in the face and for a moment the officials questioned whether her foul had been intentional and therefore flagrant. (After careful review, they determined that it was not.) For the last shot of the half, Kayla heaved up an off-balance three-point shot but it did not connect.

Stanford entered the locker room with its lowest first-half point total of the year, twenty-one, and trailing by nine points. It was just the third halftime that Stanford had trailed all year, and they had lost both previous games. For the first time all season, I noticed Stanford players bickering amongst themselves. On social media, a few UCLA fans began tweeting #Itshappening, as if to try and will an upset.

But in the second half, Stanford ground out yet another win, overcoming physical and psychological adversity once more. Kayla, Nneka and Chiney grabbed offensive rebounds with authority, dropped in tough and contested "put back" baskets, and made crucial free throws. UCLA was trying to take advantage of the Stanford bigs by playing pick and roll and forcing larger, less mobile players to defend smaller, more agile guards on the perimeter of the key in open space. This helped UCLA get good looks at the basket and make short-range, pull-up jumpers. But Kayla and Nneka responded with inside shots to cut into UCLA's lead, first at 36-29, and then, when Jeannette hit her first three pointer of the game, to 38-32. When Toni stole the ball, blazed court for an easy layup, and cut the UCLA advantage to three, 40-37, CSNBA's Watson called her a gamechanger.

Something *had* happened at halftime. To CSNBA's Leslie, it was credit due to Coach VanDerveer and the inspirational halftime speeches that had made her famous: "Tara got 'em in the locker room and got 'em right." It helped that UCLA's defensive strategy was no longer working: they could not contain the Ogwumike sisters inside. Kayla missed a short-range shot, but Nneka converted a put-back layup while drawing a foul to set up a three-point play. When she made the free throw, Stanford took back the lead, 47-46. On the play Nneka forced Dixon to commit her fourth foul, sending the UCLA star to the bench. Without Dixon inside the paint, the Ogwumike sisters were relatively uncontested on the boards, helping Stanford regain control of ball possession and thus the game.

Then Toni made two steals and two fastbreak buckets and put Stanford up by three, 51-48. When she nailed a three-pointer from the corner, a shot in which the ball bounced four times on the rim before falling, she prompted Watson to wail, "Toni Kokenis didn't start the game, but she may be the headline in the newspaper in the morning!" As if on cue, Kokenis hit another three to drive the Cardinal lead to nine, 57-48. Stanford made a series of free throws as the clock ran out and won the game, 64-55.

On a team of superstar upperclasswomen, it was a freshman who had saved the day.

The team was elated, donning newly minted Conference Champion hats and cutting pieces of the net as mementos of their championship. After the game, Coach VanDerveer told a CSNBA reporter that she was "proud" of how her players had "stepped up," an expression that evoked mental toughness and confidence as much as physical assertiveness. The reporter then approached Kayla and asked, "It seems like, with this team, anyone can step in at any time . . . What is it about this team?" The senior captain echoed her coach's emphasis on the mental strength that was required to win in the big time: "Everyone is a capable player," Kayla said, "Everybody's fearless."

"I Need Big Mamas Inside"

Kayla's explanation would eventually shape my own understanding of what it meant for women to buy into the big time of college basketball with their bodies—and with their minds. Big-time women athletes had to physically fight but they also had to understand the risks of fighting, and they had to be fearless, courageous, mentally tough, and psychologically immune to the pain that was an unavoidable part of this collision sport. No one forced these players to play big-time college basketball and assume these risks, and yet decisions to play were made time and time again by athletes like these who knew that they wanted to become more capable and more fearless no matter the cost.

If triumphalism, injury risk, and psychological pressure were ever-present aspects of big-time women's basketball, so too were a collective solidarity aimed at victory and with it the potential to flip these challenges on their head and choose to use big-time sports participation to strengthen one's physical and mental toughness and strengthen oneself for life's future challenges.

Many players stayed after practice was officially over and took the opportunity to help each other get better. Jos worked with Michaela on the art of faking, stepping to one side, and choosing between a jump shot or a drive the ball to hoop. Nneka helped Toni with her jump shot and her little sister with rebounding technique. Jeannette trained with Coach Tucker or Coach Paye on her ability to "post up" down low. These players understood the risks involved by putting their bodies on the line, and yet their trust in their coaches, and the prospect of a victory, seemed enough to make most forget. This potential for individual growth and collective unity became clearer to me as Stanford began its postseason campaign and geared up for the NCAA Tournament.

Basketball is a game of high energy, full of stops and starts, jumping and cutting, so it was no surprise to hear VanDerveer speak of fatigue after conference play concluded. Stanford's games were intense, hard-fought, and physical. The team endured because they were well-coached, disciplined, and had the size, versatility, and player depth to offset injuries.

Perhaps size (both height and girth) matters more in basketball than in other sports since the height of the hoop is by convention set at ten feet, giving taller players an easier chance to score, rebound, and block shots, and because space is limited in the area close to the basket called the paint, where shots are generally easier to make. Coaches customarily counsel players to exploit matchups that give their team an advantage. If, for example, a coach determines that one of her offensive players is quicker than the opponent guarding her and that as a result that player can easily go around that defender and get closer to the hoop for an easier shot, they will set up plays that will isolate the slower defender and put her "on an island." So if a taller player can perform as well as a shorter player, the taller player will routinely be picked to play because they present more matchup problems. College teams that play man-to-man defense follow one of two protocols—they either "switch" or they "stay on their man" when a screen is set. Coach VanDerveer generally asked her players to talk to each other and only switch on "likes." This meant that Stanford's 6'5" Sarah Boothe would not switch on certain opponents, especially those who were smaller in size and quicker, in part because a smaller Stanford defender wouldn't be able to defend the player that Boothe had previously been guarding.

When it came to size, Coach VanDerveer was no sentimentalist. She often said, "You can't teach height," and she had no problem announcing to the entire team that this or that player was big and therefore could not defend a guard. Coach VanDerveer seemed to have little time for tiptoeing around the issue of body size; she wanted her bigs to use what they had, saying, "I need big mamas inside."

Being a big mama meant making the most of one's size and being assertive if not aggressive with one's body. Coach VanDerveer often lamented in press interviews that her team started out games "a little casual" or the team "wasn't as aggressive" as they "needed to be early in the game." It sometimes seemed as if she expected her players to play like the Tesla Roadsters made up the street from Stanford, 0 to 60 in two seconds or less. She certainly expected her most talented and consistent players to take charge and to set the tone for the younger players. As talented as superstars like Nneka were, it could sometimes appear to the uninitiated as if her success required little effort and that it was athleticism rather than skill-building that carried her to stardom. In temperament, the Cardinal forward could also seem relatively reserved, which could be misperceived as a lack of fire, even, sometimes by her own coaches.

And yet Coach VanDerveer refused to let her star player rest on her laurels, make excuses, or boast about her abilities. Instead, she made it clear that she was determined to help Nneka become a humble fighter, a competitor, and a winner, someone who could impose her presence on her opponents and, indeed, on the game itself. Impressively, her star player followed her lead, worked tirelessly in practice, and reaped the rewards. In the month of January Nneka was named Pac-10 Player of the Week for her performances against the Arizona schools and then given the award again for her work against the Washington schools. After the team's rout of WSU in early February, Nneka told reporters, "I think . . . our best quality is we don't have an arrogant air about ourselves. We don't walk in and say, 'Oh, we're Stanford, let's just play, things will work for us.' When we're not playing or performing, it's [because of] a lack of concentration and focus."

"How the Game Should Be Played"

As important as size and assertiveness were, the coaches put just as much emphasis on consistency. There was a rational sensibility to Coach VanDerveer's passionate drive to always emerge victorious. It was a sense that became clearer to me the longer I bore witness to the efficiency of her team's practices. It was as if Coach VanDerveer lived by the mantra "Leave no stone unturned" or as if such efficiency in training represented a kind of flower blooming before her eyes. In her 1997 memoir, VanDerveer recalled the "timed, quick, and efficient" quality of Coach Bob Knight's practices at the University of Indiana, which she had observed as a young coach. She remembered that every Hoosier practice was "very well-organized" and "looked the same," with "players hustl[ing] from one drill to the next." Then she contrasted Knight's practices with the practices of other coaches and connected a line from Knight's practices to her own team's practices at Stanford.

> I've seen other coaches' practices, and you see one guy pulling down another guy's shorts. Forget that at Indiana. It was always business. There was discipline, accountability . . . Hearing the same things from Knight over and over, day after day, and watching, watching, watching . . . My brain formed patterns

for how the game should be played. My practices today are very similar to what I saw when I was 20 years old at Indiana.[7]

Every Stanford practice that I watched was as swift, efficient, and as well-planned as a factory assembly line, and every player's movements within it just as carefully choreographed. The coaches, each of whom brought specialized knowledge of basketball, were in this sense not unlike Henry Ford's early factory managers, who had read and applied the scientific management theories of the mechanical-engineer-turned-management-consultant Frederick Taylor.[8]

Even the shorthand language Stanford used illustrated the business precision of their practices and game strategy. When Coach VanDerveer talked about an offensive play, she might yell, "We're not running Tandem here! If there's nothing there, you can run Easy or Open. C'mon RED! You have to communicate!" *Red*, taken from the Cardinal red uniforms, symbolized the university and its athletic teams, and was also used to denote a particular practice squad to which a player belonged. *Easy* and *Open* were names for offensive plays and served as shorthand for in-game action when time for breathing or speaking was in short supply. The team ran many offensive and defensive plays, with each one amounting to a team trade secret and of great value to these business managers and their subordinates. Their product may not have been an automobile but rather a finely tuned basketball team and its entertaining performance, but the value of the business enterprise—and the precision needed to create it—was just as clear, nonetheless. This shorthand protected team secrets and kept the business strong in the entertainment marketplace.

"Pop 'em in the Mouth"

The business of big-time college basketball valued efficient practices, but the same efficiency required speed and size, which in combination, and in a tightly constrained space like a basketball, could also lead to pain, injury, or psychological struggle. Some hardcore sportspeople tend to say that pain, injury, or psychological struggle are "just part of the game", while others insist that they are the unacceptable collateral damage of a sports culture that can chew up its finest athletes.

Stanford coaches encouraged physical contact in practices and sometimes even showed little sympathy for its consequences, but it was not as if the coaches saw their players as replaceable machines whose bodies—or lives—did not matter. In fact, nothing could have been farther from the truth.

They cared deeply for their charges. Still their time with the players during practice was limited by NCAA rules, and there was always work to be done with the players who were healthy so it would have been a waste of that limited time to stop practice for one player's concerns even if it were a serious injury. In times of reflection, the Stanford coaches lamented the physical sacrifice, preferring to imagine the women's game as defined by finesse rather than physicality or to pine for a future in which it were. After the season, for example, I asked Coach VanDerveer if the women's game was more physical in the 2010–2011 season than it had been in her earlier years as a coach. "I am not sure what to think about this one," she replied, then paused, and then suggested that there was indeed increasing physicality in the women's game and surmised that it might be the outcome of more men being coaches at the big-time women's level, with the caveat that this was not an "end-all be-all theory." "Sometimes when they can't beat you, they want to beat you up . . . that's what they know." Finally, she called the games' increasing physicality—she dubbed it a "pop 'em in the mouth" strategy—"counterproductive" for the marketing of the sport. Coach Tucker agreed with Coach VanDerveer and said that "in a lot of ways the women's college game has mimicked the men's game," that "a physical basketball game does not favor women's basketball," and that it "takes away from the flow, movement, and finesse of the game." She explained that it was "a trickle-down effect" too in that the physicality of the men's and women's professional games put greater pressure on college women to do the same. She further explained that the process was complicated due to the game's mediated nature, especially during the postseason.

Coach Tucker: The physicality becomes more pronounced then [during the college postseason] because they [the referees] blow the whistle less because the games are on TV.

Author: Are referees told to blow the whistle less?

Coach Tucker: They won't admit that.

Author: But you are sure of that?

Coach Tucker: Oh, absolutely. The things they are calling in November, December, January . . . There are no [such] calls in the tournament. They don't want it to become a free-throw contest.

Author: Will [TV] ratings be lower?

Coach Tucker: Yeah. I think that when [7'1", 325 lbs] Shaq [Shaquille O'Neal] came into the NBA, he was the first real big guy, and he was huge, and so everyone else in the NBA needed a big guy. Not a skill guy, just a big guy to guard Shaq. So they wanted these guys who were three hundred pounds [even if they] couldn't shoot past five feet . . . Everyone wanted a big guy. Now everyone wants a big girl. So it's a trend.[9]

"Gambling with the Body"

Had the commercialization of the women's game—and thus its transformation into the big time—led to an increasingly blurry line between playing tough and playing without due concern for the human body? It was easy to see a connection between the physicality of women's college basketball today and the mediated big time since the stakes were higher than ever before. There was simply more to play for: TV exposure, potential pro contracts, status.

Still much of this reality of women's college basketball remains taboo and shrouded in the mystery created by a sports culture that will not openly discuss the size or strength of women's bodies. In women's college basketball, for example, television announcers rarely talk about the size of the players' bodies—at least not as much as they talk about it in men's basketball. This may have some impact on the ratings for the games too because sportscasters in men's college basketball often emphasize the large size and significant strength of players' bodies and the collisions between them while that kind of conversation is considered taboo in the women's game. It may also be the case that American's general gender biases still prevent them from seeing much value in women playing sports in such a physical way.

In recent years, sportscasters have euphemistically referred to this phenomenon as the "physicality" of sports. This euphemism is especially employed during college football broadcasts, as a replacement term for "violence" or "brutality" since using this tamer term sidesteps the compulsion to judge the act as violent, but the term "physicality" is also used in women's basketball, although based on my own observations, much less often than in football. It seems that what Oriard calls "the dramatic confrontation of artistry with violence," which are "both equally necessary" in the game of football, does not hold in women's basketball because those who promote the sport require that violence against women (by women) remain unmentionable.[10] Whatever it is called, the physicality of women's basketball reflects above all a great intensity and pressure to win and the corporal risk that is often accepted along with it.

One might think of playing big-time college sports that involve collision as buying in with the body. Young college athletes face a difficult choice about whether they should submit themselves to a big-time sports culture that elevates the collective value of winning games over the individual value of physical health. This seems a choice that long before the games begin requires considerable courage and fearlessness to make, the logical conclusion of a predicament that Pierre Bourdieu described when he noted that sports participation involves "gambling with the body itself."[11] And yet gamble they do, either because they are persuaded that the risk is justifiable or minimal, because they are otherwise convinced (brainwashed?) into believing that it is their best option in life, or because they genuinely appreciate that with this opportunity to play in the big time comes the chance to cultivate an individual sense of moral courage, physical fearlessness, and mental toughness. As these athletes play, and as they hope that injuries will not, too often or too severely, come their way, they also hope to learn important life lessons and earn a college degree in the process. For that final reason, it is a gamble that is perhaps easier to take at some universities than others.

"Who Do You Want in Your Bunker?"

Was women's basketball going the way of men's basketball or becoming as violent as college football? On the level of language, at least, it seemed like a relevant question. A quasi-militaristic language of battle was common among coaches and players of both genders and thus supported if not outright encouraged physical play. Coach VanDerveer was no outlier, having said, among other things, "Who do you want in your bunker?" "Who do you want to go to battle with?" "We need to nail people." "I loved boxing out. I played against boys and they hated when I would box them out."

Language, however, was just one part of the story. The language of battle colors the talk of basketball coaches as much as football coaches, and that is the case whether the games are played by males or females. And yet the received cultural wisdom is that if the financial stakes are higher in the big time, then men must be tougher than women. Basketball is, like football, a highly physical sport, with banging bodies and the ever-present risk of injury, including head injury. Young women who involve themselves in this sport know this, and many of them embrace it. But while the injuries of football—particularly, head injuries—beg for a deep public urgency,[12] that does not mean the injuries of basketball are insignificant and unworthy of similar concern.

Unfortunately, the routine stamp of the big time on men's basketball and not on women's basketball, as well as the comparatively more prevalent media attention that comes with that stamp, encourages men to see themselves as the tougher gender even as women voluntarily subject themselves to similar physicality and violence and just as valiantly endure it.

Violence in sports remains taboo, perhaps more so in women's sports because some want to believe that women are the nurturing gender and therefore incapable of hurting others. Historically and cross culturally, aggressiveness is encouraged in young males more than it is in young females.[13] But female athletes also can be aggressive, inflict physical pain, and endure physical sacrifice in much the same way male athletes do—that is, some lament it, some embrace it, and some are indifferent.

It is also clear that as sports, football and basketball are different in many important ways, and the physicality of football and women's basketball are far from equivalent. For one, the media that cover football arguably encourage its violence, and the fans who watch it also seem to crave it. Many football fans want to see the big hits, and they want to believe that sporting heroes let nothing faze them, not even physical pain. To some, that's part of the game's allure. Only the most catastrophic injuries force fans to take a step back and look at the prevalence and severity of injuries in football.[14] Otherwise, football fans are relatively desensitized to football violence and in awe of the toughest football players who find new ways to overcome the game's painful consequences,[15] thereby reinforcing the view that the game is not inherently problematic.

That was not my experience observing women's college basketball. The sense I got watching women's basketball was that the kind of violence that may cause catastrophic injury or significant pain happens with far less frequency, and when it does, it is not glorified to the same degree. By the late 2000s, there were a few examples[16] of women playing violently on sports courts and fields, losing their ability to control their behavior in exactly the same ways that men in big-time sports have been doing for many decades.[17] Acts of violence appear to be more limited in women's college sports (the NCAA does not maintain data for four-year colleges but there is data that suggests as much, at least at the junior college level[18]). The relative lack of media money is a factor too. After all, potential coaching salaries are so much less in women's basketball, and the media is so much less involved in hyping up the games.

The question of mental, rather than physical, well-being is an even tougher question to answer since so often the problem is difficult to even see. In 2016 the NCAA instituted for the first time a mental health task force, which published best practices for "everything from protocols for athletes in crisis to promoting overall well-being." Since the 2000s according to research by Rachel Bachman of the *Wall Street Journal*, the number of sports psychologists employed by big-time college athletic departments has increased too, suggesting that athletic directors and other administrators recognize the increasing pressures on athletes to perform and the psychological toll such pressure may take.[19] After Kevin Love, an NBA star, spoke out about suffering a panic attack in 2017, more professional athletes have spoken out about mental illness. (Love himself donated 850 subscriptions of the meditation guidance app "Headspace" to UCLA, which offers the service for free to its athletes.) Increasingly, college administrators also acknowledge that in-house mental health services offer athletes "an alternative to overflowing university clinics" and "more privacy than general student counseling centers," where athletes may be recognized and face social stigma.[20]

Do physical injuries and psychological damage heighten the stakes of women playing college basketball and would these pressures increase if the money generated were to someday become comparable to the men's game? It is hard to say, but there will always be women for whom that higher level of competition will make any risk seem worth taking. After all, the Stanford players themselves kept coming back to practice each day, proving with their actions that they did not consider these physical and psychological costs too considerable to bear. After observing the team for a season and taking an informal inventory of injuries to players on the Stanford team and on the teams of their conference competitors, I stopped counting the number of times I heard women's basketball players say that as young women they sought out the physicality of the game as a way to "release energy" or overcome childhood ridicule. It was a common theme that I noticed and so I came to realize that the bruises were in fact like badges of honor to some players, physical symbols of their willingness to sacrifice themselves for a team victory.[21] In that regard, at least, it seemed that they were no different from the male athletes I had grown up alongside.

But in big-time college sports, it is victories that align the interests of players and coaches, coaches and athletic directors, athletic directors and university presidents, athletic departments and faculties, and myriad commercial and alumni organizations as well. For that reason, athletes not only risk their physical health for the sake of their teammates but also for communal unity and corporate profit. Must we then judge their injuries as the collateral damage generally accepted by mainstream American society?

Moreover, the pursuit of victory—and the physical risks taken to achieve it—seemed more complicated for a coach like VanDerveer than it might have been for the coach of a big-time men's college team since the society that surrounded her did not readily recognize the fact that women still have to deal with enduring forms of sexism. In a sports culture that remains male-dominated, winning was loaded with an extra layer of meaning for female coaches. Like all basketball coaches, regardless of gender, winning games was Coach VanDerveer's ultimate purpose and what she was hired by Stanford University to do. Yet each victory seemed emblematic not only of her relentless preparation and fierce competitiveness and therefore, by some measure, a metric of her essence as a human being, but also of her philosophy to never apologize for being a competitive sportswoman.

Her halftime speech against Cal underscored all of this to me. Each word roared from her mouth like the fire of a dragon. And as I listened to my recording of the speech, it occurred to me that while her level of passion wasn't technically necessary—after all, the Cardinal would have likely won the Pac-10 conference title without the Cal victory nor would a loss to the Bears have had a significant impact on her team's postseason tournament seeding in the NCAA tournament—her enthusiasm enunciated how much winning *every* game meant to her.

Sometimes Coach VanDerveer made light of this passion, saying to her players, "You want to have fun? Try winning. Now *thaaaat's* fun," but instilling a VanDerveerian fire to win in her players was undoubtedly core to her professional purpose. Coach VanDerveer later explained to me that she wanted the "perfect kinda team"—disciplined, high energy, humble, emotionally and physically tough—and that she liked women who were "consistent, want to get better, and . . . aren't moody or selfish."

I could personally see little problem with Coach VanDerveer's determined desire to win even if it may have, in some indirect-but-impossible-to-quantify way, led to a higher risk of physical injury or psychological damage for her players and the players of opposing teams, so long as her players continued to buy in to her way of doing things. I believed her when she said she did not appreciate the increasing physicality of the women's game even though I could also easily note the many instances of her imploring her team to play more aggressively. I believed her when she insisted that there was a key difference between aggression and violence. I could equally see the sense in her assertion that it was the male coaches who coached women's teams that caused much of the physicality since men's sports are relatively more physical—and more routinely brutal—than women's. (For example, female athletes do not engage in physical skirmishes or brawls as often as male athletes do.)

But even if VanDerveer were culpable for the seemingly increasing level of physicality in women's sports, could she be blamed for this arguably key aspect of the big time? Historically, female athletes like VanDerveer had been forbidden from being competitive, from pushing their bodies and minds to the limit in intercollegiate sport and from prioritizing victory as men did for too long. They had been restricted from intense, physical, and competitive sports play and from games that required physicality, assertiveness, aggressiveness, toughness, and an immunity to pain, so it made little sense for me or anyone else to criticize them if they chose to play in a physical manner. Although I had never personally restricted any woman or girl from playing sports, I both benefited from a sports culture that by default excluded girls from the kind of competition I enjoyed, and I could also easily recognize how it would have likely stung for a woman like VanDerveer to hear any man questioning her team's aggressive play, whatever its consequences.

Conclusion

Long before I observed her team, Coach VanDerveer had determined that her coaching strategy would be to build teams that exuded an unparalleled work ethic and a steadfast determination to practice the right way. In short, as VanDerveer would later write in her memoir, "battles are won before they're fought."[22] Before her Stanford team won its first NCAA championship, in 1990, VanDerveer's mother sent her *The Art of War*, the famous Chinese military treatise penned by Sun Tzu sometime around the fifth century BCE. VanDerveer recalled that her mother "saw, accurately, the connections between war and sport . . . If we were going to win the NCAA title, we would win it on the strength of our three-hour practices, our video work, our scouting, our drills." Big-time women's college basketball was certainly not the same thing as war, but to VanDerveer there were reflections in the water, and ripples of "strategy, motivation, discipline, preparation and leadership" ebbing out to the same sea. For a coach like her, whose temperament and approach in many ways bore a striking resemblance to that of a general asking her soldiers to sufficiently prepare the day before battle, the victories could only be assured before the games began. Her work was to prepare her players for the battle against an aggressive opponent, of course, but also to prepare their minds to be ready for the moment when the elbows began to fly, when the opponents' "pop 'em in the mouth" tactics began to take a physical form. Coach VanDerveer trained her players hard to be mentally and physically tough in the face of long-distance travel, physical opponents, rowdy fans, and intrusive media, too.[23] While any of these could create pressure, Coach VanDerveer liked to say that "pressure created diamonds," which was her way of encouraging her players to think the same way she did: that with the right attitude and the willingness to buy in, all the necessary sacrifices of the big time would ultimately pay off.

The Pac-10 championship was another feather in the Cardinal cap, but the players, especially senior leaders like Jeannette Pohlen, were trying their best to live in the moment even though the television networks that covered women's basketball had a hype-train to fuel. "Are you looking forward to the chance to 'rematch' UCONN again, perhaps this time with a national title on the line?" a reporter asked Pohlen, looking ahead to the upcoming NCAA Tournament. "Well," Jeannette replied, "We just take it one game at a time." Jeannette was named Pac-10 Player of the Year that day, a remarkable achievement for a player who had once been considered a role player for Stanford and someone who battled chronic back problems. She had heeded her coaches' advice and adopted a no-nonsense, and positive, attitude that her coaches had made seem eminently normal. In doing so, Jeannette had stoked inside herself the will to grow and the fire to fuel it, which gave her the physical strength and self-confidence to lead her team to conference supremacy. Pohlen's was a story of triumph in the face of adversity and, in my mind at least, a story well worth telling in a positive way.

Notes

1. Brohm, *Sport*, 23.
2. Rich, *Of Woman Born*, 39.
3. Associated Press," Nnemkadi Ogwumike."
4. Associated Press," Nnemkadi Ogwumike."
5. Hyman, *Until It Hurts*, 73; Trojian and Collins, "The Anterior Cruciate Ligament"; Arendt, Agel, and Dick, "Anterior Cruciate Ligament," 86.
6. Personal communication, May 8, 2018.
7. VanDerveer and Ryan, *Shooting from the Outside*, 76–77.
8. Taylor, *Scientific Management*.
9. Personal communication, 2011.
10. Oriard, *Reading Football*.
11. Bourdieu, "How Can One Be a Sports Fan?" 438.
12. Fainaru-Wada and Fainaru, *League of Denial*; Bachynski, *No Game for Boys*.
13. Ember, Pitek, and Ringen, "Adolescence."
14. See, for example, Finley, "They Basically Reset my Brain."
15. Football players often play through injury, and some now take powerful painkillers to get back on the field. Toradol was a drug that was initially used after hospital operations, but since the early 2010s it has been used by college and pro players to speed up recovery even though it can cause heart attacks (Chuchmach and Ross, "Ex–USC Player").
16. In 2009, University of New Mexico soccer player Elizabeth Lambert punched a Brigham Young University opponent and then yanked her to the ground by her

ponytail. In 2010, a freshmen center at Baylor University named Britney Griner punched Jordan Barncastle of Texas Tech University in the face after the two became entangled. The NCAA suspended Griner one game, a standard suspension for a physical altercation, and Baylor's coach Kim Mulkey added another game for good measure. Similar acts by male athletes happen nearly every day in professional and college sports yet they are rarely given as much attention and often commentators argue that it is "just boys being boys," giving male athletes a pass.

17. In the 1990s, Bredemeier, Light, and Shields found that during intense competition, moral norms regarding violence and aggression are temporarily suspended and a base, low-level, and more self-interested moral reasoning overcomes participating athletes ("Applied Ethics").

18. *Inside Higher Education* reported that during the 2008–2009 academic year, there were 101 ejections in National Junior College Athletics Association sporting events for women and 648 for men. Of the 101, 37 (37 percent) were violent ejections while 177 of the 648 (27.3 percent) for the men were violent ejections (Moltz, "Decline of Sportswomanship?").

19. Bachman, "Mental Health."
20. Bachman, "Mental Health."
21. Adjepong, "They Are Like Badges."
22. VanDerveer and Ryan, *Shooting from the Outside*, 111.
23. VanDerveer and Ryan, *Shooting from the Outside*, 68–69.

CHAPTER 7

"Deep in the Woods"

> We shall nevertheless provisionally use the expression "spirit of capitalism" for that attitude which, in the pursuit of a calling, strives systematically for profit for its own sake in the manner exemplified by Benjamin Franklin.
>
> —Max Weber[1]

The Shoe Dog and the Sister Act: University of Oregon, January 27, 2011

Back in late January before Stanford had wrapped up its undefeated Pac-10 conference campaign, I joined Stanford's most faithful fans on the 550-mile road trip from Palo Alto to Eugene, Oregon. Initially I set out to see the Cardinal compete against the University of Oregon Ducks and the Oregon State University Beavers but quickly realized that the games the teams played on the court paled in comparison with the games the universities played beyond them.

That first became clear as the Cardinal walloped the Ducks 91-56 at Matthew Knight Arena, which was newly built using funds from Nike founder Phil Knight's donation to the university. Oregon had painted fir trees and the words "Deep in the Woods" on the court in an apparent attempt to remind visitors that they were far from home (and that they ought to be frightened!). But the words seemed to have frightened only the national media and local fans because once again, despite the attraction of a new arena and a matchup between the number three and number nine ranked teams in the nation, there were neither national television crews for the game nor were even half of the 12,000 seats filled. The university did not even feel the need to open all the arena's concession stands.

Oregon's new arena was named after the late son of Phil Knight, the founder and CEO of global shoe and apparel giant Nike and a self-proclaimed "shoe dog" who had earned enough money through college sports to give some of it back.[2] Knight, who was also a Stanford Business School graduate, had donated millions to the University of Oregon, and one $100 million gift he gave supplied nearly half the cost of the arena's construction, which was completed in 2010.

Knight's generosity was partly strategic: both Oregon and Stanford had deals with his company to wear its shoes and uniforms, with Nike paying the schools' athletic departments for the privilege. The deals ensured not only that talented college athletes wore Nike's shoes but also that millions of younger athletes who watched those athletes on TV thought about Nikes too. When they decided it was time to purchase new shoes, an image of the Nike swoosh might just be running through their head. By the summer of 2013, the University of Oregon was so committed to the company that it happily branded itself the University of Nike.[3]

Not that Nike owned Oregon all by itself, of course. A range of corporate advertisements hung throughout the arena concourse alongside 30 x 40-foot portraits of Oregon's historical athletic heroes. There were ads for local businesses, digital billboards that displayed automatically rotating advertisements, and a Jumbotron that was wrapped in AT&T, Pepsi, and BuyMart ads.

The University of Oregon had recently hired Paul Westhead, a former NBA coach, and was paying him handsomely to try and reinvigorate the Ducks' struggling program. One of the university's previous coaches, Jody Runge, who had fought for fairer distribution of Nike athletic gear, more-favorable practice times, and equal pay for her and her coaching staff, resigned after she was unable to secure her requests. Runge had won 70 percent of her games and two Pac-10 titles and yet few of the twenty colleges where she applied for jobs post-resignation even granted her an interview. Ultimately she left coaching to run a bed and breakfast and would later lament how hard it could be for women in the coaching profession.[4] Runge's replacement, Bev Smith, reportedly earned $206,000 per year during her tenure, before being let go herself, showing that not that much changed at the University of Nike—at least for female coaches. When Westhead was hired, he was guaranteed $3.2 million over five years.

The game was similarly lopsided, with Stanford crushing Oregon on the boards, and no player was as strong as Chiney Ogwumike. In the second half, Chiney took the game over, making a series of superb plays, ripping the ball from opponents' hands and blocking Duck shots with abandon. Chiney led all Cardinal scorers with eighteen points, controlled the boards, and an Oregon fan sitting next to me muttered to himself, "She was playing high school basketball last year? And now she is dominating this game? Wow!" At the time, Chiney was just eighteen years old but she played with the confidence of an upperclasswoman.

Chiney's maturity was so impressive, and her personality so captivating, that Stanford University wanted to rely on her to paint the institution in a positive light. In that regard, she was following in her older sister Nneka's footsteps but also in the footsteps of many big-time college athletes who had gone before her, individuals caught up in, and to some degree exploited by, an institutional battle of higher education brands.

Recruiting the Ogwumike sisters was not an easy task for Coach VanDerveer and her staff although Stanford could attract superb athletes in a way that few universities could. Then in turn their sister act helped Stanford dominate the 2010–2011 Pac-10 campaign, further cemented its elite status within the conference, and became a Cardinal storyline followed by the local and, on occasion, national media.

Toward a Qualitative Analysis of Big-Time College Sports

As college sports grew in popularity during the twentieth century, it became clear to universities that spectacular sporting events—and the great athletes and coaches who made them possible—held public relations potential for teaching the public about each university's unique offerings—in short, its brand of higher education. The American Marketing Association defines a brand as a "name, term, design, symbol, or any other feature that identifies one seller's good or service as distinct from those of other sellers," and there is little doubt that the brands of many American universities are built in part by their sports teams.[5]

Yet in recent years, scholars and journalists have raised questions about the extent to which institutions should be able to build their institutional brand by using the individual names, images, and likenesses (NILs) of their big-time athletes. Accordingly, the question of whether the NCAA's grant-in-aid—known colloquially as a full-ride scholarship—is enough compensation for an athlete's contribution to building the university brand is as hotly contested today as it has ever been.

Since at least 2011 when an essay titled "The Shame of College Sports" by civil rights historian Taylor Branch appeared in the *Atlantic*, the issue of university exploitation of big-time college athletes has been front and center in mainstream media debates about the future of American college sports and higher education. Branch, who had written a three-volume, nearly three-thousand-page biography of Dr. Martin Luther King Jr, called college sports a "shamateur" realm that had the "unmistakable whiff of the plantation." *Sports Illustrated*'s Frank Deford told NPR that Branch's story "may well be the most important article ever written about college sports," and the article led to dozens of other journalists jumping at the chance to write about the exploitation of college sports. Indeed, Branch's story led to a full public reappraisal of college sports, with writers from across the political spectrum beginning to question whether college athletes should be paid, whether universities should be in the big business of college sports in the first place, and what the educational value of an athletic scholarship amounted to for athletes who were required by coach or campus culture to spend most of their time thinking about practicing sports.

At the heart of the debate was the question of whether these athletes were being exploited by their coaches, by their universities, by the NCAA, and by sponsoring companies. One journalist, Gregg Easterbrook, argued in 2013 that many college coaches, including some at the top football programs like Nick Saban of the University of Alabama, exploited their players for their own personal gain by "elaborately nourish[ing]" a "Grand Illusion."[6] According to Easterbrook, the NCAA "apple" was "rotten" in allowing "the college football establishment to actively lure a largely African-American group of young men away from studying and graduating, by nurturing an illusion they will receive instant wealth in the NFL," adding that "the system may not have been designed to keep blacks down. But it functions that way."[7] For many African Americans, sports are seen as one of the few routes they have to succeed in what they perceive to be a "persistent racist and oppressive society."[8] In other words, a coach's pushing of the Grand Illusion may fall on eager ears.

Even before Branch and Easterbrook, scholars had long criticized big-time college sports at the biggest of the big-time athletic powerhouses, calling them "entertainment spectacles" akin to "circuses" that took place on university campuses and exploited young people.[9] They lamented that student-athletes in big-time sports play their games in multi-million-dollar stadiums, train in state-of-the-art facilities, are given free tuition, room, and board, and that these scholarships are directly tied to their labor production for the university, yet the same athletes are not included when the million-dollar profits are distributed.

The journalists' participation helped turn the public opinion in favor of what would become known as the athlete's rights movement, setting the stage for further reform proposals. Then in 2017 when a federal investigation charged ten people, including some assistant coaches of D-I men's basketball teams with bribery and accepting kickbacks,[10] the NCAA appointed former U.S. secretary of state Condoleezza Rice to oversee a new Commission on Collegiate Basketball and offer reform recommendations to NCAA president Mark Emmert. The commission concluded that the NCAA had lost the public trust and was unable to adequately deter or punish errant programs, coaches, and players. It also found that 76 percent of D-I men's basketball players believed that they would be able to parlay a college basketball scholarship into a professional contract even though their odds were closer to one in one hundred.[11]

Then in late 2019, California passed the first ever bill freeing college athletes to profit from their own names, images, and likenesses (NILs), prompting other states to draft similar bills, and prompting senators Cory Booker and Richard Blumenthal to propose national legislation to redress the economic unfairness of athletes being unable to earn anything from their own NILs. By the summer of 2021, a handful of states had passed laws forbidding colleges from preventing athletes from profiting from their NILs, and some expressed hope that Congress would step in with national legislation on the matter, too.

But even as the athlete's rights movement gained momentum, women's college teams and athletes were largely left out of the discussion (although not technically left out of California's NIL law) with the mistaken assumption being made that exploitation can only be measured in economic terms, that it is only revenue-generation that should determine who is exploited by colleges and who is not, and that women are not sufficiently big time to warrant that conclusion. Some also mistakenly consider women's college sports a relatively pure space within college sports that is not tainted by the commercialism and corruption that characterize big-time men's college sports (Dr. Rice's report, for example, makes little mention of women's sports).

But this kind of myopic thinking overlooks the reality of women's college sports like basketball, which is, at the D-I level at least, and in many qualitative respects, big time too. Moreover this kind of thinking also suggests that sexism is alive and well in our still male-dominated sports culture, though it is often hidden.

The Prospects and Perils of Going Big Time, and Staying in It: Oregon State University, January 29, 2011

Two days after the University of Oregon game, I followed that drama to Corvallis, Oregon, for Stanford's matchup with Oregon State University (OSU), which turned out to be another Stanford rout, 74-44.

I was accompanied by an old friend and Oregonian who told me that the Beavers, as OSU's sports teams were known, were widely seen as a younger stepbrother to the University of Oregon. He pointed to the fact the University of Oregon's endowment was roughly five times larger than OSU's[12] and that OSU admitted a higher percentage of applicants (83 percent versus 79 percent in 2017).[13] So significant was the rivalry between the schools that the annual football game between the teams was dubbed the "Civil War."

OSU's Ralph Miller Court at Gil Coliseum, which was completed in 1949, seemed a world away from OU's Knight Arena. In contrast to Knight's digital displays, there were drawings of Beaver athletic greats like Gary Payton and Ralph Miller on the coliseum's concourse walls. Gil was old and cavernous with a two-hundred-foot-high ceiling that allowed chilly winter gusts in and provided fans with cold, wooden, baseball-style bench seats. Traveling from Knight to Gil felt like going back in time. (OSU would begin multi-year renovations on Gil in 2013.)

Not that there weren't any advertisements in the old gym of Corvallis: Lumber Liquidators, Xfinity Cable, Sierra Mist, and Pepsi ads rotated on a manual billboard that flipped behind the courtside sports media desk, and a local Mexican restaurant hosted a half-time game in which any fan who made a half-court shot could win free burritos for a year.

Such billboards and in-game gimmicks hint at the enormous economic ecosystem that exists to promote products and services through college sports,[14] but most of the wealth that is created through college sports is created through television advertising.[15]

At Stanford's home basketball games, in-game corporate ads included those of AT&T, Nike, Muscle Milk, Outback Steakhouse, Pepsi, Wells Fargo, State Farm, and Webster House (a retirement community).

Interestingly, television ads during Pac-10 conference basketball games seemed tailored to the viewers that television executives expected to watch the game and seemed to be based on gendered stereotypes. The 2010–2011 Pac-10 Tournament Women's Basketball Final, for example, was sponsored by Pacific Life Insurance, and its television ads were for fast food, nonalcoholic beverages, insurance and banking, cable, Internet and personal

Gimmicks are common at big-time college sports events. Photo credit: *Aaron Miller*

technology, and local entertainment, while in the Pac-10 Tournament Men's Basketball Final, which was held the same day as the women's final but on a national rather than local media outlet, the advertisements were for credit cards, beer, cars, trucks and SUVs, rental cars, fantasy baseball, hardware stores, antiperspirants, and personal technology.[16]

Timeouts are even built into the game's broadcast to maximize companies' commercial opportunities. These so-called TV timeouts are taken at the first stoppage of play after the 16-, 12-, 8-, and 4-minute marks are passed in each half. That makes a total of eight TV timeouts per game and a total of 32–48 mandatory advertisements per game. Add the timeouts that the coaches call to give their players a rest and the many stoppages of play for injuries and you begin to see why sporting events have become such a highly sought-after form of corporate advertising.[17] Sometimes one sees so many ads in a college sporting event that one thinks that the sporting event is itself the sideshow.

"A Culture of Intimidation and Fear"

As I sat watching Stanford oust the Beavers with relative ease, I could see why a college or university would want to sell itself through athletes and coaches and why it would allow corporations to come along for the ride, but it seemed harder to understand why they would go to such great lengths to do so, in some cases even hiring questionable coaches to win games.

I had fully expected Stanford to win the OSU game not only because the Stanford seniors had never lost to OSU but also because the OSU women's basketball program had publicly unraveled the previous season. That year it had been reported that OSU's women's coach LaVonda Wagner had pressured players to play through serious injuries, forced them to join Weight Watchers, and even thrown a chair during a locker room meltdown. In the local press, Wagner was criticized for creating a "culture of intimidation and fear,"[18] and OSU suffered mass player and coach defections. Wagner was later fired.[19]

The OSU scandal underlined how incentives could be perverted when universities sought to brand-build through sports and especially when a coach interpreted big-time sporting culture's triumphalism as justification for an authoritarian leadership style. Wagner had come to OSU from Duke University where she had been known as a great recruiter. On the strength of that skill, Wagner was paid handsomely to make the move west—close to $500,000 dollars a year according to one account. (Even after she was fired, OSU was still required to pay her over $1 million.)[20]

But OSU was a relatively poor public university—its endowment did not routinely appear in the top 100 of the national rankings[21]—so its willingness to pay such a large sum emphasized its desire to maintain big-time status, its desire to compete against relatively rich, private, conference powerhouses like Stanford, and its willingness to take considerable risks to ensure the opportunity.[22]

Even if a university could justify such costs financially, one had to wonder about the emotional cost to players who played for coaches like Wagner not to mention the university's black eye after the scandal broke. Was the marketing value that big-time sports provided and the corporate sponsorship dollars they secured worth that much?

"It Is Our Aspiration to Compete, Not Just to Play": UC Davis, March 19, 2011

These issues resurfaced in my mind again in mid-March, as the Cardinal prepared to begin their title run to another NCAA Championship for VanDerveer and Stanford. Now with a Pac-10 conference title and a Pac-10 conference tournament championship on their resume, the 29-2 Cardinal had secured not only an automatic entry but also a number one seed in the illustrious NCAA tournament, where they met yet another university bent on being part of the big time. Their first-round opponent, the sixteenth-seeded University of California, Davis (UCD), would give Stanford a run for its money, but its ascent to D-I play was indicative of the high stakes associated with the rarified air. In 2003–2004, the university's students had voted to transition from D-II to D-I college athletics,[23] with some in the Aggie community arguing that the university would never be considered "a first-class university without a Division I sports program."

When I asked a friend and retired UCD professor why UCD was trying to go big time, he told me it was because a former chancellor named Ted Hullar had recommended "shedding the Aggie image" despite pushback from "many faculty." Hullar's proposed change was indicative of an ambitious, university-wide rebranding campaign, which ultimately failed, and Hullar was transferred to a temporary job at the University of California head office after six years.

The result was a sort of compromise between those who wanted UCD to join the big time and those who wanted the university to remain true to its educational roots as an agricultural academy. According to a strategic audit commissioned by UCD Athletics and performed by an outside consultancy, UCD had worked to maintain an "educational model" of intercollegiate athletes, which would be generally more typical of a D-II or D-III university, when it made the transition to D-I in 2007. This decision, the audit suggested, was not in harmony with the realities of competitively successful D-I programs, which follow a business model and operate on a principle of self-sufficiency for their inter-collegiate athletic programs. The audit referred to athletic departments at elite, top-tier universities as "auxiliary enterprises," noting that these enterprises invest whatever profits they earn one year in the sports that they expect will generate revenue the next year. Charged with the task of making recommendations for what UCD Athletics ought to do next, the audit advised UCD to make a "cultural shift" toward this business model if it hoped to fully integrate with D-I athletics, adding that this shift would compromise neither the university's long-standing commitment to education nor its financially committed fan base and that there needed to be a mixture of staff with the athletic department, half of whom continued to value "noble amateurism" and half of whom were "willing to transition to a more contemporary model in the pursuit of greater athletic performance." Finally, the report concluded that UCD would have to reconsider and adjust the eight principles commonly referred to as the Davis Way in order to "more closely coincide with NCAA Division I . . . philosophies and practices."[24] The audit thus recommended UCD only make the transition to the D-I level when they had the budget and facilities necessary to compete and when UCD's cherished conception of the teacher-coach role—that of an educator first and a coach second—had been reconsidered to "better serve students who want to develop athletic skills and increased fitness levels."

If UCD had accepted all the consultancy's recommendations, it would have marked a dramatic change in the method and purpose of sports at the public university. Ultimately though, UCD joined D-I but in the Big Sky Conference instead of the bigger time Mountain West or Pac-12 conferences, which would have required higher capital outlays for improved facilities. It was a decision that left some Aggie alumni unhappy. Mike Belotti, who had played football for the Aggies before becoming a college football coach and television analyst, told the *Sacramento Bee* in 2015, "You can't hide in Utopia and expect to compete with people who are spending more money and giving their coaches more resources." He then added,

> If you want football to be the flagship, to be the bell cow, which it typically is at most universities, you've got to ask, are you competitive with your resources, your support, your salaries for the coaches? Are you giving them the opportunity to be successful? If you're not, then bring them up to speed so they can compete with the people in their own league, at their level of competition, on a national basis.

When Kevin Blue, a former Stanford athlete and athletic department official, took over as UCD athletic director in 2016, he seemed to echo Belotti's sentiment: "As we go forward, it is our aspiration to compete, not just to play."[25]

If their performance against Stanford in Maples was any indication, UCD was well on its way out of hiding in Utopia and was competing rather than playing. UCD began the game playing aggressively, and after 6'3" star senior Paige Mintun scored five consecutive points, Stanford led by just two, 18-16. On the CSNBA television broadcast, Mary Murphy said UCD was playing "fearless," and her partner Dave Pasch called the Aggies "pesky." The Aggies' boisterous crowd, which had traveled in droves to Palo Alto for the spectacle, relished the new level of competition too, wailing "Aiiiiiiiirball" when Jos missed a shot and cheering with raucous delight for every Aggie bucket, as if each were a game-winning shot.

But by halftime Stanford had extended its lead to 42-30, and in the second half the Cardinal pulled away to win the game convincingly. In fact, it would have been a miracle if the Aggies had pulled off the upset given Stanford's home court advantage. Unlike in the men's NCAA tournament, in which it is forbidden for schools to play any games on their home court, on the women's side it was not uncommon for top-seeded teams to play first- and second-round games in friendly confines. According to the accepted logic of NCAA tournament seedings, it was also a faceoff between one of the tournament's four best teams against one of the four worst so the chances of a UCD upset were already slim.

Still the final score—86-59—looked much more lopsided than anyone who watched the first half would have remembered. The victory margin echoed the significant disparities between the respective athletic department budgets and facilities of the two universities, but the fierce competition in the first half demonstrated just how tempting the allure of playing in the big time could be.

"A Badge of Respectability"

In fact, to the members of the UCD community, the collective desire to go big time expressed by students, fans, and alumni alike meant something important and unquantifiable, something that went beyond Xs and Os and dollars and cents. Ultimately, the Aggies wanted to do what the University of Oregon had done: take a regional university and use its sports teams to make it a national brand, maybe even ink a sponsorship deal to make it another University of Nike.

To advocates like Belotti, membership in D-I has thus become a "badge of respectability."[26] This is in part because there is no official ranking of universities in the United States and because intercollegiate sports prowess often act as a default ranking, just as gold medals in the Olympics may index national power. After all, no single official academic standard helps to differentiate one university from the next, and while it is assumed that "everyone just knows," many overlook how much the Associated Press college sports rankings, especially in football, shape these perceptions. Colleges often know the risks of trying to go big time and take them anyway, as Pennington related in 2012 in the case of the University of Massachusetts–Amherst, which took a "reasonable calculated risk" in deciding to "enhance" its football program for football bowl subdivision (FBS) eligibility and participation. As the university's chancellor explained to the *New York Times*, "If managed properly, we will come out better for it . . . There are risks to [making] academic investments, too. When we build a new research center, it is with the hope of attracting more research grants. So that is a risk [too]."[27] As former NCAA director Walter Byers recalled in his memoir, many college presidents believe that D-I status is "critical to the future of their universities."[28]

But the cost of going big time or staying big time is economically if not also spiritually significant. According to NCAA rules, schools seeking D-I status must sponsor at least fourteen varsity sports, play 60 percent of their games against D-I opponents, have a football stadium with a seating capacity over 30,000, and have had an average football attendance of over 17,000 at least once in the four years before they apply to the NCAA. Economist Andrew Zimbalist has shown that few teams make it to D-I and make serious money there and that the perceived indirect effects (e.g., "incalculable promotional value, boosting applications and donations") are often overstated. Thus, Byers concluded that "the great majority of colleges that seek to catch up and associate with the most affluent" are the ones "that have negative balances at the end of the year."[29]

Who Defines Big Time?

Where exactly do women's sports like basketball fit into all of this? In other words, what significance does the biggest time women's sport hold in the context of colleges trying to "go big"? Women athletes obviously play in the same top NCAA division as the men, and that top division similarly represents the highest level of competition for American athletes their age, but the men's and women's big time is not, and was not, created equally.

First, the gap between men's and women's sports revenue should not be glossed over. In a strict quantitative analysis, there are undeniable gaps in the income generated by men's and women's big-time college sports. For example, in 2010, ESPN paid $55 *million* for a package of rights fees that included the rights to broadcast the NCAA women's D-I basketball tournament.[30] By contrast, in the same year, various media outlets paid a combined nearly $11 *billion* to the NCAA for the men's tournament media rights.

At the same time, the Stanford–UCONN game, which was neither a postseason game nor a championship match, bore many of the major markers of a big-time college sporting event: it was nationally televised, highly commercialized by advertisers, highly professionalized by the coaches, intensely competed by the players, and raucously cheered on by the fans. And even the games against the Oregon schools, which may not have been attended as well or televised, brought in revenue and publicity for the universities involved.

Since the early 1980s, women's college basketball has gradually become a bigger deal. Even then coaches actively recruited athletes, offering them all-expenses-paid visits to campus and even joy rides in Corvettes to convince them to sign.[31] Female athletes in a range of sports are today routinely offered full-ride scholarships at a variety of institutions, and nationally televised, commercialized games may not be as commonplace as in men's sports but they are not at all uncommon and would likely make bigger headlines if not for the constant comparisons with men's sports, which are arguably unfair. After all, men's sports have had a big head start in their march to the big time. In other words, if men's college sports did not exist, you would hear a lot more about the sums of money changing hands over women's college sports.

Moreover, the money generated by big-time college sports, including big-time women's college sports, is today downright eye-popping.[32] Within that category, there are some women's sports, none more important than basketball, that drive significant economic activity and indeed create their own large industry unto themselves. Table 7.1 displays aggregated revenue figures for NCAA D-I-A women's basketball programs and compares these figures to the second-highest-grossing sport program for the years from 2003 to 2010. The combined revenue for women's basketball has consistently earned more than two times as much as the next-closest sport. The second-highest revenue-generating women's college sport varied over those years between soccer, track and field, and volleyball.

Table 7.1. Revenue for NCAA Div. I-A (Women's Basketball) 2003–2011

	Women's basketball revenue (As a percentage of total women's college sport revenue)	Second highest revenue generating women's college sport	Revenue generated by second highest revenue generating sport	Total revenue for all women's college sports
2010	$172,553,874 (24.62%)	Soccer	$79,093,483	$700,888,977
2009	$146,886,395 (26.50%)	Track and Field	$67,301,029	$563,774,243
2008	$119,584,528 (27.03%)	Track and Field	$50,901,245	$442,364,447
2007	$115,424,390 (28.00%)	Volleyball	$46,686,292	$412,295,557
2006	$93,939,593 (28.19%)	Volleyball	$38,988,694	$333,292,252
2005	$95,666,321 (33.63%)	Volleyball	$30,693,194	$284,507,311
2004	$80,631,299 (33.74%)	Volleyball	$26,578,259	$238,983,025
2003	$68,892,601 (33.45%)	Volleyball	$23,478,712	$205,980,546

Source: U.S. Department of Education, Office of Postsecondary Education, Equity in Athletics Data Analysis Cutting Tool, http://ope.ed.gov/athletics/GetAggregatedData.aspx

With more fans, bigger media rights contracts between universities and media outlets, and a larger spotlight, there have been larger revenues from television broadcasts and thus larger budget outlays for women's basketball facilities, equipment, and coaching. By 2002, D-III schools were spending on average $40,000, Ivy League schools on average $225,000, and D-I schools on average over $1 million per year on their women's basketball programs, costs that covered everything from coaching salaries and travel expenses to equipment.[33] By 2019, operating expenses for D-I schools had risen to $3–6 million per year.[34]

"The Women's Game Is a Very Different Game Than the Men's Game"

When asked what it is exactly that accounts for such gross disparities between men's and women's college sports revenue generation, you begin to see that a broader qualitative analysis of the big time is also essential. Danette Leighton, the Pac-10 marketing director, told me in 2011 that a "major challenge" for the popularity of women's college basketball was the perception in the halls of power that there were "mainstream" sports like men's football and basketball and "niche" sports like women's basketball.[35] Where a sport falls, she added, was contingent upon "who drives the national media." She dismissed the idea that the gap between women's and men's college basketball revenue could be explained solely by the number of people "who want to watch" and suggested that the women's game had been deemed niche by those who controlled what was allowed on the airwaves and television, and many of these people were men. "It is all about someone's perception about what . . . they think the product should be. The women's game is a very different game than the men's game . . . What is in people's brains is the ESPN SportsCenter highlight reel of jamming and dunking, and that's not the women's game."

In 2012 at the NCAA Final Four, Coach VanDerveer acknowledged that her team's perennial success "does kind of feed into [the notion that] 'women's basketball is top-heavy, boring.'" But while she went on to acknowledge that consistent victories by powerhouse teams could feed this perception (since if the same teams win again and again, it suggests that the sport is predictable and ostensibly less entertaining), she said she didn't "like the word parity." While she admitted that "people want to watch games when you don't know the outcome, and you don't want twenty-point and thirty-point games when you're looking at regional finals and semifinals [of the NCAA tournament]," she said she wanted there to be more "surprises . . .

more up-and-comers," and that to "develop the breadth" of women's basketball it would be important for more schools to "support women's basketball in their own community" and for every program to play the best teams they could. "[We need to] play big games not cupcake schedules," she concluded. Competition, it seemed, was the answer, and the only way to improve competition was to develop more high-quality basketball programs with more investment.

But like many of the challenges inhibiting growth in women's basketball, this lack of grassroots support can be traced back to sexism. If, for example, the male-dominated media will not provide women's sports with an equitable level of airtime, the grassroots support for the game will be harder to develop, and as a result women's basketball will continue to experience relatively lower revenue streams. If there are lower revenue streams, fewer schools will "support women's basketball in their own community," as VanDerveer suggested is important, and that limits the ability of colleges and universities to become the kind of basketball powerhouses that are necessary to host competitive and compelling big games.

Thus, while women's college basketball today enjoys the most attention, popularity, and respect among all women's college sports and arguably more attention, popularity, and respect than it ever has, it still struggles to generate mainstream public acceptance and fails to regularly be lifted to the public pedestal of being as big time as the big-time men's sports. The big time cannot therefore be defined by numbers alone. It is not only about money, budgets, revenues, and media coverage. The big time is also defined by sexism, which infiltrates sports in often hidden ways and keeps women's teams from being recognized in the same category as men's teams. In short, people struggle to avoid ascriptions of value and meaning to "intrinsic" "facts" of sex and gender, but if they could, they would see many of the same sorts of big-time markers that they see in men's sports, and they might be more willing to make the necessary investments to grow the women's game further.

Big Time: Ultimately, a Status Only Men Can Bestow

It is unfair to expect any women's college team to be considered in exactly the same echelon as the big-time men's sports not because their talent or skill or even entertainment value is subpar—it isn't—but because the determination of big-time status can only be bestowed by a sports world that is still predominantly run by men and for men—many of whom harbor a vested interest in keeping men's sports up and women's sports down—and by a male-dominated sports fan base that still looks at women's sports with derision at worst or curiosity at best.[36]

Moreover, the NCAA's determination that all college athletes under its institutional umbrella are in fact amateurs effectively limits the American public's ability to see them as professionals. In a flimsy defense of their sexist thinking, some of these men—NCAA leaders, media executives, sportscasters, journalists, administrators, and fans—have said the market ultimately decides whether women's sports, including women's college sports, should be considered big time. They conclude that it is the desires of television viewers and sports fans that dictate whether something is on television or not, and thus, while it may not be fair, it is just the way it is. To paraphrase Walter Byers, they believe that it is the "culture of the times" and not the decisions of people that keeps women down.

Yet the history of big-time college sports, including the history of women's college sports, suggests otherwise. Powerful actors and institutions, including officials from the NCAA, self-interested university officials, and athletic conferences and national oversight bodies, not to mention high-powered coaches, athletic directors and alumni boosters, most of whom were men, actively and disproportionately shaped the culture of big-time college sports as we know it today. In the process, they either deliberately or inadvertently left other sports to start well behind in the race to big-time popularity and profitability. Indeed, if the road to the big time were a 100-meter dash, then college football had a 50-meter head start and men's college basketball had a 25-meter head start on all the others.

And yet if sexist ideological exclusion from the big time continues, in some ways it is subtler than it once was. Media executives still exclude women's sports from daily highlight reels, and athletic directors still decide to hire male coaches for positions that women are qualified to assume. The sexism extends into realms of portrayal and representation too. Even when women athletes are portrayed, they are still often sexualized in a way that belittles their athleticism, objectifies their bodies, and dehumanizes them as people and diminishes their athletic accomplishments.[37] Women's college sports teams are still only getting media attention for some of their games and not others and therefore seem doomed to forever be fighting an unwinnable war to be considered big time.

Notes

1. Weber, "The Protestant Work Ethic."
2. Knight, *Shoe Dog*.
3. Bishop, "Oregon Embraces."
4. Fagan and Cyphers, "The Glass Wall."
5. One U.K. study found that marketing managers at twenty-five London universities believed that there were ten factors that together were essential to creating their brand: location, employability for graduates, educational identity (especially in terms of its level of diversity), how the campus "feels" and looks, reputation, learning environment, courses offered, links with the community, and social and sports facilities. Arguably this last factor is even more important in the United States (Bennett and Ali-Choudhury, "Prospective Students").
6. Easterbrook, *The King*, 132–35.
7. Easterbrook, *The King*, 141–42.
8. Sailes, "Betting Against the Odds," 13.
9. Sperber, *Beer and Circus*.
10. Commission on Collegiate Basketball, "Report and Recommendations," 16.
11. Commission on Collegiate Basketball, "Report and Recommendations," 6; National Collegiate Athletic Association, "So, You're Telling Me There's a Chance."
12. Newman and O'Leary, "Year-by-Year Comparison."
13. *U.S. News & World Report*, "University Comparison Tool."
14. The advertisements that one sees in arenas and stadiums are not typically sold by people working for athletic conferences such as the Pac-12 or even by individual athletic departments such as Stanford Athletic. Instead, advertising agencies like IMG College sell media rights to various Fortune 500 companies so that conferences and athletic departments do not have to concern themselves with such business and can concentrate on other matters such as development (i.e., raising funds), recruiting, and training. As of 2012, IMG College served seven Pac-12 schools (Arizona, Arizona State, California, Oregon, UCLA, Washington, and Washington State) while Stanford, Colorado, and Oregon State worked with Learfield Sports, and USC was represented by Fox Sports. The Pac-12 Conference does not own these rights—the colleges do—but it wants to be involved in the distribution of college sports content at every level so in the early 2010s, the Pac-12 agreed to pay IMG College and Learfield Sports approximately $15 million per year for them (M. Smith, "Pac-12 Buys Back Rights").
15. Novy-Williams and Crupi, "ESPN'S $793 Million."
16. Advertising during live college sporting events is more valuable than ever especially as the technology Americans use to consume their entertainment changes. Since the 2000s, DVRs have been popular, allowing consumers to record and watch shows at their leisure and skip commercials if they wish. At the same time, the Internet has in the twenty-first century increasingly displaced television, and consumers now can watch what they want to watch when they want to watch it. Live events

have therefore become an ever-greater driver of the U.S. entertainment and advertising economies (Nocera and Strauss, *Indentured*).

17. Corporations have also learned that they can sponsor both the names of the stadiums where sports are played as well as the awards that the best athletes receive. Historically most college football awards were named after great players of the past, but today, corporations put their names on many of them too. AT&T along with ESPN sponsors All-America Player of the Week and All-American Player of the Year awards while Home Depot and Liberty Mutual each sponsor a Coach of the Year Award.

18. Schnell, "Oregon State."
19. Schnell, "Oregon State."
20. Schnell, "Oregon State."
21. Sherlock, Gravelle, Crandall-Hollick, and Hughes, "College and University Endowments."
22. Something similar allegedly took place at the University of North Carolina, Chapel Hill, a few years later when longtime coach Sylvia Hatchell resigned after being accused of pushing her players to play through injury and making racially sensitive remarks (Alexander, "North Carolina Women's").
23. Furillo, "Opinion."
24. Furillo, "Opinion."
25. Furillo, "Winning Is Important."
26. Byers and Hammer, *Unsportsmanlike Conduct*, 251.
27. Pennington, "Big Dream."
28. Byers and Hammer, *Unsportsmanlike Conduct*, 330.
29. Byers and Hammer, *Unsportsmanlike Conduct*, 357.
30. The women's basketball deal also included the College (Baseball) World Series and twenty other NCAA championships (*USA Today*, "NCAA Reaches 14-Year Deal").
31. Ingalls, "The Fine Art."
32. Nocera, "The Way to Run." College sports have been estimated a $60 billion industry (Eder and Bishop, "High Stakes Games."), and college football is apparently more profitable than Major League Baseball. In 2005, sports as a whole, including professional as well as college and high school sports, were estimated to be the fifteenth-largest industry in the United States, worth about $189 billion overall, which was larger than the oil and gas industry. Nearly half of this $189 billion, or $79 billion, was spent on sports equipment apparel and footwear while $48 billion was spent by sports spectators and $14 billion was spent on television, Internet, and magazine advertisements (Milano and Chelladurai, "Gross Domestic Sport Product").
33. Shulman and Bowen, *The Game of Life*, 241–42.
34. U.S. Department of Education, "Equity in Athletics Data Analysis, Data Cutting Tool," https://ope.ed.gov/athletics/#/. Data from this website leaves a lot to be desired. There is no way to distinguish between women's and men's sports operating

expenses. To arrive at this range, I randomly selected four universities from the Power 5 coverage and examined their operating expenses.

35. Personal communication, March 17, 2011.

36. See Nelson, *The Stronger Women Get*, especially chap. 8.

37. Cooky has documented the striking gender inequalities in sports coverage in order to argue that "sports media creates demand as much as they meet it." In a 2016 Ted Talk, Cooky argued that the sports media "trivializes women's sports" with the lack of coverage it offers to women's sports and also "sexualizes their bodies" in the language they use when they do cover them. She notes that the poses that magazine cover-girls from the sports world are encouraged to take are also highly gendered. They pose for photographs in bikinis and not on the field in action. Male athletes are rarely expected to do the same. Cooky demonstrates that there are few positive images of women athletes that highlight their athleticism." And yet, she concludes, "girls need sports to grow just like boys do, and sports can help accelerate girls' leadership potential" ("The Female Athlete").

CHAPTER 8

"I Am Stanford"

The reason why I'm here is I play basketball and I bring money into the school and the community and ultimately into the NCAA's pockets.

—Ed O'Bannon

Recruiting can be a lot of propaganda, but in Stanford's case it is backed up by fact.

—Amy Tucker

The Big Three and the Front Porch

From the university's perspective, college athletes are the perfect labor force: tough, ambitious, decisive, hardworking, and often conformist team players. Universities that field big-time sports programs must also replenish their store of athletic talent each year so recruiting the best high school talent is paramount.

This is a constant process. Like any business, American colleges and universities compete to attract the best professors, administrators, students, coaches, athletes, and athletic directors, and also like any business, the best recruiting tool is word-of-mouth advertising. Unique to universities, though, is the fact that nothing else gets people talking about universities more than big-time sporting events and the stellar athletes that make them possible. Thus, universities offer scholarships to athletically talented high schoolers primarily because they are betting that these athletes will enhance the university's reputation in the marketplace and sustain their brand.

Like many universities, Stanford capitalized on the work ethic and successes of big-time athletes, hiring a sports information director to produce a media guide so journalists could learn players' names, backgrounds, and skills as well as to help disseminate the message that Stanford offered prospective students (and prospective donors) a unique education on the court and in the classroom.

As the team's media guide put it, the "Big Three" of Pohlen, Pedersen, and Nneka Ogwumike provided the Cardinal "with a truckload of talent, intelligence, courage, charisma, and confidence." In short, these were Stanford heroes, young people of whom the university and its alumni could be proud.

This media guide served as a primer for newspaper reporters and television announcers. Any time the team's games were televised, announcers used the term "Big Three" copiously as if these three players were the team itself. Never mind that basketball is a team game played by more than three players; the media had ads to sell, and the best way to do that was apparently by marketing individual players and telling stories of their greatness.

There was even a staff of several people who were entrusted with marketing Stanford athletic teams, some dedicated to the women's basketball team, including full-time staff who made creative, promotional videos for display at games and on the Internet. Midway through the season a new marketing associate was hired too, demonstrating how the business end of college sports always seemed to be growing.

If college sports are considered the front porch of American universities and often how the university wages its publicity campaigns, then calculating the value of college athletes to the university must go beyond how much revenue they generate for the university. Prospective students and would-be donors may hear the university's name through sports radio or television or read it on the newspaper sports page more than they are exposed to it in any other place.[1] The public may also see no problem in a university showcasing itself through the festivity and fun of the big-game environment, which they may view as a positive, non-threatening environment. Stellar sports teams may also serve to assure alumni that their donations to the university are going to the right place by producing winning teams that uphold the reputation of the university and by producing graduates becoming of the alumni standard. Moreover, college sports may serve as a conduit for the subsidiaries of the university to get their marketing needs met. For example, if a basketball fan sees an ad for Stanford's Cancer Center or Children's Hospital, it may lead them to choose Stanford as their own health care provider. That has significant value, even if it may be hard to quantify.

Don't all big-time athletes deserve to be paid directly for this value? Some skirt questions like this one with questions of their own such as "Does a star athlete generate more brand exposure than a role player?" and "Does a football player generate more than a women's basketball player?" But does it matter? After all, regardless of talent or public persona, any college athlete whose accomplishments are showcased by the university or one of its affiliates in some capacity is creating value. How to exactly quantify that value is another matter entirely, but building and sustaining a university brand is ultimately about drawing the collective gaze, which simply will not focus without a spectacle like sport to attract it.

The Coach and the University: "If The Team Has Success, You Have Success"

At the same time, the athlete's role is not only to draw the collective gaze. Indeed, some athletes pick the schools they do not only for the athletic programs but also for the education offered. So are the calls of exploitation tempered by the fact that at some colleges and universities, sports can and do help young people grow intellectually? In other words, the fact that some young athletes achieve fame and attain education through big-time sports participation complicates claims of universal exploitation and complicates what buying in to this system means.[2]

For example, the Texas-born Ogwumike sisters chose Stanford over Rice University, the University of Texas, and Baylor University, all institutions of higher education based in their home state. Chiney and Nneka's parents, Peter and Ify, told reporters that they wanted their daughters to attend a college with a balance between academics and athletics and that was why Stanford was appealing to them even if it was thousands of miles away from their home.

In 2011 Coach Tucker told me it took a "lot of hard work" and a lot of relationship building with Nneka's family and coaches and even her school to convince her to choose Stanford. "Obviously I think we had something that Nneka wanted, but we had to make her see that it was something that *she* wanted. And that it was something she couldn't get anywhere else." Ultimately Nneka realized that at Stanford she could play basketball at a high level and receive a solid education, and she came to agree with Coach Tucker that Stanford had what no other university could offer: superior academics, a superior environment, and an elite women's basketball program. It didn't hurt that Coach VanDerveer and her staff boasted a stellar coaching record or that the program she had built received the kind of national media exposure a star player would need to receive to attract the attention of professional scouts. "Recruiting can be a lot of propaganda," Coach Tucker told me, "but in Stanford's case it is backed up by fact." She pointed to *U.S. News & World Report* rankings and the beautiful campus but also the track record of success that the coaching staff had amassed. "You will be playing on a great team," she told me they would say to recruits. "You will be developed personally. If the team has success, you have success."

Between the 2009–2010 and 2010–2011 seasons, Coach VanDerveer enlisted Nneka to help recruit another national high school athlete of the year, a young, lanky, talented star from Texas who happened to be her younger sister Chiney. Chiney was ranked the number one basketball prospect in ESPN HoopGurlz rankings during her last year of high school, and when Chiney joined Nneka on the farm the next year, she followed in her sister's footsteps with her own charisma, flair, and determination. Indeed, Chiney's performance against Oregon punctuated an impressive and rapid ascent especially since her older sister was still considered Stanford's most talented player. By then Nneka was already a nationally recognized player-of-the-year candidate, and the reigning Pac-10 Player of the Year. Chiney met that challenge without complaint even as Coach VanDerveer asked her to change positions. She had played center in high school but at Stanford she was asked to play small forward to accommodate Nneka, who played power forward, and Sarah Boothe, whose size, strength, and skill set made her unquestionably a center. Only when Boothe rested did Chiney play power forward. The challenge to learn two new positions was no problem because Chiney was such a quick and willing study. Chiney was exceptionally confident with the basketball as well as exceptionally nimble with her body. Some of the contortions she put herself through to snag a rebound or block a shot looked painful, but she knew, uncannily, how to move her body for maximum efficiency. She was gifted around the basket, able to find the bottom of the hoop no matter which way her body was pointed. By midseason, Chiney was already a vocal team leader. "Help side [defense]!" she would yell to remind her teammates, even when she was riding a stationary bike on the sidelines to stay warm.

Stanford's historic win over UCONN put Chiney on the national map not only because Chiney had refused an offer to play for the Huskies, creating the sort of drama about which the media loved to rave, but also because she was gracious to all coaches involved in the process. In that game, Chiney emerged as one of Stanford's most powerful defensive stoppers, too, playing a key role in helping Stanford shut down Maya Moore. While diehard Stanford fans assured me that Chiney would eventually become a great scorer, few of them believed that any freshman could stop Moore. But perhaps the most significant moment came toward the end of the game when Chiney fouled out and made a special trip to the UCONN bench. There she offered a friendly hug to UCONN Coach Geno Auriemma, who had wanted this Ogwumike to enroll at his university. The hug told the crowd everything they needed to know about Chiney's character, and why any university—Stanford, UCONN, or otherwise—would want her as one of its most high-profile, public-facing students.

While Nneka carried that year's team on the court, leading the team in points scored, it was Chiney's personality that appealed not only to her teammates and coaches but also to the university public relations department. A few years after I followed the Stanford team, in 2013, during a nationally televised Stanford football game against UCLA, the university ran a publicity campaign with various members of the university. Commercials like these enable universities to market their brand of higher education during college sports broadcasts and to publicize the university's accomplishments and strengths. Of all of Stanford's thousands of students, staff, and faculty, Chiney Ogwumike, who was by then a senior, was the last person showcased in the commercial, saying, "I am Stanford" with unflinching confidence. To speak last, Stanford could have chosen a football player from its nationally prominent team, the college president, or a famous professor. Instead, Stanford chose Chiney, who embodied everything that Stanford hoped to symbolize: academic scholarship, athletic grace, cheerful perspective, and contagious charisma. In short, she was everything Stanford wanted to be.

The Conference Official: "We're Not for Profit . . . So You Want to Stay Lean"

Conferences like the Pac-10 also benefited from the presence of players like Chiney. Historically, athletic conferences were formed primarily along regional lines so that universities could challenge similarly sized colleges and their teams did not have to travel long distances to play them. But that has been changing in recent years owing primarily to the ease of air travel, the expansion of cable television channels focusing on big-time sporting events, and increased consumer access to digital media. All the while these conferences—and the universities they represent—pocket the ever-growing proceeds, capitalizing on the athletic efforts of big-time athletes and their NILs. Big-time sports universities have thus recently disregarded traditional regional sports rivalries[3] and travel inconveniences[4] to join more-lucrative athletic conferences and to sign new television broadcasting deals, all to generate more revenue.[5] Several conferences, even some individual universities, have established their own proprietary television networks too.[6] College athletic conferences have thus transformed the way they operate to enhance their brand and the brands of their member schools.[7]

Stanford's conference, the Pac-10 conference, added the universities of Utah and Colorado in 2012, renamed itself the Pac-12 conference, and since then its member universities' college sports teams have generated hundreds of millions of dollars per year in broadcast rights fees.[8] The Pac-12 marketing director, Danette Leighton, told me that before Larry Scott took over conference leadership, the conference did not have a marketing arm. Most conference offices up until that point were "structured more like governance bodies," she said, and while the Pac-10 was always strong in compliance enforcement, sports management, and officiating, they needed to make a change in the marketing of the conference and its assets. After his arrival, Scott hired Leighton, who had worked in professional sports for a decade, along with two CFOs who came from the NFL and MLB.

Leighton insisted that the Pac-10 was more of a hybrid between a traditional governance model and the new business model. This was a lean business model, she said, despite her reported $501,654 salary and Scott's $4.05 million salary (2014–2015 figures).[9] "We're not for profit," she told me, "so all of the money—TV money, whatever—gets distributed back to the schools outside of the expenses of the operating budget. So you want to stay lean. It would be silly not to be lean." Leighton noted that the Pac-10 staff was relatively small at least compared to professional sports outfits,[10] yet in the next breath she said that she was primarily concerned with the entertainment-business side of college sports and that in this regard, a comparison between the college and pro sports operations made perfect sense to her.

From an athlete's perspective, though, Leighton's comparison must appear inherently flawed because professional athletes are officially employees who are paid salaries and have the rights of employees, not to mention the ability to unionize. College athletes are also expected by NCAA rules to prioritize their education over their athletics but expected by their coaches and athletic directors and boosters to prioritize their athletic training. Big-time universities and athletic conferences thus gain more in revenue and brand exposure on the margin (here defined as the difference between a product or service's selling price and its cost of production or to the ratio between a company's revenues and expenses) than professional sports enterprises gain from the services of their employees since the reimbursement of college athletes is capped at an artificially low threshold.[11]

And yet few asked whether the salaries of big-time conference executives such as Scott and Leighton were justified since their salaries were artificially inflated given that the demand for college sports was high but the payment for the labor to meet that demand were artificially capped by NCAA rules. Were these executives forgiven because their work created a market for the exposure of these big-time college athletes that would not have otherwise existed and because that market could potentially bring those athletes fame (in professional sports or in other professions) and prepare them with an opportunity to practice dealing with that fame?

For the Pac-12, women's sports were an essential part of their own branding campaign so even if men's sports brought in the most revenue, the conference ought to have paid women's athletes if they were to use them and their example for marketing, even rhetorically. For example, Leighton told me that women's sports were a great source of pride for the conference.

> We are leaders in women's athletics . . . It is a focus of ours. It is important to us, just as our Olympic sports are. One of our differentiators is that we are not just a football or men's basketball conference. We are a broad conference that also includes women's sports and Olympic sports . . . It all boils down to committing to it. Stanford is a great example of that. They have committed to a broad-based program where their men's and women's sports are amazing. You see that at UCLA, USC, Arizona. The strength that our schools have in their men's and women's teams is very balanced.

If women's sports were important to the Pac-10 mission, didn't that also mean that these athletes should be included in any pay-for-play conversations, and what responsibility, if any, did Leighton and her employer have to put their money where their mouth was?

"You Got to Do Your Homework"

The NCAA's own television advertisements have also often shown their desire to display college athletes as students who smoothly and impressively shift between academics and athletics even if that appears to fly in the face of much research one reads in academic journals about the lived experiences of big-time college athletes.

For example, in late 2011 the NCAA ran an advertisement campaign during college football's bowl season in which it offered statistics to suggest that NCAA athletes had higher grades and graduation rates than non-athletes. At the spot's conclusion one athlete says, "You still think we're just a bunch of jocks? You got to do your homework." A narrator concludes, "Most NCAA athletes will be going pro in something other than sports."

The ad conveniently concealed the fact that "the football and men's basketball players who make money for colleges, graduate at a lower rate than students generally"[12]

This contradiction between college sports marketing and college sports reality illustrates that the NCAA and its member schools (which are simultaneously members of athletic conferences like the Pac-12) maintain the half-truth, fiction, or hoax (depending on your perspective) that college sports are amateur affairs. At the D-II and D-III levels some of this may be true, but at the big-time D-I level it may not.

In the years that the NCAA was led by former Indiana University president Myles Brand (2002–2009), the NCAA said there was one qualification of NCAA power: they provided leadership to their member universities but not always control. The idea was that the NCAA only stepped in when they were absolutely needed, and for the NCAA to succeed in its mission, it needed athletic directors and coaches to turn themselves in whenever NCAA infractions were found. The NCAA also said it expected member institutions to improve the education given to athletes (or at least improve the frequency at which they graduated).

Little changed when the NCAA hired Mark Emmert, who had previously led Louisiana State University (LSU) and the University of Washington and who continued to insist that college athletes were amateurs and that its power was limited if member institutions did not do their part.[13] Emmert said he wanted to change the NCAA's public image from that of a "cold and faceless" organization to one that was trying to make the lives of these young people better. He criticized the voluminous NCAA rulebook and in 2011 urged NCAA members to agree to give scholarship athletes $2,000 as a stipend to cover the costs of the "attendance gap." He also urged NCAA members to return to a system in which athletes were offered four-year, rather than one-year, scholarships.

But despite Emmert's acknowledgment that member schools needed to do more financially for their big-time athletes, Emmert's NCAA, like Brand's before him, continued to proclaim the importance of amateurism to its institutional mission, and for that reason Emmert's reform measures sputtered. Wondering who would pay for it, 160 schools opposed Emmert's stipend proposal. More than 60 percent of the colleges participating in D-I were against the four-year scholarship idea too. Emmert was criticized for "enjoying the trappings of being in a powerful position," including flying on the NCAA's private jet, buying an expensive Persian rug for his office, and driving a Porsche. His salary in 2013 was nearly $2 million.

As recently as 2016–2017 the NCAA officially reaffirmed its insistence that athletes should be amateurs and that they "should be protected from exploitation by professional and commercial enterprises."[14] Indeed, as of 2019 the NCAA required prospective athletes to receive an "amateurism certification." To do so, they must "register with the NCAA Eligibility Center, completely and accurately fill out the 'Sports Participation' section during registration, request final amateurism certification promptly, and monitor tasks assigned to their account."[15] Numerous NCAA rules governing college athletes further complicate matters. For example, in contracts that athletes sign with the NCAA, the NCAA warns that a variety of impermissible activities may compromise an athlete's eligibility to play college sports or receive an athletic scholarship to do so. As recently as 2017, the NCAA stated on its website that the following activities might impact amateur status and thus one's ability to receive an athletic scholarship:

- signing a contract with a professional team
- playing with professionals
- participating in tryouts or practices with a professional team
- accepting payments or preferential benefits for playing sports
- accepting prize money beyond expenses
- accepting benefits from an agent or prospective agent
- agreeing to be represented by an agent
- delaying full-time college enrollment to play in organized sports competitions[16]

In other words, the NCAA defines what amateurs and amateurism are, and they can take away an athlete's certificate proving that he or she is indeed an amateur if they believe that the athlete has violated one of their rules.

Leaving aside the legal question of whether this kind of governance should be allowed, NCAA amateurism rules leave athletes with confused notions regarding their role as students and as athletes, particularly which role ought to take precedence. Moreover, the decision for each athlete whether to apply for such certification is fraught with highly specific circumstances that only that particular athlete can decide, making generalizations difficult to draw. For example, the quality of education provided by NCAA member schools varies rather widely and the socioeconomic circumstances of prospective college athletes vary widely too so the question of whether to sign the NCAA contract in exchange for a so-called "free ride" depends on the perceived quality and value of the education promised.

Confronting each individual athlete faced with the NCAA amateurism certification process is the reality that big-time college sports at many schools are today commercial-professional affairs first and amateur-educational affairs second and driven by the entertainment side of the business more than by education.[17] For example, a 2009 U.S. Congressional Budget Office report found that big-time college sports derived 60 to 80 percent of their revenue from commercial sources. Moreover, the distinction between professional and recreational (amateur) athletes is often subjective and comes down to personal identity and intent. Sports philosopher Paul Weiss has said the difference between an amateur and a professional is that the former plays to play and for no other end while the professional has other goals in mind such as wealth or fame.[18] By this measure, of course, many college athletes would have intentions more like pro athletes than recreational athletes.

Therefore the NCAA language of amateurism appears to obfuscate a professional reality, and thereby limit calls for reform. Currently since universities do not pay salaries to big-time athletes but rather provide them with an education and require them to sign a contract promising to remain amateur, athletes can reasonably question why the so-called free market applies to conferences, universities, athletic departments, professors, and coaches but not to them. For these athletes, the ability to switch colleges (i.e., employers) in exchange for a better salary is taken for granted, yet college athletes can neither unionize nor collectively bargain for their own pay nor transfer easily from one college to another. While the NCAA statement of amateurism may ring true in some small-time sports under the NCAA umbrella, it appears at best disingenuous and at worst collusionary at the big-time level.

Big-time college sports, as they are currently managed and operated, are businesses with the primary aim of winning games, making money, and building the brand of American colleges and universities, and yet the employees who make that business possible are not given the labor rights one might expect. There may be instances of pure, unadulterated amateur play taking place within big-time American college sports, but those instances should not blind us to the reality of this economic relationship.

Shouldn't athletes be compensated in fairer proportion to how much their athletic services enrich the university (even if enrichment may be defined in numerous ways)? The star quarterback of the football team may enrich the university to a greater degree than the university swimming team's breaststroke champion given the relative media coverage of these sports and corresponding opportunity for the school to cash in, so some calibration must occur to ensure each athlete receives his or her proper due. Since they risk serious physical injury, shouldn't athletes in collision sports like football and basketball be compensated with at least the benefits of regular university employees too, including a form of worker's compensation insurance that surpasses the industry standard? At the very least, shouldn't we give them hazard pay?

Finally, the NCAA insists that its existence rests upon amateurism, but college sports do not need to be amateur to be popular. The Ted Stevens Olympic and Amateur Sports Act (TSOASA) of 1978, which required all national governing bodies to apportion 20 percent of their overall voting power to amateur athletes, ultimately led to the downfall of amateurism in Olympic sports but not their popularity. Within a decade of the TSOASA, the Olympics had removed the term "amateur" from its literature. And yet sports fans had little problem watching professional basketball players at the Summer Olympics, and billions of people around the world still watch the Winter and Summer Olympics, which suggests that amateurism rhetoric can be jettisoned, and big-time college sports will continue to attract large numbers of viewers, and continue to be profitable businesses.[19]

The Athletic Laborer: "We Were Slaves"

The cold hard truth appears to be that the NCAA is not really about amateurism but about protecting its member schools' ability to manage their college sports programs without going bankrupt.

Unfortunately though, few beyond a small group of scholars have asked whether the universities' use of big-time college athletes benefits the athletes themselves. This is not for lack of research; after all, scholars have studied the value of college sports from many other stakeholder perspectives. One study, for example, found that big-time college football victories do not actually increase alumni giving nor do they improve the test scores of the average undergraduate.[20] Other studies suggest that the branding of colleges through sports opens a university up to public scrutiny and potential scandals[21] and cover ups,[22] which run the risk of compromising a college sports team's success and therefore the university bottom line or even its overall reputation.[23] Still another study found that sexual misconduct scandals had little negative impact on fan attendance in women's college basketball.[24] Still, some colleges have turned to anonymous reporting technologies to handle internal problems that might become scandals before they become public.[25]

Rarely, though, have scholars looked at the state of affairs through the eyes of an athlete.

On one hand, branding a university through college sports may have a direct, positive impact on athletes, who may become recognizable public faces through college sports and in turn earn public exposure. This may be a highly desirable outcome for young, promising athletes who desire fame and public exposure, and it may also increase their chance of catching the eye of a pro scout or a company seeking out a future spokesman. Indeed, Chiney would ultimately become a popular ESPN basketball analyst.

But the NCAA's institutional allegiance to amateurism and the conference definition of athletes as "assets" distort the choices, perspectives, and arguably the values of young Americans, creating the impression among many that it is their athletic abilities, not their educational efforts, that primarily characterizes their formal relationship with their respective university. Ed O'Bannon, a former college basketball player and lead plaintiff in legal action against the NCAA and its corporate associates, described in early 2018 the primary role of the big-time athlete.

> With the practice schedule, the travel schedule, the playing schedule, the workout schedule, and everything that's involved in being a Division I athlete, in particular a basketball player, there's so much time dedicated to your craft, to your sport. There's not a whole lot of time left for school and life. So, when there are certain classes offered at certain times that you're interested in and you can't take, what do you do? On paper you're there as a student-athlete, you're there to get an education—and oh, by the way, also play basketball. But if you can't take those classes because you're in practice or you're traveling, what are you saying? What's the actual reason why I'm here? The reason why I'm here is I play basketball and I bring money into the school and the community and ultimately into the NCAA's pockets. That's what I'm here for.[26]

Like O'Bannon, some college athletes have protested this arrangement, which they believe effectively makes them slaves, as one University of Oregon football player related in 2013.

> I remember walking in from fall camp practice and talking to my teammates about how similar our lives were to the TV series *Spartacus*. We were slaves. We were paid enough to live, eat, and train . . . and nothing more. We went out on the field where we were broken down physically and mentally every day, only to wake up and do it again on the next. On the outside, spectators placed bets and objectified us. They put us on pedestals and worshipped us for a short time, but only as long as we were winning. In the end, we were just a bunch of dumbass [racial slur] for the owners to whip, and the rich to bet on. What I described is a business, I know. It's how it works, and it is something we understand as athletes entering the system, as [expletive] as it is. For many people entering that system, it's better than what life has to offer elsewhere. So they take it.[27]

The Journalist and the Scholar: Indentured Servants or Underpaid Professional Laborers?

When talented high school athletes find themselves recruited to play in the big-time college ranks, they have a big life decision to make. They cannot, by virtue of NBA and NFL rules, jump straight to the pro leagues. Only a select few from wealthy families or with the adventurous spirit to play their sport overseas can go around the NCAA–NBA and NFL machine. A near zero number of potentially big-time athletes eschew participation in big-time college sports altogether[28]—after all, the rewards (e.g., fame, scholarship, potential pro contract) are too great.

But those who sign the NCAA's amateurism contract soon learn that their primary role for their university is, as O'Bannon and others have shown, to work as a serious—arguably professional—athlete even though they are neither recognized nor paid as such. If their job is primarily to serve these businesses and make money for their university, conference, and the NCAA as well as for its many associated corporate and media partners, then what should journalists and scholars call these young athletes? Legally, big-time college athletes may not officially be considered employees of their institution, but it seems reasonable to at least call them underpaid professionals.[29]

Are they truly slaves, as the aforementioned University of Oregon player suggested? The economists Andy Schwarz and Jason Belzer (and Joe Nocera and Ben Strauss, who build on their argument) claim that college athletes are essentially indentured servants because they "lack the resources to pay their way to a better world." Accordingly, they face "a hard bargain—stay behind in their old lives with little prospect of advancement or else spend several years working only for room and board and training in the hope of bettering themselves." The prospect for indentured servants to capitalize on their period of indentured servitude and make a better life for themselves varies from person to person, but the problem with college athletes is that the "NCAA is the only purchaser of student athletic labor," which means the NCAA is a monopsony that colludes with colleges and universities to artificially restrain competition between colleges and to cap payment for these athletes. In such a system, Schwarz and Belzer claim, there can be no economic justice because there is no economic competition. In this regard, they argue, being a college athlete is an even more exploitative system than being a truly indentured servant of the seventeenth or eighteenth century.

As compelling as their argument may be, however, Schwarz and Belzer largely overlook the educational exchange that takes place because of college athletic scholarships, and would not in some cases occur without the athletic labor exchange, so perhaps the term "underpaid professional" better fits since it still highlights the economic injustice but also acknowledges that these athletes already receive something for their efforts: an athletic scholarship and close instruction from an expert staff of coaches in their chosen field of specialization. Zimbalist once called college athletes "unpaid professionals," but this no longer seems accurate because they *are* paid something and because they are not only exempt from paying tuition and other university fees for housing and food but they also as of 2015 receive the true cost of attendance.

The remaining question is whether all of this is enough to be considered fair and just since these athletes would likely be compensated more substantially if their employment were not governed by the universities' and the NCAA's outdated notion that they are amateurs and by the many rules that have been codified by NCAA member schools to ensure they remain as such.

To me, that question can only be answered by situating the economic argument within the broader educational context and asking questions about the quality and value of that education. In other words, asking whether the full-ride is truly full, and asking whether the education is truly higher.

The Corporate Sponsor: Be Willing to Play at Any Position

Like the universities that they partner with, companies that choose to advertise through college sports recognize the great value in affixing their name to big-time male and female athletes; indeed, many of them also see college athletes as an asset that they can use to market and sell their products. In that sense, they imagine young athletes as hard-working professionals whose athletic accomplishments can be exploited for profit. In 2012, for example, the Ford Motor Company ran a tie-in during college football telecasts promoting Ford Work Day. It was a behind-the-scenes segment highlighting "how college football players get ready for their workday" and featured several Ford trucks and their owners getting construction work done. The implication was clear: both Ford trucks and college athletes mean business, and in their business, they are nothing if not dependable.

Lowe's, a national home improvement retailer, has also tried to capitalize on college athletes by sponsoring a Senior CLASS Award (Celebrating Loyalty and Achievement for Staying in School). During the 2010–2011 NCAA Men's and Women's Basketball Championships, Lowe's used this educational platform to advertise their store, capitalizing on young athletes to market their brand on television and through the Internet. Kayla Pedersen was a finalist for the award at the end of the year. When she was nominated, her bio, which was posted on a website run by Premier Sports Management, read, "Pedersen's unselfishness and willingness to put the team's interests ahead of her own individual stats is highlighted by her total willingness to play at any position that will give the team its best chance of winning."

While true, the statement failed to acknowledge that Lowe's was building its brand on the efforts of Pedersen without directly compensating her. Perhaps the award nomination was enough to help Pedersen in her future career endeavors, but that seems besides the point. Thus, athletes like Pedersen sometimes find themselves outside the symbiotic relationship between universities and corporations, their NILs being used to infer excellence and often without their explicit consent.

Professional Play and Big-Time Exploitation

Whereas big-time athletes generate revenue for their university, and ought to be more properly compensated, they also generate the harder-to-quantify metric of favorable publicity for the university. Meanwhile, big-time athletes receive much more than just a scholarship from the university in return; they also get the chance to associate with something bigger than themselves, which may lead to other benefits that are similarly difficult to quantify. Unfortunately, too few scholars or journalists have focused on the qualitative aspects of big-time college sports and therefore have largely ignored the positive individual benefits that participation in the big time confers.

We therefore need a more qualitative and balanced assessment of big-time college sports today that acknowledges the aspects that have sustained big-time college sports over many decades especially in terms of the give-and-take between colleges and big-time athletes without sugarcoating the problems that also exist.

We also need a balanced assessment that fully accounts for the sexism that remains in college sports. After all, the same sexism that effectively prevents the public from considering women's college basketball teams big time also effectively prohibits scholars and journalists from acknowledging the exploitation—both economic and symbolic—that is done unto them. In other words, if one says that big-time men's college athletes are underpaid professionals, shouldn't one also say that women's college athletes are also underpaid professionals?

These young women are professional in the sense that they sell their services to their employers (universities like Stanford) in exchange for a full-ride and a free education. That sale may not be only an economic exchange between player and university, but it is undoubtedly partly so. Whether they are paid for their services proportionately seems to be second to, though not less important than, whether they are paid to perform services for the university. After all, many professionals outside sports are underpaid and some even choose to do work pro bono. "Professional" in this sense is a category not a degree, and the issue here is that athletes—male and female—do not have that choice. This must be remedied.

There are different definitions and types of professionalism[30] to be sure, but by and large it seems that specialized training and knowledge, earning a living through one's work,[31] and having a sense of responsibility characterize most definitions of the professional,[32] and by all these measures, albeit to differing degrees, the Stanford women I followed fit the bill. They were trained in a certain, specialized way. They prepared intensively and were required to be on time and have good time-management skills. They wore the kind of attire—a company uniform—one would expect of a professional. Crucially, they were not pursuing their sport in any meaningful recreational sense, although it would be untrue to say that they did not ever have fun.[33] Their serious intention in playing their sport seemed to be another important part of the story since their improvement benefited not only themselves but also their coach and organization.[34] Their time commitment to the sport was unparalleled. According to Sander's 2011 research, many women's basketball players spend nearly forty hours a week on basketball-related activities, which is twice what is allowed by NCAA rules. This fact has prompted the NCAA to increase staffing for women's basketball enforcement.[35]

"Professional" may connote a standard of equipment and facilities that specifically cater to athletes as much if not more than to the student body, and that was the case for Stanford's women athletes as much as men. "Professional" may also connote extensive support staff and a cadre of employees to serve the needs of the team and its coaching staff. For example, Stanford's athletic program employed dedicated development and marketing professionals charged with the task of raising money from donors (in contrast to smaller schools, which sometimes require coaches to do that work in addition to their coaching).

Thus, there are various quantitative measures—fan base, revenue, television ratings, and a higher standard of equipment and facilities as well as the availability of full-ride scholarships—that distinguish the big time from the small time and men's sports from women's, but by all these measures women's sports like Stanford basketball fit into the categories of professional and big time much more than they fit into the category of amateur and small time. Moreover, a qualitative eyeball test also suggests that professionalism goes far beyond dollars earned and work exchanged. The team I followed was nationally ranked, made up of Olympians who hailed from every corner of the nation, followed by a legion of die-hard fans and alumni, and sponsored by multinational corporations and local businesses, thus seeming eminently professional. Many of these athletes mimicked their coaches' professionalism in their own behavior, both on and off the court, and faced a similar level of pressure to carry themselves as professionals in demeanor. After all, the media most often recognized them not for their personality or classroom accomplishments but for their role in the team, program, and organization and thus for their effort and ability to win and, perhaps, give a compelling postgame interview.

To Buy In or Not To Buy In: That Is the Question

At the end of the day then, the question of whether universities should brand themselves on the backs on college athletes and whether that arrangement is good for the athletes themselves is a question that largely hinges upon one's perspective, on whether one deems college athletes professionals or amateurs or indentured servants or slaves and on whether one buys in to the notion that a college sports scholarship is mostly a good deal for the university brand and the individual or whether it is a symbiotic relationship that benefits both more or less equally. Of course, this question hinges on whether one believes that the decision to buy in to college sports will lead to something bigger for the individual athlete.

It is true that the culture of big-time women's basketball is predicated upon the physical sacrifice of athletes and that they have little choice but to give up their right to profit from their NIL in exchange for the chance to play at the big-time level, but the calculus is likely different for different athletes at different schools, and it is for that reason that we cannot paint with broad strokes.

For Stanford athletes like Nneka and Chiney who were exceptional athletes, exceptional pitchwomen for the university, and accomplished students (not to mention shoe-ins to play professional basketball), representing the Stanford brand was a complicated matter. For others who were not as talented, the calculus was different, and this is probably why for many non-star, big-time athletes, grant-in-aid and big-woman-on-campus status seems to be enough, and why they do not protest the arrangement. After all, while there has been considerable protest by some big-time college athletes, there has not yet been a mass boycott by large numbers of college athletes.

That being said, some universities do exploit big-time athletes economically and symbolically, so what can be done? Contrary to what we often read in the popular press, pressuring universities to pay players may be a misplaced effort and not the panacea that many think it would be. Instead, the best pressure should be placed on universities to improve their brand's standing in the public imagination not by improving their sports teams and their sports teams' perceived entertainment value (e.g., AP football rankings) but by increasing educational investments for their athletes (and measuring their cognitive gains with entry- and exit-testing), improving their educational offerings, and better articulating the expectations they have for a more-balanced effort from athletes in their academic and athletic pursuits. Applying such pressure may also require fans, alumni, and concerned citizens to push back against universities that spend extravagantly on college sports facilities, coaches, administrators, but also other facilities and administrative costs that limit a university's ability to hire the best professors and give them the tools they need to provide all students a high-quality education.

By improving and balancing the provision of athletic entertainment to the public and the academic education of its athletes and non-athletes, an institution can improve its brand value. Then the number of athletes benefiting in intangible and unquantifiable ways will likely increase, and more athletes may choose to buy in to the idea of trying to be the best student and athlete they can be simultaneously. More Americans (including young people and college sports fans) ought to demand a higher-quality education for all students, including but not only athlete-students, and more universities may choose to go the route of Stanford in creating a public perception that academics and athletics can and do coexist on an even plane. The details of that coexistence are the subject of the next chapter.

Notes

1. Clotfelter, *Big Time*, 58–59.
2. See for example Staurowsky, "Her Life"; Cahn, *Coming on Strong*; Grundy and Shackelford, *Shattering*; Baker, *Why She Plays*; and Betancourt, *Playing Like a Girl*.
3. In late 2012, seven schools left the Big East Conference because they believed too many conference decisions had been made based on football and instead wanted to put the interests of their basketball teams first.
4. In late 2011, the Pac-12 and Big Ten conferences inked a deal scheduling more marquee matchups between each conference's football powerhouse colleges despite significant geographic distances (Thamel, "Scheduling Partnership").
5. Most college athletic conferences, including the Pac-12, do not sell ads directly to sponsors and choose instead to have a third-party handle that for them as part of their media rights deal. Conference broadcasting decisions are increasingly inked with global considerations in mind too. In 2017, the Pac-12 sold rights to Alibaba to

broadcast games in China in an effort to advertise the athletic and academic offerings of member schools to prospective Chinese students (Soshnick, "Alibaba Buys").

6. The Big Ten Network was established first, and alongside News-Corp Fox it began airing college sports events in 2006. The University of Texas at Austin owns the Longhorn Network, which is a joint venture between ESPN and IMG College and broadcasts twenty different Longhorn sports from baseball to volleyball. BYU has its own TV network too.

7. There has also been an increase in the number of cable television channels that are dedicated to sports (e.g., ESPNU and Fox College Sports are TV channels dedicated entirely to college sports) and the amount of money networks will pay to broadcast them. In 2006, ESPN agreed to pay $1 billion over ten years for that privilege. The SEC signed a similar fifteen-year deal with CBS and ESPN for $3 billion in 2008, and the ACC signed one with ESPN that paid nearly $2 billion over twelve years (Nocera and Strauss, *Indentured*, 190–91).

8. Since 2011when the Pac-12 inked a then-historic broadcast deal with Fox and ESPN and Pac-12 Networks for $250 million per year over twelve years for a total of $3 billion, each of the conference's twelve member schools has earned approximately $21 million in annual revenue (Rosenblatt, "Breaking Down").

9. Solomon, "Pac-12 Falls Behind."

10. While the Pac-10 hosts most athletic championships in house, it outsources the men's and women's basketball and football championships to media companies like Fox and local professional teams like the Los Angeles Clippers, which it asks to help with game operations. By contrast, the conference asks member universities to host smaller events like gymnastics championships and use their own staff. Championship hosting rotates among member schools, and when a university hosts, it is required to foot the bill.

11. Investopedia, "Margin Definition."

12. Easterbrook, *The King*, 119

13. Emmert hired football coach Nick Saban to turn the LSU football program around. The Tigers had a losing record before Saban arrived, but in his first year at Baton Rouge the Tigers went 8-4 and won the Peach Bowl. At the University of Alabama, where he later coached, Saban would go on to become one of college football's most applauded—and reviled—coaches.

14. Quoted in Sage, Eitzen, and Beal, *Sociology*, 255. See also National Collegiate Athletic Association, "2016–17 NCAA Division I Manual," 4.

15. National Collegiate Athletic Association, "Amateurism."

16. National Collegiate Athletic Association, "Amateurism."

17. Staurowsky, "A Radical Proposal," 593.

18. Weiss, *Sport*, 198.

19. Finkel, Martin, and Paley, *$chooled*.

20. Using national data from the Mellon Foundation study "College and Beyond," Shulman and Bowen found that "the data flatly contradict one of the strongest myths about college athletics, that winning teams, and especially winning football

teams, have a large, positive impact on giving rate" (quoted in Feezell, "Review," 90–92). Orszag also found it difficult to prove that there is a definite link between big-time sports programs and higher alumni donations or higher-quality admissions applications: "If there's any effect, it's a blip: it doesn't persist" (quoted in Drape and Thomas, "As Colleges Compete"). Finally, there is little proof that the academic quality of an incoming student body will be better if the football team is big-time and televised on a regular basis. Dowling argues that when big-time public colleges make a "symbolic declaration of institutional purpose," they may unintentionally force otherwise promising students to leave their home state and lower the academic standard of the state's university (*Confessions*, 28). Zimbalist found in 2001 that while "there was some tendency for athletic success to increase applications," there was "no significant relationship between various measures of athletic success and average school SAT scores" and therefore concluded "the only possible institutional justification, then, for supporting athletic success is that it might enable a university to expand the size of its student body" (*Unpaid Professionals*, 169). In other words, having a football team that wins may ensure a steady stream of admissions applications and, therefore, tuition checks, but it will not necessarily better the academic quality of undergraduate students.

21. Byers and Hammer, *Unsportsmanlike Conduct*, 176.
22. The two Penn State University scandals that made national headlines illustrate how the high-profile nature of big-time sports can be a detriment to the university brand especially when university officials decide to cover up wrongdoing. See Mosbacher and Yacker, *Training Rules*; and R. A. Smith, *Wounded Lions*.
23. Prior, O'Reilly, Mazanov, and Huybers, "The Impact of Scandal."
24. Williams and Greenwell, "The Impact of Scandal."
25. In 2019 the *Wall Street Journal* reported that as many as seventy colleges were using an app called "Real Recruit," which allowed athletes to anonymously report any concerns or potentially damaging information to athletic department administrators. Incidents included "coaches having sex with athletes, inappropriate touching, bullying" (Bachman, "NCAA," A14).
26. Greene, "Ed O'Bannon."
27. Canzano, "Canzano Blog."
28. There are, however, several emerging alternatives to the NCAA, at least in men's basketball. One of them is the Professional Collegiate League (PCL), which is an organization promising to end "amateurism," which its founders call a "con" and representative of a "staggering injustice," and to pay talented men's basketball players between $50,000 and $150,000 and guarantee them a college scholarship. The PCL was set to have its inaugural season in summer 2020 contingent upon the league's ability to recruit not only talented athletes but also investors, but as of late 2021, just three of the proposed eight teams had signed on. See Costa, "College Basketball," A14); See also, https://thepcleague.com.
29. Zimbalist, *Unpaid Professionals*.

30. Freidson defines professionalism as "a set of interconnected institutions providing the economic support and social organization that sustains the occupational control of work" (*Professionalism*, 2). Lawson distinguishes between two types of professionalism: mechanical, market-driven professionalism and social-trustee civic professionalism. While the former may become fascinated by their own career aspirations and making money and lose sight of their clients' needs, the latter believe their work promotes social welfare and social justice and creates healthy people and a good society. The former may "treat clients humanely but with little feeling, believing that an objective, arm's length attitude is critical to professional success" (quoted in Hoffman, "Becoming," 336).

31. The philosopher of sport, Paul Weiss, argues that professionals cannot exist unless there is an economy in which human beings are property in whom an investment can made and from whom a return is expected. In short, professionalism presupposes a capitalist economy. Weiss writes, "The professional is a workman, an employee, a man who plays for hire under the supervision of a foreman and doubles as a guide and control. Money has been invested in him. He is property, whose primary role is to repay that investment by using his ability to play in a way that will satisfy his owners because it satisfies the spectators, usually by a victory" (*Sport*, 205).

32. Hoffman argues that professionals in sport need to master complex skills that are grounded in and guided by systematic theory and research; perform services for others (e.g., clients or patients); be granted a monopoly by the community to supply certain services to its members; be guided by formal and informal codes intended to preserve the health and well-being of clients; and meet the expectations and standards prescribed by their professional subculture ("Becoming," 327).

33. Blanchard explains that "play, unlike leisure, should not be viewed as an antidote of work . . . If work is to be treated as the polar opposite of play on an inactivity continuum, work must be consistently involuntary, and pleasurable, and real" (*The Anthropology of Sport*, 42).

34. Weiss argues that the difference between amateurs and professionals is that the former plays to play and for no other end. It is a question of intended purpose (*Sport*, 205, 198).

35. Sander, "Women's Basketball," A17.

CHAPTER 9

"I Am Not a Celebrity at Stanford"

> The public lives on the myth that if you have an outstanding academic program, you can't be excellent in athletics, and vice versa. There's also a very prevalent stereotype that a student can't be good in both academics and athletics. Our students here refute that proposition . . . By choosing to enroll here, they have accepted the challenge of playing in the major league academically as well as athletically. That decision by itself earns them my utmost respect.
>
> —Fred Hargadon[1]

"Respect, It's the Name of the Game": St. John's University, March 21, 2011 (NCAA Tournament, Round II)

Nearly six thousand fans filled their Maples Pavilion seats to take in Stanford's second-round matchup against St. John's. The heightened intensity of the postseason game could be witnessed even in warm-ups. In one pre-game drill, Chiney and Sarah Boothe took turns pushing each other in a test of balance. Their task was simple: the pusher would not tell the pushee where she was going to push. The pushee's goal was to hold her ground, a relevant drill for inside players who fight for rebounds and do not always know where their opponent will be when the shot goes up and caroms off the rim or backboard. When finished, Sarah and Chiney slapped a high five, indicating the camaraderie that came from preparing each other for the intense physicality they expected. The drill demonstrated both the toughness required to play at this level but also the social bonds created in the process.

In the first half, Coach VanDerveer used a zone defense to neutralize the quickness of the Red Storm and settle for three pointers. But Red Storm players answered with individually creative plays, beating Stanford defenders off the dribble, and creating their own shots. Stanford players presented matchup nightmares too. As she had been all year, Nneka leveraged her superior combination of size, speed, strength, and court sense. No one had stopped her all year, and no one could stop her that day, either. St. Johns tried to punish her physically when she leapt high in the air to score, but even when they forced her to take difficult shots, her sister Chiney was there to pick up an offensive rebound and put the ball back in the bucket. The sisters' power was even noticeable in their absence. When Coach VanDerveer gave them time to rest, the Red Storm went on a 9-0 run and took a 20-14 lead. Coach VanDerveer had seen enough, and sent the sisters back in. Nneka played with a fire in her belly, scoring two tough buckets, and then another to bring the Cardinal back within two, 22-20.

Chiney briefly left the game with a hand injury, and Toni followed her to the bench with a twisted ankle. Nneka remained a bulldozer inside, dropping in layup after layup, often over double-teams, or with the shot clock running down, or even when she was being fouled. One of her three-point plays put Stanford up 31-26. Toni also shifted her game to a higher postseason gear, racing the court to convert a beautiful off-balance layup, leaning into a defender. The crowd thundered, and Stanford jogged to the locker room up 38-30.

In the second half, Chiney used her long arms and nose for the ball to force turnovers and her speed to run the court in the transition game. Kayla put Stanford up by ten when she drilled a three and then nodded in Jeannette's direction with gratitude for a great assist. The Red Storm tried a full court press to keep the game close, but Stanford broke it easily. The Cardinal was too big, strong, and technically disciplined to be flustered. Nneka collected her eighteenth point on a free throw and her twentieth point following a pinpoint Jeannette pass along the baseline. The score was now 50-37.

On the next play, a Red Storm defender hammered Mikaela Ruef and sent her into a tailspin. And even though she couldn't see the basket, she found an acrobatic way to bank the ball into the bucket. The crowd roared her name—"*Ruuuuuuuuuuuuuuuuuuef!*"—and the spectacular play became the catalyst the Cardinal needed to break the game open. Two minutes later, Stanford's lead was twenty points. The final score wasn't close: 75-44.

After the game, Red Storm coach Kim Barnes Arico told the press, "Their depth, and their length, and the little combination of everything they have, wore us down . . . We got tired." Coaches had said such things about Stanford all season long, underscoring the begrudging respect they had for Coach VanDerveer and the Cardinal.

During TV timeouts, the public address announcer told the Maples crowd to be respectful and not let the madness of March carry them away. In 2011, the NCAA hosted eighty-eight NCAA championships in twenty-three sports, of which the men's March Madness tournament was the most widely known, profitable, and intense among players and among fans. But apparently there was enough madness on the women's side that the Maples announcer felt the need to remind fans, "Fans, please respect the players and coaches. Stanford and St. John's have many traditions, but bad sportsmanship is not one of them." At the same time, the NCAA flashed its own public relations message repeatedly on the Jumbotron: "Respect: It's the name of the game."

The NCAA admonitions seemed peculiar to me, having personally studied the history of the NCAA but also having watched the entire season unfold and having rarely witnessed fans fail to show their respect for the players or each other. A group of rather reserved but nonetheless knowledgeable ticket holders dominated Stanford's fan base, showing passionate spirit for a game they loved to watch but also a deep respect for those who made their entertainment possible. In my experience, it was the kind of respect that was not always apparent among fans of big-time men's college sports such as football and basketball, who sometimes treated big games as a license to drink to excess and behave in rather unsavory ways. I must confess that when I was in college, I often treated the big (men's) games that way, too.

Respect also seemed a curious notion in the context of big-time college sports especially given the intense competition that engendered physical play and given the calls of exploitation. Did Stanford University, or the NCAA for that matter, have any right to tell fans to be respectful if they themselves were economically and symbolically exploiting the athletes who were providing their entertainment? Reluctant respect expressed by an opponent was one thing; institutional respect for the players was another altogether. Did Stanford University as an institution truly respect its players, and if so, how could one tell? Was the education they provided athletes proof enough of their respect? Or was something more needed?

"Time to Put the Hammer Down": North Carolina, March 26, 2011 (NCAA Tournament, Round III)

The crowds grew larger with each advancing round of the tournament, and for Stanford's third-round matchup of the NCAA Tournament, nearly eleven thousand filed in to watch the Cardinal face the University of North Carolina Tar Heels in Spokane Arena in Washington. The competition was becoming fiercer too. UNC brought a large team: five players standing over six feet, and two towering over 6'5." Capitalizing on their inside strength, the Tar Heels raced out on a 9-0 run and took a 13-7 lead.

Once again, though, Stanford prevailed in the same manner they had all season, with a gritty second-half perseverance stoked by an inspirational VanDerveer halftime speech. Nneka took the team on her shoulders, scoring eight of the team's final fifteen points, and finishing the game with nineteen points and three rebounds. Before the Pac-10 tournament, Coach VanDerveer had urged her junior All-American to take her game to the next level: "It's time to put the hammer down," she said, and against UNC, Nneka delivered the crushing blows.

"They Were Just Better Than Us": Gonzaga University, March 28, 2011 (NCAA Tournament, Round IV)

The Cardinal remained in Spokane for the next round, an Elite Eight matchup against Gonzaga University's Zags, who were having a mighty year of their own. Their star, Courtney Vandersloot, was averaging 19.8 points per game on the season and 31 points per game in the tournament and led the country in assists at 10.1 per game. As a point guard, Vandersloot had trained with Zags legend (and Utah Jazz star, Olympian, and NBA Hall of Famer) John Stockton. By the end of her career, she would become the first player in NCAA D-I basketball history to finish her career with over 2,000 points and 1,000 assists (2,073 points and 1,118 assists), setting a record even Stockton never achieved. At the time, her star was as bright as ever, with one ESPN sportscaster calling Vandersloot "apple pie in a state that is all about apples." In November, Vandersloot had scored twenty-four points and dished out ten assists against Stanford, almost single-handedly keeping the game close.

The Zags also had home court advantage. The Associated Press deemed the advantage "unfair" since the Spokane Arena presented the Cardinal with a "deafening, unfriendly crowd in a hostile ... setting," but the day before the game Coach VanDerveer practiced with simulated crowd noise, believing that they could overcome the Zags home court edge with dogged preparation.

Stanford led 47-38 at the half, having shot 65 percent from field, a season high for a half, and in the second half their size and depth wore the Zags down. Stanford switched into a zone defense to neutralize Vandersloot's playmaking ability, too. The Zags struggled to get the ball inside the zone and began to take bad shots. In the first six minutes of the second half, they connected on 1 of 11 from the floor, and the Stanford lead grew accordingly. It was another masterful VanDerveer strategy, executed to perfection by her intelligent and fearless team. When Chiney made an acrobatic layup to extend the Cardinal lead to 61-40, the outcome seemed set in stone. Vandersloot managed twenty-five points and nine assists but Stanford still won the game handily, 83-60.

Coach VanDerveer gave high fives to each one of her players, a personal gesture to congratulate them on their upcoming trip to the Final Four, the program's fourth straight. Stanford freshmen climbed a blue and silver ladder made by Weber—an official corporate sponsor of the NCAA Tournament—to the hoop and began to cut small strands of the net. The ritual was a NCAA tournament tradition, and it followed a carefully planned order: freshmen, sophomores, juniors, seniors, staff (coaching interns, managers, trainer, strength and performance coaches, etc.), and finally, the Stanford coaches cut the last remaining threads. When Coach VanDerveer cut her part, she handed it to Jeannette, who was standing at the bottom of the ladder, looking up with equal parts reverence and appreciation.

Stanford was once again set to breathe the rarified air of one of the most culturally significant tournaments in all American sports, a winner-take-all sudden death tournament that symbolized the highest level of college basketball competition but also the highest stakes of American sports culture. Win, and your team advances. Lose, and your season is over.

Although she was stellar in defeat and would go on to have a wildly successful professional career, Vandersloot acknowledged Stanford's accomplishment with respect and matter-of-fact simplicity: "They were just better than us, they were tougher than us, they were stronger than us."

The Stanford Standard

While I was doing research for this book, many people expressed something like what Vandersloot said about Stanford: that they thought that Stanford was "just better." And by extension, some said, they did not think that Stanford's brand of balance between school and sports could be copied elsewhere.

Perhaps they were right, although I still believe that such balance is an ideal toward which others ought to strive and thus one that deserves further examination. After all, isn't the best way to judge the universities that sponsor big-time sports by their commitment to educating both athletes and non-athletes—that is to say, how they commit to being an institution of higher learning first and foremost, and how they incorporate sports into the process of honoring that commitment?

That is why, in this chapter, I examine the positive educational culture that develops because of Stanford's institutional commitment to providing quality education for all its students and how that culture influences the decision making of administrators, coaches, and athletes. Stanford's admissions policy is the most salient aspect of what I call the Stanford Standard, an impressive institutional unwillingness to admit students who do not make the cut academically even if they impress athletically.[2] But there are other aspects too, including an unwillingness to let football be crowned king on campus and the commitment to providing high quality education to all students, graduating athletes at a high rate, and to upholding the ideals of the scholar-athlete and the coach-educator.

Stanford is perennially ranked among the top academic institutions in the world, and it is one of the only top-tier universities that also regularly fields big-time sports teams.[3] Excellence in sports is, therefore, a huge part of Stanford's perceived excellence as a university.

As several scholars have found, many educational benefits may come from intercollegiate sports participation, but none are necessarily a given and indeed may depend greatly on the structure and delivery of academic and athletic programs, which of course require university investment.[4] But by establishing a university structure that prioritizes the education of athletes, college administrators can help create a culture in which education is the default priority for all students, regardless of their athletic abilities.

"Academic Performance and Intellectual Potential Are Always the Highest Priorities"

Nothing establishes Stanford's unique academic and athletic culture, and nothing ensures that true institutional respect will be given to athletes more than the Stanford policy of admitting only students who can excel in academics. According to a 2003 statement by Stanford University president John Hennessey, this policy is part of broader university effort to not allow subjectivity to distort the admissions process.

Although a wide range of considerations is taken into account, at Stanford, academic performance and intellectual potential are always the highest priorities. Historically, we have relied on consideration of race and ethnicity as one factor among many in our admission process to help achieve diversity. That said, any advantage given to a particular trait, other than some objective measure of academic merit, introduces a value that is subjective. This is true whether the trait is race, athletic skill, legacy status, leadership ability or any other attribute. Although such consideration does not legally or effectively create a quota, it is reasonable to ask why we would support any such system, even one with perceived benefits.[5]

This perspective appears to be unique among American institutions of higher education that are involved in big-time intercollegiate sports. As Branch notes, one of the most intractable problems of big-time college sport is that "high performance athletes . . . [can] be forgiven for not meeting the academic standards of their peers."[6]

"There's No Back Door"

In 2018, Coach VanDerveer said that while it was difficult to find athletes who had the ability to play basketball for her and keep up with the academic workload of Stanford, she "respected" Stanford's philosophy in saying that there was "no back door" to admissions, and that she was more than willing to accept athletics' relatively limited role on campus.

> It is difficult. There might be one hundred top players and we can only recruit five of them. I think, thankfully, academics are more and more important to young people and they might realize that if they waste the scholarship, then what are they gonna have? They are a toe jam or an ankle sprain away . . . for the most part they are not going to play professionally. Some do, but their education is really important and the young people I recruit are very serious about getting a great education and they do very well at Stanford. I respect the fact that Stanford doesn't admit someone who can't do the work. It's hard sometimes because there's a great player and I think she'd be great on the team, but if she can't do the work, then it's not fair to her . . . Just like [Stanford professors] are not telling us, "Hey, I've got a great English recruit and we need to put her on your team," I have to find players that can be on my team and can be in their classroom. I have to credit Stanford's philosophy and Stanford's mission for saying, "There's no back door. You have to get in the front door like everyone else."[7]

Stanford coaches pursued an approach they dubbed "rifle recruiting," which according to Coach VanDerveer meant they did not "spin [their] wheels recruiting a lot of players." Instead, they aggressively pursued certain likely-to-be-admitted-to-Stanford players, explaining that if they wanted a certain player, "we have got to get you if you are smart enough to get into Stanford. There's nobody else. There's nobody behind you." The second aspect of the recruiting formula Coach VanDerveer and her staff employed was to only recruit players they thought had the "higher level . . . work ethic" to keep up "in terms of conditioning and training." VanDerveer explained that she wanted players who would "buy in to playing [a fast-paced style of play]," adding that "in the old days, we didn't always have all of the TV time-outs, so we used to run people out of the gym [with superior conditioning]."

Stanford's recruiting involved extensive faculty involvement in recruiting too, which was also apparently rather unique. Athletes who pick Stanford want to know more about the education they will receive so Stanford coaches offer recruits a chance to visit campus, and when they are there encourage them to visit not only current players but also professors. It was a custom that dated back several decades. In the early 1980s, Stanford psychiatry professor William Dement, an expert on the science of sleep, helped the football team as a faculty recruiting coordinator. His job was to "organize a group of several dozen faculty who participated in the recruitment of high school athletes."[8] Condoleezza Rice, the Stanford professor, former secretary of state, and provost of the university, routinely took time away from her busy schedule to help recruit football players to the farm. Stanford head football coach David Shaw affectionately called Rice his "cleanup hitter."[9] Coach VanDerveer told me that Dr. Rice had been "very supportive" of her program too and that she met with players on recruiting trips. In the early 1980s, Stanford's recruiting coordinator was Ray Handley, who explained the rationale. "We'd be crazy not to use some of the brightest, wittiest people in the world in recruiting. The professors serve as an information source for the prospects during their recruitment and become personally involved with them during their visit."[10]

Some athletes chose Stanford because it meant being close to Silicon Valley, while for others it was the predictably sunny California weather. But for most, it was the education they would receive and the fact that they knew that the positive educational culture of Stanford would ensure that their sports coach would respect their desire to study.[11] While a coach like VanDerveer could have lamented the limitations that the Stanford Standard put on her ability to recruit, the Stanford Standard itself could also be seen an asset in the coaches' sales pitch to recruits. As Dick Gould, Stanford's former men's tennis coach, once said, "People tend to think there's something bad about recruiting. Recruiting is a not a dirty word. All we're doing is selling something we believe in, and if you're selling something you believe in, there really can't be much that is distasteful about it."[12]

Once a prospective recruit has been identified, but before they begin recruitment, Stanford coaches find out if a player is academically likely to gain admittance to Stanford. Back in the 1980s, this meant asking prospective athletes to take the SAT as soon as possible, to send a transcript, and then formally apply for admission. As an assistant football coach at the time noted, "We may be the only school to ask them to send in a transcript, and we may be the only school that asks them to formally apply for admission."[13] At that time, being a great athlete was for many college admissions offices enough to warrant being given a free admissions pass, but a prospective Stanford athlete was asked to fill out forms, take tests, ask for recommendations, and write an admissions essay like any other prospective non-athlete student. Then dean of admissions at the time Fred Hargadon explained, "What some of the coaches may regard as a drawback—the number of hoops we make recruits go through to apply here—may be a real attraction to the university. It sends out a lot of signals about the kind of school we are."[14] Being a good athlete did not give you a break, but "athletic skill was a strength that was considered" alongside other skills and the "contribution the student will make to life on campus, artistic or musical skills, or a host of other personal qualities."[15] Being a national caliber athlete could "round out one's application," so while a student had to qualify academically to get into Stanford, being able to play on one of Stanford's sports teams would undoubtedly distinguish an application.

Today, the precise way in which the admissions process unfolds is harder to pin down. While admissions officers reserved details on exactly how this process unfolds, with one telling me via email, "our process regarding athletics is an internal process and is not something I can share," everyone else I spoke with at Stanford assured me that athletic ability alone was not enough to gain admission. Assistant dean for admissions Kiyoe Hashimoto noted via an email message in 2013 that Stanford admissions officers "look for the same qualities and have the same requirements of all applicants, including student-athletes," and the admissions office website states, "In some cases, exceptional abilities in athletics may influence our decision if the applicant is otherwise well qualified, but such abilities never, by themselves, ensure admission to Stanford."[16]

Why did Stanford insist on this admissions policy for athletes? One former athletic director, Andy Geiger, explained that failing to admit the kind of student who would succeed at Stanford would amount to exploitation. "The Admissions Office admits human beings and we understand and respect that. We advocate, and they advocate, and we understand each other. We fail as an athletic department when we become of another world . . . I feel very strongly that if we bring somebody to Stanford for athletic reasons who otherwise will fail; that's exploitation."[17]

Admissions Director Hargadon agreed. "People imagine more conflict [between admissions and athletics] than there really is. I don't tell the coaches what play to call or whom to play at quarterback, and they don't tell me whom to admit."[18] Still there was a joke that went around the admissions office around that time: "If Stanford went to the Rose Bowl, it was because of good coaching. If not, it was because of poor admissions."

It seemed to me that Stanford might prefer admitting talented athletes so long as their academic record was up to a certain standard. Up until 2020, Stanford enrolled approximately 7,000 undergraduates, and approximately 850 of the total students admitted were student-athletes (11 percent) who played on one of thirty-five sports teams that Stanford fields. So long as these student-athletes do not perform significantly less well than their non-athlete counterparts in their academic courses, university officials must easily recognize the brand-building value that these talented scholar athletes provide and thus make admissions decisions accordingly.[19]

It would also be impossible to say that no exceptions have ever been made for a star athlete just as it is impossible to say that Stanford does not make admissions exceptions for families that donate money to the university. We also know from the William Rick Singer fake athlete admissions scandal of 2019 that Stanford has not been immune to shady dealings.[20] Furthermore, as a private university, Stanford can legally give more weight to any admissions factor or category of belonging they wish (e.g., high school grades, letters of recommendation, athleticism, gender, race). In 2001, Stanford's then dean of admissions told Andrew Zimbalist that he could neither confirm nor deny the use of affirmative action but that "the department of athletics may designate outstanding athletes for special attention."[21] If that is still the case, then it would seem that the best Coach VanDerveer could hope for was to walk over to the admissions office and slip a preferred application on top of the pile.

At some other institutions, where there is less priority placed on academic ability in admissions, other non-athlete students may assume that incoming athletes are as a rule underprepared for college-level academic work.[22] Moreover, even if the athlete managed to make the most of his athletic scholarship, managed to balance school with sport, and found a way to graduate, he might forever be questioned about "what he *really* learned in college." These are unfortunate stigmas that many athletes carry for life.

By contrast, Stanford's admissions policy makes it clear to athletes why they are on campus, and it assures non-athletes that athletes belong in the same classrooms, limiting the potential for such stigma to arise. Many people with whom I spoke saw Stanford's athletes as smart kids who also excelled in sports and believed that such a distinction set Stanford apart from other big-time sports colleges.

In the end, when one considers its self-imposed limitations on the admissions of athletes, Stanford's athletic success in men's and women's sports becomes that much more impressive too. Arguably no other American university has been as athletically successful as Stanford. Despite its high academic standard (or perhaps because of it), Stanford has dominated the two awards that have been awarded to college athletic programs: the Learfield Sports Directors' Cup[23] and the Capitol One Cup.[24]

Commit to the Ideal of the Student-Athlete

After they have been admitted, Stanford's athletes are expected to embrace their role as students. At Stanford, coaches are officially expected to be educators, are held to specific educational standards by the university, and are given extended tenures that allow them to develop an educator's mindset within their coaching. Stanford's institutional expectations for balance between academics and athletics thus trickle down to sports coaches, who accept the importance of maintaining high educational standards for athletes.

Sports coaches were once always seen as teachers. Before the Civil War the term "coach" was not even used in the United States in the context of sport. At the time, a coach was a private tutor responsible for training a young person in an academic subject or in some aspect of etiquette. But in recent decades, many coaches at the college level, especially the big-time college level, have become professionals whose primary aim is victory. This historical transformation has had profound consequences since some if not many big-time coaches are incentivized to care more about winning than the growth of their players.

But the Stanford Standard impacts its coaches particularly by allowing coaches to perceive themselves as teachers and masters of technical athletic skills. All Stanford coaches, including Coach VanDerveer, are tasked with executing the mission statement of DAPER, which includes the general guidelines of "teaching, leading, winning, and serving" (it is interesting to note that these goals are listed in this order). Three specific guidelines, which fall under these general guidelines, speak to Stanford's commitment to balancing academics and athletics.

- By fostering and nurturing a coaching, physical education, and recreation staff that is committed to teaching with integrity and ambition and that performs in a manner which is consistent with the academic priorities of Stanford University.
- By having an uncompromising commitment to Conference and National championships and by providing each student-athlete with the tools necessary to be successful at the highest levels of both academic and athletic performance.
- By being the model of success, of universal opportunity, and of unwavering commitment to the ideal of the scholar-athlete.[25]

In other words, Stanford mandates in official terms that it is not sufficient for Stanford coaches to win games; they must also push their players to do well in the classroom and balance sports and school.

By all accounts, Stanford coaches appear to uphold the letter and spirit of these official university statements even when it is difficult. Andy Geiger once called Stanford's balance of academics and athletics a "successful marriage"[26] although some coaches admitted that striking that balance on a day-to-day basis was difficult.[27] Still there is little doubt that Stanford's institutional commitment to admissions integrity and its educational mandate for coaches played a role in keeping coaching decisions in line with broader university norms. For example, Coach Paye told me that while she perceived the academic (and social) curiosity of individual players to be somewhat threatening to their focus on basketball, it was a "tension that made Stanford *Stanford.*"

The "Stanford Culture . . . Does a Lot of the Teaching for Us"

The institutional prioritization of education at Stanford ensured that coaches consider classroom academics and educational models of coaching in their recruiting and day-to-day decision making, which reinforced Stanford's positive educational culture in the process.

Why did Stanford coaches put up with this admission policy and the culture it created and not use their considerable public platform to advocate for an enhanced priority given to sports?

For one, this culture pays the coaches back since it helps them avoid the common annoyance of urging players to hit the books. As Coach Paye explained, the "Stanford culture," which she described as being one of "hard work, unselfishness, treating people with respect . . . does a lot of the teaching for us." Coach Paye continued, "There are many things that I don't have to spend time on as a coach because the culture takes care of it. And the kids teach themselves."

For another, Stanford's policies also unofficially provide a sense of job security and tacitly promise coaches time to build their program.[28] After all, a coach could not be expected to be a holistic educator if she were yanked from her post after one or two losing seasons. Successful athletic programs take time to develop, and for coaches to have authority that will be respected by their players, they need time to develop their program. Stanford does that, hiring coaches and giving them the time that they need to build the program their way, which allows them to build a sense of stability for their players. With this sense of job security, Coach VanDerveer and her staff have been able to help sustain Stanford's positive educational culture and foster values that they might not have been able to have sustained had they constantly been worried about producing a winning team. One thing that many big-time college coaches lament is that they must always have their bags packed because coaches are hired and fired with deplorable frequency, bouncing from one university to the next like itinerant field hands. Yet at Stanford it seems clear that coaching methods and objectives often dovetail with the university mission to prioritize education.

Perhaps Dick Gould, Stanford's long-time men's tennis coach, said it best when he once attributed his legendary coaching success—in thirty-eight years on the farm, his teams won seventeen national titles and he coached fifty All-Americans—to his ability to look at Stanford's academic standard as an opportunity, not a burden. "To succeed here," he said, "a coach has to believe that the Stanford environment is a positive thing, not an excuse for not winning."[29]

In other words, a coach will succeed if he or she buys in to the Stanford Standard and to the ideal that achieving balance between athletic and academic standards is not only possible but also that such an ideal has intrinsic value.

No Sham Classes, No Clustering and Higher Graduation Rates

Stanford's commitment to balancing academics with athletics trickles down to the player too, beginning with the campus norm that good athletes should be good students. Several non-athlete Stanford students with whom I spoke accepted the idea that being a good athlete and a good student were not mutually exclusive. "It's a 'both/and,' not an 'either/or,'" one told me, explaining that the idea that a good athlete would be admitted to any elite academic university without also having good grades was "crazy."

Unfortunately, too few big-time sports universities have demonstrated their resolve to deliver a quality education to big-time athletes, and even more troubling, the NCAA has also failed to hold them accountable when they fail.[30] At some institutions, the classes recommended to big-time athletes may be aimed at ensuring athletic eligibility, to ensure a star athlete does not miss a big game. In some instances, athletes self-segregate, or cluster, into easy classes or majors.[31] In some instances, the classes athletes take are so devoid of academic value that if a student tries to transfer to a more academically rigorous school, the credits do not transfer. These universities' failure to set a higher academic standard can also cause considerable psychological damage.[32] Worse still, instead of offering the services needed to help these athletes succeed in the field of their choosing, many universities monitor and surveil their athletes with a rigorous review of their course selections, hoping to anticipate an academic scandal before it happens.[33] Some universities even hire "janitors" to clean up "messes" before they hit the press and become public knowledge.[34] This is a dehumanizing institutional arrangement.

The ideal, of course, is for all college athletes to graduate. Yet graduation rates at big-time sports universities have remained remarkably low, likely the product of universities prioritizing sports over schoolwork. In 2017, for example, the federal graduation rate was 68 percent for all student-athletes and 48 percent for men's D-I basketball players.[35] Theoretically, big-time athletes in big-time sports should graduate at a higher rate than their non-athlete peers since they should have fewer financial struggles given their full-ride scholarships. (Most college students drop out because of a lack of funding.) Moreover, since there is considerable tutoring tailored directly to them, big-time college athletes should theoretically do as well if not better than non-athletes. In some cases, a fifth-year of free education is also available to athletes, which should also raise graduation rates (if a player is injured, he or she may "redshirt" and gain an extra year of eligibility, at the same time extending their scholarship by one year).[36] But in actuality, big-time athletes at schools where there is little institutional priority given to education find themselves putting their athletic training first and, consequently, setting themselves up for academic trouble.

The idea of a so-called sham class is unknown at Stanford. Many athletes study challenging subjects such as computer science, biology, and physics and do not usually cluster together in easy majors. Moreover, Stanford graduates most of its student athletes (in part, of course, because Stanford only admits students that it believes will be able to maintain its standard of academic as well as athletic achievement). In 2011, for example, nineteen of Stanford's thirty-five sports teams graduated 100 percent of its athletes on time, and no team graduated fewer than 80 percent of its players.[37] Most Stanford women's basketball players graduate in four years[38] (although it should be noted that many students, including many athletes, also take a fifth year (on scholarship) to pursue a master's degree so this figure may be a bit misleading). For some Stanford teams, the graduation rate is higher than it is for the general student body—at least according to the NCAA's graduation success rate (GSR).

In 2005 the NCAA created the GSR in response to public complaints that big-time college athletes were receiving scholarships but not finishing their degrees. Stanford has done extremely well in these measurements (even if the metric itself is calculated in a dubious manner).[39] For example, in 2011 nine men's teams at Stanford received perfect GSR scores: baseball, fencing, golf, gymnastics, tennis, track (outdoor and indoor), volleyball, and water polo.[40] Perfect ratings were also achieved in ten women's programs: rowing, field hockey, golf, gymnastics, softball, soccer, synchronized swimming, volleyball, water polo and swimming and diving. The GSR for Stanford women's basketball in 2011, which was 93 out of 100, was the third-highest in the country among D-I-A football schools. In fact, the team never earned a GSR under 92 in any of the years searchable in the NCAA database (2003–2010), and the lower-than-perfect scores could be traced to the fact that Stanford allowed its scholarship athletes a fifth year to pursue a master's degree.

Keep Football Grounded

There is a third factor that makes up the Stanford Standard, and that is institutional unwillingness to allow football to be crowned king of campus. Athletic department officials told me that they seek to reproduce Stanford's traditional culture and only commercialize the football team in a way that is consistent with that culture and in a way that they perceive will not have the kind of corrosive effects that football's commercialization has had on campus educational cultures elsewhere.

The Stanford Standard keeps football from becoming as big as it is in other universities, and that helps athletic department officials make sensible decisions that help moderate that sport's relative power within the athletic department and within the broader university. As we saw in chapter 2, football more than any other force has shaped the contemporary landscape of big-time college sports, impacting not only the way men and women look at themselves but also the way they perceive the relative value of education within the big time and within the world of college sports entertainment.

But at Stanford, football is not king like it is elsewhere. The needs of Stanford football are not prioritized over the needs of other sports or academics. This is reflected in the way Stanford football coaches speak. In 2012 for example, Stanford's head football coach David Shaw responded to a compliment that he and his predecessor Jim Harbaugh had done something that no other Stanford football coaches had managed to do on the farm—win—by saying that the football team was trying to keep up with all the other programs at Stanford. Shaw mentioned the swimming team and the tennis team as other teams that were perennial winners and mentioned the success of another coach by name—Tara VanDerveer.[41] Shaw's comments illustrated that the football team does not run Stanford; it sees itself as merely one of Stanford's many athletics teams.[42]

Stanford's focus on education is also reflected in housing for football players. At many universities, recruited football players occupy a separate space of campus post-admission, sometimes in literal and often in metaphoric terms, especially when they "are exclusively immersed in a sport culture in which athletic excellence is the central focus of their lives."[43] Football players were isolated from other students as early as the 1950s when sleek college dorms were built for athletes to "sweeten the recruiting deal."[44] There were various critics of athlete dorms,[45] but proponents insisted that they were an established part of the college sports landscape that was essential for building team bonding and unity. Dorms were eventually banned at the 1991 NCAA convention and officially phased out in 1996 because of the symbolic detachment of athletes from the general student body. Ultimately the NCAA decided that member schools should be required to eliminate any housing in which more than 49 percent of the occupants were athletes, but some universities still house many athletes together in the same dorm.[46] Even when they do not, the detachment is reflected in plush and often exclusive training facilities for big-time athletes. Athletes at big-time athletic colleges thus sometimes come to see themselves as big men on campus and self-segregate from their non-athletic peers.

Since the relative power of football is kept limited at Stanford, so too is the relative influence of commercialism since there's a relatively less significant need to raise money to pay an expensive football coach and his assistants. In 2011 I asked Heather Owen, who had played for Coach VanDerveer and later became a fundraiser for the Stanford athletic department, whether the pursuit of profit had any impact on Stanford education. She said, "Stanford could probably capitalize more on the commercialization of sport, but [the university is] very cognizant of maintaining its niche within the marketplace."[47] That niche, she explained, was "the ultimate coupling of academics and athletics," and the university was "very fearful of losing . . . itself in that regard."

> [We do not want to] allow . . . commercialization to . . . detract from a student athlete's experience. We are constantly grounding ourselves . . . I ask myself, What am I doing here? I'm raising money. Why am I raising money? I'm raising money so that every student-athlete that comes through here can maximize their human potential . . . That means a lot of things. I want them to be the best gymnast they can be. I want them to graduate with honors in their chosen discipline and go on and be a productive member of society . . . You never hear anyone say, "We're here to make a bunch of money at the ball game. Get them to go pro, sign a billion-dollar contract . . . and then give a bunch of money back [to the university]."[48]

Playing the Game in a Smarter Way

Stanford sought to strike a balance between the reality of college sports entertainment and the ideal of higher education. Specifically, athletic department officials said they were careful to strike a balance between building attractive and functional sports facilities without veering into the territory of opulence, which they believed might run the risk of calling into question the athletic department's and university's priorities.[49]

To the extent that Stanford did commercialize its athletics teams, its officials insisted that it did so to keep up with the ever-rising cost of running the Stanford athletic department, including the rising cost of tuition, of which the university required the athletic department pay the full cost,[50] and the cost of ever-rising coaching salaries. The athletics division of DAPER, which was protected as a legal entity, Stanford Athletics, said it had to continually find ways to pay for scholarships either by soliciting new donations, by drawing down proceeds from investments on endowed funds, or by selling new space for advertising. Moreover, the labor-market battle for coaches was fierce so Stanford kept its coaching salaries competitive and its coaching offices state-of-art. According to Joe Karlgaard, the Stanford endowment was even more important a result of these costs. He told me that Stanford began endowing scholarships before many other universities so it did not have to be as reliant on ticket sales or merchandising as other schools to make ends meet. Moreover, since athletics at Stanford were simultaneously "tethered to the university" and expected to "stand on its own two feet" financially, athletic department officials had "be somewhat creative" and embrace Stanford's "entrepreneurial culture" to balance the books. Karlgaard said the athletic department "operations were rising three to five percent a year" alongside the rising costs of travel and equipment." On top of that, he added, salaries for those within the department "were rising even faster than that" so they "had to constantly be thinking of ways to drive new revenues."

In most cases, Stanford accepted donations that were directed to athletics from alumna and sports fans, but regardless of where the money came from or why the donor said they donated it, it did not typically allow the donor to control the fundamental nature of the university mission. Stanford alumni like John Arrillaga had long been generous contributors to the university mission and its athletic programs[51] but many of them wanted to believe that their money was purely a gift. Thus, Karlgaard noted that many alumni were upset when in 2006 the athletic department decided to give the best tickets to home football games and postseason sports tournaments and bowl games to those who made donations or volunteered their services, thereby introducing a transactional tit-for-tat system. He explained that Stanford was one of the last to institute such a point system for seating at athletic events but that the Stanford alumni still rebelled. Karlgaard said some alumni believed this move was "anti-Stanford" and that they wanted the athletic department to follow a "philosophy of true philanthropy".

Karlgaard told me that ultimately the athletic department was on the horns of a dilemma: on one hand, there was a desire to be financially self-sufficient and independent of university funding, but they also had to "think long and hard about whether we want to compete with places that have big football revenue, which we don't have." He said athletic department officials felt that they had little choice but to build the most state-of-the-art facilities they could even if they were not as opulent as those of other universities. He explained that even if it could Stanford would not build a 100,000 square-foot facility for improving the strength and conditioning of the football team (as USC and Oregon had recently done). "It's crazy," he said, and added, "But we can't say, 'Oh we're fine.' We have to play the game . . . our way. That results in us thinking about how we are going to generate more revenue. I think we play it in a smarter way."

A Culture of Work, Effort, and Preparation

For their part, Stanford athletes demonstrated their desire to be great athletes and great students by working hard or, as they called it, by buying in to the grind, and by dedicating themselves to constant preparation. They also demonstrated seemingly tireless discipline and intense focus, and when I asked informants what they felt I should know about women's basketball, more than half of them asked me to write about how hard they work.

This sentiment started at the top, or at least it was encouraged by Coach VanDerveer. While Coach VanDerveer did not use the term "buying in"[52] as frequently as athletes and officials like Gold-Onwude and Karlgaard, the idea of self-investment was perhaps her coaching philosophy's most central pillar, especially in terms of her sense of ownership and work. She told me,

> I take piano lessons . . . Sometimes I don't practice as much as I should . . . [and] my teacher . . . just waits. I have to take ownership of my own game, so to speak. And I need our players to take ownership, too. To say, "Hey, I want to be a great player. Help me be a great player," and I will help . . . I am a facilitator. With each person I try to understand . . . what's gonna help them? How can I help them be as good as they can be? But they have to want it, too . . . You gotta work. A lot of these players don't know how to work. They have been good without work. So, it's also teaching them how to work.

With Coach VanDerveer there was a consistent orientation toward the process of work rather than its product. She rarely focused her language on winning or any other result (e.g., points scored, rebounds grabbed). Her goal was to stimulate the players' intrinsic motivation so that they would learn how to work, how to take ownership of that learning process themselves, and how to cultivate themselves into consistent performers. In March 2011, for example, before the NCAA tournament began, Coach VanDerveer wasn't impressed by the postseason awards that her team had collected. In a staccato breath she congratulated them but quickly added, "Don't break your arm patting yourself on the back. It's not about awards—it's about playing well and being hungry in the [NCAA] tournament." She was always coaching, challenging, and trying to motivate her players to push themselves to new heights.

Coach VanDerveer had an uncanny ability to anticipate what a player or future coach might do someday, and she wasted no unnecessary words imploring her players to get there. If that was coaching vision, then Coach VanDerveer had it in ample supply. When *New York Times* writer Karen Crouse asked whether VanDerveer was a "Tiger mother," VanDerveer conceded, "A little bit, yeah. I think it's only because I really care about them, and I would hate for them to not be able to accomplish what they're capable of."[53]

Former UCLA basketball Coach John Wooden once said, "Failing to prepare is preparing to fail," and Coach VanDerveer was living proof of that statement taken to heart. Her approach to film study was legendary. Coach VanDerveer was said to watch opponents' games twenty times, and her staff even scouted referees to determine how they might call the game. (For years, thousands of videos of games were stacked high in Coach VanDerveer's office. Later they were transferred to CD and finally, in the mid-2010s, digitized.) Coach VanDerveer made sure that every bit of practice was recorded and insisted that all players watch opponent game film as a matter of routine. After the players watched thirty minutes of film for each opponent for three days straight, they then spoke with a coach about it in an hour-long session. Her demands reflected a meticulous approach to decision making; film study gave her the data she needed to game plan.

In 2011, Coach VanDerveer accepted induction into the Naismith Basketball Hall of Fame. In her acceptance speech, she referred to Malcolm Gladwell's popular bestseller *Outliers*, which popularized the conception that one needed to log ten thousand hours of practice to achieve greatness. She said,

> [Gladwell] contends that success comes from a combination of parentage, patronage, opportunity, ten thousand hours of practice, and legacy. Instead of asking the questions "What are successful people like?" or "What kinds of personalities, talents or intellect do they have?" Gladwell says it is only by asking where they are from that we can unravel the logic of who succeeds and who doesn't. I know I logged ten thousand hours years ago. Practice is what I thoroughly enjoy. I'm not sure the players enjoy it as much as me sometimes.

Why the Myth of the Stanford Standard Needs No Proof

Coach VanDerveer embodied the core ideas of the Stanford Standard—appreciation for effort in the classroom and the court, attention to detail, and a belief that no sport was more important than other.

But there are other small things that soften the outer edges of the Stanford Standard. Each women's basketball player could, for example, invite her favorite professor to watch one home game, and she could provide that professor with a courtside seat and the chance to listen in the locker room during halftime. As one player told me, this was important "because the professor can see how hard they are working," and that playing sports was in fact serious work.

A skeptic might wonder whether Stanford's rhetoric about the importance of educational accomplishments reflects the reality of its admissions process since its admissions office is protective of its policies and procedures and will not share personal information about students with researchers. (I did hear rumblings that this or that big-time athlete was admitted to Stanford "but shouldn't have been" but this admissions confidentiality prevented me from substantiating the rumors.)

Nevertheless, this confidentiality and these exceptions to the rule seem beside the point to me, since the perception, or myth, that there is a Stanford Standard is believed widely enough that it has a real impact on the day-to-day operations and culture of the university. That Stanford insists it has an academic standard is not particularly remarkable—most universities boast of their excellence—but that its members, alumni, and the broader university culture appear to believe it, and that they believe it applies to big-time athletes, too, is.[54]

The anthropologist Mary Douglas once said a myth is "a story we tell ourselves that needs no proof." Stanford's professed standard of admission may not in fact be verifiable, but in the end it does not matter because the myth needs no proof to be reproduced over time. In fact, the myth has created a positive educational culture in which big-time college athletes are allowed if not encouraged to value their athleticism and their academic abilities and put their efforts into developing them both without fear of social stigma or critique. The myth has, in short, created an institutional norm, and that norm allows for the myth to be reproduced over time.

Moreover, even if it is a myth that Stanford only admits scholar-athletes who can make the grade and perform at a high athletic standard, that myth has created an "imagined reality"[55] that works. One might say that the Stanford community understands this myth, buys in to it as truth, and as a result creates real, positive educational consequences for all students (current and prospective), for the university's reputation and brand, and for the athletic department and its teams, coaches, and players.

In making this claim, I channel an explicitly idealistic and positive philosophical position, and I also assume that the priority of education should be the ultimate purpose of institutions that are involved in big-time college sports since I believe the modifying adjective in the expression "higher education" should mean something.[56]

In the long run, the fact that Stanford's institutional commitment to education trickles down to the coaches and the players and creates incentives for all of them to buy in to the ideal of the scholar-athlete and the coach-educator is beneficial not only for the university sports culture and the team's culture but also for the players' power vis-à-vis their coach. Big-time college coaches are officially professionals. College athletes at this level are also professionals in practice (particularly in their training, in how accept their role on the team, and in how they grind out their training regardless of their status on the team). And while the professionalized training required of big-time college athletes can pose a challenge to their academic studies if the athletes do not primarily consider themselves students, at Stanford the institutional commitment to higher standards academically means that athletes will always have the final leverage against a professional coach who may care more than they do about winning and therefore may ask too much of their time.

There is no doubt that Coach VanDerveer's success made her one of Stanford's most formidable and respected coaches, but even she was not above the institutional commitment to balancing academics and athletics, and therefore her relative power over players remained relatively limited, especially compared to the power that other coaches have over athletes at other less academically oriented institutions. The Stanford Standard thus created incentives for everyone to work hard but not become so obsessed with either academics or athletics or run the risk of becoming one-dimensional.

It is instructive to contrast Stanford's positive educational culture and its ability to cultivate growth with how some athletes at other universities have seen themselves. For example, former Detroit Pistons star Isaiah Thomas, who attended the University of Indiana, once said the term "student-athlete" was written backward. "You're an athlete-student . . . Your main purpose is not to be Einstein, but a ball player, to generate some money, to put people in the stands . . . The rest of your time you've got to motivate yourself to make sure you get something back."[57]

Can other universities learn from Stanford's balance between academic and athletic priorities? Certainly there are obstacles that prevent other institutions from adapting the standard. For one, Stanford's alumni are wealthier than the alumni of other universities and more capable of making large donations to their alma mater, which likely eases the pressure on everyone to win and make money through commercializing college sports. Stanford's alumni wealth (and philanthropic generosity with it) may also allow the university to turn down commercialization opportunities, as Stanford apparently does with football. This may not be possible elsewhere.

Still, it is remarkable how Stanford has created a myth that allows athletes to see themselves as part of the general student body and coaches to see themselves as educators, thereby creating a positive educational culture of which athletics are one part, not apart. It is equally remarkable that in turn, this positive educational culture influences the way that coaches and athletes see themselves, and so it impacts how they behave as well.

In short, balancing big-time sports with higher education is possible even if other scholars have not always seen it that way. For example, Dowling argues that corrupt big-time college sports programs are validated by a few selective universities like Stanford that "enjoy their special prominence precisely because *they serve the purpose of legitimizing the otherwise corrupt world of NCAA Division IA athletics.*" He then adds that these institutions "confidently assert" that "one does not have to choose . . . between big-time athletics and academic or intellectual values."[58] But Dowling overlooks the positive aspects of big-time college sports and so he fails to see that there is nothing in Stanford's example that legitimizes corruption elsewhere. Stanford does it its way even when it means they may not field the best team they possibly could. Athletic scholarship recipients, especially at institutions that prioritize academics, receive much more from their college experiences than Dowling cares to acknowledge, but these benefits can only be adequately measured and appreciated if they are calculated economically *and* educationally, psychologically *and* socially, and with reference not only to classroom education but also to the education that takes place within the sports setting itself and to the institutional culture and norms that allow all of the above to incubate.

Conclusion

In the 1990s in between winning several United States Golfing Association amateur titles and becoming one of the greatest professional golfers of all time, Tiger Woods attended Stanford. For a time, Woods was almost synonymous with the university, representing the same values of intellect and athleticism that the university wanted represented and much in the same way that Chiney Ogwumike would later be called on to sustain the Stanford brand in the early 2010s. At the time, though, Woods insisted that *he* was impressed by other Stanford athletes. "I thought one of the guys in my dorm was a big dumb stereotypical football player, a six-foot six lineman. He scored fifteen hundred on his SATs. You get guys like that talking intelligently to you, it's pretty shocking. Another guy, who scored 1580 on his SATs, never studies because he has a photographic memory."[59]

Woods's reaction to his fellow athletes' academic abilities illustrates the widespread and often damaging perception of big-time college athletes who play big-time sports at big-time sports schools—namely, that they must be "dumb jocks"—but it also serves as a reminder that things can be done differently. Indeed, it is telling that Woods would go on to say, "Everybody here is special in some way. You have to be special to go here . . . I am not a celebrity at Stanford."[60]

If Tiger Woods did not think of himself as a celebrity at Stanford, even though must have certainly been one, then perhaps the Stanford Standard had accomplished its mission. In other words, perhaps that demonstrated the intent of the university's admissions policy, which ensured that the subjectivity of admitting talented athletes never corrupted the uniqueness of the university's brand of balance.

Woods's normal student, non-celebrity status was no accident; it was the byproduct of many choices by generations of Stanford University leaders such as Fred Hargadon, Andy Geiger, Dick Gould, Joe Karlgaard, Heather Owen, and Tara VanDerveer, all of whom agreed to not allow commercialization to compromise the educational mission of the university.

Stanford's Standard, difficult to replicate though it may be, is perhaps fairer than the models followed by other institutions too since these other institutions may offer athletes admission despite their lack of academic accomplishments, and therefore potentially set them up for academic struggle. Some students may need extra assistance to prepare themselves for college, but if universities admit them for their athletic ability alone and do not provide them with the tools they need to do the academic job once they arrive, then they effectively perpetuate the notion that jocks get special treatment and that being a dumb jock is ultimately acceptable. (They may also perpetuate the very stereotype of the dumb jock itself.) That is unfair to the athletes themselves and does them a disservice in the long term even if the provision of an athletic scholarship may suggest the temporary provision of opportunity and resources.

Similarly, if universities forgive low academic achievement by admitting any athlete, they send the message that no amount of educational buy-in by the athlete will ever matter, and along the way they will effectively destroy the motivational power of the concept of the scholar-athlete and concede that there is little point in striving to balance one's studies with one's sport or investing in oneself cognitively. Moreover, it is hard to see how such messages could contribute positively to the maintenance of a properly functioning democracy, which requires its citizens to be able to constantly educate themselves on a range of complex political issues.

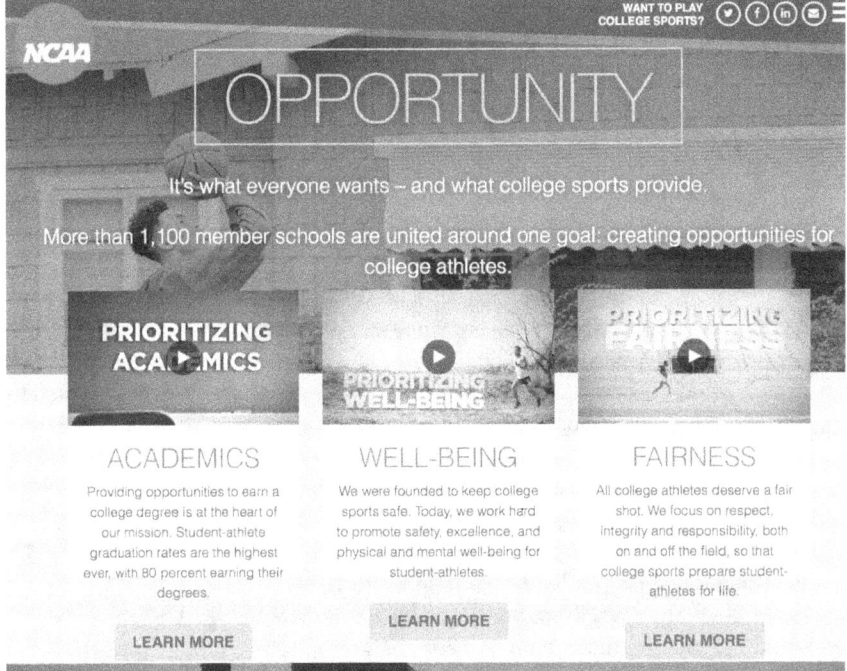

Photo 9.1. The NCAA website claims it creates opportunities for college athletes. Source: The author via screenshot, August 30, 2019.

But Stanford's Standard does offer hope in that it suggests that any university choosing to set a higher academic standard will go a long way toward establishing a campus culture in which the image of higher learning can shine more brightly and thereby make the university's educational culture more positive for all, and make the university's contribution to society that much more valuable.

Notes

1. Quoted in Cavalli, *Stanford Sports*, 155.
2. Zimbalist, *Unpaid Professionals*, 41.
3. According to the 2018 *Times Higher Education World University Rankings*, Stanford ranked number 3, trailing only the University of Oxford and Cambridge University and tied with the California Institute of Technology. It was the only American university in the top ten that also supported big-time sports teams.
4. Weight, Navarro, Huffman, and Smith-Ryan, "Quantifying."
5. Hennessey, "Committed to Diversity."
6. Branch, "The Shame."

7. Stanford University (Lagunita), "Interview."
8. Cavalli, *Stanford Sports*, 98–99.
9. Persky, "Condoleezza Rice."
10. Quoted in Cavalli, *Stanford Sports*, 98.
11. Joe Karlgaard, personal communication.
12. Quoted in Cavalli, *Stanford Sports*, 100.
13. Quoted in Cavalli, *Stanford Sports*, 97.
14. Quoted in Cavalli, *Stanford Sports*, 154. The decision to ask that forms, tests, and recommendations be sent to the admissions department was made for another, practical reason: an early review there offered coaches an educated guess as to whether a prospective athlete might be admitted, thus saving everyone time. Hargadon explained, "We save the coaches a lot of time and money. Because we let them know early what our standards are, they are not likely to waste their time on candidates who have no chance of being admitted" (quoted in Cavalli, *Stanford Sports*, 97).
15. Quoted in Cavalli, *Stanford Sports*, 155.
16. Stanford University, "Our Selection Process."
17. Quoted in Cavalli, *Stanford Sports*, 156.
18. Quoted in Cavalli, *Stanford Sports*, 156.
19. Thomas and Drape. 2010. "Stanford Dominates."
20. In 2019 the U.S. Department of Justice indicted several wealthy parents of would-be college students on bribery charges, alleging in part that they had attempted to bribe sports coaches to accept their child to the university on the condition that the parents would then make sizable donations to the university and its sports programs. The Justice department characterized the scheme as one in which parents hired a third party, William Rick Singer, to develop fake athletic profiles that the universities could use to justify preferential admission for these students. Singer pleaded guilty on all charges, several coaches were fired, and other proceedings are ongoing. See *US v. Ernst et al.*, "Investigations of College Admissions."
21. Zimbalist, *Unpaid Professionals*, 207, and preface, n. 3.
22. Grasgreen, "A Scale That Slides."
23. The Directors' Cup, started in the 1990s, run by National Association of Collegiate Directors of Athletics, and sponsored by Learfield Communications, was given annually to the best overall athletics program in the nation in each of the NCAA's three divisions. In 2011 Stanford had a huge advantage over other programs in being able to field thirty-five teams from which to select its best twenty. Stanford was so dominant in perennially winning the Directors' Cup that there were several attempts to adjust the scoring system to even the field. At one time Stanford won seventeen straight Learfield Sports Directors' Cup Awards. By the time I observed the women's basketball team, Stanford had won all but one of the nineteen Directors' championships (1994–1995 to 2011–2012 seasons).
24. The Capitol One Cup is artificially weighted toward the revenue-generating men's sports of basketball and football. In the first two years of the cup's existence (2010–2011 and 2011–2012), Stanford's female athletes won it (the Stanford men

placed fifth in 2010–2011 and thirteenth in 2011–2012). Stanford's female athletes went on to win four of the next seven titles. Karlgaard told me he was "not a huge fan" of the Capitol One Cup: "From a student-athlete perspective, you don't want to feel like what you do is less important than what somebody else does." See Stanford University, "Thinking About Sports."

25. Stanford University, "On Campus."

26. Quoted in Cavalli, *Stanford Sports*, 154.

27. Coach VanDerveer herself once admitted the frustrations of Stanford's self-imposed academic standard: "It is hard," she told me. "It's frustrating . . . Because of the academics of kids who can't get in and who you would want on the team and then who you need."

28. One Stanford athletic department official explained, "West Coast fans are not as crazy about football as some in the East, Midwest or South and therefore alumni do not put as much pressure on the university president to sack a coach who is under-performing, and the long-term tenure of many Stanford coaches leads some Stanford people to consider it a hallmark of the university." Similarly, Coach Paye told me, "Stanford is kind of unique, you know we have a lot of coaches who have been here a long time and have sustained an incredible level of success. If you look at women's tennis, or swimming, it's a pretty unique environment."

29. Quoted in Cavalli, *Stanford Sports*, 120.

30. At the University of North Carolina, Chapel Hill (UNC), for example, an educator called Mary Willingham, who was also a graduate student at the University of North Carolina, Greensboro, found that among 183 big-time athletes who played football and basketball for UNC between 2004 and 2012, 60 percent "read between fourth- and eighth-grade levels [and] between 8 percent and 10 percent read below a third-grade level" (quoted in Ganim, "CNN analysis"). After Butch Davis was hired to coach the UNC football team, Willingham found some incoming football players couldn't read. Willingham told Dan Kane of the *Raleigh News & Observer* of so-called paper classes for such big-time athletes, which also included basketball players (Finkel, Martin, and Paley, *$chooled*). UNC did its own investigation and found no wrongdoing by the academic administration or athletic department but did decide to place blame on just one individual: the chair of the African studies department. After UNC told the NCAA of the paper classes, an NCAA investigation found that there had been "a long-running scheme of suspect African and Afro-American Studies courses" at UNC that largely benefited athletes and charged the university with a "failure to monitor" and a "lack of institutional control." However, the NCAA did nothing about it, saying that they could not prove wrongdoing since they had no evidence that the paper courses were solely intended to benefit athletes (Bauer-Wolf, "NCAA Finds No Academic Fraud"). According to Kane, the failure to punish UNC as an institution "sent a message to the rest of country to do the exact same thing." The statement on the UNC Athletic Department website, boasting that they "educate and inspire through athletics" was called into question after Kane's reports (Carter, "UNC's Sylvia Hatchell"). Willingham lamented, "It's

sad . . . It's the adults who are failing the students" (quoted in Finkel, Martin, and Paley, $chooled).

31. For example, Foster and Huml found that many athletes cluster in the same academic majors or classes, which leads to a strong athletic identity but also negative outcomes educationally. By focusing on courses that help maintain their eligibility to play sports, these athletes maintain their identity as athletes but also arguably do damage to their long-term career goals since most college athletes will not become professional athletes, and therefore the degrees they receive matter that much more ("The Relationship"). Such clustering is particularly unsettling given athletes' general optimism about their academic prospects on admission.

32. In one study, Adler and Adler found that many big-time college athletes enter college with an idealism regarding the potential of their academic abilities but soon realize that their university has admitted them alongside peers with better academic preparation and therefore determine that clustering in easy courses is their best bet ("From Idealism," 241). This phenomenon is even more pronounced for black athletes at predominantly white institutions, where successful athletes have a statistically greater likelihood of having a lower graduation rate than black athletes at historically black colleges (Southall, Eckard, and Nagel, "Athletic Success").

33. In fact, measuring how athletes are doing has almost become an NCAA obsession. There are no perfect measures of athletic eligibility during college but the NCAA publishes its own measure, the academic progress rate (APR)—an "annual scorecard of academic achievement"—to compare the academic success of players and teams. According to the NCAA, the APR "is a term-by-term measure of eligibility and retention for Division I student-athletes that was developed as an early indicator of eventual graduation rates." They explain their calculation as follows.

> Each student-athlete receiving *athletically related financial aid* earns one point for staying in school and one point for being academically eligible. A team's total points are divided by points possible and then multiplied by 1,000 to equal the team's Academic Progress Rate. In addition to a team's current-year APR, its rolling four-year APR is also used to determine accountability. Currently, teams must earn a 930 four-year average APR or a 940 average over the most recent two years to participate in NCAA championships. In 2015–2016 and beyond, teams must earn a four-year APR of 930 to compete in championships (National Collegiate Athletic Association, "Academic Progress Rate").

Nationwide, women's sports teams typically receive more NCAA recognition than men's teams. In 2011, 14 percent of all D-I teams were recognized, of which 58 percent (525 of 909) of all teams that were recognized were women's teams (National Collegiate Athletic Association, "Teams Honored"). According to the NCAA, the lowest four-year average APRs (2013–2016) were found in men's basketball (966) and football (FCS: 957, FBS: 966) and in women's basketball (980) and women's bowling (974; National Collegiate Athletic Association "APR Averages and Trends"). The APR was agreed on at the 2004 NCAA convention and established in 2005 yet the metric has been controversial ever since. For example, according to Easterbrook, the APR "lacks any commonsense meaning" and is "intended to be incomprehensible" so the public does not realize just how poorly big-time athletes are performing academically. Easterbrook argues that the APR is a scale devised to illustrate smaller differences between high graduation rates and low ones. He explains, "An APR of 930 means a college is on track to graduate 50 percent of scholarship athletes. Why a proxy, rather than simply using graduation rates? Everyone knows what "failing to graduate at least 50 percent of athletes means" . . . Failing to achieve an APR of 930 is gibberish" (*The King*, 127). Using a complex metric like the APR might not help solve the underlying problem since there is no proof that the APR is a metric that itself helps improve graduation rates. While some have criticized the APR, Peter Roby, the athletic director at Northeastern University, said each school has an appeal process that a student-athlete can use to ensure that they do not have their scholarship discontinued unjustly (Trahan, "The NCAA's Academic"). The Stanford women's basketball team routinely receives NCAA recognition for achieving an APR in the top 10 percent nationwide. (See NCAA.org. "Public Recognition".) In order to be eligible to receive their scholarship, Stanford athletes need to be enrolled full-time in no less than twelve units, and they need to pass classes amounting to half of those units. But even if an athlete passes those units and fails the two other classes and sees his or her GPA dip, the NCAA can also rule a player ineligible if their GPA drops. As Coach VanDerveer explained to me, "First quarter freshmen . . . could really be in trouble" if they only pass six units but see their GPA drop." By contrast, the cumulative GPA of "a junior or senior is not gonna drop that much" so "not many kids are ineligible academically [as upperclassmen]. VanDerveer further explained using the example of a pre-med student: "Let's say I am a sophomore, and I am taking the biology core, I am pre-med. One class is 10 units. If I don't pass that one class, I haven't passed 6 units. Let's say I am only taking 14 units but 10 of 'em are in this one class. So now I am ineligible. The biology core is one of the most demanding and the sophomore year is when they have to take it. The men's team had a kid years ago who didn't pass that one core class and he was ineligible for the next quarter [right at the time] of the [NCAA] tournament. It's not that kids are just not passing." See also Zimbalist, *Unpaid Professionals*, 197–206.

34. Benedict and Keteyian, *The System*, chap. 9. Stanford's athletes do not appear to violate NCAA rules as much or as often as other college athletes. As of January 2013, Stanford was one of only three universities to participate in the highest level of athletic competition (i.e., be a member of an elite athletics conference such as the Pac-12 Conference) never to have had a major NCAA violation. In 2013, the NCAA revamped its hierarchy of violations, which had been in two-tiers (major and secondary), into four-tiers (severe breach of conduct, significant breach of conduct, breach of conduct, and incidental issues), placing emphasis on actions that violate the "integrity of college sports" (National Collegiate Athletic Association, "New Violation Structure"). Stanford coaches know that they must uphold Stanford's standard when they try to land the big-time high school recruit, as assistant athletic director for compliance Megan Boone explained to me. Boone's

job is to ensure that all operations related to financial aid, eligibility, recruiting, and amateurism uphold not only NCAA standards but also Stanford's. She also runs an educational program for Stanford coaches and student-athletes so that no major rules are violated. Boone told me that she "knocked on wood" every time she said the words "no major NCAA violations" and that if credit were to be handed out, it would have to go to "coaches, student-athletes, people who are on the front lines who decide every day to uphold the integrity of the institution." Then she added that DAPER tries to "follow the letter and the spirit of the rule" and "keep the amateurism aspect of college sports intact" by "setting a higher standard." The relative obscurity of Stanford's faculty athletic representative to the NCAA further illustrates the point. Stanford psychology professor, Ellen Markman, who was faculty athletic representative in 2008, told *Stanford Magazine* that "the position is about monitoring the integrity of the system, making sure that athletes are treated as students and ensuring student-athlete welfare," but because Stanford students and professors have a clear priority structure in their minds, Stanford rarely has problems that it must report to the NCAA or the Pac-12 Conference, and "some faculty I talk to have never heard of or known the [faculty athletic representative] position exists. It's not particularly visible, and I guess it's because there aren't that many concerns." In fact, in a recent review of its balance between academics and athletics, Markman found few major concerns. Some minor concerns were the improvement of schedule flexibility for teams to practice, including the rotation of practice times, improvement of lighting for night-time practices, and working with faculty to rework class schedules.

35. Easterbrook, *The King*, 29. There are two measures of graduation rates that are commonly used: the Department of Education's federal graduation rate (FGR), and the NCAA's graduation success rate (GSR). According to a 2018 report by the Commission on College Basketball, "the FGR and the GSR treat transferring students differently, and their differing cohorts result in dramatically different graduation rates: The 2017 FGR is 68 percent for all student-athletes and 48 percent for men's Division I basketball players. The 2017 GSR is 87 percent for all student-athletes and 82 percent for men's Division I basketball players. The meaningful graduation rate is likely somewhere between the FGR and GSR." In either case, though, and no matter the metric, the graduation rate appears much lower than it should be (National Collegiate Athletic Association Research, "Trends"; Petr and McArdle, "Academic Research," 39–40; College Sport Research Institute, "Adjusted Graduation Gap Report"; Commission on College Basketball, "Report," 2).

36. Easterbrook, *The King*, 29.

37. Cavalli, *Stanford Sports*, 98. High graduation rates have apparently been the norm at Stanford for decades and are often what makes Stanford stand out in the crowd. In the early 1980s, 90 percent of all Stanford student-athletes graduated within five years and 85 percent of them went on to do graduate work. By 2001, Zimbalist found that Stanford graduated "91 percent of all its athletes, including 94 percent of its football players and 100 percent of its basketball players," and he

called Stanford "a knight in shining armor in the world of college sports" (*Unpaid Professionals*, 3).

38. Graduation rates for female basketball players are higher than for male basketball players across the country. When Coach VanDerveer coached the 1996 Olympic team, she considered the why: "Ten of the 11 women on the national team had college degrees, a statistic few professional men's teams could match. The men are no less smart than the women; they simply have less incentive to finish their education. For the most gifted male players, college is often as much a farm league for the pros as an educational institution" (VanDerveer and Ryan, *Shooting from the Outside*, 66).

39. National Collegiate Athletic Association, "Academics."

40. The Stanford men's basketball program compiled the nation's twelfth-best rating (80). After a rule was passed prohibiting high school players from jumping directly from high school to the NBA, men's basketball players often attend a university for one year and then become what is called a "one and done," which contributes to poor GSRs.

41. Chris Townsend, "The Pulse," 95.7 FM, December 4.

42. According to several people I spoke to, Stanford presidents do not get as deeply involved in big-time sports, particularly football, as university presidents do at other schools, and they do not allow football to control the broader business of the university. Stanford tennis Coach Frank Brennan, for example, told me that while "half the presidents of the universities running the NCAA couldn't tell you what the NCAA stands for [and] couldn't tell you what city the NCAA has its headquarters in" because all of "the interactions with the NCAA are done by the athletic directors and the coaches," at Stanford, "President Hennessy is never going to be quoted about the football team." Instead, the football team at Stanford is expected to conform to the broader norms of the university.

43. Shulman and Bowen, *The Game of Life*. See also Coakley, "Studying Intercollegiate Sports," 25.

44. Byers and Hammer, *Unsportsmanlike Conduct*, 101. It was University of Alabama coach Bear Bryant who apparently demanded the construction of the first football dorms (Briley, *Career in Crisis*).

45. In 2006, Gerdy argued that athletic dorms "represent the absolute worst in college athletics—athletes treated like cogs in a machine, isolated and separated the campus community for the sole purpose of keeping them focused on playing ball." He also argued that dorms highlighted how "athletics departments have become completely divorced from the academic community" (*Air Ball*, 7).

46. Quoted in Bedell, "Not a Sporting Match."

47. Analysis by Winthrop Intelligence found that Stanford had the lowest yearly athletic spending as a percentage of endowment at 0.49 percent (*Sports Business Now*, "University Endowments"). Other universities with low rates included Duke University (1.17 percent), Texas A&M (1.43 percent) and Vanderbilt (1.46 percent). Among the ten schools that spent the lowest percentage of their endowment on sports (Stanford, Duke, Texas A&M, Rice, Vanderbilt, Michigan, Texas,

Virginia, Northwestern, and Notre Dame), three were flagship state universities, four were public, six were private, two (Stanford and Duke) were in the top ten of the *U.S. News & World Report* ranking of national universities, nine were in the top twenty-eight (Stanford, Duke, Northwestern, Vanderbilt, Rice, Notre Dame, Virginia, Michigan, and Texas), and only Texas A&M was not in the top fifty. On the other end of the spectrum, schools like Boise State (35 percent) and UNLV (33.24 percent) had considerably higher rates of spending on athletics, and none of the biggest spenders on athletics were in the top fifty national universities (*Sports Business Now*, "University Endowments"). However, Stanford's endowment was among the largest in the world. As a private university, Stanford relied upon its alumni and local philanthropists to donate the funding necessary to build athletic facilities and to provide athletic scholarships, and soliciting such donations has made Stanford one of richest universities in the world. According to 2017 figures from the Congressional Research Service, Stanford ($24.8 billion) trailed only Harvard ($36.0 billion), Yale ($27.2 billion), and the University of Texas ($26.5 billion) in terms of total endowment ("College and University"). In 2010–2011 the Cardinal spent $85 million per year on 850 athletes across 35 sports and DAPER boasted an endowment of $500 million (Stanford's budget as a whole was at the time approximately $17 billion per year). In 2012, Stanford topped a list of alumni donations to its endowment, raising $1 billion in just one year, becoming the first college to ever do so. Relative to its endowment and in comparison with its athletic competitors, Stanford's spending, which was dwarfed by other big-time universities like Texas and Oregon, who each spent over $100 million per year on sports, appeared low, but in absolute terms it was still an enormous business enterprise so these figures must be understood in context.

48. Owen added that athletic administrators at Stanford were "very happy" with their model but that they feared that things might change "from the outside in, like the NCAA or Congress or somebody else." She told me, "Pick a school, any school, we'd turn these people into employees and the money that Michigan generates from football alone allows them to go out and pay their top quarterback X, and, oh my God, we can't compete . . . We can only pay Y. Then the experience here just starts going downhill . . . You've got to keep up with the Joneses' but still maintain a sense of who you are and what you are."

49. Maples Pavilion was built in the late 1960s and named after donor Roscoe Maples, who graduated from Stanford in 1904. In addition to hosting basketball and volleyball games, including national and regional tournaments, it is occasionally used for banquets and lectures. In 2004–2005, Maples was renovated at a cost of $26 million, all funded by private donors. This renovation included new concession facilities, a new Jumbotron, new restrooms, and a new concourse encircling the pavilion. The renovation also included a new floor—at a cost of $400,000—which replaced a state-of-the-art floor that was created to bounce up and down in order to prevent injuries (Mague, "Stanford's Injury-Causing"). It also included upgraded locker rooms, student-athlete lounges, a strength and conditioning room and training room, a media workroom, a photography office, a courtside room reserved for banquets,

and padded seats for fans. Yet Maples holds the fewest fans of any Pac-12 school's arena. All other venues hold over 10,000, so while the maximum capacity at Maples is 7,233—at Utah's Jon M. Huntsman Center, the max capacity is 15,000, and the McHale Center at the University of Arizona is 14,545—Stanford had to consider ways other than ticket sales to generate revenue. The same could be said of coaching facilities. In 2011 when I visited the offices in a building next to Maples, tall glass windows encircled Stanford basketball's coaching suite in a modern architectural style one might find in a high-end corporate office, overlooking a small basketball court (with no bleachers) that was also used for alumni and media functions. Coach VanDerveer's office was spacious and included a private video room. Memorabilia from conference and national championships lined the walls in every direction. By 2018, when I visited again, these offices had been revamped to an even more sophisticated level, and a sleek athletic hall of fame had been built to showcase the historic accomplishments of Stanford athletes and coaches.

50. In Stanford's 2007–2008 budget plan, for example, Stanford expected to award $16.3 million in non-need-based scholarships to athletes and for athletics to earn revenue of $77.9 million. In 2009–2010 the budget non-need-based scholarships to athletes had risen to $18.9 million in accordance with a rise in tuition. In the 2010–2011 budget plan, the budget for non-need-based scholarships to athletes had risen to $19.6 million (Stanford University, "Budget Book," 12).

51. Much of Stanford's athletic endowment came from one leading donor, John Arrillaga, who had studied geography on the farm and played on the basketball team in the 1950s. Arrillaga then went on to make a fortune in Silicon Valley real estate, buying up fruit orchards in the Santa Clara Valley and turning them into office space for Silicon Valley technology companies. (Arrillaga-Andreessen, "John Arrillaga"). In 2006, Arrillaga made headlines when he donated $100 million to Stanford and then again in 2013 when he donated another $151 million. Over the years, his donations contributed to the construction of countless buildings on campus. Some Stanford alumni have credited Arrillaga and his "dutiful, hands-on patronage" with creating an environment in which Stanford's sports teams can thrive (Mangalindan, "The Secretive Billionaire").

52. P, Nate. "Kayla Pedersen."

53. Crouse, "Stanford's Coach."

54. See for example *In Praise of Athletic Beauty*, in which Gumbrecht hails Stanford University as the last remaining place where scholar-athletes truly exist ("Acknowledgments").

55. Here I follow the historian Yuval Harari, who argues that "any large-scale human cooperation—whether a modern state, a medieval church, and ancient city or an archaic tribe—is rooted in common myths that exist only in people's imagination," and that "an imagined reality is something that everyone believes in, and as long as this communal belief persists, the imagined reality exercises force in the world" (*Sapiens*, 27, 32).

56. Sack has argued that there are three common models that guide how scholars who study college sport view the matter: intellectual elitism, academic capitalism, and athletes' rights ("Clashing Models," 79–87).

57. Quoted in Sperber, *Beer and Circus*, 28.

58. Dowling, "Big-Time Sports," 86. Sperber follows a similar line of argument, suggesting that this calendar of seasonal spectacles, replete with pre- and post-game drinking parties, costumes, and face painting blinds us to the fact that big-time college athletics are corrupting and distorting the meaning of our institutions of higher learning (*Beer and Circus*).

59. Quoted in Strege, *Tiger*, 81.

60. Quoted in Strege, *Tiger*, 83.

CHAPTER 10

"We Need People to Take Ownership"

You can't be neutral on a moving train.

—Howard Zinn

I think everyone is a teacher. Everyone!

—John Wooden[1]

Man is an animal suspended in webs of significance he himself has spun. I take culture to be those webs, and the analysis of it to be therefore not an experimental science in search of law but an interpretive one in search of meaning.

—Clifford Geertz

"It Came Down to One Play": Texas A&M University, April 3, 2011 (NCAA Tournament, Round V)

By the time Stanford reached the NCAA's Final Four in Indianapolis, Indiana, they had tallied an astonishing 33-2 record. In the national semifinal, they were to play against the Texas A&M Aggies, a team that had cut down the mighty Baylor University Bears and their 6'8" star Brittney Griner, who was a national player-of-the-year candidate averaging 23 points, 7.8 rebounds, and 4.6 blocks per game. The Bears had tallied their own stellar season record, 34-2 and had been the nation's number one ranked team for much of the season. Indeed, since coach Kim Mulkey had taken over at

Baylor in 2000, the Bears had won at least twenty games every year, making four Sweet Sixteens and winning a national title (2004–2005) along the way, solidifying their status as a perennial women's basketball powerhouse. Had Stanford dodged a bullet by not drawing a matchup against Griner and Baylor? Or was A&M a better team than the Bears?[2]

Dave O'Brien, Doris Burke, and Rebecca Lobo called the game for ESPN on its flagship channel. The earlier rounds of the women's tournament had been relegated to ESPN2, a less-watched and less-lucrative network, but for the first time since the UCONN game, the Cardinal would have the chance to play for a national audience. O'Brien and company contended that the Aggies hoped to muscle the Cardinal around as opponents had tried all season. But Coach VanDerveer also told the press that she wanted her team to be "more physical," repeating her belief that her "team doesn't come out fighting until their nose is bloody." And as promised, the game started with intense and physical play, stifling both teams' ability to get into an offensive flow. There were six total points scored between both teams in the first six minutes of play.

In the second half, hard, physical plays sent several players to their backsides. On one play, Nneka set a hard screen on A&M's Sydney Colson, who was forced to leave the game temporarily. Kayla set her feet and selflessly took a charge, her body dropping onto the hardwood with a thud. But as soon as Stanford seemed to take control of the game, taking an eight-point lead, 40-32, they would lose it again, allowing the Aggies to cut it down to 42-41. Led by the Ogwumike sisters, Stanford stretched that lead to 54-45, but with about six minutes left in the second half, the Aggies put their foot on the accelerator again. Tyra White drove from the top of the key to the basket, drew a blocking foul on Nneka, and converted a three-point play to bring the score to 54-48. Adams converted a three-point-play of her own, driving hard to the basket and knocking Nneka over. Mel hit a jumper. White had an answer. With one minute and 25 seconds left, Stanford's lead, which had been as much as ten points, was one, 58-57. VanDerveer motioned to the referee for a timeout.

The air seemed to leave the building. The momentum had shifted to the Aggies. I found myself gnawing on a fingernail. The ball was inbounded, and the Aggies defenders glued themselves to the Cardinal players. In desperation, Mikaela Ruef heaved an off-balance three point shot that clanged and bounded far from the basket. Mel raced for, and dove after, the loose ball, but she was called for a foul. The referee could have easily called the play the other way since the Aggies' Colson had dived for the ball too and both players had equal opportunity to make a play on the ball. On the television replay, it looked like Colson had struck Mel's body first, with her left arm. But the call went the way it did, sending Mel to the bench with her fifth foul. Mel's departure left VanDerveer in a predicament. Mel had played perhaps her best game of the year and she was one of the few experienced players who had the quickness to keep up with the Aggie guards. Jeannette returned. Colson, who had been injured on the hard screen earlier in the game, stepped to the free throw line with an eye toward taking the lead for the Aggies. Calmly, she made two shots, and the Aggies led, 59 to 58. Thirty-five seconds were left in the game. Jeanette passed to Kayla. Kayla passed inside to Nneka, who was fouled by Adams. Nneka rattled in the "front end" of one and one, giving her another free shot. Nneka then hit the "back end" to put Stanford back on top, 60-59. White took a pass on the left wing, and with no hesitation drove baseline and banked in a layup. There were sixteen seconds left, and A&M had the lead, 61-60.

"Could Mel have stopped her?" I wondered. That call was huge!

Twelve seconds. Coach VanDerveer took a timeout to set up an offensive play. She called for a whirling swarm of would-be screeners to race in circles, dizzying the defense. Lindy set a screen for Nneka, and Nneka showed no hesitation on her way to the basket, scoring a tough layup across the lane and under a defender's outstretched arm: her thirtieth and thirty-first points of the game. With nine seconds left in the game, Stanford had a 62-61 lead. The Aggies had no timeouts left. Colson zigzagged up the court and dished a no-look pass to White. Lindy and Jeanette, two veteran players who had played together for years, got their signals crossed and simultaneously lunged to break up the pass. Instead, they ran into each other, opening space for the pass to reach White. White converted a bank-shot layup to put A&M back up by one. Jeanette got hurt on the play and was forced to limp off the court.

Only 3.3 seconds remained. Mikaela reared back and chucked an inbound pass the entire length of the court, but it sailed over her teammates and into the hands of an A&M player, who promptly threw it into the air as time expired.

A&M would play for a national title, and Stanford would head back to the farm with a final record of 33-3.

"The referees ruined the game!" I cried to myself. "Stanford should have won! The referees should have called the foul on White!" I was not officially part of the team, but I felt exactly like Kayla, who told the press after the game, "It's hard. I mean, it's an awful feeling."

Later, after I recovered emotionally, I would come to see that A&M had deserved the victory, having showed physical power and mental toughness not to mention impressive self-confidence in coming from ten points down in the final six minutes of play to defeat the Cardinal. They had posted heroic victories over two number one seeds to secure a seat in the NCAA Championship game, and their win over the Card seemed like destiny when, lo and behold, the Aggies won their first championship in school history two days later. When the dust had settled, they had won their NCAA tournament games by an average of 20.3 points. The Stanford win, which had been by one point, had been their closest game by far.

For VanDerveer, there was at least a silver lining in the dark clouds: "I thought we played very well to get the lead," she told the press. "We had to do some things we didn't have to do all season long against anyone else." Then in a matter-of-fact tone that to me had become her signature, she said, "It came down to one play." By saying this, she gave as clear a description of big-time college sports, maybe even sports in general, as had ever been made. The glory of victory, the agony of defeat, and every other emotion a moving body could feel, decided by one play. All the grit and perseverance, the sweat, tears, injuries, and the cut-down nets, now memories fading from the front of the mind, and only a W or an L remained.

But with VanDerveer, the statement, even in its matter-of-fact tone, also seemed hopeful, confident, and positive in that it was an interpretation of a final game and an end to a season that, for better or worse, had to be summed up. As a coach, she had to move on to the next group of young women to lead, and she had to frame this season in a light that honored the daily efforts of her players. She could not wallow in the outcome. Coach VanDerveer knew how damaging negativity could be not only to her current players but to her future ones as well. She was not about to follow some members of the media in judging teams that do not win a national title as second-best, as afterthoughts. She could have said how disappointed she was for what the loss meant to her and how she wanted her players to have done something different, but she didn't. She knew her team had battled, she knew her team had fought, and she knew that her team had bought in with all that they had and taken ownership of their journeys. Now more than ever, she knew she needed to be positive to remind her players of those efforts. She knew they needed her to remind them not to hang their heads in shame, and that despite the loss, they were still, in her heart, champions.

Coach VanDerveer's summary of the season and its final game reproduced Stanford's positive educational culture in real time, emphasizing the power of sport to build champions, both those who are crowned and those who deserve to be. It was the kind of thing a mother might say to her children in the wake of a disappointment, an acknowledgement of the pain but as much a reminder of the importance of perspective.

Thus, in this chapter I try to echo Coach VanDerveer's positivity by imagining ways in which we can be more positive about our role as scholars with an eye toward putting the college back in college sports, and the higher back in higher education.

"It Really Hurts": Texas A&M University vs. Notre Dame, April 5, 2011 (NCAA Tournament, Round VI)

Stanford did not play in the national title game. That opportunity went to Texas A&M, of course, and to Notre Dame, which beat UCONN in the other national semifinal. Another epic, big-time battle between UCONN and Stanford was not to be. After beating the Huskies, the Fighting Irish didn't have seem to have enough fight left in the tank and lost to the Aggies in the national final, 76-70.

It had been a captivating season to follow, full of excitement, surprises, upsets, and most of all, athletic beauty. Like many Americans, I had looked to star athletes like Nneka and Chiney to show me how the best players "just do it," to leaders like Kayla and Jeannette to watch how I might be more selfless, and to the Stanford coaches to learn how to manage a group of people with diverse interests, needs, and dreams. From witnessing the ways these coaches and players embraced their craft, I had personally gained an immeasurable amount.

Stanford did not win the 2011 national title, but they did win exactly ten years later, after an unprecedented season altered by the COVID-19 pandemic that required the team to travel over 7,500 miles, rarely sleep in their own beds, and endure one of the longest road trips in basketball history—sixty days. That was because of Santa Clara County's Health Guidelines, which prohibited Stanford from playing more than six home games all year. Stanford showed incredible resilience to win almost all these road games, secure the number one overall seed in the NCAA Tournament, and win six tournament games to capture the NCAA title. In the NCAA semifinal and final, Stanford won by a combined total of two points, further demonstrating their poise under pressure against other elite teams and the narrow gap between winners and losers.

The 2020-2021 team was characterized by many of the same strengths that led Stanford to the Final Four the year I followed the team—hard work, perseverance, and one of the greatest coaches of all time. As Rebecca Lobo said in the ESPN broadcast after the 2021 final, "Grit and toughness is what got Stanford through this." After the championship victory, Coach VanDerveer showed nothing but humility. In a postgame interview, she told Holly Rowe of ESPN about many different players who had contributed in different ways. Leaders who led, defenders who defended, players who stepped up. She didn't mention the importance of her coaching and instead simply said, "We are excited to win the COVID championship."

But coaching does matter, and adult leadership in college sports matters, a fact that came through when Stanford senior leader Kiana Williams said in the title game postgame interview, "We know Coach cares about us as people, not just as players."

This statement sums up the thesis of my book, which is that all adults involved in college sports need to do much better to care for the people who make these games—and the economies that depend on them—possible.

At this current moment, and for me as a fan and as a researcher, it is sometimes difficult to reconcile these moments of beauty with the ongoing conversation in the media and in the halls of academia about athlete exploitation. In many ways, watching the Stanford season unfold served my purposes well in terms of the entertainment it provided me as a fan and the information it provided me as a researcher.

But could I justify my role as a true fan if I didn't also acknowledge the exploitation that I discovered through my research? Wasn't I complicit in furthering that exploitation since without my eyeballs and those of others like me there wouldn't be the demand for college sports on television, and universities would not be encouraged to make money from them? If it wasn't true, as the colleges, conferences, and NCAA claimed, that there "just wasn't enough money to pay these athletes more" than the NCAA grant-in-aid, then didn't that imply that without my voice echoing the calls for an end to exploitation, I was selling out the athletes at the same time they brought me joy?

I thought about this contradiction between amateur rhetoric and professional reality every day I stepped foot in Maples Pavilion to watch a Stanford practice, and for the many years that followed.

If college basketball is supposed to be about the love of the game and college sports are supposed to be about college, then didn't the lessons learned in the process mean that much more? Without a focus on growth, there seemed little point in institutions of higher education supporting intercollegiate sports at this level. Unless more institutions of higher education were willing to be more honest about their role in producing profitable entertainment and branding themselves through sports while publicly accepting the professionalized approach of the athletes and the commercialized nature of their surroundings (and therefore undermining the notion of amateurism that the NCAA trumpets), that contradiction would remain.

Had the season been as positive for the athletes and coaches as it had been for me as a sports fan and researcher? Had it been as fun and productive for them as it had been for me? I couldn't shake the idea that only one team that had entered the NCAA field of sixty-four teams could say that it won its last game of the season. That fact amounted to a lot of disappointed athletes flying home each year.

After their final game, none of the Stanford players told the press how great or fun the season had been even though the team finished with an incredible 33-3 record. For Coach Paye, the end of the season brought painful reflections: "To go to the Final Four and have the best team and to not do what you are capable of doing, it hurts. It really hurts."[3] Coach Paye's comments were understandable, given that various forces in our sports culture encourage coaches to see each season in terms of how many victories you secure. In America, winning is how coaches are judged, why coaches are hired, and why coaches are paid. Winning was how coaches kept their jobs and put food on the table, and winning championships ensured a career in a volatile labor market. Far be it from me or anyone else to judge Coach Paye for feeling the way she did after a tough loss. How could she be blamed for following these cultural rules?

So it was that the end of the season challenged me as a researcher, and as a fan, to rethink my own sense of purpose. What were all these field notes for, after all? I never had plans to write a tell-all exposé about how college coaches use their players to advance their careers. But even if that had been my initial intention, that is simply not what I observed. My own observations suggested that Kiana Williams was right: Stanford coaches did care for these players as people. Still, how was I to write-up these notes, make sense of them, and share what I had learned with the world?

"We Need People to Take Ownership"

The answer to these questions, I came to realize, could only come if I faced down the prevailing winds of academia, and it had to start from a place of self-reflection, positivity, and gratitude. I needed to look past the common discourse of exploitation and figure out what to say about what this coach and her staff did, why they did it, and what it meant to their players.

I drew inspiration from Coach VanDerveer, for whom the 2011 Final Four loss was not reason enough to wallow in what had not come to pass or cause for wistful reflection on what might have been. Instead, she told me after the season that there were still ways the team could improve and that for the next season's team to win a title, they would need to "keep working."

It was not the specifics of what she said each player had to do to improve but rather the way Coach VanDerveer summed up the season, and what it meant for next year's team, that struck the deepest chord for me. After detailing each player's tasks for improvement, she said, "In order to win [a championship] we are not in the condition that we need to be in. We're not skilled enough. We need people to take ownership."

"Take ownership"? That sounded a lot like buying in to me, the sort of view one might expect a coach to have while a player talked of making an investment of sweat. But the expression could be interpreted on several levels. "Taking ownership" could be interpreted as rhetoric to reproduce a rather rigid hierarchy and status quo. "Taking ownership" could be seen as reflective of the market and its cold truths dominating the way we talk to and about each other. But for me, "taking ownership" was something else. VanDerveer's players played for a college that operated within a capitalist economy and yet it bought in to the idea that athletics and academics could be balanced. That was Stanford's brand. It was their standard and it gave that brand value in the marketplace. Moreover, it was the players who took ownership of their bodies, their training, and their education that ended up where they wanted to go. "Taking ownership" meant making choices to craft one's future self. These were facts.

Yet because of dominant trends in the humanistic social sciences today, which are dominated by postmodernist thought and particularly deconstructionism and which encourage scholars to break down the lives of the people and cultures they study so that they fit into fashionable theories, these kinds of facts are rarely highlighted, especially in academic works on college sports, where there is often a myopic, and unbalanced, focus on things negative such as economic exploitation, sexism, and racism. We need more studies that highlight both, studies that are not afraid to build up the people they study and underline the great choices they have made given the often difficult circumstances they are in. We need scholars to showcase more stories of athletes and coaches and fans and administrators who are using the power of sport to make society a better place to live.

Historically, social science scholars have examined the relationship between the individual and society, with many scholars focusing on how the latter impacts the life of the former. But for me, the reverse relationship—how the individual impacts society—is as interesting, if not more so, precisely because it offers the scholar a chance to learn something of practical value for himself and for his readers and to open the windows on a more positive side of the story.

Take for example Coach VanDerveer's coaching pedagogy. In a winning-is-everything context where victory is ultimately tied to profit, one can understand why a coach would be an authoritarian. Yes, winning was important to Coach VanDerveer, and with that goal in mind she raised her voice from time to time to get a point across to her players. But Coach VanDerveer's behavior was inexorably tied to a male-dominated big-time sports world and particularly the way that big-time male coaches set the mold for what a coach of any team can and should be. Indeed, Coach VanDerveer's authoritarian coaching was widely respected in the sports world and considered an example of how coaches could help players improve as players and as people. Was she reproducing some of the values of a commercialized culture while trying to be like the authoritarian male coaches who had set the coaching standards before her? It was tempting to draw a line from big-time football coaches such as Vince Lombardi and big-time basketball coaches like Bob Knight to VanDerveer's own coaching that, after all, involved a lot of speeches about toughness and sacrifice for the team.

But it was not as if Coach VanDerveer's coaching tactics were overbearing or abusive, so in many cases I saw her style as more authoritative than authoritarian. VanDerveer's approach challenged my sensibilities, I must admit, since my perspective on education was founded on the work of John Dewey and his idea of child-centered education, on Carl Rogers's person-centered psychology,[4] and on other scholars' work on athlete-centered sports training,[5] and these approaches to education seemed to run counter to authoritarian, though not authoritative coaching.

Furthermore, she was doing her best to buy in to a college coaching culture that she did not create. True, she was driven by a passion for victory and that drive sometimes led to yelling at an errant player, but many big-time college sports coaches are focused on winning, and many if not most have a similar passion and use similar tactics. Even if there were moments when VanDerveer's spirit appeared to reproduce the profit-minded, branding, and triumphalist values that had long characterized college football, shouldn't a scholar like me lay blame at the feet of the broader American culture and not the individual who succumbed to it? At least if one were to blame individuals, then there were many other individuals who needed to account long before VanDerveer for normalizing such behavior.

During the time I spent at Stanford observing the basketball team and studying alongside several positive psychologists of education, I came to modify my thinking about coaching styles slightly. Recent work in psychology that has been positive—that is, focused on studying what works rather than what is lacking in or deviant from what is considered normal—convinced me that studies of what exemplars do well can also shed light on what works in a particular culture, and it was easy to see that VanDerveer's approach worked well. More importantly, VanDerveer's former players said with conviction that VanDerveer's approach worked well for them. Their stories, and the research I found to contextualize them, convinced me that sports can be beneficial in terms of generating a positive self-concept and positive social relation as well as positive human development through participation[6] (and through sports team fandom too[7]). Through sports individuals can learn how to take control over their lives and determine what kind of self they want to create.[8] Whatever benefits individuals may see, the right educator, mentor, counselor, or coach can help us tease out what kinds of goals we should set for ourselves and how to achieve them while helping mitigate any quirks or idiosyncrasies that may stand in the way. In some, though certainly not all cases, an authoritarian or authoritative approach may help, and it seems to me that VanDerveer's approach, which was coupled with genuine care for her players, as well as backed up by Stanford's Standard, which ensured that athletics did not overwhelm education, combined to create the conditions in which many young students and athletes could figure out what kind of self they wanted to create.

Coach VanDerveer pushed her players from a place of support rather than from a place of anger or disappointment for what the players could not do. She channeled a positive vision of where they could be in the future. When they got there, the players looked back to say that they may not have known it at the time, but Coach VanDerveer had given them exactly what they needed. In that sense, her coaching was as positive as it was forceful, as authoritative as it was full of love.

I found VanDerveer's commitment to her craft invigorating, and I would have followed her into a foxhole even if she yelled at me to get in there. Most of all, I found her coaching remarkable because in a winning-is-everything culture where victory is ultimately tied to profit, one should not expect a coach to show the kind of positivity or humor that Coach VanDerveer exuded every day. There are too many forces, from capitalist macroeconomics to any given university's alleged "culture of excellence", working against the maintenance of that attitude.

And in the end, while winning *was* important to Coach VanDerveer and her staff, it was not in fact *the* most important thing. I saw Stanford coaches routinely treat their players with care, respect, and encouragement so perhaps what made Coach VanDerveer most unique and most legendary was not the wins or even that the players she coached often earned a college degree, a professional contract, or a coaching position but rather the gift she gave them in the way she looked at them and in the way she suggested they ought to look at themselves.

For it was unique that VanDerveer saw the pressures on big-time athletes not as an excuse to quit or complain or as a justification to adopt a negative outlook on life but as an opportunity for the athletes to choose a positive attitude, work to improve their game, and begin to take ownership of their training and their lives.

The Centerpiece of College Athletics: Prioritizing Education in the College Sports Reform Movement

My observations of the Stanford women's basketball team, along with my studies of the athletic department under whose umbrella they performed and the broader college sports culture and higher education system in which they lived, played, and studied demonstrated to me that anyone who hopes to reform this system must do so in a way that incentivizes people to achieve what Stanford University and Coach VanDerveer's teams achieved year after year: academic and athletic excellence in a balanced form.

The current economic model of NCAA D-I college sports creates a great entertainment product but it does not sufficiently allow for positive educational experiences for many college athletes either because education is not prioritized institutionally or because the broader culture encourages and incentivizes athletes to focus on their athletic pursuits.[9] In 2017, Gurney, Lopiano, and Zimbalist argued that there are two paths to college sports reform—either marketize college sports or improve the education—but I and others[10] believe that both can be accomplished and that both must be accomplished to operate both men's and women's sports ethically.

However, the way that college sports are to be marketized should be done carefully so that athletes can share in the profits of this billion-dollar entertainment industry and also so that college sports can remain a viable means of higher education. Setting up a hybrid model, which would allow each college to have a certain number of non-matriculated pros who receive a salary in explicit exchange for their athletic services,[11] does not seem fair. Moreover, other piecemeal reforms, such as limiting the numbers of scholarships available to college football teams, which often have rosters that are double that of NFL teams, or allowing the NCAA to take control of basketball summer camps,[12] or shortening the length of the season and the number of hours coaches can interact with athletes would not go far enough to ensure that education is improved for all athletes.

The distinction between revenue-generating sports and non-revenue generating sports is well-known but the distinction between athletes whose universities provide them with a high-quality education and those whose universities do not is not. I believe that this latter distinction is just as important and that for big-time college sports to operate in an ethical manner, more universities need to strive to provide a high-quality education to big-time athletes as well as free them to profit from their NILs. This chapter offers concrete suggestions for how that task may be accomplished.

One might argue that any reforms that are undertaken at the NCAA or college level should ensure that compensation to athletes is proportional to the services rendered to the university, both real and symbolic, and that these payments come directly from university coffers. Big-time athletes are, by this argument, underpaid laborers, and for this problem to be redressed, the beneficiary of their sweat must pay. After all, athletes' NILs are used by universities officially in billboards and advertisements, and as such these athletes should be compensated properly.

But college sports cease to have raison d'etre if athletes are paid salaries directly by universities as professional athletes would be. Colleges are not NCAA franchises; they are NCAA member schools, with the operative term being "schools," so they should focus their efforts on re-centering education as college sports' main priority. Many scholars and high-profile institutions have encouraged education-focused reforms, and from their work we can see that the universities' core business is and should be education, not sports entertainment.[13] Contrary to what some would say, education is as important as access to market pay because it provides an opportunity for growth for all athletes regardless of background, gender, social class, race, talent, or ability. In 2018 the Commission on Collegiate Basketball concluded that "the answer to many of college basketball's problems can be found in a renewed commitment to the college degree as the centerpiece of intercollegiate athletics." The commission concluded this because they believed intercollegiate athletics were based on "trust" and the "promise" that "athletes play for their schools and receive a realistic chance to complete a college degree in return," and "any policy or action that violates that trust" would be "morally wrong."

I am persuaded by such a moral position since the business of college sport involves human beings and human bodies to whom respect and ethical treatment should be assured and because I believe the best way to ensure this is to prioritize education and make concrete reforms that will cement that prioritization. There is a comprehensive solution that reforms college sports in a way that provides more to those who create college sports entertainment but also provides a better educational offering to those who choose to go to college to play sports *and* get an education, which is to say many if not perhaps even most college athletes.

So this chapter proposes reforms that will more sufficiently compensate the professional role big-time college athletes perform without sacrificing the educational connection that is vital to the core of college sports. Even if reclaiming college sports for higher education—while also giving the athletes proper compensation for what they do for the university and proper respect for their rights to unionize and to be treated as employees—may not be an easy project, I believe it is a necessary one.

The Reforms We Need Now for Big-Time College Athletics

Rethink Pay for Play

The first reform on every college athlete's mind is pay-for-play. Various groups and individuals such as Dick Devenzio,[14] Jeremy Bloom,[15] Jason White,[16] Ed O'Bannon,[17] Ellen Staurowsky,[18] Ramogi Huma, Shawne Alston, Nick Kindler, D. J. Stephens, Afure Jemerigbe,[19] Martin Jenkins,[20] Allen Sack,[21] Andy Schwarz, Nancy Skinner and Steven Bradford, and Jay Bilas[22] have fought for this outcome for years in the courts of law and public opinion.

Some (limited) progress has been made, most recently due to public calls that athletes be able to access the free market to sell themselves as spokesmen or sign endorsement deals (i.e., to control their NILs).[23] In 2019 the Fair Pay to Play Act (FPPA) passed the State Assembly of California. The FPPA, which was passed unanimously, will starting in 2023 effectively forbid California colleges and universities from controlling the NILs of college athletes. Some universities lobbied against the bill, but California Governor Gavin Newsom signed it into law. (As of 2020, thirty-six states had passed legislation like California's.) Predictably, the NCAA responded to the FPPA by arguing in a letter to Governor Newsom that "the bill would wipe out the distinction between college and professional athletics and eliminate the element of fairness that supports all of college sports."[24] It was a spurious argument, though, which rested on the false assumption that college sports at the big-time level are already fair, which they are not. The NCAA has drafted its own NIL measures, but voting has been delayed. In a statement, the chair of the NCAA Board of Governors announced in early 2021 that "while any postponement certainly is disappointing, we support conducting the appropriate due diligence to ensure we are effectively modernizing rules to ensure the best possible experience for our students engaged in intercollegiate athletics."[25]

The results of opinion polls regarding pay-for-play proposals are unclear sometimes because the issue of athletes earning from their NILs is often conflated with the issue of colleges paying athletes directly. While a 2017 *Washington Post*–UMASS Amherst poll found that 52 percent of Americans believe an athletic scholarship is enough to compensate athletes for their services to the university, 60 percent said they believed college athletes should be paid "based on revenue they generate." (Among African Americans, the percentage was even higher [54 percent], while among whites [32 percent] and Hispanics [41 percent] it was lower.) On the issue of NILs, the approval rate was higher, with 66 percent of Americans saying, "college athletes should be paid when their name or image is used in video games or to sell merchandise."[26] And in 2020 Knoester and Ridpath found that the "majority of U.S. adults now support, rather than oppose, allowing college athletes to be paid."[27]

Universities already do pay players, both formally and under the table. For some college athletes, what is given is perceived to a pretty good deal too.[28] However, it is open for debate whether the amount universities pay is currently enough, since "enough" depends on a variety of factors, including personal background, perceived racial category, socioeconomic class, and quality of education provided. Recruited athletes receive a uniform grant-in-aid that is essentially a stipend capped by the NCAA that is not available to non-athletes and is "awarded without regard to the financial need or the academic attainment of the recipient."[29] How much this award is worth exactly depends on the institution granting it since tuition, room, and board range widely across the country. In 2018 the Commission on Collegiate Basketball concluded that athletic scholarships were worth from "$13,392 to $71,585 for in-state students and from $18,125 to $71,585 for out-of-state students, depending on the institution." Many athletes receive ancillary benefits on top of that, some of which can be worth many more thousands of dollars.[30] (Since 2012 some NCAA athletes have been able to earn more than this too. In 2012 the NCAA drafted a reform package that included a proposal to give NCAA athletes $2,000 stipends for more financial leeway, and by 2015 that proposal had been implemented, with athletes in some sports and at some schools receiving stipends ranging from $2,000 to $7,000.[31])

What remains, then, is not the question of whether athletes should be paid by universities but who controls those payments, how much they will be, and where the additional money will come from. Paying players more than what they already earn could be achieved by either giving them more funds from university coffers or by allowing them to sell their NILs, or both. In the former case, one might expect that universities, athletic conferences, and the NCAA would accordingly seek to secure larger media rights payments to compensate.

Certainly there is a good case to be made, as Huma, Staurowsky, and Montgomery have, that certain college athletes deserve much more direct pay than they currently receive. In their 2020 study, they conclude that "the average football and basketball player at an FBS college had a fair market value of $208,208 and $370,085, respectively. Over the course of four years, football and basketball players' estimated fair market value in the highest revenue conferences range from an average of $1 million to 2.7 million."[32] They base this statement on the revenue that these athletes generated for their NCAA member schools so there is good reason to believe that they deserve a bigger piece of this pie. Moreover, if pay-for-play came directly from university coffers (direct pay-for-play), there would no longer be any need for the NCAA enforcement apparatus that currently monitors and polices athletes' reception of "impermissible benefits." There are over four hundred pages of NCAA rules, and Bishop has described the NCAA rulebook as "bigger than the Harry Potter series."[33] Eliminating this enforcement apparatus, including the salaries of many NCAA enforcement employees and athletic department compliance officials, would free up more money to pay players and diminish much of the conflict between the NCAA, its member universities, and athletes. Direct pay-for-play would also likely limit the pay gap between those who play for universities in these games and those who coach them. College coaches can earn huge sums of money, and money is power, so they often have leverage not only over their players but also over their university, which does not want to fire an expensive employee and must pay his salary as well as that of his replacement. Sometimes highly paid coaches have also abused their power over players, and that abuse would likely end if players earned salaries closer to those of the coaches.

Yet there are many problems that might arise from direct pay-for-play that are important to consider when answering the question of how players will be paid. First, direct pay-for-play might drive some colleges into bankruptcy—at least if we are to believe the veracity of college's self-reported financial statements.[34] Title IX also plays a role, as Buzuvis explains, since "paying athletes in revenue sports, coupled with the commensurate obligation under Title IX to pay female athletes, would be prohibitively expensive.[35] Next, colleges insist that if they pay players, the NCAA and universities might lose their tax exemption as not-for-profit educational organizations. Would direct pay-for-play put colleges in a "business unrelated to education," which would then eliminate colleges' entitlement to a tax break?[36] After all, why should colleges be exempt from paying the same taxes any other profitable business must pay? Finally, some see paying players directly from university coffers as a slippery slope. In 2011, Zimbalist argued that "monetizing relationships" at the university might lead to salaries for the best actor in theatrical productions or the first violinist in the school orchestra and to "allocating course enrollments slots" for the most popular professors "to those students who bid the highest."[37] In later work, Meyer and Zimbalist called for Congress to give the NCAA an antitrust exemption but stopped short of demanding that colleges and universities pay players directly.[38]

So perhaps it is best to free college athletes to profit from their NILs, which would allow the most popular athletes to profit in the free market while not being paid directly by colleges. There is no good reason why athletes should not be allowed to use their own NIL, and that decision could be universally agreed upon by all NCAA member institutions without the aid of judicial decisions.[39] NILs are the athletes' property to begin with, and there should be nothing in a NCAA contract that, in the words of economist Andy Schwarz, "abrogates" those rights.[40] Perhaps the NCAA is not the best organization to oversee transactions involving NILs and that a new "honest broker" is required,[41] but if the NCAA remains the organization of administrative record, it could encourage athletes to self-report the selling of their NIL for transparency purposes. Otherwise there would be "no involvement of institutional representatives and other controls."[42] Even as the legal prospect of such a solution remains unclear on a national level, freeing the athletes is the right thing to do.

Next, why not free athletes to access the free market and improve their education at the same time, thereby re-centering the importance of education in this ecosystem? We can tie together these reforms by requiring that NIL earnings be locked in a trust fund that the athlete can access only after graduation (waivers can be filed and exceptions can be made where necessary, e.g., in the case of a financial hardship).[43] This would, theoretically, improve graduation rates. Given that in the long run "a college diploma is substantially *more valuable* than any pay the athlete] might receive,"[44] and by some estimates a diploma "adds $1 million to the average person's lifetime earnings,"[45] this is the right move. Some young athletes today may not realize or appreciate how valuable a college degree can be. Why not reform the system in a way that more effectively incentivizes behavior that is in athletes' best long-term interest and in the interest of the society they will inevitably join? Isn't the best way to do that to free athletes with their education in mind? After all, the last thing anyone wants is a physically and mentally battered former college athlete, discarded by his or her school after his or her NCAA eligibility is gone, without a degree.

But lurking in many direct pay-for-play proposals is the sexist idea that one only need consider the pay of male athletes. This sexism is based on the mistaken premise that women do not play big-time sports, but this is not always the case. In 2011, for example, Nocera proposed paying male college athletes but suggested that women's sports such as basketball did not "occupy a [sufficiently] different role on campus" like football and men's basketball and therefore did not deserve to be paid. He added, "If the time comes when women's basketball is as commercialized and profit-driven as men's basketball, then yes, the women should be paid as well. But we're a long way from that point."[46] Nocera makes a questionable assumption here. Such a distinction may be true on some American campuses where women's basketball is not popular, but there are plenty of examples to the contrary. If big-time male athletes deserve to be paid then why shouldn't big-time women also deserve to be paid? Just because they don't generate as much money as (some) men?

Furthermore, if both male and female athletes are to be paid directly by universities, then Title IX compliance issues may arise. If NIL legislation is codified on a national level, then women athletes may be able to profit from their athleticism and personal brands. In 2021 it became clear that eight out of ten of the most-followed college athletes on social media were women, raising the prospect that these athletes could successfully monetize their NILs if allowed.[47]

Unfortunately, the courts have largely sidestepped this question of pay-for-play for big-time women's athletes. In March 2019, Judge Claudia Wilken ruled in *NCAA v. Alston* that the NCAA was in violation of the 1890 Sherman Antitrust Act and that they had to eliminate their caps on the value of grants-in-aid and allow member schools and their conferences to determine the value of the scholarships they offer athletes. (The ruling was upheld on appeal in 2020.[48]) Effectively, this meant that "schools . . . will be able to compete [with each other] by offering athletic scholarships of higher value"[49] although Wilken limited her ruling to include costs related to education (e.g., books, computers).

The Supreme Court ruled on *Alston* in the summer of 2021, shutting down the NCAA's caps on education-related expenses, but the merits of the case failed to remedy the question of whether big-time male and female athletes should receive the same or a similar amount in pay and whether it would be a violation of Title IX if they do not. The NCAA wanted the Supreme Court to determine if Wilken's decision in *Alston* "blurs the line between student-athlete and professional,"[50] but that line was blurred long ago. The more pressing issue was and remains whether NCAA member schools should pay athletes directly and if they do, whether Title IX should apply. In other words, is a grant-in-aid compensation for an athlete's efforts on the court or field, and if so, do male and female athletes deserve to be paid the same amount irrespective of how much revenue they generate for the university?[51] Buzuvis explores whether it is possible to ensure Title IX compliance and women's continued participation in college sports and concludes that colleges could improve education by returning to a system "in which financial aid is awarded based on need rather than athletic participation." She writes,

> Title IX prevents college athletic departments from using commercial objectives as the sole basis for allocating resources, and instead requires equal treatment to women's sports even though they have less potential to generate revenue.
>
> For a college athletic department that wishes to retain its association with higher education, compliance with Title IX is mandatory. Compliance with labor and antitrust law, on the other hand, is not . . . If college athletic departments replaced athletic scholarships with need-based support, they would no longer be engaging compensation or control, because an athlete could discontinue participation on the team and still be eligible for financial aid. Such reform would also signal that the institution's priority is the student's education rather than his participation in athletics. In this way, it addresses concern that college athletes are exploited, since it would restore an athlete's choice to participate in athletics without concern for economic consequences.[52]

Buzuvis adds that

> a second aspect of education-based reform is to drastically reduce the time commitment required for participation in college athletics. In addition to neutralizing . . . arguments about the presence of employer-like control, such reform would satisfy concerns about athlete exploitation by ensuring that participation in athletics does not obstruct pursuit of meaningful education. Time commitment restraints would provide athletes with the freedom to select majors and courses with less concern for conflicts with practice schedules and travel obligations. Reform that restores the priority of academics in this manner would also have the effect of subordinating a college athletic department's commercial objectives.[53]

I agree that education should be prioritized, and a return to a world where financial aid rather than athletic scholarships ruled might be ideal, but that seems like pie in the sky. Financial incentives are part of college sports and will remain, so the answer is not to eliminate them but to rebalance them with educational incentives.

In terms of how much each player will receive, it may get complicated since men's and women's college sports garner vastly different levels of fan interest, but potential complication should not override the need to operate college sports ethically. Meyer and Zimbalist conclude that if NCAA member schools were required to pay players for their NILs, "then there is little question that Title IX would apply, mandating equivalent NIL payments to women either as part of its financial-aid or benefits-and-opportunities requirements."[54]

NIL legislation has passed in many states, but it simply allows athletes to ink deals with non-university entities. What remains to be determined is whether the university must pay athletes for using their NIL, or whether the grant-in-aid is enough. If it is the former, another question is whether this necessarily means that if football player W is paid X by a university then women's basketball player Y must be paid an equivalent X by the same university. Meyer and Zimbalist rightly note that women athletes often have fewer professional opportunities than male athletes so college is a crucial time for them to maximize their time in the public spotlight and earn money while they can, which is another reason why all athletes should be freed to profit from their NIL.[55] However, that universities themselves benefit from using athletes' NILs is a fact that remains often overlooked, and it seems clear that some form of explicit compensation ought to be provided for that privilege.

Strike a Better Balance between Academics and Athletics
Many scholars have emphasized the need to improve the education of college athletes.[56] In court filings, the NCAA maintains that its "basic purpose" is to "maintain intercollegiate athletics as an integral part of the educational program and the athlete as an integral part of the student body and, by so doing, retain a clear line of demarcation between intercollegiate athletics and professional sports."[57] The NCAA has implemented branding campaigns that suggest that it provides "opportunity" to young athletes (alongside "wellbeing" and "fairness") and that it "celebrates college athletes." Still, given the enormous sums that NCAA member schools earn from their athletic efforts, more must be done to prove that the education of big-time athletes is a true priority and that these advertisements are more than obfuscatory rhetoric. The sports broadcaster Bob Costas has said that the pay-for-play idea is based on the "woeful premise" that "education doesn't matter that much,"[58] and it is true that at some big-time programs, neither athletes nor university officials are particularly concerned about education. To revolutionize the system simply by paying players directly from university coffers while also overlooking the educational element of the enterprise would amount to a shortsighted solution and would ignore

research that proves that sports participation has various educational benefits. It is a common trope that college sports participation leads to the cultivation of leadership skills, but if the nature of the educational exchange was made more explicit, more athletes would see how this exchange could benefit them in the long run.

Detail Coaching Deliverables

Here is what universities can do to prioritize education. For starters, be more explicit about the educational role college sports play and hire and fire coaches based on educational criteria. Meyer and Zimbalist argue, "The answer to the bloated spending [e.g., on college sports coaches' salaries] is not to pay the athletes a salary; it is to cap coaches' and administrators' salaries, limit the expenditures on lavish facilities used for a single sport, and reinforce the educational mission of the school,"[59] going on to say that setting these conditions would require an antitrust exemption. Similarly, universities can craft detailed statements about coaching deliverables and hold coaches to them. They can also make detailed statements about what athletes can reasonably expect from their coach-educator on and off the court or field and what will be expected of them in return. Coaches can be hired and fired on their ability to meet these criteria, rather than only on wins and losses.

Raise Eligibility Requirements

Next universities should unilaterally end special admissions consideration for exceptional athletes who do not make the grade. Currently many colleges tweak academic and admissions policies, creating "special admit" status even at academically rigorous schools that field athletically talented teams. This hurts everyone. If a student has not made the proper academic preparations for college, he may disrupt the learning of his peers or disrupt a professor's lesson plan to teach the subject at a higher level. Admitting academically underprepared students can thus have a deleterious impact on the overall learning environment, and that may lower the quality of education a particular university provides to all students. The athlete himself may also become disillusioned in a difficult classroom and give up on his education, wrongfully concluding that it is his fault. These are hardly the outcomes anyone wants. This may not be an easy step to take, but it is a step available to universities hoping to create a more positive educational culture. It would be much easier for individual universities to enact this if a regional or national association of universities did so together. Some conferences, including the Ivy League, Patriot League, and the New England Small College League have historically imposed higher admission standards and GPA requirements on their student-athletes.[60] Some individual colleges, including Stanford, Boston College, Duke, and Notre Dame insist that they keep their own academic standards higher than those of other colleges.[61] Yet few other institutions of higher education have raised academic standards beyond what the NCAA requires probably because they believe it will harm their competitive advantage on the sports field. That is a misguided priority.

In 2005, Staurowsky and Ridpath argued for the adoption of a 2.0 minimum GPA to create the "potential to empower athletes to place their educational interests above their athletic interests."[62] The NCAA has since adopted a 2.3 minimum GPA in core high school courses to ensure D-1 eligibility, but the GPA standard could be even higher given that a 2.3 GPA standard represents a C average, which hardly seems to represent the kind of excellence colleges say that they expect of student-athletes.

Provide Better Support Structures

Of course we should not simply raise the GPA without providing support structures to help athletes achieve this higher goal. Rather, we should provide extra tutoring and remedial learning whenever necessary. Gerald Gurney of the University of Oklahoma started the nation's first athletic study center, having grown concerned as he saw his university do somersaults to get underprepared athletes eligible to play even as it seemed to care little about whether they received a good education. While in 1982 there were only twenty-four athletic tutoring programs nationwide,[63] now every D-I university must have one. A national association of athletic academic advisors exists to share best practices too. Thus, additional education resources abound at most schools, with some providing big-time athletes with extra instruction, including remedial instruction, but athletes even so are often disincentivized by their institution, faculty, coaches, and peers from focusing on schoolwork. If the GPA were raised, these incentives would likely change. Therefore, new institutional decrees highlighting the primacy of education would go a long way, and raising the minimum GPA for eligibility would help these efforts considerably.

Raise Academic Standards for All Athletes and All Students

The chance to be challenged at an academically rigorous institution is beneficial for everyone, including those for whom high school may not have provided a proper challenge to help them reach their cognitive potential, those who are late bloomers, and those who may have come from a disadvantaged area where the K–12 schools were not of the highest quality.

In that sense, our society may be better off when universities take risks on athletes who may not demonstrate academic achievement before college but show academic potential. Of course, a reasonable skeptic might wonder, "Why should universities be responsible for leveling the playing field in this way?" Perhaps they should not be, at least not solely, but they can work alongside government and non-profit organizations to be the "point guards" and lead "the team" (society) there. They may also be obligated to do so. That is, if universities want to continue to receive tax exemptions while also making money and building their institutional brands using young athletic labor, don't they have an obligation to help level the playing field? The American K–12 education system is broken, and even if fixing that broken system is a political problem that we all must work together to solve, universities can help by admitting promising (but not academically underprepared) students.

And yet there is still a lingering sense that while populations underserved at the K–12 level should be given an equal opportunity to gain admission to universities, giving those opportunities primarily to athletes from such backgrounds sends the dubious message that it is balls and not books that should be the focus of a youth's free time. It is also arguably indefensible since if the goal is to offer opportunity to those historically underserved, why should an athlete rather than a stellar student receive that funding or scholarship?

In the long run, this is not the best course for any nation to take, especially not a democratic nation, and therefore not the message universities should be sending with their prioritization of athletic entertainment over education. Democracy dies in darkness, and focusing on sports to the detriment of academic pursuits can lead to an underinformed and undereducated populace.

That is why I believe that receiving an athletic scholarship should be considered a privilege that is earned through one's academic and athletic accomplishments and not something granted to talented athletes who care little about school but are stellar at sports.

Some worry that if we raise academic standards for all athletes, we might be excluding students who might have otherwise made it to college. For example, one athletic department official at Stanford told me,

> Let's [say that we] make [the GPA standard for eligibility] a 3.3, which would be a huge jump from where it's at now. Are we then excluding, and I think you would, people who, for no fault of their own, were born into a system where they just didn't have the opportunity? Is that right? I don't know how to answer that. I don't know how to start to put more value on academics, or

if we should. If you're phenomenal at football . . . Maybe it's not for me to say? . . . When you try to institutionally and across an entire policy mandate something, you're always going to have an outlier or a group of outliers that were negatively impacted . . . Somehow this country has got to back our educational system a little bit more than they are . . . I don't know the way to do that . . . The private schools have cropped up and that allows this more privileged group to get the education they deserve. That's crap, now we're just rich is getting richer, poor is getting poorer, how do we systematically across the board start to value education?

Obviously this official's comments suggest that college sports reform is only part of the solution to this systemic societal problem, but the time is ripe for reform and so it should be seized. In the long run, a failure to keep a high academic standard for all only ensures that big-time athletics will continue to have a tenuous connection to the core values of higher education, and that misguided priority structure will invariably trickle down to lower levels of education and incentivize young people to choose sports over school when what we want is a better balance between the two that better serves all students and the society.

Give Athletes More Time to Finish Their Degree
If athletes are underprepared for college schoolwork, they may take more time to graduate. Some studies have suggested that graduation rates for big-time athletes are lower than those of the average student.[64] So in 2012, members of NCAA D-I agreed to award multiyear scholarships.[65] (Previously, athletes were only given one-year scholarships subject to renewal each year.) In 2015, the Power 5 conferences instituted measures to make it less likely that athletes would have their athletic scholarships revoked "for athletic reasons," but the measures did not cover all NCAA schools. While these are steps in the right direction, no student who is recruited for sports should lose his scholarship if he is injured, does not get along with the coach, or decides that academics are more important than sports and chooses to quit the team. In 2018, the Commission on Collegiate Basketball therefore recommended that big-time colleges pay "for the degree completion of student-athletes with athletic scholarships who leave member institutions after progress of at least two years towards a degree" in order to "to restore credibility to the phrase student-athlete."[66]

Some scholars have called for guaranteed, good-for-life scholarships for big-time athletes,[67] but the commission's recommendation seems more sensible, especially given the financial struggles that academic departments at many universities now face. If athletes are to have lifetime scholarships, payment for their studies ought to be transferred from the athletic department to the academic department.

Give Athletes Freedom to Transfer without Restriction
Athletes should also be able to transfer to a new school without restriction because education rather than competitive imbalance between sports programs should be the ultimate priority. If an athlete believes he or she will be better educated elsewhere, then so be it.

For too long the NCAA required that athletes in big-time sports sit out a year before they could play again. As recently as 2019, the NCAA stated on its website that D-I athletes could only play for a new school if the athlete were transferring out of D-I into D-II or D-III or if the athlete were "transferring to a Division I school in any sport other than baseball, men's or women's basketball, football (Football Bowl Subdivision) or men's ice hockey." But this language clearly prioritized the maintenance of competitive balance between sports programs in certain revenue-producing sports rather than the education of each individual athlete.

The NCAA rules further stated, "If you are transferring to a D-I school for any of the previously-listed sports, you may be eligible to compete immediately if you were not recruited by your original school and you have never received an athletics scholarship" (i.e., if you were a walk-on rather than an official recruit). But what difference should it make? Why did the sport one plays impact one's freedom to choose where to attend college and play sports?

The rule was used to ensure that talented players did not transfer to rival schools, but players should have the right to play for whatever team they want, whenever they want. If in Olympic sports athletes can use a one-time waiver, why not in other sports?

In April 2018 the NCAA temporarily loosened the restrictions on D-I athletes' transfers but in June 2019 it tightened these rules. As the Drake Group noted in a press release at the time, the "waiver request must now have 'documented extenuating, extraordinary and mitigating circumstances outside of the athlete's control that directly impacts the health, safety, or well-being of the student-athlete' to be approved."[68] The 2020 global pandemic was certainly an extraordinary circumstance, and so many athletes were able to transfer as a result.

The rigid language regarding transfer terms points to the NCAA's prioritization of entertainment rather than education. As McCullough explains, "This transfer rule is essentially a noncompete clause like a company uses to keep an employee from hopping to a competitor . . . The NCAA wants to treat its most valued athletes as employees only when it suits the schools' agenda."[69] These rules fuel the narrative that the NCAA is not acting in the best interest of the athletes but rather in the interests of the institutions that it represents. (As of early October 2020, there were reports that suggested that the NCAA would vote to institute a one-time transfer exception for all athletes in all sports.)[70]

Certify and Give Academic Credit for Sports Training
Another way to send the right educational message would be to certify football, basketball, and other big-time sports as academically valuable subjects of study and then develop relevant curriculum to properly credit students' efforts in studying them. As Kretchmar argues, "we can be involved in acts on the dance floor and in the gymnasium that are just as insightful and brilliant as the acts of the philosopher, mathematician, or writer."[71] At Penn State University, where Kretchmar teaches, "students can even get a master's degree in a program that focuses on skillful activity such as singing, dancing, or playing the piano," and yet while "the gatekeepers of higher education apparently see these kinds of advanced motor performance as cultured, creative, and intelligent," there is "no performance major in exercise, sport, or any other kinesiology movement."[72] By taking certified courses in the strategy and tactics of sport, and sports courses regarding recruiting, advertising, history, or sociology, athletes could begin to reverse this stigma. Of course the curriculum would have to be rigorous and approved by a faculty panel that included but was not limited to coaches, but such certification could also ensure that athletes have a leg up on the competition for jobs in that sports industry. It is only an intellectual bias against kinesthetic learning that prevents these kinds of courses and degree programs from materializing.

Give Awards to Institutions and Individuals Who Take Their Duty to Educate Seriously
In 2018 the Commission on College Basketball recommended that significant punishments be implemented to disincentivize cheating and to encourage coaches, athletic directors, and college presidents to offer proper oversight to expose wrongdoing and deter bad behavior before it happens,[73] but I prefer an approach to reform that incentivizes good behavior.

One possibility is to give high-profile public awards to universities that deliver on their promises to make athlete-students into student-athletes. One could also rank universities in order of the relative priority they give to education. Easterbrook suggests that college football rankings formulas could incorporate graduation rates as 25 percent of the total formula.[74] (A group called Next College Student Athlete also produces its own proprietary "Power Rankings," which are based on "size, location, academics, and cost" and are aimed at helping recruits decide which schools are best for student-athletes [https://www.ncsasports.org]).

Faculty must be part of this process. Staurowsky and Ridpath note that while universities may not have a legal duty to educate their students, the faculty have a professional duty to advocate for their own legal interests and these interests include the securing of an environment in which all students can be educated. College faculty who are members of organizations such as the American Association of University Professors are thus theoretically obligated by their association's statement of professional ethics to "advocate for mechanisms that will protect the access athletes have to academic freedom."[75] According to Hilborn, universities fail to fulfill their own mission when they fail to fulfill their "duty to educate" and do not ensure that athletes can study and play their sports in an environment where they reasonably meet academic requirements. It is not enough for universities to provide scholarships for athletes; they should also acknowledge their duty to ensure that the scholarship can be honored by the athlete in and out of the classroom.[76]

If there existed better metrics to measure a university's fulfillment of this duty to educate, would-be freshmen athletes would be able to see if and how schools uphold their promises of providing a quality education, graduating their students, and helping them secure jobs. They might even be able to see how athletes and students differ in these regards, and they would be able to make informed decisions about their future.

Creative rewards could also be devised to incentivize individual coaches, athletic directors, and college presidents to prioritize education over winning. Awards like Lowe's CLASS award, which is given to the nation's best college scholar-athletes, already exist, and similar awards for coaches, athletic directors, and college presidents could incentivize them to balance success in academics and athletics. Why not imagine a corporate-sponsored award for big-time coaches who graduate 100 percent of their athletes each year and have 100 percent approval ratings from their players? It could come with a bonus too, which would incentivize coaches and encourage companies to donate for the positive public relations benefits. The rankings that currently exist focus too heavily on sports performance, which is indicative of entertainment value, but we should also try to measure the education received, the lessons learned, and the degree earned.[77]

Tie Coaching Pay to Graduation Rates

As it stands, too many big-time coaches today earn salaries that are vastly higher than what players receive, which creates an imbalanced power dynamic. If coaches disregard academics in favor of athletics, their players may do the same or at least feel tension if they want to disobey their coach's orders.

But there are reforms we can make. For example, coaches' compensation packages could be tied to graduation rates thereby ensuring that the educational promise of college sports is realized and positive incentives rather than negative penalties drive coaching behavior.[78] Colleges could even tie coaching bonuses to how student athletes improve academically and not necessarily to how their students perform at one given moment in time or how many graduate. Ideally, coaches would be hired and fired by how well they prepare their players for life outside sports since so few will play professionally. Easterbrook also suggests suspending coaches for a year if they oversee a program that does not graduate its players at a rate above their university's average.[79]

Colleges could also offer coaches end-of-year bonuses if their graduation rates are higher than average for their conference or equal to or higher than last year's rate and could refuse to pay severance packages to fired coaches whose players do not meet high standards for graduation rates during their tenure.[80]

The issue of college coach pay is in some ways like the issue of CEO pay in corporate America. The interests of coaches and universities rather than those of players are prioritized just as in corporate America the interests of CEOs and shareholders are prioritized over the interests of employees. But the NCAA could create a metric for coaching pay based on the ratio of scholarships given to the players who graduate along the lines of what Robert Reich has suggested in *Saving Capitalism*, arguing that America could lower CEO pay by tying corporate tax rates to the ratio of CEO pay versus average employee pay.[81] If colleges agreed to a similar metric for college coaches, they would also help incentivize coaches to do as much as they can to raise graduation rates. In the process, they might even create a more level playing field among the teams since coach pay would be effectively capped and there would not be as much competition between the best coaches for the highest paying jobs.

Encourage Big-Time Sports Universities to "Stand Up for Academic Principles in the Face of Commercial Temptations"

University leaders must be more courageous, and some are. In 2003, Michigan's former president James Duderstadt called for the shortening of college sports seasons, the re-institution of the freshman ineligibility rule, and limiting the power of celebrity coaches by deferring or restricting the amount of money they could receive from outside business dealings.[82] In 2011, Brit Kirwan, chancellor of the University of Maryland system, said "the huge TV contracts and excessive commercialization have corrupted intercollegiate athletics . . . [and] to some extent they have compromised the integrity of the universities."[83]

But Duderstadt and Kirwan do not represent the majority. So in 2001 the Knight Commission recommended that college trustees, presidents, faculty, athletic directors, and alumni "stand up for academic principles in the face of commercial temptations."[84] In practice, this might entail setting up an independent commission to better monitor contracts between media, corporate sponsors, and universities; prohibiting or limiting company logos on uniforms; controlling when games are played (e.g., not on school nights like Tuesday night); or limiting the number of hours teams can practice. It might also mean limiting roster sizes, limiting (or changing the structure of) pay for coaches, or agreeing on a coaching salary cap that all universities must abide by.

Seek Integrity

Integrity is the key here. We do not want to eliminate college sports but rather bring their operations back in line with higher education's core values. The issue of integrity exists in another sense too. While universities have championed the educational (particularly, the character-building potential of sports), they have inadvertently ignored or overlooked their own potentially powerful role as institutional paragons of moral character in the community. After all, what kind of organization can serve the greater good if it is economically exploiting young men and women, and especially in sports where the risk of bodily injury and long-term health problems is so high?

If universities are to continue producing big-time college sports (particularly if public, taxpayer-funded universities are to do so), they should be required to revise their mission statement to reflect the centrality of sport. Orleans makes this point succinctly when he argues that "we have to make the case that athletics is directly related both to institutional missions and to student-athlete development: a case that shows faculty and alumni, students and parents, and legislators and taxpayers that athletics deserves support because it is educationally and institutionally important."[85] Only then will universities hold themselves to a higher standard of ethical behavior and begin to regain their integrity. As Clotfelter argues, we need a "new candor" that will "begin with more accurate mission statements" that include the acknowledgment of the centrality of college sports to universities' bottom line and mission. These statements would also acknowledge the "century-old marriage between commercial athletics and American higher education" and its "benefits and costs."[86]

If university leaders are serious about protecting academic principles and regaining their integrity, then they must ensure that no coach, administrator, or other university official under their employ is hypocritical about, or exaggerates the power of, the educational element of big-time sports until the institution can truly prove that they deliver on such statements. Neither universities nor the NCAA should ever say that student-athletes are students first and foremost if their treatment by the university proves, or even subtly suggests, that they are not. Until true reform comes, they should explicitly acknowledge that the education athletes receive will be at best unintentional, ancillary, and insufficiently delineated as well as dependent on a particular coach and his or her commitment to the value of education.

Thus, colleges should admit they are in the business of producing entertainment for consumers and that the entertainers they contract with are athletes. Universities should also explicitly acknowledge, in their mission statement, that big-time college athletics is a central part of their marketing plan and that athletes are an (unpaid) part of it.

In concrete terms, restoring integrity would mean ensuring everyone involved in the university knows that classroom education (academic education) and education within sports participation (sports education) are both to be respected and given a central role in the broader socialization process. Students can and do benefit from learning in each realm, but they learn different things in each realm. Life in a capitalist economy undoubtedly requires perseverance, hard work, and discipline, skills that can be gained both by playing sports and by studying. But life in a capitalist democracy equally requires educational credentials and critical thinking skills, which may be less commonly developed by participation in sports especially if a grand illusion is offered to young athletes that the odds are in their favor of making the pros.[87] Higher education in the classroom can teach young people how to teach themselves just as a higher education on the court or field can teach young people how to train themselves physically (and mentally).

At the end of the day, the verdict in the public debate over the economics of opportunity versus the economics of exploitation depends largely on whether college athletes' education is evaluated highly or not. If an athlete's education lives up to the promises that universities make about it, then "exploitation" may seem like an overly dramatic term, and "opportunity" may seem to fit. Without a quality education, the term "college sports," let alone "higher education," ceases to have much meaning. Regardless of background, identity group, or political affiliation, anyone can get behind the idea of hard work paying off, and anyone can learn its value and use it as a stepping-stone to create a better life. Moreover, if quality education takes place between the coach and player on the field or court (as opposed to inside the classroom), then the athlete's overall relationship to the university, which employs the coach, cannot so easily be called exploitation.

However, if either of these kinds of education (classroom-based education or court- and field-based education) are not up to snuff, then the economic exchange between university and athlete, and between coach and player, may become the primarily level of analysis, and some may reasonably conclude that this exchange does not constitute an equitable contract but rather an exploitative relationship.

Conclusion

Universities, the NCAA, coaches, and athletic directors, can and should transparently and honestly acknowledge the professional role of labor and service that big-time college athletes provide to and for the university while also reemphasizing the primacy of the educational endeavor.[88]

Everyone has a part to play. Universities must raise academic standards for all athletes, unilaterally and without NCAA mandate if necessary, and expect coaches to perform an educative role. The NCAA and the universities must create new incentives for schools, coaches, and athletes to prioritize graduation and establish a better balance between books and balls. Athletic department officials must ensure that education is as much of a priority as enhancing the entertainment product. Coaches must be more mindful of the time required for classroom education and of the lessons learned through sports participation. Parents must more often stress the importance of striking a balance between books and balls. Finally, athletes must choose to buy in to the idea that their academic efforts are as important as their athletic efforts even if that is not the clear impression that the broader culture currently sends them. It may be hard for them to make that decision, but it is their demands as the consumers of the college education that carry the greatest leverage to advance systemic change, and especially if it is done through collective action. Finally, everyone involved in college sports should do their part because, as the late great UCLA basketball coach John Wooden once said, "everyone is a teacher." As adults, we should never forget the educational part we play when we seek to reform college sports in the recommendations we promote but also in the way we incentivize others to behave.

John Gerdy, a former college basketball player turned commissioner of the Southeastern Conference and author of various books on college sports and education, has argued that we need "institutional teamwork" in order for college athletics to "contribute more directly to higher education's three-pronged purpose of teaching, research and service."[89] Gerdy says academic management has tried an overly "defensive approach" to athletics, hoping only to keep athletes out of the news for the wrong reasons and that, as a result, universities have suffered a "decline in public trust." He calls for more integration of athletics into academics, less disdain for research on sports among academic researchers, and greater acknowledgment by college coaches of the ultimate purposes of higher education.[90] In short, Gerdy argues that college sports should be given more meaning than that of an "entertainment product" and that we should stop judging the success of athletic departments based on wins, losses, and bottom lines alone.[91]

I agree, but it is not just the different divisions of the university that must do better; each of us can in our own way help reverse these troubling trends by choosing to see "the other" not as an adversary but as a partner with whom we can work collegially. As scholars and as sports fans, we can help college athletes by being positive about the cultural and educational—not only economic—power sports hold; by being positive about the power we have to further such development; and by refocusing attention on the reason colleges have sports to begin with—to be an integral part of the higher education experience. Finally, we can help by being positive and optimistic about the potential to accomplish the aforementioned reforms.

This positive approach is not pie-in-the-sky idealism; it is, in fact, the most realistic way forward. It is implausible to expect that college sports fans will, suddenly, vanish or lose interest in these sports and equally implausible that universities will dismantle their big-time sports programs unilaterally.[92] College sports hold too much student recruiting power, potential to build community, and commercial appeal to be eliminated altogether.[93] Since big-time college sports will likely remain highly commercialized entertainment that is "thoroughly institutionalized within American higher education"[94] and a popular form of mass entertainment that cannot be legislated out of existence, as reformers we have little choice but to work within the system we have rather than seek revolution or start from scratch.

Choosing a college is a young person's first major and perhaps most meaningful life decision, and many make this selection at least in part because of the university's sports programs. In a sense, this choice amounts to a student's first choice of identity, and the ensuing allegiance to his or her school can be a powerful thing that may stay with the student their entire life.

Without throwing the baby out with the bathwater, any university can unilaterally improve the education they provide athletes, and any fan or concerned citizen can help athletes fight for the pay, respect, and education they deserve. We need not limit our options to paying players. Instead, we can choose to be positive about sports' cultural and educational power, optimistic about the prospect of achieving meaningful reform, and positive about ourselves and the power we have to make it happen.

Notes

1. Quoted in Gallimore and Tharp, "What a Coach."
2. If athletic department budget alone were considered, it seems clear that the Aggies were in similar company to Baylor. In 2008, Texas A&M Athletics spent $73.34 million on top of a $73.23 million budget, posting a loss over $100,000. Meanwhile the head coach of the women's basketball team, Gary Blair, who had won over six hundred games in his career, was said to earn approximately $800,000 per year.
3. Personal communication, 2011.
4. Rogers, *The Carl Rogers Reader*.
5. Nelson, Cushion, Potrac, and Groom, "Carl Rogers"; Light, "Positive Pedagogy."
6. Holt, *Positive Youth Development*.
7. Branscombe and Wann, "The Positive Social."
8. Ryan and Deci, "Self-Determination Theory," 68. This may include hedonistic pursuits, or mastery or flow, or outcomes beyond the self. See Seligman, Ernst, Gillham, Reivich, and Linkins, "Positive Education."
9. Sack, "Clashing Models"; Lanter and Hawkins, "The Economic Model."
10. Gurney, Lopiano and Zimbalist, *Unwinding Madness*, 209ff; see Meyer and Zimbalist, "A Win-Win."
11. Zimbalist, *Unpaid Professionals*, 200.
12. Zimbalist, *Unpaid Professionals*, 197–206.
13. See for example Gerdy, *The Successful College*; Staurowsky and Ridpath, "The Case for Minimum."
14. In the late 1980s, Dick Devenzio, who had played basketball at Duke University, where he was an academic All-American, began to argue that college athletes ought to be paid, telling Bill Moyers in the documentary *Sport for Sale*,

> Isn't it amazing that basketball players wear sneakers—Nikes, or Reeboks, or Converse or something—and the *coach* gets paid? I mean, because kids want to wear what the good players wear. I wonder . . . Does anybody ever know the type of wingtips that Dean Smith

wears? All the little kids are walking around the games in Dean Smith style wingtips. Anybody doing that? John Thompson wears hard shoes to the game. Let me see. Everybody show your feet to see if you've got John Thompson wingtips on. John Thompson in the Big East makes a half a million bucks a year. People in big-time college sports make big money. We've forced athletes in a position to claim that their number one priority is academics, when it's not. Nobody's comfortable yet with just saying that there's nothing wrong with having big-time athletics or professional athletics associated with college campus. We have weapons research. We have people studying kooky religions or abstract art, and why not professional athletics? I think to me it just comes down to people realizing that we have professional athletics on college campuses, and there's nothing wrong with that.

15. Jeremy Bloom was an All-American in football at the University of Colorado, drafted into the NFL, and a world-class Olympian skier. His all-around athletic talents and good looks made him a natural consideration for companies looking for a model and spokesman. Yet the NCAA "determined that in order for Bloom to compete as a collegiate athlete, he must forfeit his modeling and entertainment opportunities" and did not grant him an exception. Bloom argued that NCAA rules were "arbitrary and capricious" and that his modeling and entertainment opportunities were unrelated to playing football. But the trial and appellate court determined that the NCAA, as a voluntary association with a set of clear by-laws of which Bloom was aware, was entitled to declare Bloom ineligible from competing in the amateur sport of football if he chose to accept payment for activities outside the university (L. Freedman, "Pay or Play"). Freedman assessed the case and concluded that an "examination of the facts of Bloom's case reveal[ed] that a prohibition . . . does nothing to further the NCAA's goals, but only serves to injure Bloom and student-athletes like him" and that "even if the rules themselves could be saved by virtue of the fact that they support the NCAA's stated purpose of furthering amateurism, an exception should be made in Bloom's case" (710–11).

16. The case of *White v. NCAA*, which was filed in 2006, was a class-action lawsuit that asked the NCAA to pay the full cost of attendance for big-time athletes in men's basketball and football. It was settled before trial for $10 million. The settlement called for $2,500 in aid to go to each athlete in the class in order to cover "bona fide educational expenses." The settlement also suggested that another $218 million could be used by schools "for purposes allowed under the current guidelines," but that money was already earmarked for schools and the settlement merely "renamed the funds" (Nocera and Strauss, *Indentured*, 147). Stanford University economist Roger Noll, who worked with the plaintiffs on the case, said the athletes "did get something" out of the settlement but that was "small potatoes" compared to what the spirit of the case was all about. Yet *White v. NCAA* did set a legal precedent. The athletes who were plaintiffs in the case had certified a class and proved that they were big time and therefore different from their small-time college athlete counterparts. In the words of former UCLA football player Ramogi Huma, who was closely involved with the case, "it showed that football and men's basketball players could be treated differently from other athletes on campus."

17. Legal cases against the NCAA like O'Bannon's have been about the NCAA's right to use the likenesses of college athletes and their right to sell that right to third-parties. O'Bannon, a former UCLA basketball player, filed a lawsuit in 2009 against the video-game maker Electronic Arts (EA), the Collegiate Licensing Company (CLC), and the NCAA in order to receive what he believed was due compensation for the use of his likeness. O'Bannon's suit alleged that EA had profited from the creation of avatars that duplicated every aspect of student-athlete likenesses except their names. EA allegedly used players' team name, jersey number, height and weight, and relative skills with the NCAA's consent but without providing any compensation to the athletes themselves (Fainaru and Farrey, "Game Changer"). After the lawsuit was filed, internal emails from the NCAA became public records and it became apparent that officials were aware of just how far they were pushing the envelope when they chose to sell these licensing rights to EA. NCAA executives had continually held that college athletics was a voluntary activity and that the students could only be rewarded financially with athletic scholarships, yet their own correspondence in this case seemed to suggest that they were padding their own pockets at the same time (Eder and Bishop, "High-Stakes Games"). Ultimately, in 2013 the NCAA decided to end all ties with EA yet it continued to refuse to further compensate student-athletes and the case against the NCAA continued. In 2013, federal judge Claudia Wilken ruled that *O'Bannon v. EA Sports* could proceed as a class-action suit. Wilken also ruled that the NCAA could not use college athlete likenesses for profit and still maintain a rulebook that described them as amateurs (Bishop, "N.C.A.A. Dodges a Bullet"). However, Wilkin only certified the class for future college athletes and stopped short of certifying a damages class that could have led to enormous NCAA payments to former college athletes. In June 2014, *O'Bannon v. EA Sports* moved to trial and Wilkin ruled that the NCAA amateurism rules violated the nation's antitrust laws and that "the NCAA's compensation rules were an unlawful restraint of trade." She determined that the NCAA changed its definition of the term "amateurism" whenever it was convenient for them, allowing certain types of payments for certain athletes when it deemed necessary. Accordingly, she concluded that schools should not "block players from sharing broadcast and video game money" and "that there was a clear market for their names and images" (Nocera and Strauss, *Indentured*, 277), and she ruled that the NCAA had a flawed rationale when it contended that college sports were popular precisely because they weren't paid. Her verdict held that the NCAA's legal reliance on obscure *dicta* in the case of *Regents v. NCAA* was not valid. At the same time, Wilkin stopped short of saying players should endorse products in a free market, arguing that doing so "would undermine the efforts of both the NCAA and its member schools to protect against the commercial exploitation of student athletes." Instead, Wilken ruled that the NCAA put $5,000 per player in a trust fund that could only be accessed after graduation, which effectively ensured that the NCAA practice of fixing a cap on possible wages during college would continue. Yet in an appeal, the Court of Appeals of the Ninth Circuit refused to rule in a way that would change the way the

NCAA did business. First, the court of appeals reversed Wilken's determination that the NCAA put away $5,000 in a trust fund for players to access after graduation and concluded that the cost of attending college was enough payment for the services these athletes provided to their universities. The court of appeals rationale was that compensation was "not related to education," would not preserve amateurism, and that amateurism was indeed "the thing" that made college sports what it was (Nocera and Strauss, *Indentured*, 288–90). O'Bannon would ultimately settle out of court with CLC and EA Sports. EA agreed to pay $40 million to players who had been on rosters in EA games dating to 2003. EA vice president Andrew Wilson affirmed that his company would continue to develop college football games just without the NCAA logo emblazoned on the cover (Eder, "As Legal Battle Continues"). It was the first time any commercial entity had agreed to pay anything directly to college players. For their part, the Commission on Collegiate Basketball concluded in 2018 that "if a college or university is using a student-athletes' NIL for commercial purposes, the school must ask that student-athlete for consent, which must be voluntarily given" (Commission on Collegiate Basketball, "Report and Recommendations," 8).

18. Staurowsky has led studies that have sought to determine how much earnings big-time male athletes lose in the current system. For example, in 2013, Staurowsky and the National College Players' Association (NCPA) co-authored a report titled "The $6 Billion Heist: Robbing College Athletes under the Guise of Amateurism." The report found that "if not for the NCAA's prohibition of a fair market," football and men's basketball players in the Football Subdivision (FBS) would have received "full athletic scholarships plus an additional $6 billion between 2011–2015." In addition, the average football player in the FBS lost $456,612; the average men's basketball player lost $1,063,307, and "the [total] lost value over a four-year career for the average football and men's basketball player in the six [Bowl Championship Series] conferences [was] $715,000 and $1.5 million, respectively." Staurowsky later told *Drexel Now*, "the NCAA's principle of amateurism continues to be used as a mechanism to deny the dignity, humanity and worth of the athletes whose hard work and commitment gives value to the product that others profit from" (quoted in McKechnie, "Drexel and NCPA").

19. In 2014, attorneys for four NCAA athletes filed cases in which they argued that the NCAA "violated national laws in unlawfully capping the value of athletic scholarships or Grants-in-Aid (GIAs)" (Hagens Berman Law Firm, "Student-Athletes Reach"). The case was settled in 2017 for $208 million, and Judge Claudia Wilken approved the settlement in which over forty thousand D-I athletes would receive approximately $5,000–$7,500 directly from the NCAA. Eligible athletes included anyone who played men's or women's basketball or college football in the Football Bowl Subdivision between March 5, 2010, and March 21, 2017, and "who received from an NCAA member institution for at least one academic term (such as a semester or quarter) (1) a full athletics GIA required by NCAA rules to be set at a level below the cost of attendance, and/or (2) an otherwise full athletics GIA" (Hagens Berman Law Firm, "Student-Athletes Reach").

20. Sports labor lawyer Jeffrey Kessler, who represents Martin Jenkins, was successful in negotiating a settlement that forced the NCAA to pay cost of attendance stipends to players, but *Jenkins v. NCAA* "essentially seeks a free market for athletes in top football and Division I men's basketball programs"; to "strip the N.C.A.A. of the right to set compensation limits for college athletes"; and to "prevent the NCAA and a group of 11 major conferences from collectively confining athletes to receiving scholarships covering tuition, fees, room, board, books and incidental costs of attending college" (Berkowitz and Kreighbaum, "Judge Rules"). According to Kessler, "In no other business—and college sports is big business—would it ever be suggested that the people who are providing the essential services work for free. Only in big-time college sports is that line drawn" (quoted in Farrey, "Jeffrey Kessler Suit"). Judge Claudia Wilken ultimately decided that the NCAA had not given a sufficient definition of what amateurism was nor did they adequately argue for why there should be a cap on how much athletes should be able to earn through college sports participation. And yet she stopped short of forcing the NCAA to do anything about it. Kessler had won the battle but lost the war. Tracy said,

> How can a judge rule that a law is being broken but allow the lawbreaking to continue? According to [sports law expert Gabe] Feldman, the answer includes a much-disputed antitrust principle known as the rule of reason. In some cases—including this one—the rule calls for anticompetitive activity to be overturned only if there is a different system that could provide the positive benefits of the anticompetitive system without suppressing other competition as much. Wilken determined that amateurism was crucial to college sports' commercial appeal and allowed it to compete with professional sports, even if doing so required it to apparently violate antitrust ("The N.C.A.A. Lost in Court").

21. In 2009, Sack argued that "big-time college athletes should be able to endorse products, get paid for speaking engagements, and be compensated for the use of their likenesses on licensed products." Furthermore, he concluded, "they should be able to negotiate an actual contract with the NBA as part of a final project in a finance class and have an agent. These athletes are working their way through college by playing professional college sports. It is time to accept this reality and move on" ("Let Athletes Be Entrepreneurs").

22. The NIL controversy took place outside court too. In 2013, for example, Jay Bilas, a former college basketball star at Duke University turned ESPN analyst, publicly criticized the NCAA for selling jerseys of popular college basketball and football players on its website. Bilas decided to take on the NCAA in the court of public opinion (i.e., via his Twitter account). He found that if you typed the name of a famous college football player such as Johnny Manziel into the search box on the NCAA website, your search would lead you to a page where you could buy a replica of Manziel's Texas A&M jersey (although without the name "Manziel" stitched to the back of the jersey). The same was true of many other star college athletes. He tweeted images of these searches to his then 500,000 followers, which engendered public rage against the NCAA. A few days later, NCAA president Mark Emmert announced that the NCAA would stop selling the jerseys on the site and admitted

that the NCAA had made a mistake in doing so in the first place. His statement, though, was less than apologetic, noting dryly, "I can certainly understand how people can see that as hypocritical" (quoted in Nocera and Strauss *Indentured*, 232). See also Schlabach, "NCAA Puts End."

23. Even Byers once suggested that student-athletes should be allowed to endorse products, with the money earned first going to a trust fund that they could only access after graduation. Byers argued that such a system would allow athletes to tap into the free market, sell their NIL, get a larger piece of what was an ever-increasing financial pie, and maintain their amateur status until graduation. He also said he believed that "athletes deserved the same access to the free market that the coaches enjoyed" (Byers and Hammer, *Unsportsmanlike Conduct*, 13). In his 1995 memoir, Byers demanded that Congress "free the athletes" and enact a "comprehensive College Athletes' Bill of Rights," and he suggested that "the federal government should require deregulation of a monopoly business operated by not-for-profit institutions contracting together to achieve maximum financial returns, going on to say that doing so would treat the "twin curses of exploitation and hypocrisy that have bedeviled college athletics" and "prevent[ed] colleges from denying players the freedoms available to other students." Finally, he claimed "collegiate amateurism is not a moral issue; it is an economic camouflage for monopoly practice" and one that operates "an air-tight racket of supplying cheap athletic labor'" (Byers and Hammer, *Unsportsmanlike Conduct*, 376, 388).

24. National Collegiate Athletic Association, "NCAA Responds."
25. National Collegiate Athletic Association, "Board of Governors."
26. Hobson and Guskin, "Poll."
27. Knoester & Ridpath, "Should College Athletes Be Allowed?"
28. Danley, "Give Athletes Five-Year Scholarships."
29. Byers and Hammer, *Unsportsmanlike Conduct*, 373.
30. Commission on College Basketball, "Report and Recommendations," 7.
31. Berkowitz and Kreighbaum, "Cincinnati Athletes Lead."
32. Huma, Staurowsky, and Montgomery, "How the NCAA's Empire."
33. Bishop, "N.C.A.A. Dodges a Bullet."
34. Zimbalist, "Short of Paying Players."
35. Buzuvis, "Athletic Compensation," 297.
36. Edelman, "From Student-Athletes."
37. Zimbalist, "College Athletes Should Get Paid."
38. Meyer and Zimbalist, "A Win-Win."
39. Drake Group, "The Drake Group Finds."
40. Aspen Institute, "Future of College Sports."
41. Drake Group, "Position Statement."
42. Lopiano et al., "The Drake Group Position Statement."
43. *Drexel Now*, "Study"; McKechnie, "Drexel and NCPA Study."
44. Easterbrook, *The King of Sports*, 138.
45. Easterbrook, *The King of Sports*, 141.

46. Nocera, "Let's Start Paying."
47. Manza Young, "Women Hurt Most."
48. Murphy, "Appeals Court Upholds."
49. McCann, "Why the NCAA Lost."
50. Remy, "NCAA Statement."
51. Staurowsky, "A Radical Proposal."
52. Buzuvis, "Athletic Compensation," 336.
53. Buzuvis, "Athletic Compensation," 336.
54. Meyer and Zimbalist, "A Win-Win," 265–66.
55. Meyer and Zimbalist, "A Win-Win," 265.
56. See for example Ridpath, "Can the Faculty Reform Intercollegiate Athletics?"; and Gerdy, *The Successful College*.
57. *NCAA v. Alston*, "Defendants' Joint Opening Brief," 6.
58. Quoted in Finkel, Martin, and Paley, *$chooled*.
59. Meyer and Zimbalist, "A Win-Win," 262.
60. Easterbrook, *The King of Sports*, 128.
61. Easterbrook, *The King of Sports*, 129.
62. Staurowsky and Ridpath "The Case for Minimum," 118.
63. Zimbalist, *Unpaid Professionals*, 43–44.
64. Southall, "2012 Adjusted Graduation Gap Report: NCAA Division-I Football"; Southall, "2012 Adjusted Graduation Gap: NCAA Division-I Baseball and Softball."
65. Sack, McComas, and Cakan, "The Revival."
66. Commission on Collegiate Basketball, "Report and Recommendations," 7.
67. See for example Jackson, "Take It from a Former."
68. Lopiano et al., "The Drake Group Position Statement."
69. McCullough, "Days of NCAA Having."
70. Auerbach, "Sources."
71. Kretchmar, *Practical Philosophy of Sport*, 116.
72. Kretchmar, *Practical Philosophy of Sport*, 112.
73. Commission on Collegiate Basketball, "Report and Recommendations," 10–11.
74. Easterbrook, *The King of Sports*, 317ff.
75. Staurowsky and Ridpath "The Case for Minimum," 121.
76. Hilborn, "Student-Athletes," 769.
77. Gerdy, *The Successful College*, 7.
78. Easterbrook, *The King of Sports*, 139.
79. Easterbrook, *The King of Sports*, 140.
80. Easterbrook, *The King of Sports*, 317ff.
81. Reich, *Saving Capitalism*, 196.
82. Duderstadt, *Intercollegiate Athletics*.
83. Quoted in Nocera, "Let's Start Paying."
84. Quoted in Clotfelter, *Big-Time College Sports*, 215.

85. Orleans, "The Effects of the Economic Model," 83.
86. Clotfelter, *Big-Time College Sports*, 221.
87. Pappano, "How Big-Time Sports Ate."
88. Mitten, Musselman, and Burton, "Commercialized Intercollegiate Athletics," 229.
89. Gerdy, *The Successful College*, 7.
90. Gerdy, *The Successful College*, 10.
91. Gerdy, *The Successful College*, 13.
92. This could happen if a few like-minded universities decided to re-emphasize their academic focus as members of the Ivy League chose to do in 1954. Duke, Vanderbilt, Northwestern, and Stanford would be candidates for such a league but these universities are wealthy and private and routinely field strong athletic teams, so it seems unlikely. Furthermore, it seems unlikely because many assume that this would forego money and public recognition and invite alumni ire. Thus, returning to the small-time is as daunting a prospect as would be the disarming of nuclear powers to which it is often compared.
93. As Zimbalist argues, it is not possible to begin with a clean slate because "college sports are too popular and too ingrained in our culture," "have powerful support constituencies," and after over a century of commercial tie-ins there is just too much money at stake for such a plan to ever gain the support it needs (*Unpaid Professionals*, 196). In 2000, members of the Drake Group suggested a reduction in the number of intercollegiate games and matches, but you don't need to study this topic long to see how unlikely that prospect is. There's just too much demand for these games. Indeed, the group has since done away this reform proposal and now focuses its efforts on mitigating the "corrosive aspects of commercialism in college sports."
94. Shulman and Bowen, *The Game of Life*, 1.

Conclusion: Give Women's Sports a Chance

> I am an elite athlete. I am an MVP. I am a daughter. I am a sister. I am a No. 1 draft pick. I am a WNBA player and I am the president of the WNBPA. And I want young female athletes to dream about playing in a vibrant and thriving WNBA. I want them to dream of having it all.
>
> —Nneka Ogwumike

For many months it was a thing of beauty to watch the Stanford team play, and although I knew there were drawbacks to big-time college sports being part of a juggernaut entertainment industry, I had to admit that I did not want the fun to end. These women were exceptionally talented, patient, and hard-working, and they always played unselfishly as a team. They played the kind of basketball I had grown to admire and exemplified the kind of teamwork I had come to respect. They had a coach I considered a heroine on and off the court.

In writing up what I had seen, I wanted to highlight the best of sport pioneers like VanDerveer particularly for having been part of the cultural push for landmark social and legal change and for having become advocates for the further liberation of women. In my mind, coaches like VanDerveer who both won games and made education a priority in the daily lives of their players should be hailed as symbols of college sports done the right way. If that amounts to hagiography, it is also the truth of what I saw, heard, and read.

In the context of Lean In and Me Too, which have become the new buzzwords indexing women's ongoing battle for equality, pay equity, and respect, VanDerveer's biography illustrates that on the one hand, sexism is still reproduced in many different realms, but on the other hand, individuals like her can do and are doing heroic work to overcome it. Indeed, it is courageous individuals like her who decide not only to embrace the market and its power but also to buy in to the idea that sport itself has power and that sport can be a positive force for social change. In the end, it was observing Coach VanDerveer and reflecting on her circumstances and her actions that convinced me that scholars can also do more to be part of the social solutions we need.

I also wanted to applaud the young women I watched play basketball. There is much to admire about their choice to buy in to the big-time college sports culture even if it may not be a perfect realm. Athletes' efforts to secure a higher education through hard work and sports performance should be lauded not only for the tough decisions that must be made every day (e.g., to rise early and hit the gym, field, or court, and stay up late to finish their studies) but also because it is a choice to improve one's self-discipline, polish one's ability to communicate, cultivate one's time management skills, and raise one's self-confidence while also providing inspirational entertainment for the masses and a sense of camaraderie for the college community.

These are conscious choices that are not easy to make, and yet too few scholars ever seem to give them their proper due. What's more, they constitute an integral part of the long and ongoing journey of women fighting for equal rights and opportunities in sports.

In the end it may be that the positives of women in big-time college sport are hard to acknowledge because so much sexism remains and so much still needs to be done. After all, revenue generation and the question of big time are but two of the many unfair comparisons to which sporting women have historically been subject: how much money they make, how much value they create for the university brand, and how popular or entertaining their sports are vis-à-vis men's sports. Perhaps most painfully, men's continued denigration of women's sports only serves to hinder its growth further and reinforces the harmful notions that women coaches should be paid less and that women's sports are not as popular because they are "boring".

A change in our attitude as male sports fans is in order. If we fight the urge to compare women's sports to the men's game, then perhaps we will treat the achievements of female athletes for what they are—and as we do the achievements of male athletes: as stepping-stones to *their* growth and not only sources to satisfy our excitement or make our colleges money.

While laws may be sand and custom may be rock, to paraphrase Mark Twain, the way we choose to interpret history, assess the present, and imagine the future matters too. Such interpretations may be wholly immaterial, but they are no less consequential than law or custom. We can choose to see the positives in history and contemporary society and to be optimistic about what may be yet to come, or we can choose to ignore the positive gains and focus primarily on past problems, leaving ourselves with nowhere to go and no idea how to get there.

I have chosen to take a different path, being positive by believing in my own power to stoke positive social change. I have gained inspiration by looking to hard working (female) athletes and coaches who rise early every day and put one foot in front of the other despite considerable obstacles.

At the same time, I am hardly a Polyanna. I know that sexism remains because most of us allow it to and because most of us allow ourselves to treat men and women differently in instances where there is no good reason to do so.

Men can begin to reverse this trend by changing the way we see and talk about male and female athletes, male and female coaches. We can do our best to avoid unjustified comparisons between boys' and girls' sports and men's and women's sports since such comparisons are inherently flawed, unfair, and potentially damaging. We can acknowledge the male allies of these great female pioneers, too few though they may be. For example, in 1967, Syracuse University student Kathrine Virginia Switzer used her initials, K. V., to enroll in the Boston Marathon, which was at the time an all-male event. Switzer knew that she would be forbidden from running if she used her full name, which would have given away her gender. In those days, the marathon was considered a male-only event since the long race stoked fears that women would "get big legs, grow mustaches or your uterus would fall out,"[1] but Switzer knew she could run it. When the race director found her on the marathon course part way through the race and physically tried to remove her from the race, yelling, "Get the hell out of my race," Switzer's boyfriend Tom Miller, who was running the race alongside Switzer, pushed the director to the side and allowed Switzer to finish the race.[2] Few though they may be, men have also helped along the way since the fight for true equality and justice for all can never be won without allies who hail from the majority, powerful groups.

We can appreciate the value in encouraging girls and women to move their bodies and compete in sweaty sports like basketball. We can do what we can—as individuals and as members of collective movements—to ensure that girls and women will always be the bosses of their own bodies.

Women's sports like women's college basketball must be judged on their own terms and not in quantitative contrast to sports like college football or men's basketball and in terms of how much money is made. Perhaps there is less dunking in the women's game, but that does not mean the game is any less exciting. The women's game, like the men's game, includes the same drama of athletes playing through pain, underdogs taking down favorites, and the constant pursuit of excellence in performance. Isn't that what makes sports exciting anyway?

Judge the big-time nature of women's sports on its own terms too. As Coach Paye explained, it is a concept that was shaped by the media but could be changed if the right measures are taken.

> A lot of it is trying to change perceptions. A lot of people have an idea about what women's basketball is like . . . Some of them you're never going to catch their interest . . . But if you get them to one game, they are surprised by what they see. They see Nneka jumping out of the gym and the athleticism and the skill.

Statements like "women's sports are boring" are born of ignorance, the sad product of the mass media conditioning us to believe that sports are for males and that sexism is not a social scourge. The implication is that if women want real equality in basketball, they must mimic men and our dunking, showboating, and trash talking, and money-making.

But statements like "women's sports are boring" are also born of our own sad laziness to change the channel and give women's sports a chance. After all the sexism our forefathers put them through, should the onus be on them to catch up to our game, or should it be on us to give them equal airtime and rethink how we look at their sports?

Male sports fans need to seriously question the dismissiveness that they have for women's sports especially since it may be their eyeballs that most impact the state of women's sports. Many spectators, most of whom are male, have been dismissive of women's college basketball and often are ignorant of the game. But if such spectators attempt to overcome their ignorance and turn the channel to a women's game, they will be actively ignoring the biases that the media and market forces have over many years created and in turn creating new demand that will help women's sports like basketball grow.

Indeed, if we truly reconsider the women's game by taking a closer look at it, then perhaps we can finally persuade media executives to give these sports the attention they deserve.

For women to thrive in sports, they need a groundswell, and it must come from male sports fans.[3]

Notes

1. Switzer, quoted in PBS, "*Women Who Make America.*"
2. Switzer, quoted in PBS, "*Women Who Make America.*"
3. See, for example, Connell, "Change among the Gatekeepers" for a more robust argument in more general terms.

Epilogue: Big-Time College Sports amid Two Pandemics

Depending on who ultimately writes it, history may recall it as a curiosity that the COVID-19 pandemic and Black Lives Matter protests spread so widely in the same year, but both are linked in significant ways. After all, it wasn't just the COVID-19 pandemic that put the nonexistence of college athletes' labor rights in the national spotlight as never before—it was also the Black Lives Matter movement.

Just like the virus itself, big-time colleges and universities disproportionately exploit and sometimes devastate black lives since the big-time college athlete work force is made up of many young people of color who play violent sports like basketball and football. COVID-19, the disease caused by the novel coronavirus, disproportionately impacts communities of color too since health care in America tracks socioeconomic status and since American blacks earn only a fraction of what whites earn and therefore cannot live healthy lives as easily.

On top of all that, there is the astonishing lack of legal care for black lives. Horrific footage of police brutality, such as that of the brutal murder of George Floyd on May 25, 2020, hints at how difficult it must be for any athlete, but especially black athletes, to focus their attention on playing a game at a time in which there seems to be a war against black bodies.

The confluence of these issues came to a head in the summer of 2020 when these two viruses—the novel coronavirus and the centuries-old racism against people of color—reminded college athletes that they could be activists for their own cause and that they had a latent power that was in some cases going unused. More athletes began to see connections between police brutality and the rights of black college athletes as well as the need to fight for the rights of any other black person whose experience was marked by discrimination or bigotry.

The prospect of playing any game for the entertainment of others, especially at a time when non-athlete peers were not expected to attend classes in person, seemed like a bridge too far, and many athletes, from revenue-generating sports to non-revenue generating sports, began to speak out with unprecedented urgency and considerable courage. Many of these outspoken athletes were black, and they began to organize their protests in ways that they never had before. They took to the streets alongside Black Lives Matter activists. They seized digital platforms to speak directly to the public via social media and outlets like the Players' Tribune to protest injustice against people of color and to protest their working conditions.

Athletes of the Pac-12, for example, published a detailed statement of grievances in early August 2020 on the Players' Tribune highlighting their desire to be "treated fairly"; to be allowed to opt out of play during a pandemic; to profit from their NILs; and to be protected from long-term health care expenses incurred from play. In sum, they concluded, "we are united." Then on August 9, 2020, athletes from the Power 5 conferences posted an image on Twitter demanding "universal mandated health and safety procedures and protocols to protect college athletes against COVID-19"; giving "players the opportunity to opt out and respect their decision"; guaranteeing "eligibility whether a player chooses to play the season or not"; and creating "a college football players' association." About a month later, the same group of athletes revised their demands to include assurances that players would have no athletic requirements on November 3, election day. They added a desire to "discuss with our presidents and administrators to further raise awareness about racial injustice and creative initiatives to further empower our communities" and "normalize having routine conversations about change (policing, legal rights, addressing racial injustice, etc. between college football teams and our respective police departments, local governance, and community leaders to build trust and empathy." They also added that on game days they would use their platform "to raise awareness via wearing shirts, utilizing statements on our helmets and jerseys, and playing tribute videos to recognize victims of racial injustice."

For decades, college athletes had been remarkably absent from college sports reform debates in part because the adults in control had not bothered to give them a seat at the table but also because their situation was, perhaps to some, "not bad enough." Before the age of the Internet and the age of the smartphone, perhaps some were also ignorant of the sums of money being made from their athletic efforts and the number of black lives being devastated by police.

But by summer 2020, all of that was changing. As the Stanford football player Dylan Boles, who helped organize the August 2020 message, said, "The beautiful thing is now we're all on the same page. We made history tonight." Boles's statement recalled one by Ramogi Huma, the executive director of the National College Players Association, who told *Time* in June 2020, "This is a moment where the outrage of players is stronger than their fear of speaking out. This has not been the case in modern times."[1] Scholars knew long before the pandemic that big-time college sports needed serious reform, but we did not know that college athletes themselves might lead it, at least not in this way.

The protests by the athletes themselves raise important questions such as Just how essential is college sport to American life? Just how essential is college football, and how essential is women's college basketball? These are the two most important sports, respectively, for male and female athletes, as each draws more attention and generates more revenue than any other sport.

In 2020 Mayhew and Shaheen argued that "college football may be an essential element of our functioning democracy," quoting an Ohio State football fan who said, "The world needs college football." They argued that "few, if any, have addressed the essential role that college football may play toward healing a democracy made more fragile by disease, racial unrest and a contested presidential election cycle," adding that "college football holds a special bipartisan place in the American heart."[2]

Andrew McGregor took issue with these claims, arguing that Mayhew and Shaheen's views were "simply inaccurate and conjecture and not grounded in historical research or empirical fact." To McGregor, college football was not an "essential part of American society and our political system . . . but rather a symptom of the deep-seeded [sic] issues that have contributed to political polarization, racial unrest, the devaluation of education, and prolonged devastation of the COVID-19 pandemic."[3]

Mayhew and Shaheen make several important points. College football *is* an important part of American society and culture, if not also democracy—at least in the sense that it brings people from diverse backgrounds together and into conversation. That has been the case for decades, and without such conversation, Americans today would be limited in their options for interacting with others with whom they might not share the same political views.

And yet promoting any sport—much less one that disproportionately exploits black men without proper compensation and protection and at a time in which a pandemic is still raging and when expecting them to play only serves to deepen the wounds caused by this exploitation—is not an acceptable response. In fact, this prioritization of entertainment over not only education but also basic health care only serves to exacerbate the injuries of a flawed society and education system and legal system since not all of us are impacted by public health crises in the same way.

McGregor picks apart Mayhew and Shaheen's argument claim by claim,[4] including their view that college sports should be judged by their ability to boost a university or generate revenue. Above all, he takes Mayhew and Shaheen to task for not listening to the voices of the players, especially those who had been speaking up against the idea of playing during a pandemic and for ending the "racial injustice, exploitation of athletes by draconian NCAA rules." "If football represented a 'functioning democracy,'" McGregor explains, "then the voices of players and the lives of these players would matter. The truth is, however, the NCAA and its members are not democratic; they value athletes for their bodies, not their minds."[5]

When I finished drafting this book at the end of 2019, the state of college sports did not seem that much different from when I began my fieldwork in late 2010. Men's sports still dominated the media conversation, football still dictated the business terms of the big time, and women's sports like basketball still lived in the cultural shadows. Scholars of college sport still rightly focused on questions of exploitation, racism, violence, and sexism, and journalists followed suit.

But then the 2020 global pandemic hit, people began to get sick and die, the longstanding cracks in the college sports system began to widen, and more people began to see the structure that is NCAA college sports begin to fall. What had been normal economic activity in 2019 came to a screeching halt. Most education went online, and sports of all kinds, college or otherwise, stopped.

One thing stayed the same, though, even when the balls stopped flying, and it struck me as very telling. Although many focused on the players whose seasons had been cut short, few gave much attention to the education that would have been taking place on the now empty courts and fields not to mention in the classrooms. Instead, if anyone talked about college sports in the public sphere, they mostly talked about how to get the "players" back to their "work" in the entertainment industry.

Then in the autumn, sports did come back as the colleges, the universities and their trade associations, and the NCAA found ways to push revenue-generating athletes back onto fields and courts even though vaccines to fight the pandemic had not been rolled out and even though there were considerable health risks involved. Eager to continue to exploit athletes' bodies for institutional gain, these organizations of higher learning literally forced the big-time show to go on even as a pandemic raged on. (Some athletes opted out but most did not.) Still, rarely a peep about college athlete education could be heard let alone what the impact might be of adults forcing young athletes to see themselves as essential workers.

In the mass media and corridors of power in higher education, the question was not "How can we protect these young people or how can we help them continue to be educated?" but rather "How can we play football in a pandemic and still earn money if our athletes are not officially employees?"

So in the year 2020—a numerical synonym for perfect eyesight—the laborer reality of many college athletes, regardless of revenue generation, race, and gender, came into clearer focus and with it the realization that few adults involved in college sports really care that much about the education of college athletes.

The NCAA may not officially acknowledge it, but these big-time athletes are expected to perform just as an employee would—and their scholarships are directly tied to their willingness to play for their institution. And even though these athletes continued to work for the universities' benefit and continued to be treated like underpaid laborers, they were still not covered by employee labor laws and did not have the legal power to form a union to fight for better employment terms.

Which returns us to the central arguments of this book: (1) Adults involved in college sports should expect college athletes to be students first; (2) These athletes should be paid; and (3) A better balance must be struck between providing an education to athletes and entertainment to the public. In short, colleges must work harder to find ways to pay athletes as laborers, enhance their education as students, and respect their rights as people. Toward this end, institutions and individuals that exploit athletes for their gain could learn from the Stanford Standard, particularly the idea that academics and athletics need not be imagined as an either-or but rather as a both-and.

There is reason to be optimistic that change is on the way, but it is not enough to simply free the athletes to make money on their NILs or allow the richest colleges to provide more education-related benefits like computers to the most talented athletes. For college sports to be a justifiable part of higher education, we need to do more to put the college back in college sports.

Athletes from the Pac-12, who led the protest in August 2020, included in their demands the right to profit from their own NILs. For years scholars and journalists have been pushing for this right to be returned to athletes, but it seems that the athletes' protest had the greatest impact on swaying public opinion because various states have enacted NIL laws and there is talk of a national NIL law too. Indeed, one might argue that it was the athletes themselves, by standing up for themselves in 2020 and 2021, who were instrumental in convincing the Supreme Court to rule in their favor in *NCAA v. Alston* and to convince the NCAA to strike down its own NIL restrictions.

There is some hope that national legislation on college sports might come soon. In August 2020, Senators Cory Booker and Richard Blumenthal sponsored legislation that aimed to address the various indignities of college sports. On August 3, 2020, Senators Cory Booker, Richard Blumenthal, Christopher Murphy, Kirsten Gillibrand, Ron Wyden, Mazie Hirono, and Kamala Harris issued a college athletes bill of rights statement that sought to advance justice and opportunity for college athletes and promised future legislation to realize their position. On August 13, 2020, they were joined by Senators Bernie Sanders, Chris Van Hollen, and Brian Schatz. The bill promised to give college athletes full outside employment and NIL rights, a strong voice in the governance of college sports, comprehensive coverage for medical costs related to athletic injuries, protection from abusive coaches, mandated five-year athletic scholarships, and other academic protections to improve educational outcomes." At the time, Senator Booker, who had played football at Stanford and had maintained close ties to the university, said,

> The NCAA has failed generations of young men and women even when it comes to the most basic responsibility—keeping the athletes under their charge safe and healthy. The NCAA continues to fight tooth and nail, excuse after excuse, to ensure that college athletes, specifically Black athletes, who generate an outsized amount of college sport revenue and aren't able to share in the $15 billion industry that college sports has become.[6]

Senator Blumenthal put health and safety first, arguing that the pandemic "has highlighted the need to enact strong health and safety protections across the country. Schools are now rushing to bring students back on campus. We are watching a slow-motion potential catastrophe. We all want college sports. We all want colleges to reopen. It has to be done safely, putting athletes first."[7]

Then in December 2020, Booker and Blumenthal introduced legislation that would establish a pay-for-play model for college athletes as well as guarantee no infringement of their ability to profit from selling their own NILs. California, Colorado, and Florida had led the way in the latter category of reform, challenging the NCAA to revise its policy on the matter. Although NCAA rules still prohibit athletes from receiving endorsement money, in April 2020 the NCAA said its board of governors was willing to make rule changes that would allow that to occur, and by 2021 they had begun the process to change their bylaws. Soon thereafter the NCAA reached out to Congress asking for help drafting the rules, arguing that legal liability might be incurred if this weren't done on a national level.

Debate remains on issues such as how exactly athletes will be allowed to sell their NILs, whether those deals will have to be made public, and whether an individual athlete's NIL deal could conflict with a term in the athlete's team contract. It certainly seems wise for universities to educate athletes and offer financial literacy and life-skill workshops before entering such NIL deals, but who will pay for them? For many athletes, college is the only time they will ever have earning power as athletes so the NIL issue is important to them.[8] Even though they may want to, these athletes will not go pro. For Senator Booker, it is therefore "plainly hypocritical" for the NCAA to argue that they need congressional regulation to ensure that athletes only earn fair market value for their NIL and that without such a cap "wealthy boosters could funnel money to players, creating a competitive advantage."

While some also believe that universities need to pay players directly for their labor to the university (in addition to being allowed to profit from their NIL), the Drake Group has argued that Congress should legislate to "grant full outside employment and NIL rights for enrolled college athletes overseen by an independent NIL Commission, rather than the NCAA" but stops short of requiring universities to pay players directly.[9] This is because the group believes that doing so would strain university finances, create "adverse implications for the education of those athletes," and establish a "revenue-sharing agreement that creates an ill-disguised employer/employee relationship between the institution and college athlete that changes the nature of the university-student relationship and produces a variety of destructive effects." It would also establish a "pay for play professional sports business contrary to its tax-exempt purpose."[10] Finally, the group argues that Booker's bill will violate Title IX.[11]

And it is here that we must return to the issue of gender imbalance in college sports. College sports are disproportionally discussed with the male athlete in mind, which has led even the NCAA itself to treat female athletes as second-class citizens. One recent example came during the 2021 March Madness basketball tournament, when images of subpar training facilities and unequal amenities for women's basketball teams emerged on social media, highlighting how female athletes remain unjustifiably underserved. Then a few days later, when Coach Tara VanDerveer led Stanford to its first title in twenty-nine years, she spoke to the media about the many changes that remained to truly level the playing field. Even NCAA president Emmert agreed that it was "exactly the right moment" for gender equity reform, promising the Women's Basketball Coaching Association that they had his "personal commitment" to work to fix "stark" inequities. The NCAA has appointed a Commission on Gender Equity in College Sports Commission, but their unequal treatment of these players in 2021 reminds us that women athletes are often cast aside or overlooked not only by the sports media but also by the very organizations that insist that they are giving them opportunity.

At the end of the day, widespread striking by college athletes themselves, particularly by black and female athletes, to fight for better working conditions may be more powerful than any other reform measure,[12] but these are young men and women who are already doing a great deal to voice their opinions and stand up for their rights and the rights of others, while also balancing the rigorous demands of school and sports. Certainly we should applaud them for the activism, but should we expect it?

As adults, we must accept that we have not done right by them and accept our responsibility to lead the reform movement in a way that puts their interests above our own. Let us find ways to protect athletes' right to protest and implement the changes they demand and deserve but also to create an educational system that can put the student back in student-athlete and the college back in college sports. With proper respect for athletes' rights and without economic or symbolic exploitation, we can prioritize the minds, bodies, and the mental health of these athletes. And we must.

Notes

1. Quoted in Gregory, "College Athletes Are Realizing."
2. Mayhew and Shaheen, "Why America Needs College Football."
3. McGregor, "College Football Is a Symptom."
4. First, McGregor takes issue with the idea that college football is "important in demonstrating the 'values and purpose of higher education to the American people.'" He notes that this claim has a "long history, where college football is framed as a middlebrow culture that makes seemingly elite institutions more palatable to citizen

". . . This argument builds on the concept of the 'Booster University' where sport emerges as one of the most important 'products' that colleges offer to 'taxpayers.'" Should taxpayers expect to see their ROI from the football team? McGregor says no. "Emphasizing college football as the most prized output of a university de-emphasizes the true 'value and purpose of higher education.' If athletic competition is more important than seeking and transferring knowledge through teaching and research, why do universities exist at all?" Furthermore, McGregor argues that Mayhew and Shaheen forget that professional athletes "who negotiated their working conditions and receive compensation for their labor, are providing the very entertainment and morale lifting they are seeking." McGregor concludes, "During a moment when our democratic institutions are plagued with anti-intellectualism that denies basic facts, dismisses scientific data, and denounces the roles of experts, one has to wonder how [playing college football] helps democracy? One might argue it does quite the opposite." There are, however, problems with McGregor's arguments too. First, McGregor forgets that college athletes are compensated for their labor, it is just not called compensation. It is called a grant-in-aid or, colloquially, an athletic scholarship. Further, many states do not have professional sports teams and want college football (or basketball) to be their sport of choice. In those states, big-time college athletes are treated with a great deal of respect, and the big game is a big part of the broader regional culture. On the other hand, McGregor rightly notes that the argument that sports are integral to the university above all else misses the mark so we cannot accept Mayhew and Shaheen's argument either. College sports are an important part of our culture and democracy and they offer athletes a massive political platform that they might not otherwise have, but if athletes are not being listened to when they use that platform, then there is a problem, and McGregor is right to conclude that they are often prized more for their bodies than minds ("College Football Is a Symptom").

5. Miller and Tummalapalli, "Being a Basketball Fan."
6. Giambalvo, "As the NCAA Asks."
7. Giambalvo, "As the NCAA Asks."
8. As former college football player George Wrighster put it, "You're actually causing economic injury because all of us have a finite time in life that we are going to have our highest earning potential. It's completely un-American to cut off the free market system. The NCAA, at this point in time, wants to put undue restrictions on student-athletes" (quoted in Giambalvo, "As the NCAA Asks").
9. The Drake Group has been active in lobbying and advising Congress on how to reform college sports. In 2020 it wrote,

> The Drake Group proposes a College Athletes Rights and Protection Act (CARPA) to accomplish all of the promises made in the "College Athletes Bill of Rights." Using the carrot of institutions continuing to receive funding under the Higher Education Act of 1965 ($130 billion annually in federal loans and grants in 2019), the proposed bill includes the following mandates: Granting full outside employment and NIL rights for enrolled college athletes overseen by an independent NIL Commission, rather than the NCAA; Establishing a private National College Athlete Medical Trust Fund with an

independent Board of Directors charged with implementing a long-term athlete disability insurance program that addresses the latent medical cost impact of brain trauma or other athletics injuries that do not manifest before the end of enrolled athlete basic athletic injury insurance policy coverage; Allowing athletes and institutions to enter into licensing arrangements with third parties conditioned on proceeds being donated to the National College Athlete Medical Trust Fund and further funding the trust with assessments derived from gross annual media rights fees from national collegiate championships, conference championships, regular season and special events; Requiring national athletic governance associations to adopt and enforce consensus statements on standards of health care and coaches' codes of conduct as membership obligations and to initiate investigations of athlete deaths by independent panels of medical experts; Guaranteeing athletic scholarships for five years or until graduation, whichever occurs first; Permitting college athletes to transfer to other institutions without athletic participation ineligibility; Closing the loopholes in rules that limit the athletics-related time demands of coaches and creating limits on classes missed to ensure college athletes have the time to study and for adequate sleep; Requiring tenured faculty oversight and transparent reporting of college athlete educational outcomes; Providing a governance association athlete welfare advocate at no cost to the athlete to provide legal advice on the application of association rules and due process rights; Requiring that thirty percent of any national association's independent governing board of directors be former athletes appointed by currently enrolled athletes; Prohibiting excessive employee compensation and construction of lavish athletes-only facilities; and Requiring annual reports to Congress electronically available to the general public" ("Position Statement").

10. Drake Group, "Position Statement."

11. Booker's bill is based on the notion that no women's sports meet the bill's "revenue-sharing formula"—only FBS football, men's basketball, and men's ice hockey do. Accordingly, the Drake Group writes,

> Even if in future years, women's basketball or other sports become revenue-producing pursuant to the formula, there will still be a Title IX problem because the number of women athletes receiving royalty benefits and the amount per woman athlete predictably would be a small fraction of the amounts received by male athletes. The revenue-sharing provision violates Title IX because Title IX requires educational institutions that are the recipients of federal funds to provide equal treatment and benefits to male and female athletes without regard to sources of revenues. Indeed, shortly after Title IX was passed, amendments that would exclude the revenue sports of football and men's basketball from Title IX were expressly rejected on multiple occasions. Either institutions will be subject to the ultimate Title IX penalty of withdrawal of governmental funding, or, in order to comply, institutions will be required to revise the royalty distribution formula to equally benefit male and female athletes. Further, using the conference or athletic association as the "pass through banker" with athletes being paid by the conference instead of the institution, doesn't obviate institutions' Title IX obligations. Alternatively, even if the NCAA were deemed the legitimate source of the payments for various legal purposes, Title IX regulations are clear that the source of the funding is not relevant—institutions have an obligation to equally treat male and female athletes in the provision of benefits in addition to the provision of athletic scholarships. While the bill includes a catch-all pro-

vision that Title IX applies, it overlooks the crucial Title IX flaw in the revenue-sharing provision ("Position Statement").

12. Bissinger, "Buzz Bissinger."

Bibliography

Ackerman, Val. "Is Gender a Factor When It Comes to Leadership?" ESPN, April 26, 2011. http://m.espn.go.com/wireless/analysis?columnistId=val_ackerman&wjb.

Acosta, R. Vivian, and Linda Jean Carpenter. "Women in Intercollegiate Sport: A Longitudinal, National Study. Thirty-Five Year Update, 1977–2012," 2012. https://eric.ed.gov/?id=ED570883.

———. "Women in Intercollegiate Sport: A Longitudinal, National Study. Thirty-One Year Update, 1977–2008," 2008. https://eric.ed.gov/?id=ED570885.

———. "Woman in Intercollegiate Sport: A Longitudinal, National Study. Thirty-Seven Year Update, 1977–2014," 2014. https://eric.ed.gov/?id=ED570882.

———. "Women in Intercollegiate Sport: A Longitudinal, National Study. Thirty-Three Year Update, 1977–2010," 2010. https://eric.ed.gov/?id=ED570886.

———. "Women in Intercollegiate Sport: A Longitudinal, National Study. Twenty-Nine Year Update, 1977–2006," 2006. https://eric.ed.gov/?id=ED570884.

Adams, Stephen B. "Regionalism in Stanford's Contribution to the Rise of Silicon Valley." *Enterprise & Society* (2003): 521–43.

Adjepong, Anima. "'They Are Like Badges of Honour': Embodied Respectability and Women Rugby Players' Experiences of Their Bruises." *Sport in Society* 19, no. 10 (2016): 1489–502.

Adler, Peter, and Patricia A. Adler. "From Idealism to Pragmatic Detachment: The Academic Performance of College Athletes." *Sociology of Education* (1985): 241–50.

Alan-Fine, Gary. "Review of Elias, N. and Dunning, E. *Quest for Excitement: Sport and Leisure in the Civilizing Process*." *American Journal of Sociology* 93, no. 6 (1988): 1520–22.

Alexander, Jonathan. "North Carolina Women's Coaches Sylvia Hatchell Has Resigned amid Investigation." *News & Observer*, April 19, 2019. www.newsobserver.com/sports/article228892914.html.

Allen, Rick. 2016. "The Facts About Guaranteed Multi-Year Scholarships." https://informedathlete.com/the-facts-about-guaranteed-multi-year-ncaa-di-scholarships/.

Allison, Lincoln. *Amateurism in Sport: An Analysis and Defence*. London: Routledge, 2012.

Almond, Eliot. "Stanford's VanDerveer Famous for Her Work Ethic." *San Jose Mercury News*, August 9, 2011b.

———. "Stanford Women's Coach Still a Student of Game at 58." *Contra Costa Times*, August 10, 2011a.

Altenberg, Lee. "Beyond Capitalism: Leland Stanford's Forgotten Vision." *Sandstone and Tile* 14, no. 1 (Winter 1990): 8–20.

American Anthropology Association. "Statement on Race." www.americananthro.org/ConnectWithAAA/Content.aspx?ItemNumber=2583.

Anderson, Kelli. "The Fight for Play." *Stanford Magazine*, September 1, 2016. https://alumni.stanford.edu/get/page/magazine/article/?article_id=88434.

———. "Nine for IX: The Power of Play" and "Olympic Movement." *Sports Illustrated*, May 7, 2012.

Andrews, Vernon L. "Black Bodies—White Control: The Contested Terrain of Sportsmanlike Conduct." *Journal of African American Men* 2, no. 1 (June 1, 1996): 33–59. https://doi.org/10.1007/BF02733939.

Antonucci, Mike. "Game On: Tara VanDerveer Took the Cardinal from Doormat to Dynamo and Helped Boost Women's Athletics; But as Far as She Is Concerned, It's Still a Work in Progress." *Stanford Magazine*, January–February 2010. https://stanfordmag.org/contents/game-on.

Araton, Harvey. *Crashing the Borders: How Basketball Won the World and Lost Its Soul at Home*. New York: Free Press, 2007.

———. "Lieberman Is Back in Men's Game, in New Role." *New York Times*, December 23, 2010b.

———. "Moore Leads Connecticut to Women's Title." *New York Times*, April 6, 2010a.

Arendt, Elizabeth A., Julie Agel, and Randall Dick. "Anterior Cruciate Ligament Injury Patterns among Collegiate Men and Women." *Journal of Athletic Training* 34, no. 2 (1999): 86.

Aronson, Emily. 2014. "Fred Hargadon, Former Dean of Admission, Dies." Princeton University, January 16, 2014. www.princeton.edu/news/2014/01/16/fred-hargadon-former-dean-admission-dies.

Arrillaga-Andreessen, Laura. "John Arrillaga and Stanford: Generosity Begets Generosity." *Stanford Report*, July 1, 2013. http://news.stanford.edu/news/2013/july/arrillaga-major-gift-070113.html.

Aspen Institute. "Future of College Sports: Reimagining Athlete Pay," May 1, 2018. www.aspeninstitute.org/events/future-college-sports-reimagining-athlete-pay/.
Associated Press. "Kayla Pedersen, Stanford Hand Texas First Loss of Year." ESPN, November 28, 2010. www.espn.com/ncw/recap/_/gameId/303320024.
———. "Nnemkadi Ogwumike Scores 24 as Stanford Uses Huge 2nd Half to Roll Past Arizona." ESPN, January 6, 2011. www.espn.com/ncw/recap/_/gameId/310060024.
———. "No. 5 Stanford Women Top Washington in Pac-12 Play." *Contra Costa Times*, January 6, 2020, C2.
———. "No. 6 Tennessee Outlasts No. 2 Stanford in Overtime." ESPN, December 19, 2010. www.espn.com/ncw/recap/_/gameId/303532633.
———. "USC Falls to No. 4 Stanford 95-51." University of Southern California Athletics, January 22, 2011. https://www.google.com/search?client=safari&rls=en&q=USC+Falls+to+no.+4+Stanford+95-5&ie=UTF-8&oe=UTF-8.
———. "Women's Hoops Sets Attendance Mark." ESPN, May 17, 2011. www.espn.com/womens-college-basketball/news/story?id=6559525.
Association for Intercollegiate Athletics for Women v. NCAA, 558 F. Su 487—Dist. Court, Dist. of Columbia 1983.
Association for Intercollegiate Athletics for Women v. NCAA, 735 F. 2d 577—Court of Appeals, Dist. of Columbia Circuit 1984.
Association for Intercollegiate Athletics for Women, A Non-profit Corporation, Appellant, v. National Collegiate Athletic Association, an Unincorporated Association, Appellee, 735 F.2d 577 (D.C. Cir. 1984), U.S. Court of Appeals for the District of Columbia Circuit—735 F.2d 577 (D.C. Cir. 1984). Argued Jan. 11, 1984. Decided May 18, 1984. https://law.justia.com/cases/federal/appellate-courts/F2/735/577/212153/.
Atkin, Charles, and Walter Gantz. "Promotion and Prevention of Drinking in U.S. College Sports." In *Sport, Beer, and Gender: Promotional Culture and Contemporary Social Life*, edited by Lawrence A. Wenner and Steve Jackson. New York: Peter Lang, 2009, 261–78.
Atwell, Robert. "The Only Way to Reform College Sports Is to Embrace Commercialization." *Chronicle of Higher Education*, July 13, 2001. www.chronicle.com/article/the-only-way-to-reform-college-sports-is-to-embrace-commercialization/.
Auerbach, Nicole. "Sources: NCAA One-Time Transfer Proposal, Notification Deadlines Being Finalized." *Athletic*, October 6, 2020.
Auletta, Ken. "Annals of Higher Education: Get Rich U." *New Yorker*, April 30, 2012.
Austin, Brad. *Democratic Sports: Men's and Women's College Athletics during the Great Depression*. Fayetteville: University of Arkansas Press, 2015.
Austin, J. L. "Performative Utterances." In *The Semantics-Pragmatics Boundary in Philosophy*," edited by Maite Ezcurdia and Robert Stainton (Peterborough, Canada: Broadview Press, 2013).
Axthelm, Pete. *The City Game: Basketball in New York from the World Champion Knicks to the World of the Playgrounds*. New York: Harper's Magazine Press, 1970.

Bachman, Rachel. "Mental Health: College Sports' Newest Need, Psychologists." *Wall Street Journal*, November 9, 2018, A16.

———. "NCAA: Firms Collecting College Secrets—How Can Athletic Departments Avert scandal?" *Wall Street Journal*, March 5, 2019, A14.

Bachynski, Kathleen. *No Game for Boys to Play: The History of Youth Football and the Origins of a Public Health Crisis*. Chapel Hill: University of North Carolina Press, 2019.

Bailey, Steve. *Science in the Service of Physical Education and Sport: The Story of the International Council of Sport Science and Physical Education, 1956–1996*. Chicester, UK: J. Wiley & Sons, 1997.

Bailey, Wilford S., and Taylor D Littleton. *Athletics and Academe: An Anatomy of Abuses and a Prescription for Reform*, New York: American Council on Education, 1991.

Bain, Linda L., and Janice C. Wendt. "Undergraduate Physical Education Majors' Perceptions of the Roles of Teacher and Coach." *Research Quarterly for Exercise and Sport* 54, no. 2 (June 1, 1983): 112–18. https://doi.org/10.1080/02701367.1983.10605282.

Bain-Selbo, Eric. "Sport as the 'Opiate of the Masses': College Football in the American South." *Philosophy & Religion Faculty Publications*, paper 1, 2008. http://digitalcommons.wku.edu/phil_rel_fac_pub/1.

Baker, Christine A. *Why She Plays: The World of Women's Basketball*. Lincoln: University of Nebraska Press, 2008.

Barber, Nigel. "Is Sport a Religion?" *Psychology Today*, November 2009. www.psychologytoday.com/us/blog/the-human-beast/200911/is-sport-religion.

Barton, Bob. "Honoring Walter Camp." *College Football Historical Society Newsletter* 21, no. 4 (August 2008).

Bauer-Wolf, Jeremy. "NCAA Finds No Academic Fraud at UNC." Inside Higher Ed, October 16, 2007. www.insidehighered.com/news/2017/10/16/breaking-ncaa-finds-no-academic-fraud-unc.

Baxter, R. "Directions for Amusements and Recreations." www.gracegems.org/28/directions_for_amusements.htm.

Baysinger, Tim. "ESPN Reaches 12-Year Deal for New College Football Playoff." Broadcasting+Cable, November 21, 2012. www.broadcastingcable.com/news/espn-reaches-12-year-deal-new-college-football-playoff-64874.

Bearak, Barry. Where Football and Higher Education Mix. *New York Times*, September 16, 2011.

Beard, Richard. *Muddied Oafs: The Soul of Rugby*. New York: Random House, 2018.

Beck, Howard. "World Will Be More Like N.B.A." *New York Times*, August 25, 2008.

Bedell, Doug. "Not a Sporting Match." *Chicago Tribune*, March 23, 1997. www.chicagotribune.com/news/ct-xpm-1997-03-23-9703230048-story.html.

Beech, Hannah. "Crazy for Gold." *Time*, 2008.

Bell, C. C. "Using Sports to Strengthen Resiliency in Children." *Child and Adolescent Psychiatric Clinics of North America* 7, no. 4 (1988): 859–65. https://europepmc.org/article/med/9894046.
Belson, Ken. "Abuse Scandal Inquiry Damns Paterno and Penn State." *New York Times*, July 13, 2012.
———. "A Star College Quarterback Is Worth . . ." *New York Times*, November 13, 2010.
Benedict, Jeff, and Armen Keteyian. *The System: The Glory and Scandal of Big-Time College Football*. New York: Knopf Doubleday, 2014.
Bennett, Roger, and Rehnuma Ali-Choudhury. "Prospective Students' Perceptions of University Brands: An Empirical Study." *Journal of Marketing for Higher Education* 19, no. 1 (May 28, 2009): 85–107. https://doi.org/10.1080/08841240902905445.
Bennett, William. *Is College Worth It?* Nashville, TN: Thomas Nelson, 2013.
Benson, Martin T. *A Statistical Comparison of College Graduation of Freshman Student-Athletes Before and After Proposition 48*. NCAA Research Report 92-02, 1993. https://eric.ed.gov/?id=ED381044.
Berenson, Senda. *Basketball for Women*. Park Place, NY: American Sports Publishing, 1903.
Berkowitz, Steve. "Duke's Krzyzewski Credited With $9.7 Million in Pay for 2011." *USA Today*, May 15, 2013. www.usatoday.com/story/sports/ncaab/2013/05/15/mikekrzyzewski-coach-k-duke-salary-pay-2011/2156231.
Berkowitz, Steve, and Andrew Kreighbaum. "Cincinnati Athletes Lead in Benefit Boost from Cost of Attendance." *USA Today*, August 20, 2015. www.usatoday.com/story/sports/college/2015/08/20/ncaa-cost—attendance-cincinnati-bearcats/32062729/.
———. "Judge Rules NCAA Must Defend Limits on Compensation to College Athletes in New Trial." *USA Today*, March 28, 2018.
———. "NCAA Unveils Proposed Rule Changes Related to Athletes' Name, Image, and Likeness." *USA Today*, Nov. 13, 2020.
Berri, David. "Exploitation Is Everywhere in Men's College Basketball." *Time*, November 14, 2014.
Besnier, Niko, Susan Brownell, and Thomas F. Carter. *The Anthropology of Sport: Bodies, Borders, Biopolitics*. Oakland: University of California Press, 2018.
Betancourt, Marian. *Playing Like a Girl: Transforming Our Lives Through Team Sports*. Contemporary Books, 2016.
Bishop, Greg. "N.C.A.A. Dodges a Bullet, but Change Is On the Way." *New York Times*, November 10, 2013. http://nyti.ms/1Ly9Nm6.
———. "Oregon Embraces 'University of Nike' Image." *New York Times*, August 2, 2013. www.nytimes.com/2013/08/03/sports/ncaafootball/oregon-football-complex-is-glittering-monument-to-ducks-ambitions.html?_r=0.
Bissinger, Buzz. "Buzz Bissinger: College Football Players Should Threaten to Boycott." *New York Times*, August 25, 2020.

Blanchard, Kendall. *The Anthropology of Sport: An Introduction.* Westport, CT: Bergin & Garvey, 1995,

Blinde, Elaine M., Susan L. Greendorfer, and Rebecca J. Shanker. "Differential Media Coverage of Men's and Women's Intercollegiate Basketball: Reflection of Gender Ideology." *Journal of Sport and Social Issues* 15, no. 2 (September 1, 1991): 98–114. https://doi.org/10.1177/019372359101500201.

Bok, Derek. *Universities in the Marketplace: The Commercialization of Higher Education.* Princeton, NJ: Princeton University Press, 2009.

Boren, Cindy. "Obama: NCAA's Basketball Farm System 'Not a Sustainable Way of Doing Business.'" *Washington Post*, February 27, 2018.

Bourdieu, Pierre. "How Can One Be a Sports Fan?" In *The Cultural Studies Reader*, edited by Simon During. Hove, UK: Psychology Press, 1993, 427–40.

Bowen, William G., and Sarah A. Levin. *Reclaiming the Game: College Sports and Educational Values.* Princeton, NJ: Princeton University Press, 2005.

Bowlby, John. *Attachment.* New York: Basic Books, 2008.

Boykoff, Jules. *Celebration Capitalism and the Olympic Games.* New York: Routledge, 2013.

Brake, Deborah. "The Struggle for Sex Equality in Sport and the Theory Behind Title IX." *University of Michigan Journal of Law Reform*, 2001. https://core.ac.uk/download/pdf/76622262.pdf.

Branch, Taylor. "The Shame of College Sports." *Atlantic Monthly*, October 2011. www.theatlantic.com/magazine/archive/2011/10/the-shame-of-college-sports/8643.

Branscombe, Nyla R., and Daniel L. Wann. "The Positive Social and Self Concept Consequences of Sports Team Identification." *Journal of Sport and Social Issues* 15, no. 2 (September 1, 1991): 115–27. https://doi.org/10.1177/019372359101500202.

Bredemeier, Brenda Jo Light, and David Lyle Light Shields. "Applied Ethics and Moral Reasoning in Sport." In *Moral Development in the Professions*, edited by J. R. Rest and D. Narváez. Hove, UK: Psychology Press, 1994.

Brennan, Christine. "Gender Balance Needed for Women's Coaches." *USA Today*, October 24, 2007.

Briley, John David. *Career in Crisis: Paul "Bear" Bryant and the 1971 Season of Change.* Macon, GA: Mercer University Press, 2006.

Brohm, Jean-Marie. *Sport: A Prison of Measured Time, Essays.* Translated by Ian Fraser. London: Ink Links, 1976.

Brooks, David. "The Leadership Revival." *New York Times*, January 13, 2014.

Brown, Bill. "Waging Baseball, Playing War: Games of American Imperialism." *Culture Critique* 17, no. 1 (1990–91): 51–78.

Bruni, Frank. "Women's Time to Shine." *New York Times*, July 22, 2012.

Burstyn, Varda. *The Rites of Men: Manhood, Politics, and the Culture of Sport.* Toronto: University of Toronto Press, 1999.

Burton Nelson, Mariah. "Introduction: Who We might Become." In *Nike Is a Goddess: The History of Women in Sports*, edited by Lissa Smith. New York: Atlantic Monthly Press, 1998, ix-2.

———. *The Stronger Women Get, The More Men Love Football: Sexism and the Culture of Sports*. New York: Avon, 1994.

Buzuvis, Erin E. "Athletic Compensation for Women Too: Title IX Implications of Northwestern and O'Bannon." *Journal of College and University Law* 41 (2015): 297–341, https://digitalcommons.law.wne.edu/cgi/viewcontent.cgi?article=1312&context=facschol.

Byers, Walter, and Charles H. Hammer. *Unsportsmanlike Conduct: Exploiting College Athletes*. Ann Arbor: University of Michigan Press, 1997.

Caccese, Thomas M., and Cathleen K. Mayerberg. "Gender Differences in Perceived Burnout of College Coaches." *Journal of Sport and Exercise Psychology* 6, no. 3 (September 1, 1984): 279–88. https://doi.org/10.1123/jsp.6.3.279.

Cahn, Susan K. *Coming On Strong: Gender and Sexuality in Women's Sport*. Champaign: University of Illinois Press, 2015.

Cantor, Nancy E., and Deborah A. Prentice. "The Life of the Modern-Day Student-Athlete: Opportunities Won and Lost." *Princeton Conference on Higher Education*, Princeton University, Princeton, New Jersey, 1996.

Canzano, John. "Canzano Blog: Ex-Ducks Player to Oregon Fans 'Go (Bleep) Yourselves.'" *Oregonian Online*, October 29, 2013. www.oregonlive.com/sports/oregonian/john_canzano/index.ssf/2013/10/canzano_blog_ex-ducks_player_t.html#incart_flyout_sports.

Carter, Andrew. "UNC's Sylvia Hatchell: 'Hard Not to Say' Her Program Is Scapegoat." May 10, 2016. https://journalnow.com/sports/college/hatchell-hard-not-to-say-womens-basketball-is-scapegoat-in-unc-scandal/article_e30cf991-0a72-5644-acea-f65e8c2b9c46.html.

Carty, Victoria. "Textual Portrayals of Female Athletes: Liberation or Nuanced Forms of Patriarchy?" *Frontiers* 26, no. 2 (2005): 132–55.

Castelnuovo, Shirley, and Sharon Ruth Guthrie. *Feminism and the Female Body: Liberating the Amazon Within*. Boulder, CO: Lynne Rienner Publishers, 1998.

Cavalli, Gary. *Stanford Sports*. Stanford, CA: Stanford Alumni Association, 1982.

Cavallo, Dominick. *Muscles and Morals: Organized Playgrounds and Urban Reform, 1880–1920*. Philadelphia: University of Pennsylvania Press, 1981.

Chapin, Dwight. "Joe Ruetz (1916–2003), Ex-Stanford Athletic Director Dies, Credited With Bringing Shrine Game, Bill Walsh to the Farm." *San Francisco Chronicle*, January 8, 2003. http://www.sfgate.com/sports/article/JOE-RUETZ-1916-2003-Ex-Stanford-athletic-2641537.php.

Chelladurai, P., and M. Arnott. "Decision Styles in Coaching: Preferences of Basketball Players." *Research Quarterly for Exercise and Sport* 56, no. 1 (March 1, 1985): 15–24. https://doi.org/10.1080/02701367.1985.10608426.

Cheslock, J. "Who's Playing College Sports? Money, Race and Gender." East Meadow, NY: Women's Sports Foundation, 2008.

Chomsky, Noam. "Public Education: Failure by Design." *Amass* 16, no. 4 (2012): 28.
Chronicle of Higher Education. "The Almanac of Higher Education," August 28, 2009, 5.
Chu, Donald. *The Character of American Higher Education and Intercollegiate Sport*. Albany, New York: SUNY Press, 1989.
Chuchmach, Megan and Brian Ross. "Ex-USC Player: Painkiller Injections Caused Heart Attack." January 3, 2013. https://abcnews.go.com/Blotter/risks-college-football-powerful-painkiller/story?id=18114915.
Clifford, Craig, and Randolph M. Feezell. *Coaching for Character: Reclaiming the Principles of Sportsmanship*. Champaign, IL: Human Kinetics, 1997.
Clifford, James. "Introduction: Partial Truths." In *Writing Culture: The Poetics and Politics of Ethnography*, edited by J. Clifford and G. E. Marcus. Berkeley: University of California Press, 1986, 1–26.
Clotfelter, Charles. *Big-Time College Sports in American Universities*. Cambridge: Cambridge University Press, 2011.
CNBC. "Fox to Pay More Than $3 Billion to Broadcast 'Thursday Night Football' for Five Seasons, Report Says," January 31, 2018. www.cnbc.com/2018/01/31/fox-reaches-5-year-deal-with-the-nfl-to-broadcast-thursday-night-football.html.
CNN. "ESPN's $7.3 Billion College Football Gamble Pays Off." http://money.cnn.com/2015/01/12/media/espn-college-football-playoff-pays-off.
Coaches Hot Seat. "Salaries and Contracts." www.coacheshotseat.com/SalariesContracts.htm.
Coaching Association of Canada, Sport Information Resource Center. "Commercialization of Amateur Sport." Ottawa, Ontario: Coaching Association of Canada, 1990.
Coakley, Jay J. *Sport in Society: Issues and Controversies*. Maryland Heights, MD: C. V. Mosby, 1982.
———. "Studying Intercollegiate Sports: High Stakes, Low Rewards." *Journal of Intercollegiate Sport* 1, no. 1 (2008): 14–28.
———. "Youth Sport in the United States." In *Routledge Handbook of Youth Sport*, edited by Ken Green and Andy Smith. New York: Routledge, 2016, 84–97.
College Sport Research Institute. "Adjusted Graduation Gap Report: NCAA Division-I Basketball, 2017." https://www.sc.edu/study/colleges_schools/hrsm/research/centers/college_sport_research_institute/agg_reports/gap_reports/2017-basketball-agg-report.pdf.
Commission on Collegiate Basketball. "Report and Recommendations to NCAA Board of Governors, Division I Board of Directors and NCAA President Emmert," May 1, 2018. Originally retrieved from www.ncaa.org/sites/default/files/2018CCBReportFinal_web_20180501.pdf. Now available at https://wbca.org/sites/default/files/rice-commission-report.pdf.
Congressional Budget Office. "Tax Preferences for Collegiate Sports." Washington, DC: Congressional Budget Office, 2009.

Connell, R. W. "Change among the Gatekeepers: Men, Masculinities, and Gender Equality in the Global Arena." *Signs* 30, no. 3 (2005): 1801–25. www.journals.uchicago.edu/doi/abs/10.1086/427525.

Connelly, Bill. "A Better Future for College Football Players? Here's How to Make It Happen." ESPN, August 10, 2020. www.espn.com/espn/print?id=29578928.

Cooky, Cheryl. "The Female Athlete: Missing in Action." YouTube. www.youtube.com/watch?v=MPS2YoXWMSs.

Cooky, Cheryl, Michael A. Messner, and Michela Musto. "'It's Dude Time!' A Quarter-Century of Excluding Women's Sports in Televised News and Highlight Shows, 2015." https://journals.sagepub.com/doi/full/10.1177/2167479515588761.

Cooky, Cheryl, Michael A. Messner, and Robin H. Hextrum. "Women Play Sport, But Not on TV: A Longitudinal Study of Televised News Media." *Communication & Sport* 1, no. 3 (2013): 203–30. https://journals.sagepub.com/doi/abs/10.1177/2167479513476947.

Cosentino, Dom. "Why Only the NFL Doesn't Guarantee Contracts." Deadspin, August 1, 2017. https://deadspin.com/why-only-the-nfl-doesnt-guarantee-contracts-1797020799.

Costa, Brian. "College Basketball: Former NBA Star Wants to Disrupt NCAA's Model." *Wall Street Journal*, February 26, 2019, A14.

Crouse, Karen. "Stanford's Coach VanDerveer Preaches the Joy of Victory." *New York Times*, March 22, 2011.

Csikszentmihalyi, Mihaly. *Beyond Boredom and Anxiety*. San Francisco: Jossey-Bass, 1975.

———. *Flow: The Psychology of Optimal Experience*. New York: Harper Perennial, 1991.

Curtis, Bryan. "Summa Cum Madden." *New York Times*, September 13, 2008.

Cushion, Christopher. "The Coaching Process in Professional Youth Football: An Ethnography of Practice." PhD thesis, Brunel University School of Sport and Education, 2001. http://bura.brunel.ac.uk/handle/2438/5138.

Cushion, Christopher J., Kathleen M. Armour, and Robyn L. Jones. "Locating the Coaching Process in Practice: Models 'For' and 'Of' Coaching." *Physical Education and Sport Pedagogy* 11, no. 1 (February 1, 2006): 83–99. https://doi.org/10.1080/17408980500466995.

His Holiness the Dalai Lama and Howard Cutler. *The Art of Happiness: A Handbook for Living*. New York: Riverhead Books, 1998.

Damon, William. *Greater Expectations: Nurturing Children's Natural Moral Growth*. New York: Simon & Schuster, 2010.

———. *The Path to Purpose: Helping Our Children Find Their Calling in Life*. New York: Simon & Schuster, 2008.

———. *The Youth Charter: How Communities Can Work Together to Raise Standards for All Our Children*. New York: Free Press, 1997.

Dampier, William Cecil. *A History of Science and Its Relations with Philosophy and Religion*. Cambridge: Cambridge University Press, 1961.

Danley, Stephen. "Give Athletes Five-Year Scholarships." *New York Times*, March 18, 2009.

Dohrmann, George. "Chance to Be a Champion: Women Were Intramural Afterthoughts Until the AIAW Was Formed in 1971." *Sports Illustrated*, May 7, 2012. http://www.si.com/vault/2012/05/07/106189968/chance-to-be-a-champion.

Doty, Joseph. "Sports Build Character?!" *Journal of College and Character* 7, no. 3 (April 1, 2006): 1–9. https://doi.org/10.2202/1940-1639.1529.

Douglas, Mary. *Implicit Meanings: Essays in Anthropology*. London: Routledge & Kegan Paul, 1975.

———. *Natural Symbols*. New York: Vintage Books, 1973.

———. *Purity and Danger: An Analysis of the Concepts of Pollution and Taboo*. London: Routledge & Kegan Paul, 1966.

Dowling, William C. "Big Time Sports as Academic Prostitution." *Academic Questions* 14, no. 4 (2001): 82–90.

———. *Confessions of a Spoilsport: My Life and Hard Times Fighting Sports Corruption at an Old Eastern University*. University Park, PA: Penn State University Press, 2007.

———. "March Money Madness: Stop the Madness." *New York Times*, March 18, 2009.

Downey, Greg. "Scaffolding Imitation in Capoeira: Physical Education and Enculturation in an Afro-Brazilian Art." *American Anthropologist* 110, no. 2 (2008): 204–13.

Drake Group. "Defending Academic Integrity in the Face of Commercialized College Sport." www.thedrakegroup.org.

———. "The Drake Group Finds That the Independent Commission on College Basketball Missed an Opportunity to Recommend Comprehensive Reform," 2018. www.thedrakegroup.org/2011/05/04/the-drake-group-finds-that-the-independent-commission-on-college-basketball-missed-an-opportunity-to-recommend-comprehensive-reform/.

———. "Position Statement: The Drake Group Praises Proposed College Athletes Bill of Rights but Notes Significant Flaw in Massive Sorely Needed Reform Bill," December 22, 2020. www.thedrakegroup.org/wp-content/uploads/2020/12/Dec.22-Drake-Position-on-Athletes-Rights-Bill-FINAL.pdf.

Drape, Joe, and Katie Thomas. "As Colleges Compete, Money Flows to Minor Sports." *New York Times*, September 2, 2010.

Drexel Now. "Study: College Athletes Worth Six Figures Live Below Federal Poverty Line." Drexel University, September 13, 2011. http://drexel.edu/now/archive/2011/September/Study-College-Athletes-Worth-Six-Figures-Live-Below-Federal-Poverty-Line/.

Duderstadt, James J. *Intercollegiate Athletics and the American University: A University President's Perspective*. Ann Arbor: University of Michigan Press, 2009.

Dudley, Earl C. Jr, and George Rutherglen. "Ironies, Inconsistencies, and Intercollegiate Athletics: Title IX, Title VII, and Statistical Evidence of Discrimination." *Virginia Journal of Sports and the Law* 1 (1999): 177–80.
Duke University. "Site Map." www.goduke.com/ViewArticle.dbml?DB_OEM_ID=4200&ATCLID=152723.
Dunning, Eric. "Sport as a Male Preserve: Notes on the Social Sources of Masculine Identity and Its Transformations." *Theory, Culture & Society* 3, no. 1 (February 1, 1986): 79–90. https://doi.org/10.1177/0263276486003001007.
Duquin, Mary E. "Power and Authority: Moral Consensus and Conformity in Sport." *International Review for the Sociology of Sport* 19, nos. 3–4 (September 1, 1984): 295–304. https://doi.org/10.1177/101269028401900308.
Easterbrook, Gregg. *The King of Sports: Football's Impact on America*. New York: Macmillan, 2013.
Eccles, Jacquelynne S., and Janice Templeton. "Chapter 4: Extracurricular and Other After-School Activities for Youth." *Review of Research in Education* 26, no. 1 (January 1, 2002): 113–80. https://doi.org/10.3102/0091732X026001113.
Eckard, E. Woodrow. "The NCAA Cartel and Competitive Balance in College Football." *Review of Industrial Organization* 13, no. 3 (June 1, 1998): 347–69. https://doi.org/10.1023/A:1007713802480.
Edelman, Marc. "From Student-Athletes to Employee-Athletes: Why a Pay for Play Model of College Sports Would Not Necessarily Make Educational Scholarships Taxable." *Boston College Law Review* 58 (2017): 1137.
Eder, Steve. "As Legal Battle Continues, N.C.A.A. Ends Tie with Electronic Arts." *New York Times*, July 17, 2013.
Eder, Steve, and Greg Bishop. "High-Stakes Games: Critical Step for Suit Seeking Payment for College Athletes." *New York Times*, June 19, 2013.
———. "NCAA Admits Mishandling Miami Inquiry." *New York Times*, January 24, 2013a.
———. "For ESPN, Millions to Remain in Connecticut." *New York Times*, December 26, 2013b.
Edwards, Elise. "Theorizing the Cultural Importance of Play: Anthropological Approaches to Sports and Recreation." In *Blackwell Companion to Anthropology of Japan*, edited by J. Robertson. Oxford: Blackwell, 2005, 279–96.
Edwards, Harry. "The Collegiate Athletic Arms Race: Origins and Implications of the 'Rule 48' Controversy." *Journal of Sport and Social Issues* 8, no. 1 (March 1, 1984): 4–22. https://doi.org/10.1177/019372358400800103.
———. "The Revolt of the Black Athlete." In *Sport and Society: An Anthology*, edited by John T. Talamini and Charles H. Page. New York: Little Brown, 1973.
———. *Sociology of Sport*. Homewood, IL: Dorsey Press, 1973.
Edwards, Harry, and Van Rackages. "The Dynamics of Violence in American Sport; Some Promising Structural and Social Considerations." *Journal of Sport and Social Issues* 1, no. 2 (June 1, 1977): 3–31. https://doi.org/10.1177/019372357700100201.

Eikleberry, Sarah Jane. "More Than Milk and Cookies: Reconsidering the College Play Day." *Journal of Sport History* 41, no. 3 (2014): 467–86.

Eisenhart, Margaret A., and Elizabeth Finkel. *Women's Science: Learning and Succeeding from the Margins*. Chicago: University of Chicago Press, 1998.

Eitzen, D. Stanley. "The Sociology of Amateur Sport: An Overview." *International Review for the Sociology of Sport* 24, no. 2 (June 1, 1989): 95–105. https://doi.org/10.1177/101269028902400201.

Eitzen, D. Stanley, and Stephen R. Pratt. "Gender Differences in Coaching Philosophy: The Case of Female Basketball Teams." *Research Quarterly for Exercise and Sport* 60, no. 2 (June 1, 1989): 152–58. https://doi.org/10.1080/02701367.1989.10607430.

Elias, Norbert. *Quest for Excitement: Sport and Leisure in the Civilising Process*. Oxford: Blackwell, 2008. www.cabdirect.org/cabdirect/abstract/20093110385.

———. "The Quest for Excitement in Unexciting Societies." In *The Cross-Cultural Analysis of Sport and Games*, edited by G. Luschen. Champaign, IL: Stipes, 1970, 31–51.

Ellis, Blake. "Ex-Penn State President Tops Highest-Paid List." CNN, May 12, 2013. http://money.cnn.com/2013/05/12/pf/college/university-president-pay/.

Ember, Carol R., Emily Pitek, and Erik J. Ringen. "Adolescence." Human Relations Area Files, December 8, 2017. https://hraf.yale.edu/ehc/summaries/adolescence.

Emery, Lynne Fauley, and Margaret Toohey-Costa. "Hoops and Skirts: Women's Basketball on the West Coast, 1892–1930s." In *A Century of Women's Basketball*, edited by Joan Hult and Marianna Trekell. Reston, VA: NAGWS.

Entine, Jon. *Taboo: Why Black Athletes Dominate Sports and Why We're Afraid to Talk About It*. New York: Public Affairs, 2008.

Epstein, David J. *The Sports Gene: Inside the Science of Extraordinary Athletic Performance*. New York: Penguin, 2014.

Erskine, Chris. "Title IX Has Benefited Anyone Who Loves Sports." *Los Angeles Times*, September 3, 2012.

ESPN. "Chapel Hill Still About Dorrance Dynasty," August 23, 2008. http://espn.go.com/ncaa/s/preview00/wsoccer/unc.html.

———. "ESPN to Televise College Playoff," November 21, 2012. http://espn.go.com/college-football/story/_/id/8660304/espn-televise-college-football-playoff-12-year-deal.

———. "Geno Auriemma: UConn Fans Spoiled," March 23, 2011. http://sports.espn.go.com/ncw/tournament/2011/news/story?id=6249777.

———. "Gerald Ford Obituary Video Broadcast," December 26, 2006.

———. "Ralph Nader: Replace Scholarships," April 4, 2011. https://www.espn.com/college-sports/news/story?id=6254572.

———. "Stanford's Amy Tucker Retiring From Coaching, to Stay On in Administrative Role," April 12, 2017. www.espn.com/womens-college-basketball/story/_/id/19146673/amy-tucker-stanford-cardinal-retiring. http://sports.espn.go.com/ncaa/news/story?id=6254572.

———. "Twins Postpone Thursday's Game After Bridge Collapses Near Metrodome." August 1, 2007. https://www.espn.com/mlb/news/story?id=2957912

———. "Women Coaching Men," October 14, 2001. www.espn.com/page2/tvlistings/show81transcript.html.

Estler, Suzanne E., and Laurie J. Nelson. "Who Calls the Shots? Sports and University Leadership, Culture, and Decision Making." *ASHE Higher Education Report* 30, no. 5 (2005): 1–125. https://doi.org/10.1002/aehe.3005.

Fagan, Kate, and Luke Cyphers. "The Glass Wall: Women Continue to Shatter Stereotypes as Athletes. So How Come They Can't Catch a Break as Coaches?" ESPN. http://sports.espn.go.com/espn/eticket/story?page=theGlassWall&src=mobile.

Fainaru, Steve, and Tom Farrey. "Game Changer." ESPN, July 24, 2014. www.espn.com/espn/otl/story/_/id/11255945/washington-attorney-michael-hausfeld-most-powerful-man-sports.

Fainaru-Wada, Mark, and Steve Fainaru. *League of Denial: The NFL, Concussions, and the Battle for Truth*. New York: Three Rivers Press, 2014.

Farred, Grant. *Phantom Calls: Race and the Globalization of the NBA*. Chicago, IL: Prickly Paradigm Press, 2006.

Farrey, Tom. "Jeffrey Kessler Suit against NCAA." ABC, March 17, 2014. https://abcnews.go.com/Sports/jeffrey-kessler-suit-ncaa/story?id=22939019.

Fastbreak Club. "Tara's New Title. Stanford FBC: Stories of the Summer," December 8, 2010. http://fbccardinalnews.blogspot.com/2010/12/taras-endowment.html.

Feezell, Randolph M. "Review." *Academe* 87, no. 5 (2001): 90–92. https://doi.org/10.2307/40252073.

Feinstein, John. *The Last Amateurs: Playing for Glory and Honor in Division I College Basketball*. Boston, MA: Little, Brown, 2008.

———. *Season on the Brink*. New York: Simon & Schuster, 2012.

Festle, Mary Jo. *Playing Nice: Politics and Apologies in Women's Sports*. New York: Columbia University Press, 1996.

Fields, Sarah. "Review of Ying Wushanley, *Playing Nice and Losing: The Struggle for Control of Women's Intercollegiate Athletics, 1960–2000*." *Aethlon* 23, no. 1 (2005): 189.

Finley, Jermichael. "They Basically Reset My Brain." Players' Tribune, May 24, 2017. www.theplayerstribune.com/en-us/articles/jermichael-finley-packers-injury-retirement.

Foley, Douglas A., Bradley A. Levinson, and Janise Hurtig. "Anthropology Goes Inside: The New Educational Ethnography of Ethnicity and Gender." *Review of Research in Education* 25, no. 1 (January 1, 2000): 37–98. https://doi.org/10.3102/0091732X025001037.

Foley, Douglas E. "The Great American Football Ritual: Reproducing Race, Class, and Gender Inequality." *Sociology of Sport Journal* 7, no. 2 (June 1, 1990): 111–35. https://doi.org/10.1123/ssj.7.2.111.

Follansbee, Geoff. "Excellence, Community, and Belonging: Tara VanDerveer on the Lessons of Chautauqua." *Chautauqua Pillars* (2010 Fall). www.chautauquasportshalloffame.org/taravanderveer2010b.php.

Foster, Kevin Michael. "Panopticonics: The Control and Surveillance of Black Female Athletes in a Collegiate Athletic Program." *Anthropology & Education Quarterly* 34, no. 3 (2003): 300–323. https://doi.org/10.1525/aeq.2003.34.3.300.

Foster, Sayvon J. L., and Matt R. Huml. "The Relationship between Athletic Identity and Academic Major Chosen by Student-Athletes." *International Journal of Exercise Science* 10, no. 6 (October 1, 2017): 915–25.

Foucault, Michel. *Discipline and Punish: The Birth of the Prison*. Durham, NC: Duke University Press, 2007.

Frank, Anna Marie. *Sports and Education: A Reference Handbook*. Santa Barbara, CA: ABC-CLIO, 2003.

Frederickson, F. S. "Sport in the Cultures of Man." In *Science and Medicine in Exercise in Sports*, edited by W. R. Johnson. New York: Harper & Row, 1960, 633–38.

Freedman, Josh. "Subsidized Saturdays: The Tax-Free World of College Football," *Forbes*, December 23, 2013. www.forbes.com/sites/joshfreedman/2013/12/23/subsidized-saturdays-the-tax-free-world-of-college-football/.

Freedman, Laura. "Pay or Play—The Jeremy Bloom Decision and NCAA Amateurism Rules." *Fordham Intellectual Property, Media & Entertainment Law Journal* 13 (2003): 673–711.

Freidson, Eliot. *Professionalism, the Third Logic: On the Practice of Knowledge*. Chicago: University of Chicago Press, 2001.

French, Roger Kenneth. *Medicine before Science: The Rational and Learned Doctor from the Middle Ages to the Enlightenment*. Cambridge: Cambridge University Press, 2003.

Frey, James H., and D. Stanley Eitzen. "Sport and Society." *Annual Review of Sociology* 17, no. 1 (1991): 503–22. https://doi.org/10.1146/annurev.so.17.080191.002443.

Fried, Barbara H. "Punting Our Future: College Athletics and Admissions." *Change* 39, no. 3 (January 1, 2007): 8–15. https://doi.org/10.3200/CHNG.39.3.8-15.

Funk, Daniel C., and Jeffrey D. James. "Consumer Loyalty: The Meaning of Attachment in the Development of Sport Team Allegiance." *Journal of Sport Management* 20, no. 2 (April 1, 2006): 189–217. https://doi.org/10.1123/jsm.20.2.189.

Fuoss, Donald, and R. J. Troppman. *Effective Coaching: A Psychological Approach*. New York: John Wiley & Sons, 1981.

Furillo, Andy. "Opinion: It's Time for UC Davis to Reexamine Its 'Principles.'" *Sacramento Bee*, April 19, 2015. www.sacbee.com/sports/spt-columns-blogs/andy-furillo/article19001964.html.

———. "Winning Is Important to New UC Davis AD Kevin Blue." *Sacramento Bee*, May 20, 2016. www.sacbee.com/sports/spt-columns-blogs/andy-furillo/article78975662.html.

Gaines, Cork. "The Amount Networks Are Paying to Broadcast NFL Games Is Skyrocketing." Business Insider, November 23, 2015. www.businessinsider.com/nfl-tv-rights-revenue-2015-11.

Gaines, Judith. "Young Athletes Can Pay High Price for Injuries." *Boston Globe*, April 13, 2003.

Gallico, Paul. *Farewell to Sport*. New York: Knopf, 1941.

Gallimore, Ronald, and Roland Tharp. "What a Coach Can Teach a Teacher, 1975–2004: Reflections and Reanalysis of John Wooden's Teaching Practices." *Sport Psychologist* 18, no. 2 (June 1, 2004): 119–37. https://doi.org/10.1123/tsp.18.2.119.

Ganim, Sara. "CNN Analysis: Some College Athletes Play Like Adults, Read Like 5th-Graders." CNN, January 8, 2014. www.cnn.com/2014/01/07/us/ncaa-athletes-reading-scores/.

Gardiner, E. Norman. *Athletics of the Ancient World*. London: Oxford University Press, 1930.

Garrido, Augie. *Life Is Yours to Win: Lessons Forged from the Purpose, Passion, and Magic of Baseball*. New York: Touchstone, 2012.

Gavora, Jessica. *Tilting the Playing Field: Schools, Sports, Sex and Title IX*. San Francisco: Encounter Books, 2002.

Geertz, Clifford. "Deep Play: Notes on the Balinese Cockfight." In *Culture and Politics: A Reader*, edited by Lane Crothers and Charles Lockhart. New York: Palgrave Macmillan, 2000, 175–201. https://doi.org/10.1007/978-1-349-62965-7_10.

Geiger, Roger, and Donald E. Heller. "Financial Trends in Higher Education: United States." Penn State Center for the Study of Higher Education, Working Paper no. 6, 2011.

Gems, Gerald R. *The Athletic Crusade: Sport and American Cultural Imperialism*. Lincoln: University of Nebraska Press, 2006.

———. "Football and Cultural Values." *College Football Historical Society* 10, no. 4 (August 1997): 1.

———. *For Pride, Profit, and Patriarchy: Football and the Incorporation of American Cultural Values*. Lanham, MD: Scarecrow Press, 2000.

Gentry, James K., and Raquel Meyer Alexander. "Pay for Women's Basketball Coaches Lags Far Behind That of Men's Coaches." *New York Times*, April 2, 2012.

George, Christeen, Andrew Hartley, and Jenny Paris. "The Representation of Female Athletes in Textual and Visual Media." *Corporate Communications* 6, no. 2 (January 1, 2001): 94–101. https://doi.org/10.1108/13563280110391007.

George, Nelson. *Elevating the Game: Black Men and Basketball*. Lincoln: University of Nebraska Press, 1999.

Gerdy, John R. *Air Ball: American Education's Failed Experiment with Elite Athletics*. Jackson: University Press of Mississippi, 2009.

———. "For True Reform, Athletics Scholarships Must Go." *Chronicle of Higher Education* 52, no. 36 (2006).

———. *Sports: The All-American Addiction*. Jackson: University Press of Mississippi, 2010.

———. *The Successful College Athletic Program: The New Standard*. Phoenix, AZ: Oryx Press, 1997.

Giambalvo, Emily. "As the NCAA Asks Congress for Help on NIL Legislation, Lawmakers Want More Rights for College Athletes." *Washington Post*, July 23, 2020.

Gibson, John H. *Performance versus Results: A Critique of Values in Contemporary Sport*. Albany, NY: SUNY Press, 1993.

Gill, Rosalind. "Breaking the Silence: The Hidden Injuries of Neo-Liberal Academia." In *Secrecy and Silence in the Research Process: Feminist Reflections*, edited by R. Flood and R. Gill. London: Routledge, 2009, 228–44.

Giulianotti, Richard. "Sport, Globalization and Development: Making the Global Civil Society." *ISSA 2008*, Kyoto, Japan, July 26–29.

Gladwell, Malcolm. "The Order of Things: What College Rankings Really Tell Us." *New Yorker*, February 14 and 21, 2011, 68–75.

Glamser, Francis. "School Sport in England: A Comparative View." *Journal of Sport Behavior* 11, no. 1 (1988): 193–208.

Gmelch, George. *Inside Pitch: Life in Professional Baseball*. Lincoln: University of Nebraska Press, 2006.

———. "Magic in Professional Baseball." In *Games, Sports and Power*, edited by Gregory P. Stone. New Brunswick, NJ: Dutton, 1972, 128–37.

Goffman, Erving. *Asylums: Essays on the Social Situation of Mental Patients and Other Inmates*. Piscataway, NJ: Aldine Transaction, 1968.

———. *The Presentation of Self in Everyday Life*. Garden City, NY: Doubleday Anchor, 1959.

Goldstein, Dana. *The Teacher Wars: A History of America's Most Embattled Profession*. New York: Anchor Books, 2015.

Golfweek. "Title IX Has Bolstered Women's College Golf, But Not Without Cost," November 9, 2002. https://golfweek.com/2002/11/09/2002-title-ix-has-bolstered-womens-college-golf-no/.

Goodhart, Philip, and Christopher John Chataway. *War Without Weapons*. London: W. H. Allen & Company, 1968.

Gootman, Elissa, and Catherine Saint Louis. "Maternity Leave? It's More Like a Pause." *New York Times*, July 20, 2012.

Gould, Daniel, and Nicole Damarjian. "Mental Skills Training in Sport." In *Training in Sport: Applying Sport Science*, edited by Bruce Elliot. Chicester, UK: John C. Wiley & Sons, 1998, 69–116.

Gould, Daniel, and Elizabeth M. Wright. "Psychology of Sports Coaching." In *Oxford Handbook of Sports and Performance Psychology*. Oxford: Oxford University Press, 2012, 343–63.

Graham, Hugh Davis. "The Storm over Grove City College: Civil Rights Regulation, Higher Education, and the Reagan Administration." *History of Education Quarterly* 38, no. 4 (1998): 407–29. https://doi.org/10.2307/369849.

Grasgreen, Allie. "A Scale That Slides . . . Too Much." Inside Higher Ed, January 9, 2012. www.insidehighered.com/news/2012/01/09/ncaa-convention-presentation-says-some-athletes-lack-basic-academic-skills.

Green, Andy. "Education, Globalisation and the Role of Comparative Research." *London Review of Education* 1, no. 2 (2003): 84–97.
Greene, Dan. "Ed O'Bannon: How to Fix College Sports and Revamp the Student-Athlete Experience." *Sports Illustrated*, February 9, 2018. www.si.com/college-basketball/2018/02/09/ed-obannon-interview-court-justice-ncaa-lawsuit-college-athletes-paid.
Greenstone, Michael, and Adam Looney. "Where Is the Best Place to Invest $102,000—In Stocks, Bonds, or a College Degree?" Brookings Institution. www.brookings.edu/research/papers/2011/06/25-education-greenstone-looney.
Gregory, Sean. "College Athletes Are Realizing Their Power amid the George Floyd Protests and COVID-19." *Time*, June 18, 2020. https://time.com/5855471/college-athletes-covid-19-protests-racial-equality/.
Grundy, Pamela, and Susan Shackelford. *Shattering the Glass: The Remarkable History of Women's Basketball*. Chapel Hill: University of North Carolina Press, 2017.
Grundy, Pamela, and Benjamin Rader. *American Sports: From the Age of Folk Games to the Age of Televised Sports*. New York: Pearson, 2015.
Gumbrecht, Hans Ulrich. *In Praise of Athletic Beauty*. Cambridge, MA: Harvard University Press, 2006.
Gurney, Gerald, Donna A. Lopiano, and Andrew Zimbalist. *Unwinding Madness: What Went Wrong with College Sports and How to Fix It*. Washington, DC: Brookings Institution Press, 2017.
Gutting, Gary. "The Real Humanities Crisis." *New York Times*, November 30, 2013.
Guttmann, Allen. *From Ritual to Record: The Nature of Modern Sports*. New York: Columbia University Press, 2004.
———. *Sports Spectators*. New York: Columbia University Press, 1986.
———. *Women's Sports: A History*. New York: Columbia University Press, 1991.
Haag, Herbert. "Research in 'Sport Pedagogy'—One Field of Theoretical Study in the Science of Sport." *International Review of Education* 35, no. 1 (March 1, 1989): 5–16. https://doi.org/10.1007/BF00597680.
Hacker, Jacob S., and Paul Pierson. *Winner-Take-All Politics: How Washington Made the Rich Richer—And Turned Its Back on the Middle Class*. New York: Simon & Schuster, 2010.
Hagens Berman Law Firm. "Student-Athletes Reach $208 Million Settlement with NCAA over Scholarship Antitrust Claims." http://www.hbsslaw.com/press/ncaa-scholarships-class-action/student-athletes-reach-208-million-settlement-with-ncaa-over-scholarship-antitrust-claims.
Hall, Granville Stanley. *Jesus, the Christ, in the Light of Psychology*. Boston, MA: D. Appleton, 1923.
Hall, Kita. "Performativity." *Journal of Linguistic Anthropology* 9, nos. 1–2 (June 1999): 184–87.
Harari, Yuval Noah. *Sapiens: A Brief History of Humankind*. New York: Harper Perennial, 2018.

Hardin, Marie, Erin Whiteside, and Erin Ash. "Ambivalence on the Front Lines? Attitudes Toward Title IX and Women's Sports among Division I Sports Information Directors." *International Review for the Sociology of Sport* 49, no. 1 (February 1, 2014): 42–64. https://doi.org/10.1177/1012690212450646.

Hargreaves, Jennifer. *Sporting Females: Critical Issues in the History and Sociology of Women's Sports*. London: Routledge, 1994.

Harris, S. J. "Sport Is New Opium of the People." *Democrat and Chronicle*, November 3, 1981, 3B.

Hart, Barbara A., Cynthia A. Hasbrook, and Sharon A. Mathes. "An Examination of the Reduction in the Number of Female Interscholastic Coaches." *Research Quarterly for Exercise and Sport* 57, no. 1 (March 1, 1986): 68–77. https://doi.org/10.1080/02701367.1986.10605390.

Harvey, David. *A Brief History of Neoliberalism*. Oxford: Oxford University Press, 2007.

Hatteberg, Sarah J. "Under Surveillance: Collegiate Athletics as a Total Institution." *Sociology of Sport Journal* 35, no. 2 (June 1, 2018): 149–58. https://doi.org/10.1123/ssj.2017-0096.

Head, Fay A. "Student Teaching as Initiation into the Teaching Profession." *Anthropology & Education Quarterly* 23, no. 2 (1992): 89–107. https://anthrosource.onlinelibrary.wiley.com/doi/abs/10.1525/aeq.1992.23.2.05x1260l.

Heath, Shirley Brice, and Juliet Langman. "Shared Thinking and the Register of Coaching." In *Perspectives on Socially Shared Cognition*, edited by L. Resnick, J. Levine, and S. D. Teasley. Washington, DC: American Psychological Association, 1994, 101–24.

Henderson, Robert W. *Ball, Bat and Bishop: The Origin of Ballgames*. New York: Rockport Press, 1947.

Hennessey, John. "Committed to Diversity in Many Forms: Expanding the Intellectual Base Helps All Students." *Stanford Magazine*, May–June 2003. https://stanfordmag.org/contents/committed-to-diversity-in-many-forms.

Henricks, Thomas S. "Sport and Social Hierarchy in Medieval England." *Journal of Sport History* 9, no. 2 (1982): 20–37.

Heyman, Brian. "W.N.B.A. Internships Put Players to Work." *New York Times*, December 5, 2010.

Higgs, Robert. *Sports: A Reference Guide*. Westport, CT: Greenwood Press, 1982.

Hilborn, Harold B. "Student-Athletes and Judicial Inconsistency: Establishing a Duty to Educate as a Means of Fostering Meaningful Reform of Intercollegiate Athletics." *Northwestern University Law Review* 80 (1995): 722–66.

Hoberman, John M. "History of the Science of Human Performance and Sport." www.sportsci.org/encyc/drafts/History_sport_science.doc.

———. *Mortal Engines: The Science of Performance and the Dehumanization of Sport*. New York: Free Press, 1992.

Hobsbawm, Eric, and Terence Ranger. *The Invention of Tradition*. Cambridge: Cambridge University Press, 2012.

Hobson, Will, and Emily Guskin. "Poll: Majority of Black Americans Favor Paying College Athletes, 6 in 10 Whites Disagree." *Washington Post*, September 4, 2017. www.washingtonpost.com/sports/colleges/poll-majority-of-black-americans-favor-paying-college-athletes-6-in-10-whites-disagree/2017/09/14/27fa5fc2-98df-11e7-87fc-c3f7ee4035c9_story.html?noredirect=on&utm_term=.7b3d68b3b15a.

Hobson, Will, and Steven Rich. "Colleges Spend Fortunes on Lavish Athletic Facilities." *Washington Post*, December 23, 2015. http://www.chicagotribune.com/sports/college/ct-athletic-facilities-expenses-20151222-story.html.

Hoffman, Shirl. "Becoming a Physical Activity Professional." In *Introduction to Kinesiology: Studying Physical Activity*, edited by Shirl Hoffman. Champaign IL: Human Kinetics, 2013, 323–56.

Hollands, Robert G. "The Role of Cultural Studies and Social Criticism in the Sociological Study of Sport." *Quest* 36, no. 1 (January 1, 1984): 66–79. https://doi.org/10.1080/00336297.1984.10483802.

Holmes, Douglas R. *Cultural Disenchantments: Worker Peasantries in Northeast Italy*. Princeton, NJ: Princeton University Press, 1989.

Holt, Nicholas L. *Positive Youth Development through Sport*. London: Routledge, 2007.

Holt, Richard. *Sport and the British: A Modern History*. Cambridge: Clarendon Press, 1990.

Homans, Jennifer. "A Woman's Place." *New York Times*, September 13, 2012.

Horger, Marc Thomas. "Play by the Rules: The Creation of Basketball and the Progressive Era, 1891–1917." PhD dissertation, Ohio State University, 2001.

Horkheimer, Max. "New Patterns in Social Relations." In *Philosophical Inquiry and Sport*, edited by W. J. Morgan and K. V. Meier. Champaign, IL: Human Kinetics Publishers, 1964.

Horne, John, Alan Tomlinson, and Gary Whannel. *Understanding Sport: An Introduction to the Sociological and Cultural Analysis of Sports*. New York: E. & F.N. Spon, 1999.

Horner, Matthew, Neal Ternes, and Christopher McLeod. "Not Going Pro: On Seeking Lasting Returns from College Sports." *Journal of Amateur Sport* 2, no. 1 (February 29, 2016): 188–213. https://doi.org/10.17161/jas.v2i1.5017.

Hughson, John. "Special Issue: The Making of Sports Cultures." *Sport in Society* 12, no. 1 (2009): 1–140.

Huizinga, Johan. *Homo Ludens*. New York: Roy Publishers, 1950.

Hult, Joan S., and Marianna Trekell, eds. *A Century of Women's Basketball: From Frailty to Final Four*. AAHPERD Publications, 1991.

Huma, Ramogi, and Ellen Staurowsky. "TV Money Windfall in Big Time College Sports." http://assets.usw.org/ncpa/pdfs/TV-Money-Windfall-in-Big-Time-College-Sports.pdf.

Huma, R., E. J. Staurowsky, and L. Montgomery. "How the NCAA's Empire Robs Predominantly Black Athletes of Billions in Generational Wealth." Riverside, CA: National College Players Association, 2020. https://drive.google.com/file/d/1z97vhcjErrHIvuO3Nu2wUWbG90bFKnm_/view.

Humphreys, Brad R. "Equal Pay on the Hardwood: The Earnings Gap between Male and Female NCAA Division I Basketball Coaches." *Journal of Sports Economics* 1, no. 3 (2000): 299–307. https://journals.sagepub.com/doi/abs/10.1177/152700250000100306.

Hurn, Christopher. "Changes in Authority Relationships in Schools: 1960–1980." *Research in Sociology of Education and Socialization* 5, no. 1 (1985): 31–57.

Hyman, Mark. *Until It Hurts: America's Obsession with Youth Sports and How It Harms Our Kids*. Boston, MA: Beacon Press, 2009.

Ingalls, Zoë. "The Fine Art of Recruiting Superstars for Big-Time Women's Basketball." *Chronicle of Higher Education* 26, no. 5 (1983): 21–24.

Ingham, Alan. "Review of Goldstein, J. H. *Sports Violence*." *Contemporary Sociology* 13, no. 3 (1984): 298–300.

Ingold, Tim. "Editorial." *Man* 27, no. 4 (1992): 693–96.

Inside Higher Ed. "North Carolina and Coach Settle Sexual Harassment Suit," January 15, 2008. www.insidehighered.com/news/2008/01/15/north-carolina-and-coach-settle-sexual-harassment-suit.

Investopedia. "Margin Definition." www.investopedia.com/terms/m/margin.asp.

Irick, Erin. "NCAA Sports Sponsorship and Participation Rates Report: 1981-82- 2015-16." Indianapolis, IN: National Collegiate Athletic Association, 2015.

Isaacs, Neil. D. *All the Moves: A History of U.S. College Basketball*. New York: HarperCollins, 1984.

Jackson, Victoria. "Take It From a Former Division I Athlete: College Sports Are Like Jim Crow." *Los Angeles Times*. www.latimes.com/opinion/op-ed/la-oe-jackson-college-sports-20180111-story.html.

———. "Title IX and the Big Time: Women's Intercollegiate Athletics at the University of North Carolina." PhD dissertation, Arizona State University, 2015.

Jacobs, Peter. "Here's the Insane Amount of Time Student-Athletes Spend on Practice." Business Insider, January 27, 2015. www.businessinsider.com/college-student-athletes-spend-40-hours-a-week-practicing-2015-1.

James, C. L. R. *Beyond a Boundary: 50th Anniversary Edition*. Durham, NC: Duke University Press, 2013.

James, Wendy. *The Ceremonial Animal: A New Portrait of Anthropology*. Oxford: Oxford University Press, 2005.

———. "Human Worlds Are Socially Constructed: For the Motion." In *Key Debates in Anthropology*, edited by Tim Ingold. London: Routledge, 2003, 105–11.

———. *The Writings of William James*. Chicago: University of Chicago Press, 1977.

Jenkins, Richard. *Pierre Bourdieu*. London: Routledge, 1992.

Jenkins, Simon P. R. *Sports Science Handbook: The Essential Guide to Kinesiology, Sport and Exercise Science, Volumes 1 and 2*. Brentwood, UK: Multi-Science Publishing, 2005.

Jenkins, Wesley. "Hundreds of Colleges May Be Out of Compliance with Title IX. Here's Why." October 23, 2019. https://www.chronicle.com/article/hundreds-of-colleges-may-be-out-of-compliance-with-title-ix-heres-why/.

Jet. "Ex-Georgetown University Coach John Thompson Supports Female Coaches for Male Sports Teams," March 29, 1999.
Johnson, Gary. "Women's Basketball Attendance Sets All-Time High," June 6, 2012. https://www.ncaa.org/about/resources/media-center/news/women-s-basketball-attendance-sets-all-time-high.
Johnson, Robert Carl. "Walter Camp and James Naismith: The Shapers of a Culture." *North American Society for Sport History, Proceedings and Newsletter*, 1989. https://digital.la84.org/digital/collection/p17103coll10/id/11051/rec/1, p. 16.
Jones, Robyn L., ed. *The Sports Coach as Educator: Re-conceptualising Sports Coaching*. London: Routledge, 2006.
Jones, Robyn L., Kathleen M. Armour, and Paul Potrac. *Sports Coaching Cultures: From Practice to Theory*. Hove, UK: Psychology Press, 2004.
Jones, Robyn L., and Kieran Kingston. *An Introduction to Sports Coaching: Connecting Theory to Practice*. London: Routledge, 2013.
Jurewitz, Ross A. "Playing at Even Strength: Reforming Title IX Enforcement in Intercollegiate Athletics." *American University Journal of Gender, Social Policy & the Law* 8 (2000): 283–351.
Kawakami, Tim. "VanDerveer, Mullin Bring Grace to Hall." *San Jose Mercury News*, August 13, 2011.
Keenan, Matthew. "Stanford Tops Harvard, Yale with $911 Million in Private Gifts." *Arkansas Democrat–Gazette*, February 21, 2007. https://www.arkansasonline.com/news/2007/feb/21/stanford-tops-yale-harvard-911-million-private-gif/.
Kent, Michael, ed. *Oxford Dictionary of Sports Science and Medicine*. Oxford: Oxford University Press, 1998.
Kenyon, Gerald S., and John W. Loy, eds. *Sport, Culture, and Society: A Reader on the Sociology of Sport*. New York: Macmillan, 1969.
Kiley, Kevin. "Playing Different Games." Inside Higher Ed, January 16, 2013. www.insidehighered.com/news/2013/01/16/universities-spend-more-athletics-athlete-academics-student-report-finds#ixzz2IeIy6rhS.
Kindberg, Scott. "VanDerveer Loves Her Time Here." Chautauqua Sports Hall of Fame. https://www.chautauquasportshalloffame.org/taravanderveer2010.php.
King, Billie Jean, and Frank Deford. *Billie Jean*. New York: Viking, 1982.
Kirk, David, Carlton Cooke, Anne Flintoff, and Jim McKenna. *Key Concepts in Sport and Exercise Sciences*. Thousand Oaks, CA: Sage Publications, 2008.
Kirk, Jason. "Here's Exactly How Josh Rosen Wants to Modernize Amateurism." SBNation, July 16, 2018. www.sbnation.com/platform/amp/college-football/2018/7/16/17577578/josh-rosen-ncaa-amateurism-plan.
Kissoudi, Penelope. "Antidote to War: The Balkan Games." In *Military, Sport, Europe: War Without Weapons*, edited by J. A. Mangan. London: Frank Cass, 2001, 145–68.
Klein, Alan M. *Little Big Men: Bodybuilding Subculture and Gender Construction*. Albany, New York: SUNY Press, 1993.

———. *Sugarball: The American Game, the Dominican Dream*. New Haven, CT: Yale University Press, 1991.
Klein, Naomi. *The Shock Doctrine: The Rise of Disaster Capitalism*. New York: Henry Holt & Company, 2010.
Knapp, Gwen. "Women's NCAA Tournament." Associated Press, March 29, 2010.
Knight Commission on Intercollegiate Athletics. "A Call to Action: Reconnecting College Sports and Higher Education (2001)." www.knightcommission.org/images/pdfs/2001_knight_report.pdf.
———. "Restoring the Balance: Dollars, Values, and the Future of College Sports (2010)." www.knightcommission.org/images/restoringbalance/KCIA_Report_F.pdf.
Knight, Phil. *Shoe Dog: A Memoir by the Creator of Nike*. New York: Simon & Schuster, 2016.
Knoester, Chris, and David B. Ridpath. "Should College Athletes Be Allowed to Be Paid? A Public Opinion Analysis." *Sociology of Sport Journal* 1 (2020): 1–13. https://journals.humankinetics.com/view/journals/ssj/aop/article-10.1123-ssj.2020-0015/article-10.1123-ssj.2020-0015.xml.
Knoppers, Annelies. "Gender and the Coaching Profession." *Quest* 39, no. 1 (1987): 9–22.
Koch, James V., and Wilbert M. Leonard. "The NCAA: A Socio-Economic Analysis: The Development of the College Sports Cartel from Social Movement to Formal Organization." *American Journal of Economics and Sociology* 37, no. 3 (1978): 225–39.
Kohn, Alfie. *No Contest: The Case Against Competition*. New York: Houghton Mifflin Harcourt, 1992.
Kohn, Marek. *The Race Gallery: The Return of Racial Science*. London: Jonathan Cape, 1995.
Kosloski, Philip. "How a Christian Invented Basketball and Made It an Evangelization Tool." Aleteia, December 21, 2016. https://aleteia.org/2016/12/21/how-a-christian-invented-basketball-and-made-it-an-evangelization-tool/.
Krause, Karen. "Augusta National Adds First Two Female Members." *New York Times*, August 20, 2012.
Kretchmar, Robert Scott. *Practical Philosophy of Sport and Physical Activity*. Champaign, IL: Human Kinetics, 2005.
Kyle, Donald G. *Sport and Spectacle in the Ancient World*. New York: John Wiley & Sons, 2014.
Lambert, Craig, and John T. Bethell. "First and 100." *Harvard Magazine*, September 2003. http://harvardmagazine.com/2003/09/first-and-100.html.
Lancy, David, and B. Tindall. "The Anthropological Study of Play: Problems and Prospects." *Sociology, Social Work and Anthropology Faculty Publications*, January 1, 1976. https://digitalcommons.usu.edu/sswa_facpubs/103.
Landicho, Marisa. "Athletics Budget on Stable Ground." *Stanford Daily*, July 29, 2010. www.stanforddaily.com/2010/07/29/athletics-budget-on-stable-ground/.

Lannin, Joanne. *A History of Basketball for Girls and Women: From Bloomers to the Big Leagues*. Minneapolis, MN: Lerner Publishing Group, 2000.

Lanter, Jason R., and Billy J. Hawkins. "The Economic Model of Intercollegiate Athletics and Its Effects on the College Athlete Educational Experience." *Journal of Intercollegiate Sport* 6, no. 1 (2013): 86–95.

Lapchick, Richard Edward. *Broken Promises: Racism in American Sports*. New York: St. Martin's Press, 1984.

Lapchick, Richard Edward, and D. Baker. "The 2015 Racial and Gender Report Card: College Sport." Institute for Diversity and Ethics in Sport. https://43530132-36e9-4f52-811a-182c7a91933b.filesusr.com/ugd/7d86e5_9969908c0d7d49caa793b14ae8d954ec.pdf.

Larmer, Brook. "Fast Living." *Time*, June 18, 2008. http://content.time.com/time/specials/2007/article/0,28804,1815747_1815707_1815673,00.html.

Lave, Jean, and Etienne Wenger. *Situated Learning: Legitimate Peripheral Participation*. Cambridge: Cambridge University Press, 1991.

LeCompte, Margaret. "Learning to Work: The Hidden Curriculum of the Classroom." *Anthropology & Education Quarterly* 9, no. 1:22–37. https://anthrosource.onlinelibrary.wiley.com/doi/abs/10.1525/aeq.1978.9.1.05x1748z.

Lenk, Hans. *Social Philosophy of Athletics: A Pluralistic and Practice-Oriented Philosophical Analysis of Top Level Amateur Sport*. Champaign, IL: Stipes, 1979.

Leseth, Anne. "The Use of *Juju* in Football: Sport and Witchcraft in Tanzania." In *Entering the Field: New Perspectives on World Football*, edited by G. Armstrong and E. Giulianotti. Oxford: Berg, 1997.

Lesser, Alexander. "The Pawnee Ghost Dance Hand Game: A Study of Cultural Change." *Columbia University Contributions to Anthropology, Volume 16*. New York: Columbia University Press, 1933.

Lewis, J. Lowell. *Ring of Liberation: A Deceptive Discourse in Brazilian Capoeira*. Chicago: University of Chicago Press, 1992.

Liberti, Rita M. "'Gendering the Gym': A History of Women in Physical Education." *Kinesiology Review* 6, no. 2 (May 2017): 153–66.

———. "Trailblazing in Marin: Women's Dipsea Hikes, 1918–1922." *California History* 81, no. 1 (2002): 54–65.

———. "'We Were Ladies, We Just Played Basketball Like Boys': African American Womanhood and Competitive Basketball at Bennett College, 1928-1942." *Journal of Sport History* 26, no. 3 (1999): 567-584.

Lickona, Thomas. *Educating for Character*. New York: Bantam Books, 1991.

Lidz, Franz. "Tennis, Everyone?" *Sports Illustrated*, October 16, 1991. https://www.si.com/vault/1991/10/16/125154/tennis-everyone-when-helen-wills-and-suzanne-lenglen-clashed-on-the-riviera-in-1926-the-whole-world-awaited-the-news.

Liebendorfer, Don E. *The Color of Life Is Red: A History of Stanford Athletics, 1892–1972*. Stanford, CA: Department of Athletics, Stanford University, 1972.

Light, Richard. *Positive Pedagogy for Sport Coaching: Athlete-Centred Coaching for Individual Sports*. London: Routledge, 2016.

Light, Richard L., and Stephen Harvey. "Positive Pedagogy for Sport Coaching." *Sport, Education and Society* 22, no. 2 (February 17, 2017): 271–87. https://doi.org/10.1080/13573322.2015.1015977.

Light, Richard, and David Kirk. "High School Rugby, the Body and the Reproduction of Hegemonic Masculinity." *Sport, Education and Society* 5, no. 2 (October 1, 2000): 163–76. https://doi.org/10.1080/713696032.

Lock, Daniel, Tracy Taylor, Daniel Funk, and Simon Darcy. "Exploring the Development of Team Identification." *Journal of Sport Management* 26, no. 4 (July 2012): 283–94. https://doi.org/10.1123/jsm.26.4.283.

Longman, Jeré. "Before Games, Wins for Women." *New York Times*, July 14, 2012a.

———. "Education First, Beating UCONN a Close Second." *New York Times*, March 21, 2010c.

———. "For Lolo Jones, Everything Is Image." *New York Times*, August 4, 2012b.

———. *The Girls of Summer*. New York: HarperCollins, 2009.

———. "A History of Fearlessness." *New York Times*, August 24, 2011c.

———. "Problem Child Becomes Complete Player." *New York Times*, April 5, 2010d.

———. "Stanford Beats UCONN to Halt Streak at 90." *New York Times*, December 30, 2010b.

———. "Stanford Pushes, But Not Far Enough." *New York Times*, April 6, 2010a.

Lopiano, Donna, Gerald Gurney, Mary Willingham, Brian Porto, David B. Ridpath, Allen Sack, and Andrew Zimbalist. "The Drake Group Position Statement: Rights of College Athletes." Drake Group, 2018. http://thedrakegroup.org.

Lopiano, Donna, Brian Porto, Gerald Gurney, David B. Ridpath, Allen Sack, Mary Willingham, and Andrew Zimbalist. "The Drake Group Position Statement: Compensation of College Athletes Including Revenues from Commercial Use of Their Names, Likenesses, and Images." Drake Group. http://thedrakegroup.org.

Lovejoy, A. *The Great Chain of Being: A Study of the History of an Idea*. London: Routledge, 2017.

Loy, John W. "The Nature of Sport." In *Sport and Social Systems*, edited by John W. Loy and Gerald Kenyon. Reading, MA: Addison-Wesley, 1969.

Loy, John W., Douglas Booth, and Richard Giulianotti. "Consciousness, Craft, Commitment: The Sociological Imagination of C. Wright Mills." *Sport and Modern Social Theorists* (2004): 65–80.

Loy, John W. and Gerald Kenyon, eds. *Sport, Culture and Society: A Reader on the Sociology of Sport*. London: Macmillan & Co, 1969.

Lumpkin, Angela. *Modern Sports Ethics: A Reference Handbook*. Santa Barbara, CA: ABC-CLIO, 2009.

Luschen, Gunther. "Sociology of Sport: Development, Present State, and Prospects." *Annual Review of Sociology* 6, no. 1 (1980): 315–47.

Luschen, Gunther, and George H. Sage. *Handbook of Social Science of Sport*. Champaign, IL: Stipes, 1981.

Luxbacher, Joseph A., and Shirl J. Hoffman. "Careers in Coaching and Sport Instruction." In *Introduction to Kinesiology: Studying Physical Activity*, edited by S. Hoffman. Champaign IL: Human Kinetics, 2013, 447–47.

Lyle, John. "The Coaching Process: An Overview." In *The Coaching Process: Principles and Practice for Sport*, edited by N. Cross and J. Lyle. Oxford: Butterworth-Heinemann, 1999.

MacAloon, John. *This Great Symbol: Pierre de Coubertin and the Origins of the Modern Olympic Games*. London: Routledge, 2007.

Macleod, D. I. *Building Character in the American Boy: The Boy Scouts, YMCA, and Their Forerunners, 1870–1920*. Madison: University of Wisconsin Press, 1983.

MacMillan, Margaret. *The Uses and Abuses of History*. New York: Profile, 2009.

Mague, Anthony. "Stanford's Injury-Causing, Springy Floor to Be Removed." *Daily Orange*, February 2004. http://dailyorange.com/2004/02/stanford-s-injury-causing-springy-floor-to-be-removed/.

Mahiri, Jabari. "African American Males and Learning: What Discourse in Sports Offers Schooling." *Anthropology & Education Quarterly* 25, no. 3 (1994): 364–75. https://doi.org/10.1525/aeq.1994.25.3.04x0150t.

Malina, Robert M. "Anthropology, Growth, and Physical Education." In *Physical Education: An Interdisciplinary Approach*, edited by Robert Singer et al. New York: Macmillan, 1972, 239–309.

Malinowski, Bronislaw. *A Diary in the Strict Sense of the Term, 1914–1918*. London: Routledge & Kegan Paul, 1967.

Mandelbaum, Michael. *The Meaning of Sports*. New York: Public Affairs, 2005.

Mangalindan, J. P. "The Secretive Billionaire Who Built Silicon Valley." *Fortune*, July 7, 2014. http://fortune.com/2014/07/07/arrillaga-silicon-valley/.

Mangan, J. A. *Europe, Sport, World: Shaping Global Societies*. London: Routledge, 2013.

———. *The Games Ethic and Imperialism: Aspects of the Diffusion of an Ideal*. London: Frank Cass, 1986.

———, ed. *Militarism, Sport, Europe: War Without Weapons*. London: Frank Cass, 2003.

———. "Prologue: Combative Sports and Combative Societies." In *Military, Sport, Europe: War Without Weapons*, edited by J. A. Mangan. London: Frank Cass, 2003, 1–9.

Mangan, J. A., and Callum McKenzie. "'Pig-Sticking Is the Greatest Fun': Martial Conditioning on the Hunting Fields of Empire." In *Military, Sport, Europe: War Without Weapons*, edited by J. A. Mangan. London: Frank Cass, 2003, 97–119.

Mangan, J. A., and Hamad S. Ndee. "Military Drills—Rather More Than 'Brief and Basic': English Elementary Schools in English Militarism." In *Military, Sport, Europe: War Without Weapons*, edited by J. A. Mangan. London: Frank Cass, 2003, 67–99.

Mann, Leon. "Sport Crowds Viewed from the Perspective of Collective Behavior." In *Sports, Games and Play*, edited by Jeffrey H. Goldstein. Hillsdale, NJ: Lawrence Erlbaum Associates, 1979, 337–68.

Manning, Frank. "Celebrating Cricket: The Symbolic Construction of Caribbean Politics." *American Ethnologist* 8, no. 3 (1981): 616–32.

Manza Young, Shalise. "Women Hurt Most by Lack of NIL, Social Media Money." Yahoo! March 29, 2021. https://sports.yahoo.com/on-top-of-tournament-inequities-the-nca-as-arcane-nil-rules-hurt-womens-basketball-players-most-too-204948049.html.

Marcus, George E. *Ethnography Through Thick and Thin*. Princeton, NJ: Princeton University Press, 1998.

———. *Lives in Trust: The Fortunes of Dynastic Families in Late Twentieth-Century America*. Boulder, CO: Westview Press, 1992.

———. "The Uses of Complicity in the Changing Mise-en-Scène of Anthropological Fieldwork." *Representations* 59, no. 1 (1997): 85–108.

Marcus, Ruth, and Helen Dewar. "Reagan Vetoes Civil Rights Restoration Act." *Washington Post*, March 17, 1988.

Marcuse, Herbert. *One-Dimensional Man: Studies in the Ideology of Advanced Industrial Society*. Boston, MA: Beacon Press, 1964.

Markula, Pirkko. "Firm but Shapely, Fit but Sexy, Strong but Thin: The Postmodern Aerobicizing Female Bodies." *Sociology of Sport Journal* 12, no. 4 (1995): 424–53.

Martens, Rainer. *Coaches Guide to Sport Psychology*. Champaign, IL: Human Kinetics, 1987.

———. *Social Psychology and Physical Activity*. New York: Harper & Row, 1975.

———. *Successful Coaching*. Champaign, IL: Human Kinetics Press, 1997.

Martens, Rainer et al. *Coaching Young Athletes*. Champaign, IL: Human Kinetics Publishers, 1981.

Martin, Adam, and Mary G. McDonald. "Covering Women's Sport? An Analysis of *Sports Illustrated* Covers from 1987–2009 and *ESPN The Magazine* Covers from 1998–2009."

Marx, Karl. "*Capital* Volumes 1 and 3." In *The Marx-Engels Reader*, edited by R. C. Tucker. New York: W. W. Norton, 1978, 294–442.

———. "Economic and Philosophic Manuscripts of 1844." In *The Marx-Engels Reader*, edited by R. C. Tucker. New York: W. W. Norton, 1978, 66–125.

Mason, Andrew. "MacIntyre on Modernity and How It Has Marginalized the Virtues." In *How Should One Live?* edited by R. Crisp. Oxford: Clarendon Press, 1996, 191–209.

Mastrich, Jim. *Really Winning: Using Sports to Develop Character and Integrity in Our Boys*. New York: St. Martin's Press, 2002.

Mauss, Marcel. "Les Techniques du Corps." *Journal de Psychologie* 32, no. 1 (1934): 3–4.

Mayhew, Matthew, and Musbah Shaheen. "Why America Needs College Football." Inside Higher Ed, September 24, 2020. https://www.insidehighered.com/

views/2020/09/24/college-football-can-help-americans-get-through-current-difficult-times-opinion.

McCann, Michael. "Why the NCAA Lost Its Latest Landmark Case in the Battle Over What Schools Can Offer Athletes." *Sports Illustrated*, March 8, 2019. www.si.com/college-football/2019/03/08/ncaa-antitrust-lawsuit-claudia-wilken-alston-jenkins.

McClancy, Jeremy. "Sport, Identity and Ethnicity." In *Sport, Identity and Ethnicity*, edited by Jeremy McClancy. Oxford: Berg, 1996.

McCullick, Bryan, Don Belcher, and Paul Schem. "What Works in Coaching and Sport Instructor Certification Programs? The Participants' View." *Physical Education and Sport Pedagogy* 10, no. 2 (2005): 121–37.

McCullough, J. Brady. "Days of NCAA Having It Both Ways Should Be Nearing an End." *Los Angeles Times*, June 28, 2019.

McDonald, Mary G. "The Marketing of the Women's National Basketball Association and the Making of Postfeminism." *International Review for the Sociology of Sport* 35, no. 1 (2000): 35–47.

McGregor, A. "College Football Is a Symptom of Many of Society's Worst Problems, Not Central to the Democracy." Inside Higher Ed, September 27, 2020. https://www.insidehighered.com/views/2020/09/27/college-football-symptom-many-societys-worst-problems-not-central-democracy-letter.

McIntosh, P. C. *Physical Education in England since 1800*. London: G. Bell & Sons, 1952.

McKechnie, Alex. "Drexel and NCPA Study Shows NCAA's Use of 'Amateurism' Denies College Athletes Billions in Revenue." Drexel Now, March 25, 2013. http://drexel.edu/now/archive/2013/March/NCPA%20Study/.

McLaughlin, Thomas. *Give and Go: Basketball as a Cultural Practice*. Albany, New York: SUNY Press, 2008.

McMorris, Terry, and Tudor Hale. *Coaching Science: Theory into Practice*. Chicester, UK: John C. Wiley & Sons, 2006.

Mead, Margaret. *Coming of Age in Samoa*. New York: Mentor, 1949.

———. "Our Educational Emphases in Primitive Perspective." *American Journal of Sociology* 48, no. 6 (1943): 633–39.

Mechikoff, Robert A. *A History and Philosophy of Sport and Physical Education: From Ancient Civilizations to the Modern World*. New York: McGraw-Hill Higher Education, 2010.

Melnick, Ralph. *Senda Berenson: The Unlikely Founder of Women's Basketball*. Amherst, MA: University of Massachusetts Press, 2007.

Menand, Louis. "Glory Days: What We Watch When We Watch the Olympics." *New Yorker*, August 2012, 64–72.

Messner, Michael. "Boyhood, Organized Sports, and the Construction of Masculinities." *Journal of Contemporary Ethnography* 18, no. 4 (January 1, 1990): 416–44. https://doi.org/10.1177/089124190018004003.

———. *Power at Play: Sports and the Problem of Masculinity*. Boston, MA: Beacon Press, 1992.

———. "Sports and Male Domination: The Female Athlete as Contested Ideological Terrain." *Sociology of Sport Journal* 5, no. 3 (September 1, 1988): 197–211. https://doi.org/10.1123/ssj.5.3.197.

Messner, Michael, and Cheryl Cooky. "Gender in Televised Sports: News and Highlights Shows, 1989–2009." Center for Feminist Research, University of Southern California.

Messner, Michael A., Margaret Carlisle Duncan, and Cheryl Cooky. "Silence, Sports Bras, and Wrestling Porn: Women in Televised Sports News and Highlights Shows." *Journal of Sport and Social Issues* 27, no. 1 (February 1, 2003): 38–51. https://doi.org/10.1177/0193732502239583.

Meyer, Jayma, and Andrew Zimbalist. "A Win-Win: College Athletes Get Paid for Their Names, Images, and Likenesses and Colleges Maintain the Primacy of Academics." *Harvard Journal of Sports and Entertainment Law* 11 (2020): 247.

Milano, Michael, and Packianathan Chelladurai. "Gross Domestic Sport Product: The Size of the Sport Industry in the United States." *Journal of Sport Management* 25, no. 1 (January 1, 2011): 24–35. https://doi.org/10.1123/jsm.25.1.24.

Mill, John S. *On Liberty and Other Writings*. Cambridge: Cambridge University Press, 1859[1994].

———. 1869[1988]. *The Subjection of Women*. Indianapolis, IN: Hackett.

Miller, Aaron L. "Beyond the Four Walls of the Classroom: 'Real' and 'Imagined' Change in Japanese Sports and Education." In *Reimagining Japanese Education: Borders, Transfers, Circulations, and the Comparative*, edited by David Blake Willis and Jeremy Rappleye. Oxford: Symposium Books, 2011, 171–91.

———. "Corporal Punishment in Japan: One Path to Positive Anthropological Activism." *Anthropology in Action* 23, no. 1 (2016): 39–45.

———. "For Basketball Court and Company Cubicle: New Expectations for University Athletes and Corporate Employees in Japan." *Japanese Studies* 33, no. 1 (May 1, 2013): 63–81. https://doi.org/10.1080/10371397.2013.785627.

———. "Foucauldian Theory and the Making of the Japanese Sporting Body." *Contemporary Japan* 27, no. 1 (March 1, 2015): 13–31. https://doi.org/10.1515/cj-2015-0002.

———. "From Bushidō to Science: A New Pedagogy of Sports Coaching in Japan." *Japan Forum* 23, no. 3 (September 1, 2011): 385–406. https://doi.org/10.1080/09555803.2011.597054.

———. "Pan-Asian Sports and the Emergence of Modern Asia 1913–1974, by Stefan Huebner." *Japan Forum* 29, no. 3 (July 3, 2017): 429–31. https://doi.org/10.1080/09555803.2016.1269826.

———. "Taibatsu: From Educational Solution to Social Problem to Marginalized Non-issue." In *A Sociology of Japanese Youth: From Returnees to NEETs*, edited by R. Goodman, Yuki Imoto, and Tuukka Toivonen. London: Routledge, 2011, 81–97.

———. "*Taibatsu ni Kansuru Kokusaiteki Dōkō*" [International Trends Regarding Corporal Punishment]." *Sports Journal* 282, no. 1 (2009): 14–15.

———. "*Taibatsu*: Towards a Theory of Corporal Punishment in Schools and Sports in Japan." *Japan Forum* 21, no. 2 (2009): 233–54.

Miller, Aaron L., and Tuukka Toivonen. "To Discipline or Accommodate? On the Rehabilitation of Japanese 'Problem Youth.'" *Asia-Pacific Journal: Japan Focus*, May 31, 2010. www.japanfocus.org/-Aaron-Miller/3368.

Miller, Aaron L., and Z. Tummalapalli. "Being a Basketball Fan during the Black Lives Matter Movement and a Global Pandemic." Society Pages, October 6, 2020. https://thesocietypages.org/engagingsports/2020/10/06/being-a-basketball-fan-during-the-black-lives-matter-movement-and-a-global-pandemic/#comments.

Miller, Ted. "Stanford Football: Character, Cruelty." ESPN, September 22, 2010. http://espn.go.com/blog/ncfnation/post/_/id/27797/stanford-football-character-cruelty.

Miller, Toby. *Greenwashing Sport*. London: Routledge, 2017.

Miracle, Andrew W., and C. Roger Rees. *Lessons of the Locker Room: The Myth of School Sports*. Amherst, New York: Prometheus, 1994.

Missanelli, M. G. "Chaney Still a Strong Foe of Proposition 48." *Philadelphia Inquirer*, December 21, 1987.

Mitten, Matthew J., James L. Musselman, and Bruce W. Burton. "Commercialized Intercollegiate Athletics: A Proposal for Targeted Reform Consistent with American Cultural Forces and Marketplace Realities." *Journal of Intercollegiate Sport* 2, no. 2 (2009): 202–32.

Moe, Terry. "Introduction." In *A Primer on America's Schools*, edited by Terry Moe. Stanford, CA: Hoover Press, 2001.

Moltz, David. "Decline of Sportswomanship?" Inside Higher Ed, March 8, 2010. https://www.insidehighered.com/news/2010/03/08/decline-sportswomanship.

Moncure, John. *Forging the King's Sword—Military Education between Tradition and Modernization: The Case of the Royal Prussian Cadet Corps, 1871–1918*. New York: Peter Lang, 1993.

Morgan, Kevin. "Pedagogy for Coaches." In *An Introduction to Sports Coaching: From Science and Theory to Practice*, edited by Robyn L. Jones, Mike Hughes, and Kieran Kingston. Abingdon, UK: Routledge, 2008, 3–15.

Morgan, William J. "Habermas on Sports." In *Sports and Modern Social Theorists*, edited by R. Giulianotti. London: Palgrave MacMillan, 2004, 173–86.

Mrozek, Donald J. "The 'Amazon' and the American 'Lady': Sexual Fears of Women as Athletes." In *From "Fair Sex" to Feminism*, edited by J. A. Mangan and Roberta J. Park. London: Frank Cass, 1987, 282–98.

———. *Sport and American Mentality, 1880–1910*. Knoxville: University of Tennessee Press, 1983.

Muller, Shawn. "Muller: Geno Auriemma Needs to Stop Talking, Period." CBS, March 23, 2011. http://chicago.cbslocal.com/2011/03/23/muller-gino-auriemma-needs-to-stop-talking-period/.

Murphy, Dan. "Appeals Court Upholds Ruling That Colleges Can Pay for All NCAA Athletes' Education Expenses." ESPN, May 18, 2020. www.espn.com/college-sports/story/_/id/29191519/appeals-court-upholds-ruling-colleges-pay-all-ncaa-athletes-education-expenses.

Nader, Laura. "Anthropology!" *American Anthropologist* 103, no. 3 (2001): 609–20.

Nathan, Daniel A. "Review Essay: Traveling, Notes on Basketball and Globalization; Or, Why the San Antonio Spurs Are the Future." *International Journal of the History of Sport* 25, no. 6 (2008): 737–50.

National Coalition for Women and Girls in Education. "Title IX at 40: Working to Ensure Gender Equity in Education." Washington, DC: National Coalition for Women and Girls in Education, 2012. www.ncwge.org/PDF/TitleIXat40.pdf.

National College Players' Association and Drexel University Department of Sport Management. "National College Players' Association." www.ncpanow.org/.

———. "The $6 Billion Heist: Robbing College Athletes under the Guise of Amateurism." https://www.ncpanow.org/studies-and-revenue/study-the-6-billion-heist-robbing-college-athletes-under-the-guise-of-amateurism.

National Collegiate Athletic Association. "Academic Progress Rate Explained." www.ncaa.org/aboutresources/research/academic-progress-rate-explained.

———. "Academics." http://fs.ncaa.org/Docs/newmedia/public/rates/index.html.

———. "Amateurism." www.ncaa.org/student-athletes/future/amateurism.

———. "APR Averages and Trends." www.ncaa.org/about/resources/research/apr-averages-and-trends.

———. "Board of Governors Supports Postponing Name, Image and Likeness Votes." www.ncaa.org/about/resources/media-center/news/board-governors-supports-postponing-name-image-and-likeness-votes.

———. "Budget Statistics, 2010." www.ncaa.org/wps/portal/ncaahome?WCM_GLOBAL_CONTEXT=/ncaa/NCAA/About+The+NCAA/Budget+and+Finances/index.html.

———. "Estimated Probability of Competing in Athletics beyond the High School Interscholastic Level." www.ncaa.org/wps/portal/ncaahome?WCM_GLOBAL_CONTEXT=/ncaa/NCAA/Academics+and+Athletes/Education+and+Research/Probability+of+Competing/Methodology+-+Prob+of+Competing.

———. "14-Year Trends in Division I Athletics Finances." www.ncaa.org/sites/default/files/2019RES_D1-RevExp_Report_Final_20191107.pdf.

———. "NCAA Responds to California Senate Bill 206."

———. "NCAA Statement on Improving Student-Athlete Experience." www.ncaa.org/about/resources/media-center/news/ncaa-statement-improving-student-athlete-experience.

———. "New Violation Structure." www.ncaa.org/about/resources/media-center/news/new-violation-structure.

———. "1999–2000 Attendance Figures." http://fs.ncaa.org/Docs/stats/w_basketball_RB/reports/Attend/00att.pdf.

———. "1999–2000 NCAA Women's Basketball Attendance." http://fs.ncaa.org/Docs/stats/w basketball_RB/reports/Attend/00att.pdf.
———. "Participation Statistics Report, 1982–1995," 90–117.
———. "Public Recognition Awards Database," https://web3.ncaa.org/aprsearch/aprawards.
———. "So, You're Telling Me There's a Chance." www.ncaa.org/about/resources/research/so-you-re-telling-me-there-s-chance.
———. "Teams Honored for Top Grades in DI." https://www.ncaa.org/about/resources/media-center/news/teams-honored-top-grades-division-i.
———. "Transfer terms." www.ncaa.org/student-athletes/current/transfer-terms.
———. "Trends in Graduation Success Rates and Federal Graduation Rates at NCAA Division I Institutions." www.ncaa.org/about/resources/research/graduation-rates.
———. "2016–2017 NCAA Division I Manual." Indianapolis, IN: National Collegiate Athletic Association.
———. "2016–2017 Attendance Figures." http://fs.ncaa.org/Docs/stats/w_basketball_RB/reports/Attend/2017.pdf.
NCAA v. Alston. "Defendants' Joint Opening Brief in re: National Collegiate Athletic Association Athletic Grant-in-Aid Cap Antitrust Litigation" (Appeal of the Alston Case), US Court of Appeals for the Ninth Circuit.
National Collegiate Athletic Association Research. "Division I Men's Basketball Study on Youth Sport, Recruiting and College Choice." December 2017.
National Federation of High School Sports. "2014–15 High School Athletics Participation Survey," 2015. http://www.nfhs.org/ParticipationStatics/PDF/2014-15_Participation_Survey_Results.pdf.
National Public Radio. "Back to School #474." *This American Life*, September 14, 2012. www.thisamericanlife.org/radio-archives/episode/474/back-to-school.
National Science Foundation, National Center for Science and Engineering Statistics. "Women, Minorities, and Persons with Disabilities in Science and Engineering: 2013." Special Report NSF 13-304. www.nsf.gov/statistics/wmpd/.
National Women's Law Center. "Title IX History." www.titleix.info/history/the-living-law.aspx.
Nelson, Lee, Christopher J. Cushion, Paul Potrac, and Ryan Groom. "Carl Rogers, Learning and Educational Practice: Critical Considerations and Applications in Sports Coaching." *Sport, Education and Society* 19, no. 5 (July 4, 2014): 513–31. https://doi.org/10.1080/13573322.2012.689256.
New York Times. "Eliot Against Basket Ball: Harvard President Says Rowing and Tennis Are the Only Clean Sports," November 28, 1906.
———. "N.C.A.A. to Indianapolis," June 1, 1997. www.nytimes.com/1997/06/01/sports/ncaa-to-indianapolis.html.
———. "Room for Debate Blog: March Money Madness," March 18, 2009. https://roomfordebate.blogs.nytimes.com/2009/03/18/march-money-madness/.

Newman, Jonah, and Brian O'Leary. "Year-by-Year Comparison of College and University Endowments 2007–12." www.chronicle.com/interactives/endowments-overtime.

Newton-Smith, W. H. *The Rationality of Science*. London: Routledge, 1981.

Nixon, Howard L. *The Athletic Trap: How College Sports Corrupted the Academy*. Baltimore, MD: Johns Hopkins University Press, 2014.

Nocera, Joe. "Let's Start Paying College Athletes." *New York Times*, December 30, 2011b.

———. "The NCAA's Double Standard." *New York Times*, April 8, 2011a.

———. "The Way to Run College Sports." *New York Times*, June 5, 2013.

Nocera, Joe, and Ben Strauss. *Indentured: The Inside Story of Rebellion against the NCAA*. Portfolio, 2016.

Novak, Michael. *The Joy of Sports: End Zones, Bases, Baskets, Balls, and the Consecration of the American Spirit*. New York: Basic Books, 1976.

Novy-Williams, Eben, and Anthony Crupi. "ESPN'S $793 Million in Ad Sales on the Line with College Football." Sportico, July 24, 2020. www.sportico.com/leagues/college-sports/2020/espn-college-football-billion-1234609615/.

O'Bannon v. NCAA 802 F.3d at 1076.

O'Gorman, F. "How Academe Breeds Anxiety." *Chronicle of Higher Education*, July 12, 2015. http://chronicle.com/article/How-Academe-Breeds-Anxiety/231441.

Opler, Morris. "The Jicaralla Apache Ceremonial Relay Race." *American Anthropologist* 41, no. 1 (1944): 75–97.

———. "A Sumo Tournament at Tule Lake Center." *American Anthropologist* 46, no. 1 (1945): 134–39.

Oppenheimer Fund. "Game Face: From the Locker Room to the Boardroom, A Survey on Sports in the Lives of Women Business Executives."

O'Reilly, Jean, and Susan Cahn, eds. *Women and Sports in the United States: A Documentary Reader*. Lebanon, NH: University Press of New England, 2012.

Orenstein, Peggy. *Schoolgirls: Young Women, Self-Esteem and the Confidence Gap*. New York: Doubleday, 1994.

Oriard, Michael. *King Football: Sport and Spectacle in the Golden Age of Radio and Newsreels, Movies, and Magazines, the Weekly and the Daily Press*. Chapel Hill: University of North Carolina Press, 2005.

———. *Reading Football*. Chapel Hill: University of North Carolina Press, 2000.

———. "Review of Smith, R. *Pay for Play: A History of Big-Time College Athletic Reform*." *Journal of Intercollegiate Sport* 4 (2011): 158–65.

Orleans, Jeffrey H. "The Effects of the Economic Model of College Sport on Athlete Educational Experience." *Journal of Intercollegiate Sport* 6, no. 1 (2013): 79–85.

Orszag, Jonathan, and Peter Orszag. "The Empirical Effects of Collegiate Athletics (Commissioned by the National Collegiate Athletic Association)." www.ncaa.org/sites/default/files/empirical_effects_of_collegiate_athletics_update.pdf.

Ortiz, Araceli, and Enoch Shih. "Media Contracts in College Football: A Look at the Pac-12." Stanford Graduate School of Business Report, May 23, 2011.

Oxendine, Joseph. *American Indian Sports Heritage*. Champaign, IL: Human Kinetics, 1988.

Ozanian, Mike. "The Most Valuable NFL Teams." *Forbes*, August 14, 2013. www.forbes.com/sites/mikeozanian/2013/08/14/the-most-valuable-nfl-teams/.

P, Nate. "Kayla Pedersen: The Calming Force of Stanford's 'Three-Headed Monster.'" SB Nation Swish Appeal, February 18, 2010. www.swishappeal.com/2010/2/18/1315507/kayla-pedersen-the-calming-force.

Paish, Wilf. *The Complete Manual of Sports Science: A Practice Guide to Applied Sports Science*. London: A & C Black, 1998.

Palmer, Catherine. "Introduction: Anthropology and Sport." *Australian Journal of Anthropology* 13, no. 3 (2002): 253–56.

———. "A Life of Its Own: The Social Construction of the Tour de France." PhD thesis, University of Adelaide, 1996.

Pappano, Laura. "How Big-Time Sports Ate College Life." *New York Times*, January 22, 2012. www.nytimes.com/2012/01/22/education/edlife/how-big-time-sports-ate-college-life.html.

Park, Roberta J. "From Football to Rugby—And Back, 1906–1919: The University of California–Stanford University Response to the 'Football Crisis of 1905.'" *Journal of Sport History* 11, no. 3 (1984): 5–40.

———. "Research and Scholarship in the History of Physical Education and Sport: The Current State of Affairs." *Research Quarterly for Exercise and Sport* 54, no. 2 (1983): 93–103.

———. "Review of Massengale and Swanson, eds. *The History of Exercise and Sport Science*." *Journal of Sport History* 24, no. 1 (1997): 221–23.

Pells, Eddie. "Bowl-Bound Schools Spend Millions on Football." Associated Press, December 30, 2010.

Pennington, Bill. "Big Dream, Rude Awakening." *New York Times*, December 29, 2012.

Persky, Jana. "Condoleezza Rice Leads Football Recruitment Efforts. *Stanford Daily*, March 13, 2013.

Petr, Todd A., and John J. McArdle. "Academic Research and Reform: A History of the Empirical Basis for NCAA Academic Policy." *Journal of Intercollegiate Sport* 5, no. 1 (2012): 27–40.

Plaschke, Bill. "Nikki Caldwell Heats Up UCLA Women's Basketball." *Los Angeles Times*, December 12, 2010. http://articles.latimes.com/2010/dec/11/sports/la-sp-plaschke-20101212.

Poliakoff, Michael. *Combat Sports in the Ancient World: Competition, Violence and Culture*. New Haven, CT: Yale University Press, 1987.

Porto, Brian. *A New Season*. New York: Praeger, 2003.

Positive Coaching Alliance. www.positivecoach.org/.

Postman, Neil. *Amusing Ourselves to Death: Public Discourse in the Age of Show Business*. New York: Penguin, 2006.

Pratt, Stephen R., and D. Stanley Eitzen. "Differences in Coaching Philosophies between Male Coaches of Male and Female Basketball Teams." *International Review for the Sociology of Sport* 24, no. 1 (1989): 151–61.

Prior, Daniel D., Norm O'Reilly, Jason Mazanov, and Twan Huybers. "The Impact of Scandal on Sport Consumption: A Conceptual Framework for Future Research." *International Journal of Sport Management and Marketing* 14, nos. 1–4 (January 1, 2013): 188–211. https://doi.org/10.1504/IJSMM.2013.060647.

Puma, Mike. "Bear Bryant Simply the Best There Ever Was." ESPN. http://espn.go.com/classic/biography/s/Bryant_Bear.html.

Purdy, Mark. "Tara VanDerveer's Victory Total a Milestone Worth Many 'Wows.'" *Spokesman Review*, February 4, 2017. www.spokesman.com/stories/2017/feb/04/tara-vanderveers-victory-total-a-milestone-worth-m.

Rader, Benjamin G. *American Sports: From the Age of Folk Games to the Age of Televised Sports*. London: Routledge, 2004.

Radke-Moss, Andrea G. *Bright Epoch: Women and Coeducation in the American West*. Lincoln: University of Nebraska Press, 2008.

Ramachandran, Neel. "Jerod Haase Introduction Ushers in New Era for Men's Basketball." *Stanford Daily*, March 28, 2016.

Ramgopal, Kit. "Steffens, Women's Water Polo Live Out Legacy in Title Win." *Stanford Daily*, May 16, 2017.

Redmond, G. "The First Tom Brown's Schooldays: Origins and Evolution of 'Muscular Christianity' in Children's Literature, 1762–1857." *Quest* 30, no. 1 (1978): 4–18.

Reed, William. "A New Proposition." *Sports Illustrated*, January 23, 1989.

Rees, C. Roger, Frank M. Howell, and Andrew W. Miracle. "Do High School Sports Build Character? A Quasi-experiment on a National Sample." *Social Science Journal* 27, no. 3 (1990): 303–15.

Reich, Robert. *Saving Capitalism: For the Many, Not the Few*. New York: Vintage, 2016.

Reichart-Smith, Lauren. "The Less You Say: An Initial Study of Gender Coverage in Sports on Twitter." In *Sports Media: Transformation, Integration, Consumption*, edited by A. Billings. New York: Routledge, 2011, 146–61.

Reilly, Thomas, and Mark Williams. *Science and Soccer*. London: Routledge, 2003.

Remy, Donald. "NCAA Statement Regarding Supreme Court Petition for Alston Case." www.ncaa.org/about/resources/media-center/news/ncaa-statement-regarding-supreme-court-petition-alston-case.

Rhode, Deborah L., and Christopher J. Walker. "Gender Equity in College Athletics: Women Coaches as a Case Study." *Stanford Journal of Civil Rights & Civil Liberties* 4 (2008): 1.

Rhoden, William. "For N.C.A.A.'s Myles Brand, Tough Battles Behind and Ahead." *New York Times*, April 6, 2009.

———. "In B.C.S., No Reward for Sportsmanship." *New York Times*, November 16, 2010.

Rich, Adrienne. *Of Woman Born: Motherhood as Experience and Institution.* New York: W. W. Norton & Company, 2021.

Ridpath, B. D. "Can the Faculty Reform Intercollegiate Athletics? A Past, Present, and Future Perspective." *Journal of Issues in Intercollegiate Athletics* 1 (2008): 11–25.

Riess, Steven A. *City Games: The Evolution of American Urban Society and the Rise of Sports.* Champaign: University of Illinois Press, 1991.

———. "Class and Sport." In *A Companion to American Sport History*, edited by Steven A. Riess. New York: John Wiley & Sons, 2014, 454–78.

———. *Sport in Industrial America, 1850–1920.* New York: John Wiley & Sons, 2012.

Riegelhaupt, Joyce. "Untitled." *American Anthropologist* 75, no. 2 (1973): 378–81.

Rintala, Jan. "*The Sociology of Sports: An Introduction by Delaney, Tim and Tim Madigan.*" *Journal of Sport History* 37, no. 2 (2010): 296–99.

Roberts, John M., Malcolm J. Arth, and Robert R. Bush. "Games in Culture." *American Anthropologist* 61, no. 1 (1959): 597–605.

Roberts, Selena. "With Few Frills, VanDerveer Focuses on Winning." *New York Times*, July 14, 1996.

Robson, Garry. *No One Likes Us, We Don't Care: The Myth and Reality of Millwall Fandom.* London: Berg Publishers, 2000.

Rogers, Carl R. *The Carl Rogers Reader.* New York: Houghton Mifflin Harcourt, 1989.

Rosen, Lee. 2000. "Proposition 16 and the NCAA Initial-Eligibility Standards: Putting the Student Back in Student-Athlete." *Catholic University Law Review* 50, no. 1:175–218.

Rosenberg, Alyssa. "The *New York Times* Goes After Hurdler Lolo Jones and Gets Olympic Sexism Wrong." Slate, August 6, 2012.

Rosenblatt, Ryan. "Breaking Down the Pac-12's New TV Deal With ESPN/Fox & the Pac-12 Network." Bruins Nation, May 4, 2011. www.bruinsnation.com/2011/5/4/2153940/breaking-down-the-pac-12s-new-tv-deal-with-espn-fox-pac-12-network.

Rovell, Darren. "Matt Barkley Had No Insurance." ESPN, April 30, 2013. http://espn.go.com/nfl/story/_/id/9228764/matt-barkley-returned-usc-trojans-insurance-sources.

———. "Verizon, NFL Agree to New 5-Year Deal Worth Nearly $2.5 Billion." ESPN, December 11, 2017. www.espn.com/nfl/story/_/id/21737823/verizon-nfl-agree-new-5-year-deal-worth-nearly-25-billion.

Rowe, David. "Sport and the Repudiation of the Global." *International Review for the Sociology of Sport* 38, no. 3 (2003): 281–94.

Rudd, Andy, and Michael J Mondello. "How Do College Coaches Define Character? A Qualitative Study with Division IA Head Coaches." *Journal of College and Character* 7, no. 3 (March 2006): 1–9. https://doi.org/10.2202/1940-1639.1524.

Russell, Bertrand. *A History of Western Philosophy.* London: Routledge, 2013.

Ryan, Kevin, Karen E. Bohlin, and Judith O. Thayer. *Character Education Manifesto*. Boston, MA: Boston University Center for the Advancement of Ethics and Character, 1996.

Ryan, Richard M., and Edward L. Deci. "Self-Determination Theory and the Facilitation of Intrinsic Motivation, Social Development, and Well-Being." *American Psychologist* 55, no. 1 (2000): 68–78. https://doi.org/10.1037/0003-066X.55.1.68.

Sabo, D. F., and J. Panepinto. "Football Ritual and the Social Reproduction of Masculinity." In *Sport, Men, and the Gender Order: Critical Feminist Perspectives*, edited by M. A. Messner and D. F. Sabo. Champaign, IL: Human Kinetics, 1990, 115–26.

Sabock, R. J. *The Coach*. Champaign, IL: Human Kinetics, 1985.

Sack, Allen. "Big Time College Football: Whose Free Ride?" *Quest* 27, no. 1 (1977).

———. "Clashing Models of Commercial Sport in Higher Education: Implications for Reform and Scholarly Research." *Journal of Issues in Intercollegiate Athletics* 2 (2009): 76–92.

———. "Let College Athletes Be Entrepreneurs." *New York Times*, March 18, 2009a.

———. "Sport: Play or Work?" In *Studies in the Anthropology of Play*, edited by Phillips J. Stevens. West Point, NY: Leisure Press, 1977, 186–95.

Sack, Allen, and Ellen J. Staurowsky. *College Athletes for Hire: The Evolution and Legacy of the NCAA's Amateur Myth*. Westport, CT: Praeger, 1998.

Sack, Allen, A. E. McComas, and E. Cakan. "The Revival of Multiyear Scholarships in the Twenty-First Century: Which Universities Supported and Opposed This Legislation and Why?" *Journal of Issues in Intercollegiate Athletics* (2014): 207–23.

Sage, George. "The Coach as Management." In *Sport and American Society*, edited by George Sage. Reading, MA: Addison Wesley, 1974, 429–36.

———. *Globalizing Sport: How Organizations, Corporations, Media, and Politics Are Changing Sport*. London: Routledge, 2015.

———. "The Social World of High School Athletic Coaches: Multiple Role Demands and Their Consequences." *Sociology of Sport Journal* 4, no. 3 (September 1, 1987): 213–28. https://doi.org/10.1123/ssj.4.3.213.

———. "United Students Against Sweatshops: Social Protests and Global Activism Against Sweatshops Where Sporting Goods for Universities Are Made." *International Sports Sociology Association World Congress*, Vancouver, CA, June 13, 2013.

Sage, George Harvey, D. Stanley Eitzen, and Becky Beal. *Sociology of North American Sport*. Oxford: Oxford University Press, 2018.

Sailes, Gary A. "Betting Against the Odds: An Overview of Black Sports Participation." *Journal of African American Men* 2, nos. 2–3 (1996): 11–22.

Salinas, Alejandro. "Two Podiums for Cross Country." *Stanford Daily*, November 24, 2017.

San Jose Mercury News. "Stanford Football Coach David Shaw's Salary Nearly Doubled." www.mercurynews.com/2016/07/18/stanford-football-coach-david-shaws-salary-nearly-doubled/.

Sander, Libby. "Women's Basketball Matures, But Not Without Growing Pains." *Chronicle of Higher Education*, December 9, 2011.

Sands, Robert R. *Anthropology, Sport and Culture*. Westport, CT: Bergin & Garvey, 1999a.

———. *Gut Check! An Anthropologist's Wild Ride into the Heart of College Football*. San Francisco: Rincon Hill Books, 1999b.

———. *Instant Acceleration: Living in the Fast Lane, The Cultural Identity of Speed*. Lanham, MD: University Press of America, 1994.

Sansone, David. *Greek Athletics and the Genesis of Sport*. Berkeley: University of California Press, 1988.

Santoro, Marco. "Cultural Turn." In *Encyclopedia of Consumer Culture*, edited by Dale Southerton. Thousand Oaks, CA: Sage Publications, 2011, 401–2.

Saunders, Daniel. "The Impact of Neoliberalism on College Students." *Journal of College & Character* 8, no. 5 (2007): 1–9.

Saury, Jacques, and Marc Durand. "Practical Knowledge in Expert Coaches: On-Site Study of Coaching in Sailing." *Research Quarterly for Exercise and Sport* 69, no. 3 (September 1, 1998): 254–66. https://doi.org/10.1080/02701367.1998.10607692.

Sawyer, R. Keith. "The New Anthropology of Children, Play, and Games." *Reviews in Anthropology* 31, no. 2 (January 1, 2002): 147–64. https://doi.org/10.1080/00988150212940.

Schechner, Richard. "Preface." In *The Anthropology of Performance*, edited by Victor Turner. Baltimore, MD: Johns Hopkins University Press, 1987, 7–20.

Schlabach, Mark. "NCAA Puts End to Jersey Sales." ESPN, August 9, 2013. https://www.espn.com/college-sports/story/_/id/9551518/ncaa-shuts-site-jersey-sales-says-hypocritical.

Schlager, Brandon. "More People Watched Super Bowl XLIX Than Voted in Presidential Election—Again." *Sporting News*, February 5, 2015. http://www.sportingnews.com/nfl/news/more-people-watched-super-bowl-xlix-than-voted-in-presidential-election/1x5qpbnnwvsyr1l6v8yf1va3bl.

Schnell, Lindsay. "Oregon State Coach LaVonda Wagner Built Culture on Fear and Intimidation, Sources Say." *Oregonian*, January 10, 2019. https://www.oregonlive.com/behindbeaversbeat/2010/05/osu_coach_lavonda_wagner_built.html.

Schwartz, Larry. "Didrikson Was a Woman Ahead of Her Time." http://espn.go.com/sportscentury/features/00014147.html.

———. "More Info on Babe Didrikson." http://www.espn.com/classic/s/000804babedidriksonadd.html.

Schwartz, Stuart B. *Implicit Understandings: Observing, Reporting and Reflecting on the Encounters between Europeans and Other Peoples in the Early Modern Era*. Cambridge: Cambridge University Press, 1994.

Schwarz, Andy. "Wait, the NCAA Can Pay Players' Parents Now?" Deadspin, January 7, 2015. https://deadspin.com/wait-the-ncaa-can-pay-players-parents-now-1677853402.

Scott, Harry Alexander. *Competitive Sports in Schools and Colleges*. New York: Harper, 1951.

Scraton, Sheila, and Anne Flintoff. "Sport Feminism: The Contribution of Feminist Thought to Our Understandings of Gender and Sport." In *Gender and Sport: A Reader*. Hove, UK: Psychology Press, 2002, 30–46.

Sedgwick, Hubert M. "Walter Camp—Maker of Watches and Football Players." *Baseball Magazine* 2, no. 2 (December 1908).

Seligman, Martin E. P., Randal M. Ernst, Jane Gillham, Karen Reivich, and Mark Linkins. "Positive Education: Positive Psychology and Classroom Interventions." *Oxford Review of Education* 35, no. 3 (June 1, 2009): 293–311. https://doi.org/10.1080/03054980902934563.

Serazio, Michael. "Just How Much Is Sports Fandom Like Religion?" *Atlantic*, January 29, 2013.

Shaw, Stephanie J. *What a Woman Ought to Be and to Do*. Chicago: University of Chicago Press, 2010. www.degruyter.com/document/doi/10.7208/9780226751306/html.

Sherlock, Molly F., Jane G. Gravelle, Margot L. Crandall-Hollick, and Joseph S. Hughes. "College and University Endowments: Overview and Tax Policy Options." Congressional Research Service. https://sgp.fas.org/crs/misc/R44293.pdf.

Shetler, Matt. "Lamar Odom and the 8 Biggest Prima Donnas in the NBA." Bleacher Report, March 2, 2012. http://bleacherreport.com/articles/1088729-lamar-odom-and-8-biggest-prima-donnas-in-the-nba.

Shi, Winston. "Shannon Turley, Part III: The Student Teaches the Master." *Stanford Daily*, April 26, 2013.

Shibley, Robert L. *Twisting Title IX*. San Francisco: Encounter Books, 2016.

Shields, David Lyle Light, and Brenda Jo Light Bredemeier. *Character Development and Physical Activity*. Champaign, IL: Human Kinetics, 1995.

Shulman, James, and William Bowen. *The Game of Life: College Sports and Educational Values*. Princeton, NJ: Princeton University Press, 2001.

Silk, Michael. "Sporting Ethnography: Philosophy, Methodology, and Reflection." In *Qualitative Methods in Sports Studies*, edited by David L. Andrews, Daniel S. Mason, and Michael L. Silk. London: Berg, 2005.

Silva, Derek, Nathan Kalman-Lamb, and Johanna Mellis. "Cancelling the College Football Season Is About Union Busting, Not Health." *Guardian*, August 12, 2020.

Singell, Larry D. Jr. "Baseball-Specific Human Capital: Why Good But Not Great Players Are More Likely to Coach in the Major Leagues." *Southern Economic Journal* 58, no. 1 (1991): 77–86.

Sipes, Richard. "War, Sports, and Aggression: An Empirical Test of Two Rival Theories." *American Anthropologist* 75, no. 1 (1973): 64–86.

Smith, Christopher. "Full Cost of Attendance: What Will It Mean for Power Five Players?" www.saturdaydownsouth.com/sec-football/full-cost-of-attendance-explained/.

Smith, Dennis. "The Civilizing Process and the History of Sexuality: Comparing Norbert Elias and Michel Foucault." *Theory and Society* 28, no. 1 (1999): 79–100.

Smith, Gary. *Beyond the Game: The Collected Sportswriting of Gary Smith*. New York: Grove Press Books, 2000.
Smith, Jay M. "How Sports Ate Academic Freedom." *Wall Street Journal*, May 1, 2018.
Smith, Jay M., and Mary Willingham. *Cheated: The UNC Scandal, the Education of Athletes, and the Future of Big-Time Sports*. Lincoln: University of Nebraska Press, 2015.
Smith, Michael. "Pac-12 Buys Back Rights, Clears Way for New Channel." Sports Business Daily, November 7, 2011. www.sportsbusinessdaily.com/Journal/Issues/2011/11/07/Media/Pac12.aspx.
Smith, Michelle. "Inductee VanDerveer Feels Right at Home." ESPN, August 12, 2011.
———. "Nneka Ogwumike Fits Right In." ESPN, July 13, 2012.
Smith, Ronald A. *Pay for Play: A History of Big-Time College Athletic Reform*. Champaign: University of Illinois Press, 2011.
———. "The Rise of Basketball for Women in Colleges." *Canadian Journal of History of Sport and Physical Education* 1, no. 2 (1970): 18–36.
———. *Sports and Freedom: The Rise of Big-Time College Athletics*. Oxford: Oxford University Press, 1988.
———. *Wounded Lions: Joe Paterno, Jerry Sandusky, and the Crises in Penn State Athletics*. Champaign: University of Illinois Press, 2016.
Smith, Ronald Edward, Frank L. Smoll, and Robert E. Smith. *Way to Go, Coach! A Scientifically Proven Approach to Youth Sports Coaching Effectiveness*. Forest Knolls, CA: Warde Publishers, 2002.
Smith, Shelley. "Basketball." In *Nike Is a Goddess: The History of Women in Sports*, edited by Lissa Smith. New York: Atlantic Monthly Press, 1999.
Sokolove, Michael. "Is It Dunk and Done for Perry Jones?" *New York Times*, March 8, 2011.
Solomon, Jon. "Pac-12 Falls Behind SEC in Money Even With Commissioner at $4 Million in Salary." CBS, May 18, 2016. www.cbssports.com/college-football/news/pac-12-falls-behind-sec-in-money-even-with-commissioner-at-4-million-in-salary/.
Soshnick, Scott. "Alibaba Buys Broadcast Rights to Slate of Pac-12 College Sports." Bloomberg, October 15, 2017. www.bloomberg.com/news/articles/2017-10-05/alibaba-buys-broadcast-rights-to-slate-of-pac-12-college-sports.
Southall, Richard. "A Real-World Collegiate Model." HuffPost, January 12, 2012. www.huffpost.com/entry/college-athletes-pay_b_1210932.
———. "2012 Adjusted Graduation Gap: NCAA Division-I baseball and softball." https://www.sc.edu/study/colleges_schools/hrsm/research/centers/college_sport_research_institute/agg_reports/gap_reports/csri_2012_agg_ncaa_d-i_ba-sb2.pdf.
———. "2012 Adjusted Graduation Gap Report: NCAA Division-I football." https://exss.unc.edu/wp-content/uploads/sites/779/2011/07/2012_FB_D-I_AGG_Report_Post-Embargo_Copy_9-25-2012.pdf.

Southall, Richard M., and Mark S. Nagel. "A Case-Study Analysis of NCAA Division I Women's Basketball Tournament Broadcasts: Educational or Commercial Activity?" *International Journal of Sport Communication* 1, no. 4 (2008): 516–33. https://journals.humankinetics.com/view/journals/ijsc/1/4/article-p516.xml.

Southall, Richard M., E. Woodrow Eckard, Mark S. Nagel, and Morgan H. Randall. "Athletic Success and NCAA Profit-Athletes' Adjusted Graduation Gaps." *Sociology of Sport Journal* 32, no. 4 (December 1, 2015): 395–414. https://doi.org/10.1123/ssj.2014-0156.

Spencer, Herbert. *Education: Intellectual, Moral and Physical*. London: Routledge, 1993.

Sperber, Murray. *Beer and Circus: How Big-Time College Sports Is Crippling Undergraduate Education*. New York: Henry Holt & Company, 2000.

———. "College Sports, Inc.: The Athletic Department vs. the University." In *Contemporary Issues in Sociology of Sport*, edited by A. Yiannakis and M. J. Melnick. Champaign, IL: Human Kinetics, 2001, 147–58.

———. "College Sports, Inc.: How Big-Time Athletic Departments Run Interference for College, Inc." In *Buying In or Selling Out? The Commercialization of the American Research University*, edited by Donald G. Stein. New Brunswick, NJ: Rutgers University Press, 2004, 17–31.

———. "March Money Madness: What Bonanza? Most Colleges Lose Money." *New York Times*, March 18, 2009.

Splitt, Frank G. "Are Big-Time College Sports Good for America?" Drake Group. www.thedrakegroup.org/2005/12/21/are-big-time-sports-good-for-america/.

———. "The Knight Commission on Intercollegiate Athletics: Why It Needs Fixing." Drake Group. www.thedrakegroup.org/2009/01/10/the-knight-commission-on-intercollegiate-athletics-why-it-needs-fixing/.

Sports Illustrated. "For 2nd Straight Year, Player Declares Early for WNBA Draft." April 5, 2016.

Sports Business Now. "University Endowments vs Athletic Spending: Stanford Reigns." November 5, 2012.

St. Louis, Brett. "Sport, Genetics and the 'Natural Athlete': The Resurgence of Racial Science." *Body & Society* 9, no. 2 (2003): 75–95.

Staffo, Donald F. "The History of Women's Professional basketball in the United States with an Emphasis on the Old WBL and the New ABL and WNBA." *Physical Educator* 55, no. 4 (1998): 187. www.proquest.com/openview/1451cfd0405e3067dbb1f16874ebd770/1?pq-origsite=gscholar&cbl=35035.

Stagg, Amos Alonzo. 1926[1971]. "Touchdown." *Saturday Evening Post*, October 23, 1926, 31. Reprinted as "Football in Its Cradle Days." In *Oh, How They Played the Game: The Early Days of Football and the Heroes Who Made It Great*, by Allison Danzig. New York: Macmillan, 1971, 27–47.

Stanford Digital Repository. Grant founding and endowing the Leland Stanford Junior University (SC1445) Dept. of Special Collections and University

Archives, Stanford University Libraries, Stanford, Calif. https://purl.stanford.edu/rb803rc6397

Stanford Magazine. "When Every Moment Is Savored." November–December 2008. http://alumni.stanford.edu/get/page/magazine/article/?article_id=30759.

Stanford University. "Facts." https://facts.stanford.edu/about/.

———. "On Campus: History/Traditions." www.gostanford.com/sports/2013/4/17/208445349.aspx.

———. "Our History—Our Mission." https://gostanford.com/sports/2016/6/25/b-cc-about.aspx.

———. "Our Selection Process." www.stanford.edu/dept/uga/basics/selection/index.html.

———. "Thinking About Sports." http://news.stanford.edu/news/multi/features/sports/fullstory.html.

Stanford University Historical Society. "Title IX," October 11, 2012.

Stanford University (Lagunita). "Interview by Blakey Vermeule of Tara VanDerveer" for Massive Open Online Course: Sports and the University, 2018. Unit 5.2.

Staples, Andy. "How Television Changed College Football—And How It Will Again." In *The Reference Shelf: Sports in America*, edited by H. W. Wilson (Ipswich, MA: H. W. Wilson) 2013.

Staurowsky, Ellen J. "Her Life Depends on It III: Sport and Physical Activity in the Lives of American Girls and Women." Women's Sports Foundation, 2015.

———. "'A Radical Proposal': Title IX Has No Role in College Sport Pay-for-Play Discussions." *Marquette Sports Law Review* 22, no. 2 (Spring): 575–95. https://heinonline.org/HOL/LandingPage?handle=hein.journals/mqslr22&div=24&id=&page=.

———. "Where the Amateurs Are." *New York Times*, March 18, 2009.

Staurowsky, Ellen J., and B. David Ridpath. "The Case for Minimum 2.0 Standard for NCAA Division I Athletes." *Journal of Legal Aspects of Sport* 15, no. 1 (2005): 113–38.

Stein, Donald G., ed. *Buying In or Selling Out? The Commercialization of the American Research University*. New Brunswick, NJ: Rutgers University Press, 2004.

Stevenson, C. L. "Socialization's Effects on Participation in Sport: A Critical Review of the Research." *Research Quarterly* 46, no. 1 (1975): 287–301.

Stevenson, Harold W., and James W. Stigler. *The Learning Gap: Why Our Schools Are Failing and What We Can Learn from Japanese and Chinese Education*. New York: Simon & Schuster, 1992.

Stiglitz, Joseph E. 2012. *The Price of Inequality: How Today's Divided Society Endangers Our Future*. New York: W. W. Norton & Company.

Stoney, Emma. "Cal's Varsity Squad Emerges from a Scrum Only as a Club Team." *New York Times*, December 20, 2010.

Strauss, Ben. "N.L.R.B. Rejects Northwestern Football Players' Union Bid." *New York Times*, August 15, 2015.

Strauss, Claudia. "Beyond 'Formal' versus 'Informal' Education: Uses of Psychological Theory in Anthropological Research." *Ethos* 12, no. 3 (1984): 195–222.

Strege, John. *Tiger: A Biography of Tiger Woods*. New York: Broadway Books, 1997.

Stringer, Vivian, and Laura Tucker. *Standing Tall: A Memoir of Tragedy and Triumph*. New York: Three Rivers Press, 2008.

Stripling, Jack, and Andrea Fuller. "On Campuses, the Income Gap Widens at the Top." *Chronicle of Higher Education*, December 5, 2011. http://chronicle.com/article/On-Campuses-the-Income-Gap/129980.

Stubbs, Michael. *Discourse Analysis: The Socio-linguistic Analysis of Natural Language*. London: Wiley-Blackwell, 1991.

Suggs, Welch. "Foes of Title IX Try to Make Equity in College Sports a Campaign Issue." *Chronicle of Higher Education*, February 4, 2000. https://listserv.uwindsor.ca/cgi-bin/wa?A3=ind0002a&L=9550101-L&E=0&P=594&B=--&T=text%2Fplain;%20charset=us-ascii&header=1.

———. *A Place on the Team: The Triumph and Tragedy of Title IX*. Princeton, NJ: Princeton University Press, 2006.

Summitt, Pat, and Sally Jenkins. *Raise the Roof*. New York: Broadway Books, 1999.

Sutton-Smith, Brian. "Commentary: At Play in the Public Arena." *Early Education and Development* 3, no. 4 (1992): 390–400.

———. "Foreword." In Kendall Blanchard, *The Anthropology of Sport: An Introduction*. Westport, CT: Bergin & Garvey, 1995, xi–xiv.

———. "Notes Toward a Critique of Twentieth-century Psychological Play Theory." In *Homo Ludens: Der Spielende Mensche II*, edited by Günther G. Bauer. Munich-Salzburg: Emil Katzbilchler, 1992, 95–107.

Taylor, Frederick Winslow. *Scientific Management*. London: Routledge, 2004.

Taylor, Kathleen, and Dean Elias. "Transformative Learning: A Developmental Perspective." In *The Handbook of Transformative Learning: Theory, Research, and Practice*, by Edward W. Taylor and Patricia Cranton. San Francisco: Jossey-Bass, 2012, 147–61.

Taylor, Sandra C. *Advocate of Understanding: Sidney Gulick and the Search for Peace with Japan*. Kent, Ohio: Kent State University Press, 1984.

Taylor, Tom. "W. Basketball: Gold-en Guard." *Stanford Daily*, February 10, 2010. www.stanforddaily.com/2010/02/23/w-basketball-gold-en-guard/.

Templeton, Josh. "Elevate Your Team: Buy In." Coach T Hoops, October 18, 2016. www.coachthoops.com/elevate-team-buy/.

Templin, Thomas J., Robert Woodford, and Carol Mulling. "On Becoming a Physical Educator: Occupational Choice and the Anticipatory Socialization Process." *Quest* 34, no. 2 (July 1, 1982): 119–33. https://doi.org/10.1080/00336297.1982.10483771.

Thamel, Pete. "Scheduling Partnership Links Pac-12 and Big Ten." *New York Times*, December 28, 2011.

Thamel, Pete, and Duff Wilson. "The Quick Fix: Easy Grades for Athletes—Poor Grades Aside, Top Athletes Get to College on $399 Diploma." *New York Times*, February 25, 2006.

Theberge, Nancy. "The Construction of Gender in Sport: Women, Coaching and the Naturalization of Difference." *Social Problems* 40, no. 3 (1993): 301–13.

———. "Toward a Feminist Alternative to Sport as a Male Preserve." *Quest* 37, no. 2 (1985): 193–202.

Thelin, John. "Front Sports Page to Front Page." In *Introduction to Intercollegiate Athletics*, edited by Eddie Comeaux. Baltimore, MD: Johns Hopkins University Press, 2015, 3–13.

Thomas, Katie. "Colleges Cut Men's Programs to Satisfy Title IX." *New York Times*, May 1, 2011.

———. "ESPN Slowly Introducing Online Brand for Women." *New York Times*, October 15, 2010. www.nytimes.com/2010/10/16/sports/16espnw.html.

Thomas, Katie, and Joe Drape. "Stanford Dominates the Director's Cup." *New York Times*, September 2, 2010.

Thompson, E. P. "Time, Work-Discipline, and Industrial Capitalism." *Past & Present* 38 (1967): 56–97.

Thompson, John Jr. "Let's Drop the Charade and Pay College Athletes." *New York Times*, November 12, 2020. www.nytimes.com/2020/11/12/opinion/ncaa-sports-paying-college-players.html.

Thurmond, Raymond Clyde. "The History of Sport and Physical Education as a Field of Study in Higher Education." PhD dissertation, University of Oklahoma, 1976.

Tindall, B. Allan. "The Cultural Transmissive Function of Physical Education." *Council on Anthropology & Education Quarterly* 6, no. 2 (1975): 10–12.

Todorov, Tzvetan. *On Human Diversity: Nationalism, Racism, and Exoticism in French Thought*. Cambridge, MA: Harvard University Press, 1993.

Tracy, Marc. "The N.C.A.A. Lost in Court, But Athletes Didn't Win, Either." *New York Times*, March 11, 2019. www.nytimes.com/2019/03/11/sports/ncaa-court-ruling-antitrust.html.

Tracy, Marc, and Tim Rohan. "What Made College Football More Like the Pros? $7.3 billion, for a Start." *New York Times*, December 30, 2014.

Trahan, Kevin. "The NCAA's Academic Progress Rate Punishes HBCUs More Than It Promotes Education." Vice, April 29, 2016,. https://sports.vice.com/en_us/article/qky8qw/ncaa-apr-punishes-hbcus-more-than-it-promotes-education.

Trail, Galen T., Dean F. Anderson, and Janet S. Fink. "A Theoretical Model of Sport Spectator Consumption Behavior." *International Journal of Sport Management* 1, no. 3 (2000): 154–80.

Travis, Clay. "How Much Do the NFL and TV Partners Make a Year?" March 1, 2017.

———. *Republicans Buy Sneakers, Too: How the Left Is Ruining Sports*. New York: Broadside Books, 2018.

Trojian, Thomas H., and Seamus Collins. "The Anterior Cruciate Ligament Tear Rate Varies by Race in Professional Women's Basketball." *American Journal of Sports Medicine* 34, no. 1 (2006): 895–98. https://journals.sagepub.com/doi/abs/10.1177/0363546505284384.

Tsitsos, William, and Howard L. Nixon. "The Star Wars Arms Race in College Athletics: Coaches' Pay and Athletic Program Status." *Journal of Sport and Social Issues* 36, no. 1 (2012): 68–88. https://journals.sagepub.com/doi/abs/10.1177/0193723511433867.

Turner, Victor. *The Anthropology of Performance*. New York: PAJ Publications, 1986.

———. *The Forest of Symbols: Aspects of Ndembu Ritual*. Ithaca, NY: Cornell University Press, 1967.

———. *From Ritual to Theatre: The Human Seriousness of Play*. New York: Performing Arts Journal Publications, 1982.

———. "Symbolic Studies." *Annual Review of Anthropology* 4, no. 1 (1975): 145–61.

———. "Symbols and Social Experience in Religious Ritual." In *Worship and Ritual: In Christianity and Other Religions*. Studia Missionalia, Rome: Gregorian University Press, 1974.

Turner, Victor, and Edith Turner. *Image and Pilgrimage in Christian Culture: Anthropological Perspectives*. New York: Columbia University Press, 1978.

Turrini, Joseph. *The End of Amateurism in Track and Field*. Champaign: University of Illinois Press, 2010.

Tuttle, Jane P. "Setting the Mark: Lucile Godbold and the First International Track Meet for Women." *South Carolina Historical Magazine* 102, no. 2 (April 2001): 135–52.

Tylor, Edward Burnett. "The History of Games." *Fortnightly Review* 25 (1879): 735–47.

———. *Primitive Culture: Researches into the Development of Mythology, Philosophy, Religion, Language, Art, and Custom*. London: J. Murray, 1871.

Ullian, David M. "A Rope, a Tree, Hang the Referee: Exploring the First Amendment Boundaries of Offensive Fan Speech Regulation in College Sports." *Sports Lawyers Journal* 23 (2016): 1.

UNESCO, Institute for Education. "UNESCO's Decade of Commitment to Physical Education and Sport." *International Review of Education* 35, no. 1 (1989): 99–102.

UNESCO. *International Charter of Physical Education and Sport*, 1978.

U.S. General Accounting Office. "Intercollegiate Athletics: Four-Year Colleges' Experiences Adding and Discontinuing Teams."

———. "Intercollegiate Athletics: Recent Trends in Teams and Participants in National Collegiate Athletic Association Sports." www.gao.gov/new.items/d07535.pdf.

U.S. Internal Revenue Service. "Identifying Full-Time Employees." www.irs.gov/affordable-care-act/employers/identifying-full-time-employees.

U.S. News & World Report. "University Comparison Tool." www.usnews.com/best-colleges/compare?xwalk_id=209551&xwalk_id=209542.

USA Today. "An Analysis of Salaries for Women's College Basketball Coaches." http://usatoday30.usatoday.com/sports/college/womensbasketball/2011-coaches-salary-database.htm.

———. "Men's Basketball Coaches Salary Database." http://usatoday30.usatoday.com/sports/college/mensbasketball/story/2012-03-28/ncaa-coaches-salary-database/53827374/1.

———. "NCAA Reaches 14-Year Deal with CBS/Turner for Men's Basketball Tournament, Which Expands to 68 Teams for Now," April 22, 2010. http://content.usatoday.com/communities/campusrivalry/post/2010/04/ncaa-reaches-14-year-deal-with-cbsturner/1#.UdRxMODj_ZQ.

Van Gennep, Arnold. *The Rites of Passage*. Chicago: University of Chicago Press, 1960.

VanDerveer, Tara, and Joan Ryan. *Shooting from the Outside*: New York: Avon Books, 1997.

Veblen, Thorstein. *Theory of the Leisure Class*. New York: Macmillan & Company, 1899.

Verbrugge, Martha H. *Active Bodies: A History of Women's Physical Education in Twentieth-Century America*. Oxford: Oxford University Press, 2012.

Voepel, Mechelle. "Stage Set for Uconn-Stanford Clash." ESPN, December 29, 2010a.

———. "Stanford Snaps UConn's Win Streak." ESPN, December 30, 2010b. http://sports.espn.go.com/ncw/columns/story?columnist=voepel_mechelle&id=5973237.

———. "Wooden Saw Value in Women's Hoops." ESPN, June 9, 2010c.

Wagner, Eric A., ed. *Sport in Asia and Africa: A Comparative Handbook*. Westport, CT: Greenwood Press, 1989.

———. "Sport in Asia and Africa: Americanization or Mundialization?" *Sociology of Sport Journal* 7, no. 1 (1990): 399–402.

Walton, Bill. "March Money Madness: My Priceless Opportunity." *New York Times*, March 18, 2009.

Wang, Chih-ming. "Capitalizing the Big Man: Yao Ming, Asian America, and the China Global." *Inter-Asia Cultural Studies* 5, no. 2 (2004): 263–78.

Watson, Nick J, Stuart Weir, and Stephen Friend. "The Development of Muscular Christianity in Victorian Britain and Beyond." *Journal of Religion & Society* (2005): 1–21.

Watterson, John S. "The Gridiron Crisis of 1905: Was It Really a Crisis?" *Journal of Sport History* 27, no. 2 (2000): 291–98.

Weber, Max. "The Protestant Work Ethic and the Spirit of Capitalism." Translated by Peter Baehr and Gordon C. Wells. New York: Penguin Books, 2002.

Weight, Erianne A., Coyte Cooper, and Nels K. Popp. "The Coach-Educator: NCAA Division I Coach Perspectives about an Integrated University Organizational Structure." *Journal of Sport Management* 29, no. 5 (2015): 510–22.

Weight, Erianne, Kristina Navarro, Landon Huffman, and Abbie Smith-Ryan. "Quantifying the Psychological Benefits of Intercollegiate Athletics Participation." *Journal of Issues in Intercollegiate Athletics* 7 (2014): 390–409.

Weil, Elizabeth. "Nobody Ever Remembers the Skinny Girl's Name." *New York Times Magazine*, June 21, 2012.

Weiss, Paul. *Sport: A Philosophical Inquiry*. Carbondale: Southern Illinois University Press, 1969.

Weistart, John. "Equal Opportunity? Title IX and Intercollegiate Sports." *Brookings Review* 16, no. 4 (1998): 39.

Westney, Eleanor. *Imitation and Innovation: The Transfer of Western Organizational Patterns to Meiji Japan*. Cambridge, MA: Harvard University Press, 1987.

Wetzel, Dan, and Don Yaeger. *Sole Influence: Basketball, Corporate Greed, and the Corruption of America's Youth*. New York: Warner Books, 2000.

Whannel, Garry. *Media Sport Stars: Masculinities and Moralities*. London: Routledge, 2002.

White, Leslie. "Anthropology 1964: Retrospect and Prospect." *American Anthropologist* 67, no. 1 (1965): 629–37.

Whiteside, Erin, Marie Hardin, and Erin Ash. "Good for Society or Good for Business? Division I Sports Information Directors' Attitudes toward the Commercialization of Sports." *International Journal of Sport Communication* 4, no. 4 (December 1, 2011): 473–91. https://doi.org/10.1123/ijsc.4.4.473.

Will, George. "A Train Wreck Called Title IX." *Newsweek*, May 26, 2002.

Willard, F. E., and C. O'Hare. *How I Learned to Ride the Bicycle: Reflections of an Influential 19th-Century Woman*. San Francisco: Fair Oaks Publishing, 1991.

Williams, Alex. "Saying No to College." *New York Times*, November 30, 2012.

Williams, Claire. "Bay to Breakers: The Original Fun Run." In *San Francisco Bay Area Sports: Golden Gate Athletics, Recreation, and Community*, edited by R. Liberti and M. Smith. Fayetteville: University of Arkansas Press, 2017.

Williams, J. G. P. "Rowing: Art or Science." In *Rowing: A Scientific Approach*, by J. G. P. Williams and A. C. Scott. London: Kaye & Ward Limited, 1967.

Williams, Sarah B., and T. Christopher Greenwell. "The Impact of Scandal on NCAA Division I Women's Basketball Fan Consumption and Team Success." *Journal of Issues in Intercollegiate Athletics* 12, no. 1 (2019): 1–21.

Willis, Paul. *Learning to Labour: How Working-Class Kids Get Working-Class Jobs*. London: Routledge, 1977.

———. "Women in Sport and Ideology." In *Sport, Culture and Society*, edited by Jennifer Hargreaves. London: Routledge and Kegan Paul, 1982, 117–35.

Wilner, Jon. "Pac-12 Salaries: Men's Basketball Coaches." *San Jose Mercury News*, April 12, 2013. www.mercurynews.com/2013/04/12/pac-12-salaries-mens-basketball-coaches/.

Wolff, Alexander. *Big Game, Small World: A Basketball Adventure*. New York: Warner Books, 2002.

Wolverton, Brad. "At Private Colleges, 33 Coaches and Athletic Directors Top $1 Million." *Chronicle of Higher Education*, December 13, 2013. http://chronicle.com/blogs/players/at-private-colleges-33-coaches-and-athletic-directors-top-1-million-in-pay/34003.

Women's Sports Foundation. "Coaching—Do Female Athletes Prefer Male Coaches? The Foundation Position." www.womenssportsfoundation.org/home/advocate/foundation-positions/equity-issues/do_female_athletes_prefer_male_coaches.
Wright, Eric. "Comparative Studies in Physical Education and Sport." *Comparative Education* 9, no. 2 (1973): 67–71.
Wright, Trevor, Pierre Trudel, and Diane. Culver. "Learning How to Coach: The Different Learning Situations Reported by Youth Ice Hockey Coaches." *Physical Education and Sport Pedagogy* 12, no. 2 (2007): 127–44. www.tandfonline.com/doi/abs/10.1080/17408980701282019.
Wushanley, Ying. *Playing Nice and Losing: The Struggle for Control of Women's Intercollegiate Athletics, 1960–2000.* Syracuse, NY: Syracuse University Press, 2004.
Yost, Mark. *Var$ity Green: A Behind the Scenes Look at Culture and Corruption in College Athletics.* Palo Alto, CA: Stanford University Press, 2020.
Young, T. R. "The Sociology of Sports: Structural Marxist and Cultural Marxist Approaches." *Sociological Perspectives* 29, no. 1 (1986): 3–28.
Zeitlyn, David. "Life-History Writing and the Anthropological Silhouette." *Social Anthropology* 16, no. 2 (2008): 154–71.
Zimbalist, Andrew. "College Athletes Should Get Paid." *Atlantic*, September 20, 2011. www.theatlantic.com/entertainment/archive/2011/09/college-athletes-should-not-get-paid/245390/.
———. "Short of Paying Players, Fix the Rules." *New York Times*, March 18, 2009.
———. "Taxation of College Sports." In *An Introduction to Intercollegiate Athletics*, edited by Eddie Comeaux. Baltimore, MD: Johns Hopkins University Press, 2015.
———. *Unpaid Professionals: Commercialism and Conflict in Big-Time College Sports.* Princeton, NJ: Princeton University Press, 2001.
Zimbalist, Andrew, Donna Lopiano, Fritz Polite, Brian Porto, Janet Blade, Gerald Gurney, B. David Ridpath, Allen Sack, Julie Sommer and Mary Willingham. "The Drake Group Position Statement: Compensation of College Athletes Including Revenues Earned from Commercial Use of Their Names, Images and Likenesses and Outside Employment." Drake Group. https://www.thedrakegroup.org/wp-content/uploads/2020/08/8-3-20-FINAL-Drake-NIL-Position-Paper.pdf.
Zirin, David. *A People's History of Sports in the United States: 250 Years of Politics, Protest, People, and Play.* New York: New Press, 2008.
Zschoche, Sue. "Dr. Clarke Revisited: Science, True Womanhood, and Female Collegiate Education." *History of Education Quarterly* 29, no. 4 (1989): 545–69.

Documentary Films

Earp, Jeremy, dir. *Not Just a Game*. Media Education Foundation, 2010.
Ellwood, Allison, dir. *Women of Troy*. HBO, 2020.
Finkel, Ross, Trevor Martin, and Johnathan Paley, dirs. *$chooled: The Price of College Sports*. Strand Releasing and Makuhari Media, 2013.
Mosbacher, Dee, and Fawn Yacker, dirs. *Training Rules*, 2009.

Moyers, Bill, dir. *Sports for Sale*.
PBS. *American Masters: Billie Jean King*.
———. *League of Denial*.
———. *Media Coverage & Female Athletes*, 2013. https://video.tpt.org/video/tpt-co-productions-media-coverage-female-athletes/.
———. *This Is a Game*.
———. *Women Who Make America: Kathrine Switzer*.

Index

AAA. *See* American Anthropology Association
AAGBL. *See* All-Americans Girls Baseball League
ABL. *See* American Basketball League
academic progress rate, 242n33
academic standards, 269–71
accountability, 37
Active Bodies (Verbrugge), 89
activism, 90, 115, 289–90, 295–97, 300
Adams, John, 49, 53
Adidas, 22
administration, 135, 193–94, 220–21, 245n42, 246n48
admissions, 223–24, 240n14, 240n20
adolescence, 92n39
advertisements, 45–46, 189n14, 189n16, 267–68
AIAW. *See* Association for Intercollegiate Athletics for Women
All-Americans Girls Baseball League (AAGBL), 79
Alston, Shawne, 261
alumni, 6, 63–64, 117, 208–9, 232

amateurism: in college sports, 254; for NCAA, 199–203; politics of, 260, 284n20; professionalism and, 205–6; in sports, 53–54; TSOASA, 203; for women, 78
American Anthropology Association (AAA), 67n19
American Association (baseball), 52
American Basketball League (ABL), 107, 130
Anthony, Susan B., 76–77
Appel, Jayne, 147
Arico, Kim Barnes, 217
Arizona State University, 145–46
The Art of War (Sun Tzu), 169
Association for Intercollegiate Athletics for Women (AIAW), 101, 109–13, 118, 123n18
athletes: academic standards for, 269–71; activism by, 300; admissions for, 223–24; California for, 177; coaching, 10; college sports for, xiii–xiv, 22–23, 36–42, 38, 43n11, 242n32, 284n21; compensation for, 202–3, 280n14, 283n18; competition

355

for, 155–56; conditioning for, 11; data from, 211n20; development of, 54–55; Drake Group for, 302, 303n9; economics of, 8; education for, 65, 221–25, 242n31; eligibility requirements for, 268–69; exploitation of, xvi, 203–4; fans and, 266–67; feminism for, 86–89; football for, 70n75; GPAs for, 243, 269–71; graduation rates for, 245n40; growth-mindsets for, xviii–xix; higher education for, xvi, 24–25, 277–78; housing for, 230–31, 245n45; injuries for, 61–62, 147–48; jerseys for, 284n22; NCAA and, 29, 187–88, 197–99, 238–39, 239, 242n33, 283n19; NILs for, 22–23, 175, 197–98, 264, 285n23; in Olympics, 118; professionalism for, 43n9; psychology of, 36, 170, 215–16, 290, 295–302; race for, 190n22, 302; recruitment of, 195–96; reform for, 267–68; risk for, 164–65; scholarships for, 14–15, 30n8, 175–77, 228–29, 238–39; sexism for, 80–81, 291; social media for, 37; sociology of, 78; Stanford University for, 35–36, 130, 162–64, 195–97, 209, 233–34, 237–39, 239; student-athletes, 221–22, 225–26, 234–37, 241n27; support for, 269; Title IX for, 263–64; training for, 4–5, 45–46; tramp, 60–61; transfers, 272–73; Twitter for, 39; at University of North Carolina, 241n30; VanDerveer for, 10–11, 145, 160, 233–34, 289; Victorianism for, 79; video games for, 282n17; Weight Watchers for, 180; women as, 168–69
athletic budgets, 8–9
athletic conferences, 197–99, 210nn3–5, 211n6, 211n8, 211n10
athletic departments, 280n2
Auriemma, Geno, 2, 131, 135–37, 197
Austin, B., 92n20
awards, for education, 273–74

Bachman, Rachel, 166–67
Barncastle, Jordan, 170n16
baseball, 15; AAGBL, 79; American Association, 52; Chicago White Stockings, 52; Cincinnati Red Stockings, 52; culture of, 51–52; economics of, 52–53; newspapers for, 52–53; professionalism in, 53–54; San Francisco Giants, 43n9
Basic Educational Opportunity Grants (BEOG), 113
basketball: ABL, 107, 130; Commission on College Basketball, 244n35, 273; competition in, 90; football and, 14–15; Golden State Warriors, 38; Hall of Fame, 234; history of, 93n44; in Japan, xiv; masculinity and, 85–86; for men, 19; men's, 21; NBA, 38, 139, 157, 284n21; PCL for, 212n28; popularity of, 16–17, 31n14; for Tucker, 163–64; for women, 36–37, 93n72. *See also specific topics*
Baxter, Richard, 49–50
Bayh, Birch, 100
Baylor University, 170n16, 249–50, 280n2
Beecher, Catherine, 75–76
Belotti, Mike, 182
Belzer, Jason, 205–6
Bennett College, 78–79
BEOG. *See* Basic Educational Opportunity Grants
Berenson, Senda, 82–84
bicycles, 76–77
Bilas, Jay, 261, 284n22
Black Lives Matter, 295–97
Bloom, Jeremy, 261, 281n15
Blue, Kevin, 182

Blumenthal, Richard, 22, 177, 300–301
Bochy, Bruce, 43n9
Boles, Dylan, 297
Booker, Cory, 22, 177, 300–301, 304n11
booster clubs, 134, 302n4
Boothe, Sarah, 7, 11, 33–34, 72–73, 149, 160, 196, 215. *See also* Stanford University
Boston Marathon, 291
Bourdieu, Pierre, 165
Boyle, Joanne, 152
Bradford, Steven, 261
Branch, Taylor, 22, 176
Brand, Miles, 200
branding, 203–4
Brennan, Frank, 245n42
bribery, 240n20
Brigham Young University, 170n16
Brohm, Jean Marie, 143
Brown, John, 50
Burke, Doris, 250
Butts, Niya, 145
Byers, Walter, 110, 114, 183, 285n23

Cahn, Susan, 79, 86, 94n77
Cal. *See* University of California Berkeley
Calhoun, Jim, 135–37
California, 177, 261
California Institute of Technology, 239n3
Cambridge University, 239n3
Cammeyer, William H., 51–52
Camp, Walter, 55–56, 58, 60
Campbell, Talia, 144
Capitol One Cup, 225, 240–41n24
Cardinal Sports, xvii
Carnegie, Andrew, 54
Carnegie Report, 65
Cavalli, Gary, 107–8
Chicago White Stockings, 52
children, 24

Cincinnati Red Stockings, 52
civil rights, 113, 122n1. *See also* Title IX
Civil Rights Restoration Act, 113
Clotfelter, Charles, 16–17
clothing, 78–79
coaching: athletes, 10; in college sports, 140, 160; economics of, 127–28, *137*; education and, 278–79; graduation rates and, 275; in higher education, 181–82; history of, 58; for media, 40–41, 138–39; in NCAA, 245n42; in Olympics, xx; for Paye, 241n28; pedagogy, 256–57; for Pohlen, 5; professionalism in, 58, 60–61, 131–39, *132*, *136–38*; psychology of, 43n11, *129*, 129–31; reform in, 268; for Reid, 57–58; research on, 134; rowing, 69n56; sexism in, 128–29; at Stanford University, 36–42, *38*, 141n22, 161–62; by VanDerveer, xiv–xx, *14*, 102–3, 119–20, 131, 162–63, 216, 253
college sports: administration for, 246n48; advertisements for, 189n14, 189n16; amateurism in, 254; for athletes, xiii–xiv, 22–23, 36–42, *38*, 43n11, 242n32, 284n21; athletic budgets for, 8–9; athletic conferences for, 197–99; Bill of Rights in, 303n9; Capitol One Cup for, 225; coaching in, 140, 160; coaching pedagogy, 256–57; commercialism of, 32n38, 59–60, 69n61, 228–30; community in, 143–44; competition in, 133–34; COVID-19 for, 253–54, 295–302; culture and, 21–22, 31n11, 164–65, 179–80, 233–34, 287n92; economics of, *136*, 190n32, 291–92; education and, 235–36; exploitation in, 224; for fans, 48, 58–60; feminism in, 76–78, *77*; fieldwork on, 41–42; football for, 39–40, 70n92, 183;

gender equality and, 92n20, 119–21, 171n18, 289–92; graduation rates in, 228–29; for higher education, xv–xvi, 41, 183–84, 209–10, 248n58; history of, 53–54, 89–90; IAA, 62; integrity in, 276–78; Learfield Sports Directors' Cup for, 240; for media, 12; mental health task force for, 166–67; NCAA and, 14–15, 55–58, 184–86, *185*, 267–76, 278–80; newspapers for, 59; PCL for, 212n28; popularity of, 47; professionalism in, 61–62; qualitative analysis of, 175–77; reform in, 259–67, 299–300; research on, 211n20; SATC, 63; scholarship on, 175–77, 205–6, 237, 248n56; sexism in, 78–80, 88–89, 264–65; sponsorship for, 206–7; at Stanford University, 45–47, 231–33; Title IX for, 86–89, 117–19, *119*; *White v. NCAA* for, 281n16; for women, 76–77, *77*; at Yale, 55–56. *See also specific sports*

The Color of Life is Red (Liebendorfer), 88–89

Colson, Sydney, 250–51

Columbia University, 61

commercialism: of college sports, 32n38, 59–60, 69n61, 228–30; in higher education, 277; for men's sports, 109–14, *110*; reform in, 275–76; for sports, 53–54; for women, 48; for women's basketball, 164–65

Commission on College Basketball (2018), 244n35, 273

community: in college sports, 143–44; in higher education, 58–62, 70n91, 268–69; in Ivy League schools, 287n91; scholarship on, 247n55; at Stanford University, 108–9, 125n68, 133

compensation, 202–4, 280n14, 281n15, 283n18

competition: for athletes, 155–56; in basketball, 90; in college sports, 133–34; ethics and, 171n17; for fans, 187; psychology of, 74; in sports, 76–77; for VanDerveer, 144

conditioning, for athletes, 11

Conradt, Jody, 72

Cooky, Cheryl, 20, 191n37

Cooper, Cynthia, 122n7

Corbett, Sara, 120

Costas, Bob, 267

Coubertin, Pierre de, 75

COVID-19, 253–54, 295–302

Crouse, Karen, 233

culture: of baseball, 51–52; college sports and, 21–22, 31n11, 164–65, 179–80, 233–34, 287n92; cultural hegemony, 68n22; in education, 220; football in, *15*, 15–16, 64–65; gender equality in, xx, 89–90; masculinity in, 301–2; men's sports in, 23, 187–88; modernism for, 75; posture in, 78–79; religion for, 67n19; of scholarship, xvi–xviii; sexism in, xv, 85–86, 186–87; social class in, 51; social Darwinism, 55; social media in, 39; sports, xviii, 17–18, 28, 70n81; of Stanford University, 193–95, 225–27; Title IX for, 114–15, 124n44; of United States, 65–66; Victorianism, 51–53; women in, 17–18; women's basketball and, 18–19, 37–38

Daley, Arthur, 90

DAPER. *See* Department of Athletics and Physical Education and Recreation

data: analysis, xvii–xviii; from athletes, 211n20; on gender equality, 137; interpretation of, xiii–xiv; for research, xiii–xiv

Dawkins, Johnny, 137–38

Deford, Frank, 176
democracy, 270–71, 297–98
Department of Athletics and Physical Education and Recreation (DAPER), 8–10, 9, 30n2, 107–8, 225, 231–32
DePaul University, 71–72
Devenzio, Dick, 261, 280n14
Didrikson, Mildred, 80–81
Dixon, Jasmine, 158
Donaghe, Hannah, 156
donations, 232
Douglas, Mary, 235
Drake Group, 302, 303n9, 304n11
Duderstadt, James, 275–76
Duke University, 16, 134, *136–37*, 180, 284n22

Easterbrook, Gregg, 176
economics: advertisements, 45–46; alumni donations, 117, 232; of athletes, 8; in athletic departments, 280n2; of baseball, 52–53; booster clubs, 134, 302n4; for Cardinal Sports, xvii; of coaching, 127–28, *137*; of college sports, *136*, 190n32, 291–92; compensation, 202–3; education and, 26–27; endowments, 245n47, 247n51; for ESPN, 18–19, 31n16; of exploitation, xx; of football, 31n11, 134; in Great Depression, 92n20; intellectualism and, 28; of merchandise, xxin1; of NCAA, *15*, 15–19, 118–19, *119*, 284n20; of NILs, 25–26; of professionalism, 213n30; quantitative analysis of, 19–20; scholarship on, 16–17, 26, 275; sexism and, 86; sponsorship, 174, 178–79, 190n17; of sports, 199–203; at Stanford University, 8–9, 30nn2–3, *136–37*, 246n48; of women's basketball, 13–17, *14–15*, 184–86, *185*. See also commercialism

education: academic progress rate, 242n33; for athletes, 65, 221–25, 242n31; awards for, 273–74; BEOG, 113; of children, 24; coaching and, 278–79; college sports and, 235–36; culture, 220; economics and, 26–27; in England, 51–52, 67n14; ethics in, 68n24; for NCAA, 259–67; patriarchy for, 75–76; from sports, 48; at Stanford University, 228–29; student-athletes, 225–26; in United States, 25, *110*, 110–11, 269–70; for women, 91n8
Electronic Arts, 282n17
eligibility requirements, 268–69
Eliot, Charles, 57, 62, 65
elitism, 31n13, 69n42
Emerson, Ralph Waldo, 69n42
Emmert, Mark, 200, 302
endowments, 231–32, 245n47, 247n51
England: Cambridge University, 239n3; education in, 51–52, 67n14; ethics in, 51; football in, 53; higher education in, 189n5; sports in, 68n24; United States and, 50; University of Oxford, 239n3
Equal Pay Act (1963), 137
ESPN: economics for, 18–19, 31n16; ESPNw, 18; NFL on, 32n28; Schaap for, 13–14; sports, 21; SportsCenter, 12; sports on, 2–4; for women, 32n23, 184; women's basketball on, 17–18, 250
ethics: competition and, 171n17; in education, 68n24; in England, 51; for fans, 61–62; professional, 274; Puritan, 49–50; in recruitment, 279
exploitation: of athletes, xvi, 203–4; in college sports, 224; economics of, xx; by NCAA, 22; politics of, 209–10; professionalism and, 207–9; of race, 176

Faculty Committee on Athletics (FCA), 87–88
Faculty Committee on Women's Athletics (FCWA), 87–88
Fainaru, Steve, 72
Fainaru-Wada, Mark, 72
Fair Pay to Play Act, 261
fans: alumni as, 63–64, 208–9; athletes and, 266–67; college sports for, 48, 58–60; competition for, 187; ethics for, 61–62; football for, 65–66; gimmicks for, 178–79, *179*; masculinity for, 291–92; social media for, 158; of Stanford University, 6–7, 124n60, 241n28; technology for, 189n16; timeouts for, 217; in United States, 54–55; violence for, 166; women's basketball for, 187–88
FCA. *See* Faculty Committee on Athletics
FCWA. *See* Faculty Committee on Women's Athletics
federal graduation rates, 244n35
Feinstein, John, 103
feminism: for athletes, 86–89; bicycles for, 76–77; in college sports, 76–78, *77*; femininity, 74; history of, 75–76, 94n83, 97–102, *99*; Mink, P., for, 97–100, *99*, 122n3; politics of, 291–92; sexism and, 91n19, 301–2; in sports, 114–15; Tucker for, 106; VanDerveer and, 90, 128–29; for women, 81–86
fieldwork, xvi–xviii, 41–42
Final Four, 249–53
Floyd, George, 295
football, 18–19; for athletes, 70n75; basketball and, 14–15; college, 297–98; for college sports, 39–40, 70n92, 183; in culture, *15*, 15–16, 64–65; democracy in, 297–98; economics of, 31n11, 134; in England, 53; for fans, 65–66; for higher education, 78; history of, 53–58; injuries in, 170n15; for NCAA, 263, 297–98, 302n4; psychology in, 45; rugby and, 62–63; at Stanford University, 46–47, 229–31; in United States, 58–66; women's basketball compared to, 48; at Yale, 69n61. *See also* National Football League
Football Facts and Figures (Camp), 56
Ford (company), 206
Ford, Henry, 54
Frederico, Rachelle, 151–52
Fresno State University, 71

Gallico, Paul, 65, 80
Gavora, Jessica, 121
Geertz, Clifford, 249
Geiger, Andy, 105, 108–9, 223–24, 226, 238
gender equality: college sports and, 92n20, 119–21, 171n18, 289–92; in culture, xx, 89–90; data on, 137; disparity in, 18; history of, 77, 123n11; for media, 191n37; revenue-generation and, 139; in scholarships, 208–9; in sports, 115–16; at Stanford University, 127–28, 135; in tennis, 76–77, 80–81; Title IX for, 27; at UCONN, 135–36; in United States, 114–15, 140; for VanDerveer, 132–33; for women, 89–90
General Accountability Office, 116
Gerdy, John, 279
Gillibrand, Kirsten, 300
Gladwell, Malcolm, 234
Goestenkors, Gail, 135
Gold, Patricia, 37
Golden State Warriors, 38
Gold-Onwude, Rosalyn, 36–39, *38*, 41
golf, 80–81, 237–38
Gonzaga University, 218–19
good-for-life scholarships, 271–72

Gould, Dick, 222–23, 227, 238
grade point averages (GPAs), 243, 269–71
graduation rates, 228–29, 244n35, 245n40, 245nn37–38, 271–72, 275
Grants-in-Aid, 283n19
Great Depression, 92n20
Green, Edith, 97–100, 99
Griner, Britney, 170n16, 249–50
growth-mindsets, xviii–xix
Gulick, Luther, Jr., 81–82
Gulick, Luther, Sr., 81–82
Gulick, Sydney, 82
Gumbrecht, Hans Ulrich, xix
Gurney, Gerald, 269
Guthrie, Luell Weed, 88
gymnastics, 82–83

Haase, Jerod, 42n8
Hall, Edward K., 58
Hall, G. Stanley, 81–82, 92n39
Handley, Ray, 222
Harari, Yuval, 247n55
Harbaugh, Jim, 141n22
Hargadon, Fred, 215, 223–24, 238, 240n14
Harris, Kamala, 300
Harvard University, 53–54, 57–58, 106
Hashimoto, Kiyoe, 223
Hatchell, Sylvia, 72, 190n22
hegemony, 68n22
Helser, Brendra Mersereau, 89
Hennesey, John, 220–21
Higginson, Thomas Wentworth, 50
higher education: academic progress rate, 242n33; administration in, 135, 193–94; admissions for, 240n14; advertisements for, 267–68; for athletes, xvi, 24–25, 277–78; athletic departments, 280n2; branding in, 203–4; coaching in, 181–82; college sports for, xv–xvi, 41, 183–84, 209–10, 248n58; commercialism in, 277; community in, 58–62, 70n91, 268–69; elite athletics in, 31n13; endowments in, 231–32; in England, 189n5; football for, 78; graduation rates in, 244n35, 244n37, 245n38, 245n40; Higher Education Act, 100; housing in, 245n45; masculinity in, 56, 64; media in, 40; men's sports for, 19, 25; for non-athlete students, 224–25; for Paye, 227; reform in, 273–74, 278–80, 287n91; research on, 171n18, 211n20, 234–37; SATC, 63; scholarship in, 25; sports and, 23–24, 123n18; at Stanford University, 219–21, 239n3; for student-athletes, 225–26; for students, 279–80; in United States, 17, 183, 259–67; for women, 26, 76–78, 77; women's basketball for, 28
high school sports, 117–18
Hirono, Mazie, 300
Hoover, Herbert, 60–61
Hughes, Thomas, 50
Hullar, Ted, 181
Huma, Ramogi, 281n16, 297
Hutchins, Robert Maynard, 65

IAA. *See* Intercollegiate Athletic Association
identity, 40–41, 70n91
Indiana University, 11
injuries: for athletes, 61–62, 147–48; concussions, 71–72; in football, 170n15; for Ogwumike, N., 144–45; sexism with, 74, 85; for Stanford University, 147–48
integrity, in college sports, 276–78
intellectualism, xix, 28
Intercollegiate Athletic Association (IAA), 62
Ivy League schools, 268–69, 287n91

James, Sarah, 5, 33, 72, 77
Japan, xiv, xviii–xix
Jefferson, Thomas, 49, 53
Jemerigbe, Afure, 261
Jenkins, Martin, 261
jerseys, 284n22
Johnson, Lyndon, 122n1
Jurewitz, Ross, 115, 124n44

Kane, Dan, 241n30
Karlgaard, Joe, 33, 39–41, 232–33, 238
Kelly, Mike, 52
Kelsey, Bobbie, 10–11, 130, 133, 148–49, 152–53
Kessler, Jeffrey, 284n20
Kindler, Nick, 261
King, Martin Luther, Jr., 176
Kingsley, Charles, 50
Kirwan, Brit, 275–76
Knight, Bob, 103, 161–62
Knight, Phil, 173–74
Kokenis, Toni, 5, 7, 33–34, 72–73, 158–59
Krzyzewski, Mike, 134

Lambert, Elizabeth, 170n16
LaRocque, Lindy, 11, 34
Lawson, Kara, 12
leadership: in NCAA, 188; of Ogwumike, N., 33; of Pohlen, 170; of Tucker, 195–96; of VanDerveer, 34–35, 71–72, 97, 158, 218; for women, 97–102, 99
League of Denial (Fainaru and Fainaru-Ward), 72
Learfield Sports Directors' Cup, 240
Leighton, Danette, 186, 198–99
Lenglen, Suzanne, 80
Leslie, Lisa, 122n7
Lewellen, Mel, 101
Liberti, Rita, 78–79
Liebendorfer, Don, 88–89
Linfield College, 30n8

Lobo, Rebecca, 250, 253
Lombardi, Vince, 45
Los Angeles Clippers, 157, 211n10
Los Angeles Lakers, 157
Los Angeles Sparks, 157
Louisiana State University, 211n13
Louisville, 124n60
Love, Kevin, 167
Lowe's, 206–7, 274
Luck, Andrew, 46

Mahan, Alfred T., 54
Manziel, Johnny, 284n22
Maples, Roscoe, 247n49
Maples Pavilion. *See* Stanford University
marginalization, 26
Marx, Karl, 27
masculinity: basketball and, 85–86; in culture, 301–2; for fans, 291–92; in higher education, 56, 64; in psychology, 57; in religion, 54–55; sexism and, 47–49; in sports, 164–65; for women, 66, 191n37
McGregor, Andrew, 297–98, 302n4
media: athletic conferences for, 210n5; coaching for, 40–41, 138–39; college sports for, 12; gender equality for, 191n37; in higher education, 40; NCAA and, 31n12, 199–200; newspapers, 52–53, 59; for Paye, 292; Pohlen with, 35; sexism in, 13–17, *14–15*; in sociology, 20; sponsorship and, 178–79; sports for, xvi, 17–18, 70n92, 112, 118–19, *119*, 211n7; timeouts for, 66n1, 179; UCONN for, 13–14; VanDerveer with, 250, 252–54; women in, 38–39; women's basketball for, 3–4, 8, 20–21
Medill, Joseph, 52–53
men's sports: commercialism for, 109–14, *110*; in culture, 23, 187–88; graduation rates in, 245n40; for

higher education, 19, 25; popularity of, xv; at Stanford University, 21; at UCLA, 2; in United States, 109–14; women's basketball and, 16–17, 19–23, 84, 165–69, 186–87
mental health task force, 166–67
merchandise, xxin1
Meyer, Urban, 134
Meyerhoff, Arthur, 79
Miller, Cheryl, 122n7
Miller, Ralph, 178
Miller, Tom, 291
Mill's College, 88
Mink, John, 99
Mink, Patsy, 97–100, 99, 122n3
Minnesota Lynx, 3, 130
Mintun, Paige, 182
MLB. *See* baseball
modernism, 75
Monson, Don, 104
Moore, Harold, 61
Moore, Maya, 2–4, 7, 11–12, 196–97
Morris, Darxia, 150–51, 157
Mosher, Duel, 87–88
Mulkey, Kim, 127, 170n16, 249–50
Murphy, Christopher, 300
Murphy, Mary, 144, 182
Murphy, Mel, 145–47, 151
Muscle Milk, 45–46

NAIA. *See* National Association of Intercollegiate Athletics
Naismith, James, 71, 77, 81–84. *See also* basketball
names, images, and likeness (NILs): for athletes, 22–23, 175, 197–98, 264, 285n23; for Booker, 300–301; economics of, 25–26; for NCAA, 260, 284n22; politics of, 261–62; Title IX and, 265–67; in United States, 177, 299–300
National Association of Intercollegiate Athletics (NAIA), 30n7

National Basketball Association (NBA), 38, 139, 157, 284n21
National Collegiate Athletic Association (NCAA): accountability with, 228; AIAW for, 109–13, 118; alternatives to, 212n28; amateurism for, 199–203; athletes and, 29, 187–88, 197–99, 238–39, 239, 242n33, 283n19; coaching in, 245n42; college sports and, 14–15, 55–58, 184–86, 185, 267–76, 278–80; Commission on College Basketball for, 244n35, 273; compensation for, 281n15; for Drake Group, 304n11; economics of, 15, 15–19, 118–19, 119, 284n20; education for, 259–67; exploitation by, 22; football for, 263, 297–98, 302n4; graduation rates in, 271–72; history of, 62; leadership in, 188; media and, 31n12, 199–200; mental health task force for, 166–67; NAIA and, 30n7; *NCAA v. Alston*, 265–66, 300; *NCAA v. Board of Regents of the University of Oklahoma*, 116–17; NFL and, 259; NILs for, 260, 284n22; politics for, 295–302; reform for, 276–78; reputation of, 42, 237; Rice for, 22; rules, 163, 166–67, 183–84, 217, 283n18; scandals for, 179–80, 200–201, 241n30; scholarship on, 21–22, 175–77; scholarships for, 8–10, 9; sports for, xiii, 116–17; Stanford University for, 243n34; TCOA for, 22–23; Title IX for, 109–14, 110; video games for, 282n17; *White v. NCAA*, 281n16; women and, 109–10, 128; women's basketball for, 184–86, 185. *See also* NCAA tournament
National Football League (NFL), 18–19; on ESPN, 32n28; history of, 54; NBA and, 139; NCAA and, 259; scandals for, 72; training for, 42n8

nationalism, xx, 54–55, 67n16
National Organization of Women (NOW), 115
National Section on Women's Athletics (NSWA), 83, 85–86
NBA. See National Basketball Association
NCAA. See National Collegiate Athletic Association
NCAA tournament: round II of, 215–17; round III of, 218; round IV of, 218–19; Round V of, 249–52; Round VI of, 253–55
Nelson, Mariah Burton, 48
New England Small College League, 268–69
Newsom, Gavin, 261
newspapers, 52–53, 59
NFL. See National Football League
Nike, 174
NILs. See names, images, and likeness
Nixon, Richard, 98
Nocera, Joe, 205
Noll, Roger, 281n16
non-athlete students, 224–25, 228
Notre Dame, 253–55
NOW. See National Organization of Women
NSWA. See National Section on Women's Athletics

O'Bannon, Ed, 193, 204, 261, 282n17
O'Brien, Dave, 250
Ogwumike, Chiney, 7, 11–12, 175; in NCAA tournament, 215–17, 219; reputation of, 45–46, 195–97; with teammates, 33–34; teamwork for, 71. See also Stanford University
Ogwumike, Nneka, 6–7, 7, 11–12; injuries for, 144–45; leadership of, 33; in NCAA tournament, 218, 250–51; reputation of, 160–61, 194–96; teamwork for, 71; WNBA for, 289. See also Stanford University
Ohio State, 11, 103–5, 104, 134
Olympics, 75; athletes in, 118; coaching in, xx; for Stanford University, 5–6; TSOASA, 203; for women, 120; women's basketball in, 119–20
Oregon State University (OSU), 178–80, 179
Outliers (Gladwell), 234
Owen, Heather, 231, 238, 246n48
Oxford University, 239n3

Park, Roberta, 62
Pasch, Dave, 182
patriarchy, 75–76
patriotism, 67n16
Patriot League, 268–69
Paye, Kate, 10–11, 20, 130–31, 152–56; coaching for, 241n28; higher education for, 227; losing for, 255; media for, 292; Tucker and, 159. See also Stanford University
Payton, Gary, 178
PCL. See Professional Collegiate League
pedagogy, 256–57
Pedersen, Kayla, 206–7; concussion for, 71–72; defense for, 11; Pohlen and, 6–7, 12, 73, 145, 194; recovery for, 73. See also Stanford University
Penn State, 212n22
Pepperdine University, 131
Pohlen, Jeanette, 149; coaching for, 5; leadership of, 170; with media, 35; Moore, M., and, 11–12; Pedersen and, 6–7, 12, 73, 145, 194. See also Stanford University
politics: of amateurism, 260, 284n20; of exploitation, 209–10; of feminism, 291–92; for NCAA, 295–302; of NILs, 261–62; sexism in, 121; sports in, 116–17; of Title IX, 115–17,

127–28, 301, 304n11; United States, 22–23
posture, 78–79
practice, 4–10, 5–7, 9, 218–19
prejudice, 128, 186–87, 236
Princeton, 53, 61
Professional Collegiate League (PCL), 212n28
professionalism: amateurism and, 205–6; for athletes, 43n9; in baseball, 53–54; in coaching, 58, 60–61, 131–39, *132*, 136–38; in college sports, 61–62; economics of, 213n30; exploitation and, 207–9; professional ethics, 274; in sports, 55–58, 69n56, 213n32; for VanDerveer, 132–33; for women, 207–8; in women's basketball, *132*
PSAL. *See* Public School Athletic Leagues
psychology: accountability, 37; of athletes, 36, 170, 215–16, 290, 295–302; of coaching, 43n11, *129*, 129–31; of compensation, 204; of competition, 74; in football, 45; of identity, 40–41; masculinity in, 57; research on, 171n17; sports, 166–67; of VanDerveer, 255–59; of women's basketball, 158–60
Public School Athletic Leagues (PSAL), 81
Pullman, George, 54
Puritanism, 49–50

qualitative analysis, 19–20, 175–77
quantitative analysis, 19–20

race, 67n19; for athletes, 190n22, 302; exploitation of, 176; prejudice with, 128; in research, 262; in sports, 256
Reagan, Ronald, 123n35
recruitment: of athletes, 195–96; at Duke University, 180; ethics in, 279; scholarships and, 37; for Stanford University, 221–25; technology for, 212n25; by VanDerveer, 175, 222–23
reform: in academic standards, 269–71; for athletes, 267–68; in coaching, 268; in college sports, 259–67, 299–300; in commercialism, 275–76; with eligibility requirements, 268–69; for graduation rates, 271–72; in higher education, 273–74, 278–80, 287n91; for NCAA, 276–78
Reich, Robert, 275
Reid, William, 57–58
religion: adolescence in, 92n39; for culture, 67n19; masculinity in, 54–55; sports and, 67n13, 67n16; in United States, 49–53, 56, 68n23, 81–82, 84
research: on coaching, 134; on college sports, 211n20; data for, xiii–xiv; fieldwork for, xvi–xviii; on higher education, 171n18, 211n20, 234–37; on psychology, 171n17; qualitative analysis in, 175–77; race in, 262; scholarship and, xiv–xvi; for sociology, 17–18; on sports, 23–28; from University of Minnesota, 18; on women, 94n77; by Women's Sports Foundation, 141n4
revenue-generation, 139
Rice, Condoleezza, 1, 22, 177, 222
Rich, Adrienne, 143
Richter, Ally Hudson, 123n11
risk, 164–65
Rogers, Carl, 257
Rogers, Regina, 149
Roosevelt, Theodore, 57, 65
Rowe, Holly, 253–54
rowing, 58, 69n56
Ruef, Mikaela, 5, 33, 72, 153, 216, 250–51
Ruetz, Joe, 107–8

rugby, 56, 62–63
Runge, Jody, 174

Saban, Nick, 176, 211n13
Sack, Allen, 261
St. John's University, 215–17
Sanders, Bernie, 300
San Diego State University, 131
San Francisco Giants, 43n9
SATC. *See* Student Army Training Corps
Saving Capitalism (Reich), 275
scandals: admissions, 224, 240n20; for NCAA, 179–80, 200–201, 241n30; at Penn State, 212n22
Schaap, Jeremy, 13–14
Schatz, Brian, 300
scholarship: on college sports, 175–77, 205–6, 237, 248n56; on community, 247n55; culture of, xvi–xviii; on economics, 16–17, 26, 275; in higher education, 25; intellectualism in, xix; on NCAA, 21–22, 175–77; research and, xiv–xvi; in social sciences, 35–36; from sociology, 27; on sports, xviii–xix; on Title IX, 115; on women's basketball, 23–28
scholarships: for athletes, 14–15, 30n8, 175–77, 228–29, 238–39; gender equality in, 208–9; good-for-life, 271–72; Grants-in-Aid for, 283n19; for NCAA, 8–10, 9; recruitment and, 37; sexism in, 114–15; at Stanford University, 25, 123n15, 247n50
Schwarz, Andy, 205–6, 261
Scott, Larry, 198–99
A Season on the Brink (Feinstein), 103
Seattle Reign, 130
self-investment, 233–34
sexism: activism against, 289–90; for athletes, 80–81, 291; clothing in, 78–79; in coaching, 128–29; in college sports, 78–80, 88–89, 264–65; in culture, xv, 85–86, 186–87; economics and, 86; feminism and, 91n19, 301–2; history of, 91n8; with injuries, 74, 85; masculinity and, 47–49; in media, 13–17, *14–15*; in politics, 121; in scholarships, 114–15; in sports, 13–14, 17–18, 94n77, 187–88; in United States, 49–53, 89–90; for VanDerveer, 29, 167–68; for women, 83–84, 91n4; for women's basketball, 94n75; women's liberation against, 90
"The Shame of College Sports" (Branch), 176
Sharp, 122n7
Shaw, David, 134, 141n22, 222, 230, 231
Sherman Antitrust Act, 265–66
Shibley, Robert L., 121
Simmons, Meighan, 73
Singer, William Rick, 224, 240n20
Skinner, Nancy, 261
Skipper, John, 19
slavery, 67n19
Smith, Bev, 174
Smith, R. A., 53–54, 57–58
social class, 51, 74
social Darwinism, 55
social media, 37, 39, 158
social sciences, 35–36
sociology: of athletes, 78; media in, 20; research for, 17–18; scholarship from, 27; Weber for, 68n23; women in, 35–36
Spalding, Albert, 52
sponsorship, 174, 178–79, 190n17, 206–7
sports: amateurism in, 53–54; commercialism for, 53–54; competition in, 76–77; culture, xviii, 17–18, 28, 70n81; economics

of, 199–203; education from, 48; in England, 68n24; feminism in, 114–15; gender equality in, 115–16; hegemony in, 68n22; higher education and, 23–24, 123n18; high school, 117–18; history of, 49–53; management, 21–22; masculinity in, 164–65; for media, xvi, 17–18, 70n92, 112, 118–19, *119*, 211n7; as nationalism, 54–55; for NCAA, xiii, 116–17; in politics, 116–17; professionalism in, 55–58, 69n56, 213n32; psychology, 166–67; race in, 256; religion and, 67n13, 67n16; research on, 23–28; scholarship on, xviii–xix; sexism in, 13–14, 17–18, 94n77, 187–88; for Stanford University, xiv–xv, xvii, 24, 49, 105–6; television contracts for, *15*, 15–17; time outs in, 45, 66n1; in United States, 190n32, 202; for VanDerveer, 20; violence in, 166, 170n16; for women, xx, 30n4, 75–76, 117–18, 289–92; Women's Sports Foundation, 141n4; YMCA for, 81–82. *See also specific sports*

Sports and Freedom (Smith, R. A.), 53–54

SportsCenter, 12

Standing Tall (Stringer), 127–28

Stanford, Jane, 86–88, 95n84

Stanford, Leland, 86–87, 94n83

Stanford University: administration, 220–21, 245n42; alumni from, 6; Arizona State University and, 145–46; for athletes, 35–36, 130, 162–64, 195–97, 209, 233–34, 237–39, *239*; Cal and, 60–65, 143–44, 150–57, 168; Capitol One Cup at, 225, 240–41n24; coaching at, 36–42, 38, 141n22, 161–62; college sports at, 45–47, 231–33; community at, 108–9, 125n68, 133; culture of, 193–95, 225–27; DAPER at, 8–10, *9*, 30n2, 107–8, 225, 231–32; DePaul University and, 71–72; Duke University and, 134; economics at, 8–9, 30nn2–3, *136–37*, 246n48; education at, 228–29; endowment, 231–32, 245n47, 247n51; fans of, 6–7, 124n60, 241n28; FCA at, 87–88; FCWA at, 87–88; football at, 46–47, 229–31; gender equality at, 127–28, 135; golf at, 237–38; Gonzaga University and, 218–19; graduation rates at, 244n37, 245n40; higher education at, 219–21, 239n3; history of, 106–7, 247n49; housing at, 230–31; injuries for, 147–48; men's basketball at, 21; for NCAA, 243n34; Olympics for, 5–6; OSU and, 178–79, *179*; practice at, 4–10, 5–7, 9; recruitment for, 221–25; reputation of, 60–61, 210, 299–300; roster, *5*; St. John's University and, 215–17; scholarships at, 25, 123n15, 247n50; sports for, xiv–xv, xvii, 24, 49, 105–6; for student-athletes, 225–26, 234–37; tennis at, 86, 101, 107–8, 123n15, 222–23, 227, 229–30; Texas A&M University and, 249–52; Title IX at, 106–9; UC Davis and, 180–83; UCLA and, 146–47, 157–59, 167; UCONN and, 2–4, 11–13, *13*, 21, 37, 47, 184, 196–97; University of Arizona and, 144–45; University of North Carolina and, 218; University of Oregon and, 173–75; University of Tennessee and, 73–74; University of Texas and, 45–46; University of Washington and, 148–49; VanDerveer for, 10–11, 302; for Voepel, 14; water polo at, 42n8; WNBA and, *132*; for women, 86–89,

94n83, 95n84; women's basketball at, xiii–xix, 33–35, 105, 159–61, 169–70, 234–35, 255–59, 289–92
Stanton, Elizabeth Cady, 77
Staurowsky, Ellen J., 21–22, 261, 269
Stockton, John, 218
Strathairn, Pamela, 107
Strauss, Ben, 205
Stringer, C. Vivian, 72, 127–28
Student Army Training Corps (SATC), 63
students: academic standards for, 269–71; GPAs for, 243, 269–71; higher education for, 279–80; housing, 230–31, 245n45; non-athlete students, 224–25, 228; self-investment for, 233–34; student-athletes, 221–22, 225–26, 234–37, 241n27; transfers, 272–73
Summitt, Pat, 72, 135
Sun Tzu, 169
support, for athletes, 269
Switzer, Katherine Virginia, 291

Taylor, Frederick, 58
TCOA. *See* true cost of attendance
technology, 189n16, 212n25
Ted Stevens Olympic and Amateur Sports Act (TSOASA), 203
Teevens, Buddy, 46
television contracts, 15, 15–17
tennis: gender equality in, 76–77, 80–81; at Stanford University, 86, 101, 107–8, 123n15, 222–23, 227, 229–30; for women, 90
Texas A&M University, 249–55, 280n2, 284n22
Texas Tech University, 170n16
Thompson, Tina, 122n7
Thorne, Charli Turner, 11, 146
timeouts, 45, 66n1, 179, 217
Tinkle, Joslyn, 6, 11. *See also* Stanford University

Title IX: for athletes, 263–64; for college sports, 86–89, 117–19, *119*; for culture, 114–15, 124n44; Equal Pay Act and, 137; for gender equality, 27; history of, 98–100, 99, 123n35; for NCAA, 109–14, *110*; NILs and, 265–67; politics of, 115–17, 127–28, 301, 304n11; scholarship on, 115; at Stanford University, 106–9; for Supreme Court, 265–66; for women, xvii, 119–21, 140n3
Tobin, Becca, 145–46
training, 4–5, 42n8, 45–46, 63
tramp athletes, 60–61
transfers, 272–73
Treloar, Al, 85
true cost of attendance (TCOA), 22–23
TSOASA. *See* Ted Stevens Olympic and Amateur Sports Act
Tucker, Amy, 10–11, 149, 152–56, 193; basketball for, 163–64; for feminism, 106; leadership of, 195–96; Paye and, 159; VanDerveer and, 30n4, 104
Turley, Shannon, 42n8
Twain, Mark, 97, 290–91
Twitter, 39

UC Davis. *See* University of California Davis
UCLA. *See* University of California Los Angeles
UCONN. *See* University of Connecticut
United States: BEOG in, 113; civil rights in, 122n1; Civil Rights Restoration Act in, 113; college football in, 297–98; culture of, 65–66; democracy in, 270–71; education in, 25, *110*, 110–11, 269–70; elitism in, 69n42; England and, 50; Equal Pay Act in, 137; fans in, 54–55; federal graduation

rates in, 244n35; football in, 58–66; gender equality in, 114–15, 140; General Accountability Office in, 116; Great Depression, 92n20; Higher Education Act in, 100; higher education in, 17, 183, 259–67; identity in, 70n91; Japan and, xviii–xix; marginalization in, 26; men's sports in, 109–14; nationalism in, xx; NILs in, 177, 299–300; politics, 22–23; religion in, 49–53, 56, 68n23, 81–82, 84; sexism in, 49–53, 89–90; Sherman Antitrust Act in, 265–66; sports in, 190n32, 202; TSOASA in, 203; Victorianism, 51–53; women's basketball in, xiii–xx, 106–9
University of Arizona, 144–45
University of California Berkeley (Cal): budget at, 135, *136–37*; reputation of, 60–65, 91n14; Stanford University and, 60–65, 143–44, 150–57, 168; for women, 91n14
University of California Davis (UC Davis), 180–84
University of California Los Angeles (UCLA), 2, 146–47, 157–59, 167
University of Connecticut (UCONN): attendance for, 124n60; gender equality at, 135–36; for media, 13–14; Notre Dame and, 253; reputation of, 14, 36; Stanford University and, 2–4, 11–13, *13*, 21, 37, 47, 184, 196–97; women's basketball at, 1–2
University of Idaho, 104
University of Indiana, 101–3
University of Iowa, 106
University of Maryland, 276
University of Minnesota, 18
University of New Mexico, 170n16
University of North Carolina, 218, 241n30

University of Oklahoma, 116–17
University of Oregon, 173–75
University of Oxford, 239n3
University of Tennessee, 73–74, 124n60, 135
University of Texas, 45–46, 117
University of Washington, 148–49
Unsportsmanlike Conduct (Byers), 114
USC, 122n7

Valvrojenski, Senda, 82–83
Vandersloot, Courtney, 218–19
VanDerveer, Tara: for athletes, 10–11, 145, 160, 233–34, 289; career of, 100–102, 112, 120, 129–30; coaching by, xiv–xx, *14*, 102–3, 119–20, 131, 162–63, 216, 253; with colleagues, 152–56; competition for, 144; Dawkins compared to, 137–38; feminism and, 90, 128–29; gender equality for, 132–33; for Gold-Onwude, 36–39, *38*; graduation rates for, 245n38; Knight, B., for, 161–62; leadership of, 34–35, 71–72, 97, 158, 218; with media, 250, 252–54; motivation for, 160–61, 169; Ohio State for, 103–5, *104*; practices for, 218–19; professionalism for, 132–33; psychology of, 255–59; recruitment by, 175, 222–23; reputation of, 2, 5, 11–13, *13*, 108–9, *129*, *138*, 195–96, 230, 236; as role model, 290; sexism for, 29, 167–68; sports for, 20; for Stanford University, 10–11, 302; student-athletes for, 221–22, 241n27; Tucker and, 30n4, 104; women's basketball for, 102–6, *104*, 186–87. *See also* Stanford University
Van Hollen, Chris, 300
Venable, F. P., 57
Venus to the Hoop (Corbett), 120
Verbrugge, Martha, 89
Victorianism, 51–53, 75, 79

video games, 282n17
violence, 166, 170n16
Voepel, Michelle, 14

Wade Trophy, 3
Wagner, LaVonda, 180
Walker, Francis A., 57
water polo, 42n8
Weber, Max, 27, 68n23, 173
Weight Watchers, 180
Weiss, Paul, 213n31, 213n34
Westhead, Paul, 174
White, Jason, 261
White v. NCAA, 281n16
Whitney, Caspar, 58
Whittemore, John, 60
Wicks, Courtney, 1
Wilbur, Ray Lyman, 63
Wilken, Claudia, 282n17
Will, George, 121
Willard, Frances, 77
Williams, Kiana, 254–55
Willingham, Mary, 241n30
Wills, Helen, 80
WNBA. *See* Women's National Basketball Association
women, 91n19; AIAW, 101, 109–13, 118, 123n18; amateurism for, 78; as athletes, 168–69; basketball for, 36–37, 93n72; Cal for, 91n14; college sports for, 76–77, 77; commercialism for, 48; in culture, 17–18; education for, 91n8; ESPN for, 32n23, 184; ESPNw for, 18; feminism for, 81–86; gender equality for, 89–90; golf for, 80–81; graduation rates for, 245n38; gymnastics for, 82–83; higher education for, 26, 76–78, 77; leadership for, 97–102, 99; masculinity for, 66, 191n37; in media, 38–39; Mill's College for, 88; NCAA and, 109–10, 128; NOW for, 115; NSWA, 83, 85–86; Olympics for, 120; positive anthropology of, xix; prejudice against, 186–87; professionalism for, 207–8; research on, 94n77; sexism for, 83–84, 91n4; social class for, 74; in sociology, 35–36; sports for, xx, 30n4, 75–76, 117–18, 289–92; Stanford University for, 86–89, 94n83, 95n84; tennis for, 90; Title IX for, xvii, 119–21, 140n3. *See also specific topics*
women's basketball: commercialism for, 164–65; culture and, 18–19, 37–38; economics of, 13–17, *14–15*, 184–86, *185*; on ESPN, 17–18, 250; for fans, 187–88; Final Four in, 249–53; football compared to, 48; for higher education, 28; history of, 81–86; for media, 3–4, 8, 20–21; men's sports and, 16–17, 19–23, 84, 165–69, 186–87; for NCAA, 184–86, *185*; in Olympics, 119–20; professionalism in, *132*; psychology of, 158–60; records in, 1–2; scholarship on, 23–28; sexism for, 94n75; at Stanford University, xiii–xix, 33–35, 105, 159–61, 169–70, 234–35, 255–59, 289–92; at UCONN, 1–2; in United States, xiii–xx, 106–9; at USC, 122n7; for VanDerveer, 102–6, *104*, 186–87; Wade Trophy, 3. *See also specific topics*
Women's National Basketball Association (WNBA): draft, 3; history of, 119–20; Los Angeles Sparks, 157; Minnesota Lynx, 3, 130; for Ogwumike, N., 289; Stanford University and, *132*
Women's Sports Foundation, 141n4
Wooden, John, 2, 13, 234, 249, 278
Woods, Tiger, 237–38
Wrighster, George, 303n8
Wrigley, William, 79

Wyden, Ron, 300

Yale University, 53–58, 61, 69n61
Young Men's Christian Association (YMCA), 81–82

Zimbalist, Andrew, 184, 206, 224, 263–64, 287n92
Zinn, Howard, 249

About the Author

Aaron L. Miller, PhD (Oxon), is lecturer in the Department of Kinesiology, California State University, East Bay, and associate adjunct faculty, Department of Kinesiology, St. Mary's College of California. Previously he was assistant professor and Hakubi Scholar at Kyoto University, affiliated with the Graduate School of Letters, visiting scholar at Stanford University's Center on Adolescence, and visiting professor at Waseda University, Faculty of Sports Sciences. A trained sociocultural anthropologist, he is the author of *Discourses of Discipline*, a translated version of which was published in Japanese in 2021, and dozens of other essays, journal articles, and book chapters about education, sports, culture, power, violence, and social justice. He is also host of the podcast *The Power of Sports*, which can be found at https://podcasts.apple.com/us/podcast/the-power-of-sports/id1574997548.

www.ingramcontent.com/pod-product-compliance
Lightning Source LLC
Chambersburg PA
CBHW072118290426
44111CB00012B/1701